Peasants in Power

Philip Verwimp

Peasants in Power

The Political Economy of Development
and Genocide in Rwanda

 Springer

Philip Verwimp
Solvay Brussels School of Economics and Management
Université Libre de Bruxelles
Brussels
Belgium

ISBN 978-94-007-6433-0   ISBN 978-94-007-6434-7   (eBook)
DOI 10.1007/978-94-007-6434-7
Springer Dordrecht Heidelberg New York London

Library of Congress Control Number: 2013935771

Printed on acid-free paper

Springer is part of Springer Science+Business Media (www.springer.com)

Advance Praise for Peasants in Power

"This book will make a major impact not only on the scholarship of the Rwandan genocide but also on our knowledge of agrarian societies and their susceptibility in times of economic crisis to state or elite manipulation, particularly those societies that are densely-populated, smallholder-dominated, and ethnically divided. It is a striking intervention on a topic of global concern that is not likely to diminish in the future, given current trends of population growth, resource exhaustion, ecological crisis, ethnopolitical polarization, and proliferation of weaponry."

Ben Kiernan, A. Whtiney Griswold, Professor of History, professor of international and areas studies, and founding director of the Genocide Studies Program at Yale University, author of Blood and Soil

"Rather than an act of inter-ethnic madness, this books shows how the Rwandan genocide emanated directly from the development path the country had chosen after independence. Verwimp's argument brings genocide into the study of development in the same way that Barrington Moore's integrated democracy into it. Indeed in a sense he has provided us with a new "path into the modern world.""

James A. Robinson, Florence Professor of Government at Harvard University, co-author of Why Nations Fail and the Economic Origins of Dictatorship and Democracy

"For everyone willing to understand how apparently kind and calm people can suddenly lead their society to a nightmarish descent into chaos and genocidal killings, reading "Peasants in Power" will be an invaluable step. The author has worked for more than ten years on the issue and is now a world expert in the field."

Jean-Philippe Platteau, Professor of Development Economics in Namur and at the Centre for the Study of African Economies, Oxford University, author of Institutions, Social Norms and Economic Development

"Philip Verwimp's deeply researched book is an important addition to the growing body of literature on the Rwandan genocide addressing its complex dynamics of violence. Verwimp explores the entanglement between the developmental state, the institutions of the regime and ordinary Rwandans "in the hills". He shows how the emergence of specific moral 'reference frames' is intricately linked to the political and economic set-up. The book deserves a wide reading among scholars and practitioners interested in African politics, economics, and genocide more generally."

Anna-Maria Brandstetter, Ph.d. in Anthropology and Senior Researcher at the Center for African Studies, Johannes Gutenberg University, Mainz, author of Die Rhetorik von Reinheit, Gewalt and Gemeinschaft: Bürgerkrieg and Genozid in Rwanda

"To be ruled is to be kept an eye on, inspected, spied on, regulated, indoctrinated, sermonized, listed and checked off, estimated, appraised, censured, ordered about... To be ruled is at every operation, transaction, movement, to be noted, registered, counted, priced, admonished, prevented, reformed, redressed, corrected".

Pierre-Joseph Proudhon, quoted in
Guérin D., *Anarchism: From Theory to Practice*,
Translated by Mary Klopper,
New York, Monthly Review Press, 1970

Preface

Over the past 15 years I have published a dozen scientific articles on the political economy of development and genocide in Rwanda. I would not have found the energy to do that if the event I was studying would not have had the magnitude that it did. When I first heard about the genocide I was blown away by its horror, its speed and its sheer complexity. What had happened in that small country in Central Africa seemed incomprehensible. Were humans really capable of doing this to one another on the eve of the twenty-first century?

I was fortunate to be able to channel my energy, curiosity, incomprehension, and thrust for understanding in a doctoral program and dissertation in economics. At the time, we speak of 1998, this was not straightforward. Doctoral Schools in Economics in the late 1990s were known for their unified approach to teaching economics and learning how to do economic research. Most of my fellow graduate students were skilled theorists whose mathematical skills I could hardly match. While several graduate students wrote empirical dissertations only the development economists would go out to the field to collect their own data. The idea to collect data in a developing country, learn how to do development economics in practice, combined with the chance to investigate the causes and consequences of one of the most horrific crimes of the twentieth century provided the energy necessary to finish the doctoral course work and embark on a dissertation. I am still grateful to my doctoral advisers at the time as well as to the Fund for Scientific Research (FWO) for the support they gave to start this intellectual journey.

During my years in high school, at the university and till today I entertain a broad interest in history and politics. I never saw this as a waste of time as some believe it is for an economist who needs to write academic articles. In fact, history and politics provide the framework to ask questions on the economy. I was an institutional economist before I knew what that meant. Luckily, by the end of the 1990s we saw the first signs of a renewed interest in political economy in economics. For a young economist interested in history, politics and development, this interest was great because it gave the feeling that there were many scholars out there who were interested in the political economy of development. Today, writing this preface in 2012, this seems obvious as political economy approaches in general and development economics in particular have gained center ground in economics.

Throughout the years and with each academic article on Rwanda I gained a deeper understanding of the forces that lead to the genocide. The constraints proper to an article, however, rarely allow a researcher to explain what (s)he wants to explain in depth and at length. I therefore wrote this book. The reader will notice that I am sharing insights that I have never published earlier in the form of an academic article. The book is far from a collection of previously published papers. Rather, I integrate several previously published papers with new chapters in an attempt to increase our overall understanding of development and genocide in Rwanda. More than half of the content of this book is new. The Chaps. 1, 3, 5, 7–9 as well as the conclusion presented in Chap. 11 are researched uniquely for this book.

I would like to thank the publishers of different journals for the permission to use previously published articles for this book. An early version of the first chapter was published in the Journal of Genocide Studies in 2000 as well as in a monograph on genocide in Cambodia and Rwanda edited by Susan Cook in 2004. The version published in the book is revised and updated. Chapter 4 was first published in the European Journal of Political Economy in 2003 with a completely new version in the Journal of Theoretical Politics in 2012. Chapter 6 was published in the Journal of Agrarian Studies in 2011 and has not been changed since then. A part of Chap. 10 has been published as a Working Paper on the Households in Conflict website in 2007. I draw on several of my other, in particular econometric articles on the causes and consequences of the genocide in this book, but these articles are not reproduced here.

The following persons merit a special word of gratitude for their support to the research for the chapters published in this book: Stefan Dercon and Lodewijk Berlage, my thesis advisors at the Catholic University of Leuven; Ben Kiernan, renowed genocide scholar at Yale University where I studied one year (1999) and one semester (2004). I benefited from a Fellowship from the Belgian American Educational Foundation and from a Fulbright-Hays Grant to support both stays at Yale. The late Alison Desforges was not only a profound expert on Rwanda and a human rights activist but also one of the most inspiring persons I have ever met. Victor Ginsburg emeritus professor of economics at the Université Libre de Bruxelles gave valuable advice on the structure of the manuscript. I could rely on the skills of my editor at Springer-Verlag Hendrinkje Tuerlings throughout the production process. I am grateful to Francois Bart for the permission to reproduce three maps from his 1993 book. Chapter 4 benefited from the insights of my co-author Bart Capéau with whom I wrote the 2012 article on the political economy of dictatorship mentioned above. Chapter 9 is co-authored by Jacob Boersema. Chapter 10 is co-authored by all graduate students who performed fieldwork in

Rwanda in 2004, in alphabetical order Jacob Boersema, Arlette Brone, Jerome Charlier, Bert Ingelaere, Shanley Pinchotti, Inge Thiry, Cecelle Meijer, and Marij Spiesschaert. I express my deep appreciation for the many Rwandans and non-Rwandans who have shared their stories and insights with me over the years.

Brussels, May 2012   Philip Verwimp

Contents

Map of Rwanda

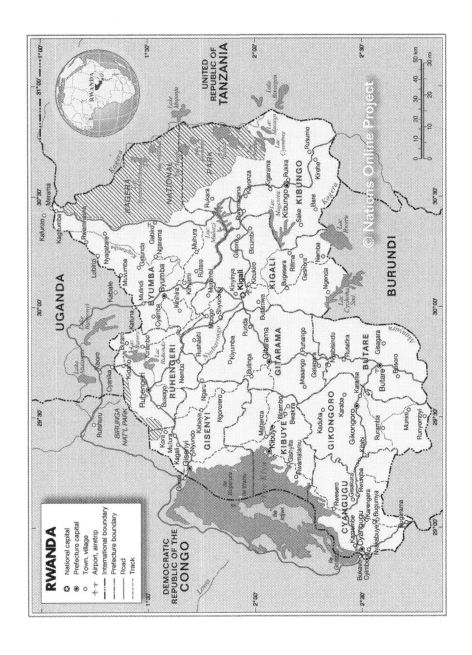

Chapter 1
Development, Dictatorship and Genocide

1.1 Genocide in Rwanda: A Campaign Unlike Anything Else

A small, hilly and landlocked country in Central Africa became front page news in April 1994 when soldiers, youth militia and ordinary citizens slaughtered fellow citizens with a brutality, speed and death toll rarely observed in human history. Early estimates of the death toll vary between at least 500,000 (Human Rights Watch 1999) and 800,000 (Prunierz 1995). Fact of the matter is that at least half a million Rwandan Tutsi were butchered to death in less than three months. Incited by a virulent hate radio, supported by their wives and lead by local and national politicians, Rwandan Hutu men killed Tutsi, raped Tutsi women and pillaged their property. Tutsi were killed in the street and in their homes, in large scale massacres in schools, hospitals, churches and other public spaces. People who had sought shelter and protection in these places hoped that the designated authorities would protect them from evil. The contrary happened: the local and national administrative, political and military authorities were implementing a policy of genocide on a national scale.

According to the 1991 Census, 8.4 % of the population was registered as Tutsi. According to the administrative registration system in the communes it was 10.7 %. Total population in March 1994 was 7.5 million. Using the 10.7 %, which is more credible, we arrive at a total Tutsi population residing in Rwanda in March 1994 of 800,000.[1] Accounting for Tutsi survivors of the genocide—estimated between 100,000 and 200,000—the death toll among Tutsi is then situated between 600,000 and 700,000 (midpoint estimate 650,000). This corresponds to between 75 and 87 % (midpoint 81 %) of the Tutsi population of Rwanda.

---

[1] We come back to this in Chap. 8 of this book when we deal with data sources. The 1991 Census underestimates the number of Tutsi. Prunier (1995) regards a 12 % estimate of Tutsi in the population as a conservative estimate. Any estimate of the death toll among Tutsi crucially depends on the percentage of Tutsi in Rwanda prior to the genocide. We also observe serious provincial level differences in the number of Hutu and Tutsi between the 1991 Census and the registration system used at the level of the commune (municipality).

P. Verwimp, *Peasants in Power*, DOI: 10.1007/978-94-007-6434-7_1,
© Springer Science+Business Media Dordrecht 2013

A post-genocide death count by the government of Rwanda in 2001 arrived at the staggering figure of between 900,000 and 1,000,000 victims (a number of 950,000 corresponds to 12.6 % of the population of Rwanda). Given the share of Tutsi in the population, it is doubtful however that this figure only includes Tutsi victims of the 1994 genocide. Such high figure must include Hutu victims. How many Hutu exactly? That depends on the percentage of Tutsi living in Rwanda on the eve of the genocide. Hutu were killed by fellow Hutu during the genocide, by the RPF in its offensive in 1994, they also died in the refugee camps or on the run in the Congo between 1994–1997 and they died during the insurgency and counter-insurgency campaign in north-west Rwanda in the 1997–1999 period. Responses given by households in the government death count can include deaths from all these episodes. If we accept that the total death count by the government correctly counts all people killed in 1994, then this count must include 250,000–350,000 (midpoint 300,000) Hutu victims. That corresponds to between 3.7 and 5.2 % (midpoint 4.4 %) of Rwanda's Hutu population.

1.2 Short History of State Formation in Rwanda[2]

The formation of the Rwandan State was the result of century long expansion of the central territory (ancient Rwanda) in which adjoining territories were put under the control of the King of Rwanda. This process took place in the 18th and 19th centuries, in particular under the reign of King Rwabugiri. The central state was characterized by a high degree of organisation in which the king and his advisors decided on all important matters. This inner circle of power was always composed of a small group of Tutsi, originating from 2 clans. The large majority of Tutsi as well as Hutu had no access to power or privilege. The two groups, differed in their main economic activity. Hutu were cultivators, whereas Tutsi were cattle-breeders. A significant part of the land was reserved for pastures (Ibikingi).

The advent of colonialism (first by Germany, then by Belgium) brought far-reaching change to the country. The colonizers observed the socio-political composition of the elite and the peasantry, and concluded that the Tutsi were a different race. Attracted by the high stature, facial characteristics and leading position in society, the coloniser (church and state) concluded that the Tutsi originated from Northern Africa and that they were related with the Caucasian race, thereby genetically predestined to rule. The Hutu on the other hand were considered Bantu-people, a black race, predestined to be ruled. Convinced of the correctness of this interpretation and in search of a mechanism to govern Rwanda

---

[2] For a detailed treatment of Rwanda's history I refer to published work by Danielle De Lame, Catharine Newbury, David Newbury, Gerard Prunier, Filip Reyntjens, Jan Vansina, Claudine Vidal and Jean-Claude Willame among others.

along clearly defined lines, the colonial administration decided to inscribe the ethnicity of each Rwandan in his/her identity card.

The Belgian colonial administration governed the country through Tutsi interlocutors. Very few Hutu were admitted to *Astrida*, the school that educated future administrators and government officials. In 1929, Hutu chiefs, often in charge of land allocation and management at the local level were removed from office and replaced by Tutsi chiefs. While the latter already occupied chieftain-ships in cattle and military affairs, the balance of power fell completely in favor of Tutsi. The Hutu peasantry regarded the Tutsi as their de facto rulers. They rep-resented the power of the state at the local level, whereas power at the national level was in the hands of the Mwami (king) and, ultimately, the colonial government.

In the wake of the pan-African independence movements in the 1950s, Tutsi leaders began to demand independence from Belgium. This was not well received by the colonial government. Aided by the Catholic Church, omni-present in Rwanda and herself influenced by a current of emancipatory struggles, the Bel-gians supported the constitution of a Hutu counter elite that would challenge Tutsi supremacy and allow Belgium to retain its influence.

From 1959 to 1962, a Hutu-lead revolution occurred in Rwanda, whereby political power was taken out of the hands of the ruling Tutsi elite. Grégoire Kayibanda, a Hutu educated in missionary schools, became president and installed the First Republic. The nature of the Hutu Revolution is much debated in the literature. To some it was a Social Revolution where the masses claimed their legitimate stake in the resources of the country. This social element clearly existed, Hutu were burdened with labour dues and taxes. They were bared from access to wealth and status (Newbury 1988). Nevertheless, research by Leurquin (1960, 203 and 278) in the 1950s showed that Tutsi who did not have a job in the adminis-tration were equally poor as Hutu farmers. When claiming their political and economic rights, Hutu rid the country of their Tutsi oppressors. Not only the elite, but thousands of Tutsi civilians were driven out of their homes and had to take refuge in neighboring countries. The revolt against the 'big Tutsi' also swept away the 'small Tutsi' and demonstrates the racial component of the revolution. The new Hutu elite trumped the cause of the masses while playing the racial card.[3] Following the Revolution, the percentage of Tutsi in the Rwandan population declined sharply.

Juvénal Habyarimana, Minister of the National Guard and the Police in the Kayibanda government, took power in a *coup d'état* in 1973 that removed pres-ident Kayibanda from power. Whereas the landed interest of the northern elite (Abakonde) was preserved by the Hutu Revolution, they were not given access to lucrative business opportunities and political power by the Kayibanda regime. According to Pottier (1993), TRAFIPRO, Rwanda's first state-run marketing

---

[3] This combination of economic claims and gains on the one hand and ethnic fears, myths and grievance on the other hand will reappear in the 1990s.

system, was at the centre of the intrigue.[4] Controlling 27 shops nationwide and 70 buying-up points for coffee (in 1966), TRAFIPRO was accused of running a monopoly and diverting rents to leading politicians in the Kayibanda government. TRAFIPRO was the economic arm of the Gitarama regime (Reyntjens 1985).[5] Nevertheless, ethnic animosities were rampant in the months before the coup: the *comité de salut public* drove Tutsi students off the campus and removed Tutsi employees from their jobs in the public and private sector. [6] As occurred a decade earlier, a new wave of Tutsi emigration took place. The new president would later say that he mounted the coup because he sensed that the Revolution went off-track (see Chap. 2).

From 1974 to 1976 Habyarimana consolidated his political power. He outlawed political parties and created his own Revolutionary Movement for Development (MRND). According to Prunier (1995), the MRND was a truly totalitarian party: every Rwandan had to be member of the MRND and all bourgmestres and préfets were chosen from among party cadres.[7] Habyarimana institutionalised *Umuganda*, the compulsory communal labour, and had peasants participate in village anima-tion sessions to honor him. He killed 56 businessmen and politicians closely related to the Kayibanda regime. All citizens were under tight administrative control. Every five years the president was re-elected with 99 % of the vote.

In October 1990, a group of several thousand Tutsi rebels (former refugees and their sons), united in the RPF (Rwandan Patriotic Front) attacked Rwanda from Uganda. The timing of this attack was determined by events in Uganda as well as by the ongoing talks to find a solution for the problem of Rwandan refugees. (1) In Uganda, the positions of influence of the Tutsi allies of president Museveni in the NRA became more and more critisized. (2) The FPR would loose its raison d'être when a negotiated solution for the refugee question would be reached. This could be permanent settlement in and conferring of the nationality of the host countries or repatriation to Rwanda. According to Guichaoua (2010, Chap. 2), these nego-tiations had made substantial progress by September 1990. In this way, Juvénal Habyarimana could claim (as he did in a speech in Abuja, 4/6/1991) before the 27th Session of the Conference of Heads of State and Government of the OAU that the RPF chose to attack because it realised that such solution would deprive it of its reason to attack. However, president Habyarimana, by September 1990 never agreed to the return of the Rwandan refugees.[8] This means that his speech in Abuja

---

[4] Pottier (1993).

[5] Reyntjens, F., 1985, Pouvoir et Droit au Rwanda, Musée Royal de L'Afrique Centrale.

[6] Committees of Public Safety. Reyntjens sees a historic line between the activism of members of these committees in 1973 and their behaviour in 1994. We come back to this in Chap. 2).

[7] Prunier (1995).

[8] In fact a right to return on an individual basis, supported by enough financial resources to sustain one's living, was recognised by the MRND since 1986, but few people (300 by 1989) had used it (Guichaoua 2010, p. 64). See below in the section 'population policy and the refugee question'in this introduction.

in 1991 was good for consumption for his African peers but does not square with his position nor that of his government or the MRND in September 1990.

The following years were marked by a low-intensity civil war and ongoing peace negotiations. In 1993, a peace-agreement was reached in Arusha whereby political power would be divided between the rebels and the government. Economic decline, political manipulation of ethnic animosities and civil war all contributed to the disintegration of Rwandan society in the 1990–1993 period. Christophe Mfizi, close supporter of the president, broke with the MRND in 1992 after discovering state-sponsored massacres in several villages in Northern Rwanda (see Chap. 6). He wrote that a group called the 'zero network' had penetrated the highest levels of government and that

> this group considers the country as an enterprise where it is legitimate to get out as much profit as possible....It is this group that has incited ethnic tensions to cover up their own interests....[9]

This is exactly what Bardhan (1997) writes about the political economy of ethnicity, namely that ethnicity is often used as a device to stake a claim in the process of rent-sharing:

> As the government has become more important in economic activities, more and more mobilised groups have used ethnicity to stake a claim in the process of rent-sharing. [10]

When, on April 6, 1994, president Habyarimana came back from a meeting in Arusha, his plane was shot down over Kigali airport. His death allowed the Hutu-extremists in his regime to turn Rwanda into hell on earth: in no less then 100 days, between 500,000 and 800,000 Tutsi and Hutu opponents of the regime were killed.

1.3 The Argument of the Book in a Nutshell

The sheer size and horror of genocide induces some people to believe that it is something beyond our comprehension, that the forces driving genocide cannot be explained, or that it is irrational. I do not share this position. I believe we have a lot of evidence to show that the forces at work during genocide are not unexplainable or irrational. I will need the whole book to explain this position. In this section I would like to make the argument in a nutshell. For a detailed and in-dept treatment of all my arguments, I refer to the different chapters. In order to study, understand and explain genocide in Rwanda, I attempt to answer four related questions in this book:

---

[9] Mfizi, C., 1992, Reseau zero, lettre ouverte à Monsieur le Président du MRND, Editions Uruhimbi, Kigali, Juillet-Aout.

[10] Bardhan (1997).

(1) *Where does the idea to commit genocide come from*? What are the origins of the intention to implement genocide?

(2) *Why* was genocide committed in Rwanda, including the related question *why was it committed then*, meaning in the period 1990–1994?

(3) *How was genocide committed*? Who was mobilised to participate? What resources where mobilised? Where did they come from?

(4) *Why was the implementation of genocide so successful?* Why did the genocidal campaign manage to kill ¾ of all Tutsi in Rwanda?

In his 1998 book *Seeing Like a State*, Scott describes how the state gradually got a handle on its subjects and their environment. Processes as disparate as the creation of permanent last names, the standardization of weights and measures, the establishment of cadastral surveys and population registers, taxation, conscription, and the construction of roads to give a few examples, contributed to the radical reorganisation and simplification of a previously unorganised world. These state simplifications, in other words the basic givens of modern statecraft, Scott argues, do not successfully represent the actual activity of the society they depict, no were they intended to do so. They represented only that slice of it that interested the official observer. They were maps that, when allied with state power, would enable much of the reality they depicted to be remade.

Scott observes that the history of Third World development is littered with the debris of huge agricultural schemes and new cities that have failed their residents. The Great Leap Forward in China, collectivization in Russia, compulsory villagization in Tanzania, Mozambique and Ethiopia are among the great human tragedies of the twentieth century. Similarly, in their 1991 book 'Vordenker der Vernichtung' Götz Aly and Susanne Heim describe how the destruction of the European Jews was the mortal outcome of a scheme to re-organize Europe's social and economic polity.

I describe and analyse Rwanda under the Second Republic in this book as a Developmental State, organised along similar lines as described by Scott. He argues that the most tragic episodes of state-initiated social engineering originate in the pernicious combination of four elements. They apply very well to the Rwandan case:

(a) *The Administrative Ordering of Nature and Society or its 'Legibility'*

Rwanda was a highly and tightly organized society. The penetration of its administration into the hills was unmatched in Africa (Guichaoua 1997; McDoom 2009). From the ethnic identity card system, the detailed registration of births, marriages and deaths at the communal level, the policy of 'ethnic equilibrium' in schools and in the administration, the parallel organisation of the Party and the State from the national down to the cellule level, to the policy to keep people in the rural areas, the Second Republic was neatly organized, as a pyramid from the top to the bottom. Many observers were stunned by the degree of organisation and thus by the presence of statecraft in the life of ordinary Rwandans. The desire to order was not limited to its inhabitants, but also applied to nature, as witnessed in the drive to re-organize agrarian space, the nationwide anti-erosion campaigns, land settlement and agrarian order all together. On the nationwide campaigns Guichaoua (1991) writes that it illustrates how a standardized, agrarian order, implemented with geometric precision, is not able to accommodate variation in soil quality, steepness and local needs and as such invites peasant resistance.

(b) *High-Modernist Ideology*

This is defined by Scott (1998, 4) as a 'muscle-bound version of the self-confidence about scientific and technical progress, the expansion of production, ... the mastery of nature ... and, above all, the rational design of social order'. It must not be confused with scientific practice. What is meant here is a coherent set of beliefs that are not open for questioning. The design of five year production plans, the mobilisation of the entire peasantry in weekly *umuganda*, the expansion of the *paysannats* and the denial of crop failure and famine conditions in the south in 1989 testify to the revolutionary beliefs held by the leaders of the Second Republic. While communist countries adopted industrialisation as their version of the developmental state, the Agrarian Nation that Rwanda would remain under the Second Republic, founded on a ruralist and peasant ideology, was Habyarimana's version of the developmental state.

(c) *An Authoritarian State*

The authoritarian character of the Second Republic is demonstrated by several of its features. Chief amongst these, we find the centralisation of power (military, executive, party) in the hands of the president; the carrot and stick policy employed in the coffee sector (Little and Horowitz 1987, 1988 and Verwimp 2003); the fact that all Rwandans were required by law to be members of the MRND; the prohibition to form other political parties; the submission of the judiciary to the authority of the single party; the weekly animation sessions in honour of the president; the forced removal of people from their land in order to create tea plantations; the organisation of mock elections; and the killing of political adversaries in 1976 and 1988.[11]

(d) *Civil Society Silenced*

This is defined by Scott as the lack of capacity to resist state plans. In his 1998 book *Aiding Violence*, Uvin paints a bleak picture of civil society in Rwanda. In Chap. 9 of his book, titled 'And Where was Civil Society', Uvin describes exactly what Scott has in mind: a weak and usurped civil society incapable of making a fist when most needed. According to Prunier (1995) the MRND was totalitarian. Its first letter 'M' stands for Movement, and the party manifest said that its task was to mobilize all living forces for the benefit of the nation. Hence there was no need for

---

[11] Animation sessions took place once a week after *umuganda* and consisted of singing and dancing in honour of president J. Habyarimana.

organisations outside the party. Even the highest religious authority; the arch-
bishop of Kigali, was a member of the Central Committee of the MRND until
ordered to resign from that position by the Pope.

My characterisation of the Second Republic as a Developmental State help us to
understand the macro-level, to wit the vision the regime espoused, its revolutionary aspirations and its monopolisation of power. This State mobilised its entire
population in weekly collective labour (umuganda), used for example to build
145 identical commune offices in every commune or to dig hundreds of km of anti-
erosion ditches in an nationwide campaign with complete disregard for local, slope
or plot level variation in the risk of erosion. This State practised a policy of land
colonisation and resettlement until every acre of land was brought under cultivation. Technological innovation to increase yields however, was completely
absent. The Developmental State encouraged all farmers to produce more food, but
solely relied on labour input to achieve it, whereas the marginal product of labour
on a farmer's small field was practically zero. This State espoused an antiintel-
lectual and anti-urban bias and decreed that only labour is the source of value.

The main purpose of the Second Republic was to safeguard the attainments of
the Hutu Revolution, in essence the post-revolutionary agrarian order, and to
cement that order with its own Moral Revolution. This agrarian order guaranteed
the hold onto power by the regime. Pastoralism all but disappeared as a way of
living during the Second Republic. Pastoral land was either converted into agricultural land or cattle were put in ranches as in the Mutara project in northern
Byumba. The Developmental State was a Peasant-State in which Habyarimana, *the
Father of the Nation*, assumed the task of government in order for the peasants to
devote themselves completely to food cultivation. Pastoralists could only belong
to the Nation-State when they changed occupation. Some did, but it is impossible
to change one's ethnic affiliation (even when some managed to do that on their
identity cards). The advent of war allowed the leaders of the Developmental State
(in essence the presidential clan or *Akazu*) to take drastic measures in order to
safeguard a regime that proclaimed itself as the guarantor of the post-revolutionary
agrarian order. The massacre of pastoralists such as the Bagogwe in 1991 and the
massacre of Tutsi from the south who settled on newly colonised land in Bugesera
in 1992 (see Chap. 6) should be regarded as instances of ethnic cleansing in areas
chosen because of their characteristics salient to the regime. The State capitalised
on ethnicity and fomemted hatred towards the Tutsi minority in an orchestrated
propaganda campaign. In 1994 genocide can be understood as a purification of the
Nation–State of all its enemies, including Hutu who did not subscribe to the cause.

The local massacres before 1994 as well as the genocide occurred in the context
of a civil war that started in October 1990. I argue in this book that the civil war
created the conditions that allowed extreme strategies such as a policy of massacres to be implemented. Civil war should not be equated with massacres or
genocide. The civil war and in particular the shooting down of the presidential
plane carrying president Habyarimana allowed extremist political and military
leaders to get the upperhand over the modest leaders, Hutu as well as Tutsi. In the

book I show that the RPF as well as the political–military nordist elite had the capability as well as the motive to kill the president. His death however was not followed by a spontaneous killing spree of outraged Hutu. Rather, his death allowed the extremists to fill the political vacuüm which they then used to orchestrate a policy of genocide. Had the modest leaders prevailed or had there be a legal and constitutional succession of president Habyarimana, there would not have been a genocide and the killings would have been limited to a few hundred. I analyse and interpret this extremist takeover in Chap. 7.

The analysis of the Second Republic as a Developmental State helps us to understand *the origins of the idea to commit genocide*, but it does not suffice to understand the remaining questions: *why* and *why then* was it undertaken, *how* was it undertaken and *why it was so successful*. To shed light on these other questions, we have to study the political and economic institutions of the Second Republic and the survival of these institutions throughout the period of the civil war and the advent of multipartism. We have to understand the political rationale to set up these institutions as well as the effect they have on the behaviour of the average Rwandan. The study of institutions is necessary because it reveals the messages elites send to their population. In this respect it is necessary to define what I call 'the institutional core' or 'core element in an institution' which lies at the centre of many systems, mechanisms, policies or institutions broadly speaking. This core element can be defined as *the overt or covert prescriptions of behaviour for today's citizens set by an institution*. Institutional cores in other words are *norms of behaviour*. And an institution in turn can be defined as *the translation of the political history of a country into rewards and penalties for administrators and, via the national and local administration, into incentives for ordinary citizens*. In that sense is, for example, the persistence of an old institution as revealing for the intention of a new regime as the change of the institution in question.

In this book, the following institutions and in particular their core element, will be studied in greater or smaller detail: the ethnic identification system, the ethnic quota system in schools and in the administration, the organisation of the MRND and the state apparatus, the organisation of coffee economy, the functioning of agricultural policy, the weekly obligatory form of communal labour called umuganda, the taxation system, and population policy.

My treatment of each of the institutions of the Second Republic will not be a chronological study of all policies enacted by the Habyarimana regime in the domain of each institution. Rather, I focus on the message these institutions conveyed, the implicit or explicit rules of behaviour for the ordinary peasants entailed and prescribed by these institutions. I will focus on the institutional core. Not all of the institutions and the policy messages emitted by these institutions will be treated in a separate chapter. Some chapters will deal with several of the mentioned institutions and their cores.

At the end of this study the following general conclusion will be reached: the quest for the origins of genocide in Rwanda, the questions 'why'and 'why then' was genocide committed in Rwanda, 'how' it was committed and 'why it was successful' are closely interlinked. It is my approach in this book, to study these

questions in one overarching way. Genocide was organised by a group of committed leaders who pushed the idelology of the Developmental State to its extreme,
to wit the inability and unwillingness to tolerate people and space outside of the
Nation–State, defined as a Peasant-State whose raison-d'être was to safeguard the
post-revolutionary agrarian order. The institutions set up by this Developmental
State where designed to tie the peasantry to the ruling elite, in good as well as in
bad times. On the eve of the civil war, these institutions were in a deadlock, they
were no longer able to uphold the promises made to the population in terms of the
producer price for coffee, schooling, access to land, food security and welfare in
general. In order to avoid institutional reform—which for the elite would mean a
loss of political power—and to jeopardize the attainments of the 1959 Social
Revolution and the 1973 Moral Revolution including its agrarian order, the
extremists, by then in control of the regime, took the ultimate step. The genocide
was implemented in the same fashion as the regime implemented its development
plans, to wit mobilising its administration, using income from tea exports to buy
weapons, financing militia from state-run companies, using radio to spread propaganda and above all mobilising the Hutu farmers. The succesfull implementation of a new killing norm by a powerful group resulted in the destruction of the
Tutsi of Rwanda. In Chap. 8, I study that success as an example of collective
action rooted in the mechanism of control over the (labour of the) peasant population. The organisation of the genocide and the path of economic development
chosen by the elite had in common that they relied on 'the people', on the collective labour of the peasant population. *This strategy for development as well as
for the genocide, was endogenous to Rwanda.* The engineering of the development
process as well as the genocide resulted from the institutions created by the revolutionary zeal of the leaders of the Second Republic. These leaders were very
aware of the force of Rwanda's only abundant factor of production and of the
options it gave to them.

My point is that we can explain a large chunk of the genocide when we take a
political economy approach to development and dictatorship in Rwanda: the
institutions of the Habyarimana Regime found themselves in a deadlock, they were
no longer able to guarantee the well-being of the population and at the same time
were highly re-distributive to the powers that be.[12] Instead of accepting and
implementing institutional reform, the elite took the institutional set-up to its
extreme: genocide. They mobilised the peasantry, directed it to serve their own
purpose and avoided the power of the masses turning against the regime. They
considered a genocide to be executed by the population itself as a form of legitimate defense, a defense against the aspirations of the feudo-monarchists. An
extermination of the Tutsi would solve Rwanda's ethnic problem which was
considered to be part of the country's institutional set-up. The regime had ample

---

[12] With the term 'Habyarimana regime' I want to clarify that it included moderate and extremist
elements. With the advent of civil war and electoral competition they engaged in fierce battles.
Ultimately, the extremists in the MRND, the presidential clan and the army overpowed the
moderates. We come back on this is Chaps. 6 and 7.

Table 1.1 Three levels to study development and genocide in Rwanda

Levels of analysis	Application to Rwanda
1. The macro level	The second republic as a developmental state
The leadership of the state, the functioning of the regime, its politicians, its ideology, its politics and policies, its budget, its fears, its plan and vision for the future	The custodian of the Hutu Revolutuion, the agrarian order, the peasant-state, the policy of food self-sufficiency, the anti-erosion campaign, population policy
2. The meso level	The institutions of the Habyarimana Regime
The relation between the regime and the citizens, its administrative apparatus, the norms it cultivates, its appeal, the organisation of the military, the school system, the rural cooperatives	The MRND party-state, the practice of collective action in umuganda, the organisation of the coffee economy, the army, the tax structure, the ethnic equilibrium in the school system, the judiciary
3. The micro level	The ordinary Rwandan
The beliefs of the citizens, their economic activities, their fears, their relationships, their conformism and protest, their uniqueness	Farm size, rural living conditions, access to off-farm jobs, hopes for a better life, vulnerability, fertility and mortality, outburst of protest, social conformism

experience with peasant mobilisation, in particular through the re-organisation of agrarian space, the peasant economy and in particular peasant labour. This experience resulted from the high levels of population density of Rwanda, a situation that requires high levels of regulation and facilitates (or better necessitates) collective action. The regime relied on the demographic majority (the great mass or rubande nyamwishi) to exectute the genocide. I will therefore argue that the genocide was *endogenous* to the development of Rwanda's institutions under the Second Republic: the genocide arises as a Final Solution to preserve the post-revolutionary agrarian order. The Tutsi did not fit into this order because the regime did not consider them as real peasants.

I argue that genocide can be understood when we study society at three crucial levels. These are, the state and political level (national as well as local), the institutional level and the individual level. Table 1.1 reformulates and expands on the three analythical levels already presented in Fig. 1.1. I consider the second level as the intermediate level, as the incorporation of policies formulated at the first level. This level translates first level policies into incentives and constraints for ordinary people.

These three levels should always be analysed in their historical context and circumstances: presence and history of the leadership, presence and history of state-citizen relationships, presence and history of the citizenry. Some examples may clarify this: in order for us to understand development and genocide in Rwanda, we have to understand the relationship between population policy, agricultural policy and ethnicity; in order for us the understand the functioning of the dictatorial regime, we have to study the coffee economy, the structure of state-run companies and the access to foreign exchange via import/export; in order for us to grasp the willingness of young Hutu to become members of a militia, we

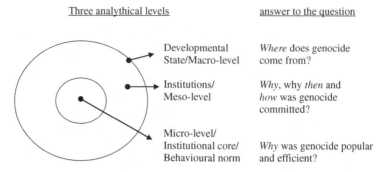

Fig. 1.1 Development, institutions and Genocide

have to look at economic conditions and the structure of social relations in Rwandan society. The relevance and contribution of one component to the whole picture only becomes clear in relationship to the other components. That is why an institutional analysis is necessary.

The historical context of the analysis is the Second Republic (1973–1994). Ideally, I should go back further in history and analyse (the institutions of) the pre-colonial period, the colonial period and the first republic (1962–1973). I will occasionally do this when I see an historic link between current and past policies and institutions. One reason to focus on the Habyarimana regime is that most of the perpetrators have lived their lives (as young adults or adults) under Habyarimana and have no experience (or only as children) of past leaders. History in this book is considered important to explain Rwanda's institutions, but it is the functioning of these institutions during Habyarimana's reign that is at the core of my interest.

1.4 A Political Economy Approach to Genocide

1.4.1 The Economic Analysis of Dictatorship

Too long economists neglected the role of politics, the form of government and more broadly institutions in the economy. Political scientists on the other hand have left economic development out of the picture. As if political choices could be explained in a world free from economic conflict. Recently, scholars in both sciences have begun to ask questions on the relationship between economic development and political power, thereby reconnecting both disciplines with the mother science of ' political economy '.

The interdependence of economics and politics are particularly apparent in economies that depend for a large part on the export of one or a few crops or on the export of one or a few minerals. Examples of the first category include coffee and cocoa in Ghana; coffee and cotton in Tanzania; coffee and tea in Rwanda and Burundi. Examples of the second category include oil in Nigeria, Iraq, Indonesia, Sudan, Angola; diamonds, coltan and gold in Congo; diamonds in Sierra Leone to name just a few. For a large part of the post world war II and the post-independence era, these countries have been ruled by authoritarian regimes, often brutal dictatorships.

I present a political economy analysis of dictatorship in Rwanda which accounts for the linkage between political power and the economy. In a model presented in Chap. 4, the ability of the dictator to amass power over the population depends on the value of the countries export crop or commodity on the world market. With the export earnings, the dictator buys political loyalty from the population and represses that part of the population that refuses to be loyal. One of the objectives of Chap. 4 is to derive the effect of changes in the world market price of the export crop or commodity on the price paid to the farmer-producers and on the level of repression.

Contrary to deep rooted beliefs, most dictators do not only (or not in the first place) rely on their repressive apparatus (which is of course a necessity to remain in power), but enjoy support from large segments of their populations. That support is not taken for granted but permanently watched. I believe that a dictator (ruler, elite or oligarchy) needs to be more concerned about the general populace when the economy is made up of many smallholder farms compared to an economy of plantations or with vast amounts of mineral wealth (oil, gold, diamonds). When the export earnings of an economy depend on the produce of smallholder farms, such as coffee in Rwanda, the dictator has a strong incentive to offer a high producer price to the farmers. In the event of low producer prices, growers will abandon the crop and switch to other crops, for example crops for the domestic market. The incentive to "care" for farmer-producers is largely absent in an economy endowed with diamond mines, gold mines or oil fields. Once the dictator controls these mines or fields, he has few incentives to "care" for the welfare of the general population. As long as he pays his repressive apparatus with the export earnings, he can remain in power. The budget of a dictator who rules a country with vast mineral resources does not depend on the welfare of his subjects. Such a dictator only needs the support of a selective group, often army officers and family members.

For that reason, we first need to take a look at the way economists treat political decision making or politics in general. Olson and Mcguire (1996) argue that there is a great gap in the economics literature.[13] Economics has not explained how the form of government—democratic rule or dictatorship—affects tax rates, income distribution and the provision of public goods. Economists take for granted that interacting parties, however much they vary in wealth and in other ways, do not use coercion to attain their objectives. This has everything to do with the degree of attention that economists have given to 'the market'. In a market, all transactions

---

[13] Olson and Mcguire (1996).

are said to occur on a voluntary basis. This is the case because market transactions are mutually advantageous. After all, this is what Adam Smiths invisible hand is all about: producers can best serve their interests by selling their output to buyers who purchase them only when that is in the buyers' best interest.[14] Economists however know very well that transaction costs hinder agents in realising mutually advantageous deals. Before the advent of the Coase-theorem, all economists agreed that laissez-faire would not deal efficiently with externalities and public goods. It was Pigou who showed long ago that in case of an externality—for example air pollution—laissez-faire cannot lead to Pareto-efficient outcomes. In his seminal article on social cost, Coase (1960) showed that the Pigouvian view was wrong. Coase explained how two parties can bargain on externalities and trough this bargain reach a Pareto-efficient outcome. The externality would be internalised, unless the bargaining costs were too high. But, if transaction or bargaining costs were zero, all externalities would be dealt with in a Pareto-efficient manner simply because rational parties would bargain until they had maximized joint gains. The Coasian bargain approach includes an awareness that some transaction costs are so high that trade will not occur. When the transaction costs of the trade exceed the gains it would bring, the parties do not make the trade, and that too is as it should be. Thus, according to this approach, any status quo resulting from the market is efficient. The logic tells us that, as long as people are free to transact, we are automatically in the most efficient of all worlds.

Olson (2000, 53–54) argues that economists and economic historians after Coase have tried to use the concept of voluntary exchange or Coasian bargains–and the transaction costs associated with them–to understand government and politics as well as the market. The voluntary exchange approach can be applied to government policies. Political transaction cost theorists argue that mutually advantageous bargaining within the political system tends to bring about socially efficient public policies. Political bargaining, they argue, leads to social outcomes that are Pareto-efficient. If an inefficient policy is chosen, it follows that changing to a more efficient policy must bring net gains, and that there is some distribution of these net gains that would leave everyone better off. Again, no matter which government policies are actually chosen, we observe an efficient outcome. Olson (2000, 58) concludes as follows:

> If you start with the assumptions of the Coasian bargain and transaction cost approach and make no logical mistakes, you inevitably keep coming back to the conclusion that the social equilibrium we are in or heading toward is Pareto-efficient, at least to an approximation. Whatever may be thought of the distribution of income that results from bargaining in the market and in the polity, when all bargaining is done it tends to leave society in a situation where it is not possible to make one person better off without making someone else worse off: all the mutually advantageous deals have been made. The Coasian bargain and transaction cost approach does not lend itself to explaining bad outcomes.

---

[14] Olson, M., Power and Prosperity, outgrowing communist and capitalist dictatorships, Basic Books, 2000, p. 48.

Here, in effect, we are interested in bad outcomes. Economic and political reality offers ample evidence of the importance of such outcomes. War, famine and genocide are just some examples of bad outcomes that have occurred very frequently in the past decades. Their existence is a strong indication that socially optimal outcomes are not realised in the present world.

As Hirschleifer (1994) has pointed out, the rationality and self-interest economists usually assume, imply that actors with a sufficient advantage in employing violence will use that power to serve their interest. Economists have not given nearly as much attention to this 'dark side' of self-interest as they have given to the social consequences of self-interested behaviour in peaceful markets.[15] We therefore need a theory of coercion, a theory of power. Indeed, the concept of rational actors, a cornerstone of economics, does not imply that actors take decisions that are beneficial for fellow human beings or for the societies in which they live. Non-economists often define rationality different from economists. Horowitz (1976) for example states that rational behavior is behavior that benefits a country's economy. Political economists believe that people in general, including politicians and especially dictators, care about their own interests first, i.e., being re-elected or seeing their power increase. The dictator (or his inner circle, the presidential clan) judges economic policies by the impact they have on his/their position and not on the welfare of the whole population.

Olson (1993) explains why a population prefers a dictator above a group of roving bandits.[16] The activity of the latter, he argues, consists of occasional plunder where the targeted population looses all its assets. A dictator on the other hand settles down, eliminates uncoordinated competitive theft and takes his income in the form of regular taxation. With a regular tax system, his subjects are aware that they can keep for themselves a known proportion of their output, thereby providing the population with an incentive to produce. The rational stationary bandit (the dictator), in Olson's view, will take only a part of income in taxes, in order to extract a larger sum in the long run. A consequence of this, important for our subject of study, is that the dictator has an incentive to prohibit murder or maiming of his subjects. Productive citizens increase tax revenue. According to Olson, a dictator has an *encompassing interest* in the territory he controls and accordingly provides domestic order and public goods. Contrary to a roving bandit, a dictator will spend resources (part of his tax receipts) to increase the productivity of his population. He is "not like the wolf that preys on the elk, but more like the rancher who makes sure that his cattle are protected and given water." This to stimulate economic growth but at the same time charge a monopoly rent on everything, including human labour. A self-interested dictator, according to Olson, avoids crushing his population and chooses a tax rate that maximizes his revenue. His encompassing interest offers the reason why he does

---

[15] Olson and Mcguire, ibidem (1996, p. 73).

[16] Olson, M., Dictatorship, Democracy and Economic Development, *American Political Science Review*, 1993, pp. 567–576.

not interfere in the economic activities of a thriving ethnic minority. A political economy model of dictatorship thus has to account for the dictator's incentive to provide public goods while maximising his tax revenue. Wintrobe (2002) however points at the problem with encompassing dictators. He writes that the worst regimes in human history such as Nazi Germany, Soviet Russia or Cambodia under the Khmer Rouge appear to have been the most encompassing. The reason is that these regimes wanted to remold the citizens and the societies under their rule and therefore intervened most thoroughly in the lives of their citizens. This is the ambiguity of the dictator's encompassing interest.

The dictator's time-horizon plays an important role in Olson's theory. The dictator only refrains from confiscating the assets of his population, because he considers the tax income he will gain from future output of the society. This means that the dictator's prospects to remain in office are crucial to Olson's theory. At the moment when the dictator has no reason to consider the future output of the society at all, his incentives become the same as those of a roving bandit. A revenue maximizing dictator who expects to be thrown out of office next year has the incentive to confiscate all assets of his population. Such a dictator, one could add, has no incentive anymore to provide security to his subjects. Again, Wintrobe points at the problem that the longer dictators are in office, the stronger their grip on power and hence the more they can mold the society and its citizens.

Olson's theory of power and Wintrobe's critique are good starting point for a political economy analysis of dictatorship. This theory however requires some complementary thoughts, remarks and expansions. The work of Bates (1981) showed that dysfunctional agricultural policies (in other words, bad outcomes) in Sub Saharan Africa are maintained because they guarantee the political survival of the elite.[17] Economically efficient policies, Bates argues, would deprive the political elite of their distributional power. Acemoglu and Robinson (2006) further explore this way of thinking.[18] They argue that policies and institutions are not the result of stupidity, ideology, incorrect expectations or rational ignorance, but can rather be understood as part of a rational strategy of political power holders to maintain and consolidate their power. While development might be desirable, these strategies may generate underdevelopment because political elites fear that economic development may disturb the political status quo and rob them of their political power. In Acemoglu and Robinson's theory, poor countries are poor because political elites fear that the benefits from promoting development are smaller than the losses they face from losing political power. These elites refuse to implement development policies when the political opposition cannot credibly promise them that their interests will not be harmed. Landed elites, according to Lewis (1995), are typically opposed to development. The process of development

---

[17] Bates, R., Markets and States in Tropical Africa, The Political Basis of Agricultural Policies, 1981.

[18] This book was written before Why Nations Fail (2012) came out, reason why I rely on earlier work by Acemoglu and Robinson. The reader will find many ideas in their new book reflected in this book.

involves capital accumulation and urbanization which increases wages and reduces land rents. On top of that, a new middle class emerges which contests the political power of the landed elite. They might e.g. introduce a land tax.

A self-serving dictator is not necessarily bad towards his population. He may enact policies that allow the population to accumulate capital (this is akin to Olson's encompassing interest). Indeed, other things equal, a prosperous economy allows the elites to tax more wealth and thus get richer themselves. One would think that elites like this. The problem however, is that economic development is very often inconsistent with the political status quo. This is an element that Olson seems to forget. According to Olson, economic development does not endanger the political power of the dictator.

Acemoglu and Robinson (2006) do not agree with that. As economic development may spur the development of a middle class, and this may lead to a call for democratization, the dictator may enact policies that are detrimental to economic development. Such predatory behavior of dictators, meaning either actions leading to a halt on the accumulation of capital by ordinary citizens (e.g., high levels of taxation) or to reluctance to take actions required to improve development (e.g., enforcement of property rights), entails costs for the dictators. They forego the benefits to themselves of a prosperous population. Such behavior is perfectly rational from the part of the dictator when, from whose own standpoint, the benefits of the political status quo outweigh the benefits of improved development. These elites prefer a poor country where they hold monopoly political power compared to a rich country were they would loose this political position. The nature of the political equilibrium induced by development thus plays an important role.

1.4.2 The Political Economy of Population Density

• Population Density and Economic Growth

Platteau (2001) adds an important variable to the discussion, namely population size and population density.[19]. He argues that population growth is the driving force behind institutional change. In areas of low population density, farming households have high transportation and high labour hiring costs. Households will therefore work on their own plot assigned to them by the village community. Self-cultivation and geographic isolation imply that, on average, everyone is self-sufficient in food. Under these circumstances, capital accumulation is very difficult and may even be considered a waste of time. Why should a self-sufficient farmer provide effort, beyond the self-sufficiency level? (Binswanger and McIntire 1987)[20].

---

[19] Platteau, J.-Ph., Institutions, Social Norms and Economic Development, Harwoord, 2001.

[20] Biswanger and McIntire, Explaining Agricultural and Agrarian Policies in Developing Countries, *Journal of Economic Literature*, December, 1997.

In areas of high population density, the contrary is true. Infrastructure develops, factor and product markets arise and farmers have incentives to produce above the self-sufficiency level. In some cases, as in Rwanda for example, a farmer's own plot often does not produce enough to feed his family, hence the need to practise intensive agriculture and to find other sources of income outside agriculture. In this sense, economic development is more likely to occur in high density regions. Several studies however, emphasize that the process of innovation, necessary to increase intensive agriculture or overall economic opportunities, only works when governments support it. Agricultural innovation can only take place when governments provide public goods. If not, farmers are not able to reach the Boserupian (1965) path of economic development through technological innovations.[21] As a result, resources will be depleted.

Here, one clearly observes the political difference between a country with low and with high population densities. In the case of low population density, not much government action is required; as a consequence less public goods will be provided and a lower level of economic development will be achieved. Under high population density, sophisticated forms of collective action and a high level of public goods (such as order and regulation) can be expected. If one believes in the Coaseian approach, one expects that bargaining will lead groups of people to efficient outcomes, meaning that the public good will be provided at an optimal level.

Returning to Acemoglu and Robinson (2006), we emphasise the role of the political leaders in this process. Political leaders are not in the first place interested in efficient outcomes. If they are convinced that the process of economic development through institutional change disturbs the political status quo and threatens their survival in office, they will block institutional reform. Throughout this book, I will try to show that it is exactly this situation of a highly populated country, where institutional change is a necessary condition for economic growth, and where this change is blocked because it would disturb the political status quo and the power position of the elite, that we found in Rwanda under Habyarimana.

• Population Policy and the Refugee Question

As I will document in the Chap. 2 of this book, president Habyarimana, throughout his entire reign, was very pre-occupied with the food-population equilibrium in Rwanda. In his many speeches on the question he emphasized the production side of the equation much more than the consumption side. He believed that the first priority for Rwanda was to increase food production in order to attain food self-sufficiency. John May, a demographer working on Rwanda in the early nineties writes that eventually the Rwandan authorities recognised that this policy response alone would not be enough to tackle rapid population growth (1993, p. 10; 1995, p. 329).

---

[21] World Bank, Managing Agricultural Development in Africa: Population Pressure, the Environment and Agricultural Intensification. Variations on the Boserup Hypothesis, DP 4, 1989.

In the course of 1990, several high profile reports on population growth in Rwanda were written and discussed by the top echelons in the regime, meaning the top brass of the MRND. These reports coincided with essays and articles on population policy in reviews such as *Imbonezamuryango* as well as with policy meetings. [22] I document the most important among them to show that they were discussed by the top leaders.

(a) *Imbonezamuryango* [*Famille, Santé, Developpement (FSD)*]

In the period 1988–1990, I count a dozen essays and statements on population growth and population policy in *Imbonezamuryango*, a review published by ONAPO, the National Population Office.[23] These articles carried alarming titles such as 'The threat of overpopulation on the environment and the living standard of Rwandans' (J.M.V Sibomana 1989, FSD, 14) or ' Malthus, Malthusianism, family planning and ONAPO' (S.Niyibizi 1991, 2). This was not new. The Belgian colonial autorities, the Kayibanda regime as well as president Habyarimana from the start of his reign has been pre-occupied with the problem. The issue is however that the problem of land scarcity became ever more problematic because population growth continued unabated and the regime only paid lip-service to family planning.

(b) *Rwanda and the problem of its refugees* (*President's Office, May 1990*)

A report, published in May 1990 by the Office of the President and written by the Special Commission on the problems of Rwandan Emigrants—chaired by Casimir Bizimungu [24]—presents an overview of the political history of Rwanda and the consequences of the 1959 Revolution (pp. 7–89) and on the position of the Kayibanda and Habyarimana governments on the question of the refugies (pp. 90–101). It then presents tables and data on the evolution of population density, agriculture and livestock since Independence (pp. 102–133).[25] The data presented in this report paint a bleak but accurate picture on the state of the Rwandan economy. We come back to the economy in Chap. 3 of this book.

---

[22] Apart from the three Rwandan publications, the international donor community also issued several reports on population growth and density in this period.

[23] This office was lead by Gaudence Nyirasafari, member of the Central Comittee of the MRND. She went to the same primary school as Juvénal Habyarimana (the parochial school of Rambura in Gisenyi) and was considered part of the presidential clan. She was married with Phocas Habimana who would in 1993 direct Radio RTLM (Guichaoua 2010, p. 107).

[24] Casimir Bizimungu, from Ruhengeri, was promoted to Minister of Health and later Minister of Foreign Affairs thanks to his promoter Dr.Séraphin Bararengana, dean of the Faculty of Medicin of the National University of Rwanda and brother of president Habyarimana. He will also be Minister in the interim government who will later implement the policy of genocide.

[25] République Rwandaise (1990). Le Rwanda et le problème de ses réfugiés. Contexte historique, analyse et voies de solution, Kigali, Présidence de la République, Commission Spéciale sur les problèmes de émigrés Rwandais, Mai. I refer to Guichaoua (2010, Chap. 2) for a discussion on the context that lead to the set-up of this Special Commission.

What is interesting about this report is that at numerous occasions its authors make a direct link between land scarcity and the inability of Rwanda to accommodate the refugees. On pages 139 and 140 the report cites president Habyarimana on this link on three different occasions:[26]

> Taking the constraints of our contry into account and avoiding unrealistic and utopian promises—while realising that the problem of Rwandan refugees concerns first and foremost the Rwandan government–we cannot tell all the refugees to return to Rwanda as we are not able to receive them in our already overpopulated country. (J.Habyarimana at the occasion of the 6th Conference of the MRND);

> And:
> When, in Semuto in Uganda, on 5 February 1988, the President of Rwanda invoked the problem of the Rwandan refugees, he stressed the constraint: land scarcity and signalled that it is one of the main reasons why Rwanda cannot repatriate all its refugees;
> And
> The Head of State has returned to this question at the occasion of the Speech he delivered for the presentation of government policy for the 1989–1994 mandate, appealing to the comprehension of the refugees themselves, their host countries as well as the international community. To the refugees, the President said that Rwanda of the 90s is not the Rwanda of the 50s or 60s. With a positive and realistic attitude they would recognize that they can earn much better their living in the host countries which generously welcomed them than to risk suffering and loss of welfare.

(c) *The Demographic Problem in Rwanda and the Framework of its Solution (ONAPO 1990)*

On June 5 and June 19 of 1990, the Central Committee of the MRND and the government held joint meetings to discuss a scientific four-volume report issued by ONAPO, the National Population Office and titled *The Demographic Problem in Rwanda and the Framework of its Solution* which presented very detailed information on population growth in Rwanda as well as several scenarios and policy options. The meeting was chaired by Bonaventure Habimana, Secretary General of the MRND (Fig. 1.2).

Thus, while the issue of population growth had been discussed for many years, by the mid eighties Rwanda had become the most densely populated country in Africa (second in the world after Bangladesh) and reached the land frontier. Two issues, central to the *raison d'être* of the regime, land scarcity and the negotiated return of the Rwandan refugees were unresolved and became ever more pressing. The policies to accomodate population growth, which focussed on increasing food production and the colonization of marginal lands, did not work anymore. By the end of the eighties Habyarimana could state that there was no space left in Rwanda and because of that he could not accommodate the refugees. In the first months of the year 1990 this situation and this political position was discussed, recognised and approved by the highest echelons of the MRND.

---

[26] Translated from the French text in the report by the author.

The Demographic Problem in Rwanda and the Framework of its solution.

Fig. 1.2 *Source* Office National de la Population, Le Problème Démographique au Rwanda et le cadre de sa Solution, Republic Rwandaise, 1990, p1

1.5 Outline of the Book

The understanding of the Rwandan situation, with its Social and Moral Revolution, with its former monarchy, with its Catholic Church, with its hilly terrain, with its temperate climate, with its beautiful lakes, with its colonial past, is far from easy. It is a very complex country. When, in this book, we try to shed some light on Rwanda and especially on the Rwandan genocide, we do this from the standpoint and the expertise of a development economist. We cannot and will not offer a complete explanation of genocide nor will we offer a full treatment of all aspects of the Habyarimana regime. This book has been written with the help of concepts and approaches drawn from two academic disciplines: political economy and agrarian studies. It is the combination of these disciplines that comes back again and again in every chapter. Readers trained in political science for example may look for a treatment of political parties and the difference in their platforms. This book does not offer this. Readers trained in anthropology may expect a detailed treatment of the history of ethnic relations. They will not find it. Instead I offer a political economy perspective to development and genocide. I am particularly interested in the relationship between the state and the peasantry. I hope this theme will run through the book like a continuous thread. One book cannot offer a full explanation of an event as complex and horrific as the Rwandan genocide. As with other books, this one stands on the shoulders of giants, hopefully allowing its readers to see things they had not seen before and to expand their understanding of the forces that have led to the genocide.

Political economy is in the first place theory, theory on the mutual relationship between economic development and political power. This discipline experienced a strong revival in the nineties. Political economy is a very powerful science, exactly because its topics are situated at the level that really matters, at the level where choices converge and where important decisions are made: at the cross-roads between politics and economics. In this book, I look at Rwanda with political economy glasses. *Agrarian Studies* is another intellectual tradition from which I borrow insights and concepts. This domain offers a rich understanding of the evolution of the peasantry through history and of the state-peasant relationship in particular. I hope this interdisciplinarity enriches this exposition.

The text is structured as follows. I discuss key elements of the Habyarimana regime in several chapters, more or less in a chronological way. For example in Chap. 5, I study the 1989 crop failure and in Chap. 6, I deal with the local massacres in the 1990–1992 period. In each chapter, the relationship between the Rwandan state and the peasantry is the central issue under discussion. This relationship was institutionalised at many different levels and contained behavioural norms, or in other words overt and covert messages on how the peasantry should behave. These norms or institutional cores will prove essential to our understanding of the Habyarimana regime and of the way development was conceived. While this central issue runs like a red fadden through the book, most chapters can also be read as stand alone chapters, a result of using several academic articles as building blocks.

In the Chap. 2, I present a detailed study of several characteristics of Habyarimana's peasant ideology that seem to me essential for our understanding of the regime. I discuss the unusual combination of pronatalist attitudes with Malthusian beliefs on the equilibrium between food production and population growth, the value attached to manual labour, the glorification of the peasantry, the politics of ethnicity and the nature of the 1973 'Moral Revolution'. Together, these elements constitute a framework that allows us to understand much of the policies that were taken or indeed not taken by the regime.

The Chap. 3 presents on overview of the Rwandan economy during Habyarimana's reign. It deals with macro-economic as well as micro-economic issues. Habyarimana was credited by the international community for the success of economic growth in the first part of his reign. This chapter looks at the fundamentals of economic growth and decline in Rwanda. It offers a discussion of taxation, public goods and income distribution.

In the Chap. 4, I model the behavior of Habyarimana vis-à-vis the coffee sector. Coffee was very important for the regime in terms of export revenue and it was also very important for the peasant cultivators in terms of monetary income. This sector thus was of prime importance to Habyarimana and the study of his behavior towards this sector will reveal the nature of his approach towards the peasantry. I use and adapt the loyalty-and-repression model advanced by Ronald Wintrobe

(1998). As all economic models, this model is a stylized version of reality, unable to capture all aspects. This chapter has benefited a lot from joint work with two colleagues from the Univesity of Leuven, Lode Berlage and Bart Capéau.[27]

Chapter 5 goes into detail on Habyarimana's agricultural and food policy in relation to the crop failure that occurred in southern Rwanda in 1989. This chapter demonstrates that the policy of food self-reliance which was the flagship policy objective of the Second Republic did not prevent hunger to occur. As with the policy towards the coffee sector, the president's agricultural policy reveals some of the key characteristics of his regime, both on the ideological as on the political level.

In the Chap. 6, I investigate the local massacres that occurred in the 1990–1992 period. Given the scale of the 1994 genocide, one may wonder why I devote space and analysis to relatively 'small' events. From the analysis however it will become clear why these events merit our attention. While other scholars have described the 'context' (i.e the civil war) of these massacres, I argue that the civil war explains the timing of these events, but cannot explain their genocidal character. I show that the early massacres should be understood as ethnic cleansing. They inscribe themselves in a logic of land colonisation, re-settlement, depredation and deprivation of cattle and land in areas where the land constraint was biting the most, where the MRND was firmly established and where peasant society was being re-modelled in a rational, geometric way. In this way these massacres can also be labeled instances of social engineering.

In Chap. 7, I relate the very tumultuous 1992–1994 period in Rwandan politics, with developments in the civil war, in the domestic scene and in the army. The attack on the plane carrying president Habyarimana is analysed from the behaviour of the key players before and just after the attack. I explain how the nordist politico-military elite imposed itself, first murdered its political opponents and then pushed a policy of nationwide genocide. This chapter relies heavily on and at the same time comments and debates the seminal work of Andé Guichaoua (2010).

Chapter 8 studies the literature on popular participation in genocide and especially the mechanisms behind the establishment of a genocidal norm and the success of collective action. I will rely on theoretical developments in political economy to explain this success and show how they apply to the Rwandan genocide. In this chapter I also discuss the explanations of participation advanced by other scholars, notably Peter Uvin, René Lemarchand and Scott Strauss.

Chapters 9 and 10 present the results of qualitative field work that I have undertaken with a group of graduate students in several areas in the province of Gitarama. We demonstrate how the organisation of the genocide is linked to the pre-existing networks of state-sanctioned power at the local level.

---

[27] In a joint paper (2003), we have outlined a complete model of a dictatorship in a single export crop economy that expands, applies and re-interprets Wintrobe's dictatorship model (1998). A full model was presented in a follow-up paper (2012) published in the *Journal of Theoretical Politics*.

In the concluding chapter of this book, I discuss the underlying logic of the Habyarimana regime, both in regard to the development of Rwanda as well as in regard to the organisation of the genocide. This underlying logic has much to do with Rwanda's institutions and with the population density of Rwanda. I reach the conclusion that the organisers of the genocide used an extremely cruel and at the same time an extremely efficient method to execute the genocide: they relied on Rwanda's sole abundant factor of production: peasant labor.

When I devote several chapters to the description and analysis of Rwanda's Developmental State and the peasant ideology of the Second Republic, it does not mean that I believe or argue that the genocide was planned before 1990 or that it had always been the objective of Habyarimana to exterminate the Tutsi population of Rwanda. My reasoning is not deterministic and I leave a lot of room for strategic behaviour, personal ambitions and ad hoc choices that determine the course of events (see Chap. 7). My point will be that without the regime's totalitarian aspirations (in essence the fusion of the interests of the elite with those of the peasant masses), without the pyramidical organisation of the MRND Party-State, and its peasant ideology, the regime would not and could not have chosen genocide as a course of action.

Chapter 2
The Nature of the Second Republic

2.1 An Unconventional Source of Information

In this chapter, I take a closer look at the ideology of the Habyarimana regime (1973–1994) as it is represented in his speeches and interviews. All speeches by and interviews with Habyarimana were published during his reign by his office and the Office of Information of Rwanda (ORINFOR). These speeches are the primary source of information regarding Habyarimana's political thought. His speeches from the years 1973, 1974, 1979, 1980, 1981, 1982, 1985, 1986, 1987 and 1988 were analyzed to determine Habyarimana's ideology.[1] The focus is on the speeches he gave on the many occasions of celebration in Rwanda. These speeches, contrary to those he made abroad, are directed at the Rwandan population and, as such, reveal the way the dictator saw his country, its population and his own task as leader. These speeches should not be considered mere rhetoric. I will show that Habyarimana actually implemented the policies that he advocated in his speeches. The focus of my analysis is on the nature of the Second Republic and more in particular on the development model the regime put in place. It will be demonstrated that the president's ideology served as a legitimation for the policies he advocated and especially for his personal hold onto power. The topics under discussion in this chapter are: population, self-reliance, ruralisation, umuganda and peasant ideology. The treatment of these concepts in this chapter has a double reason: *first*, they have all been a part of several speeches of Habyarimana and often the main subject of a speech. They are obviulsy very important in the understanding of his ideas and *second*, because of their importance, these topics all come back in the subsequent chapters of this book.

Did Habyarimana write his speeches all by himself? This question remains open, but he probably did not. According to my informants, at least three people

---

[1] I was unable to locate the speeches for the other years of his reign. The pages used in the footnotes of the sections where I cite from Habyarimana's speech, refer to the pages in the publications by ORINFOR. The speeches of Habyarimana that are used in this chapter were published in Kinyarwanda as well as in French. The author translated them from French to English.

P. Verwimp, *Peasants in Power*, DOI: 10.1007/978-94-007-6434-7_2,

helped him: Ferdinand Nahimana, professor of history and leading intellectual of the regime; Jeanneret Charles, a Swiss professor and advisor to the president; and Christophe Mfusi, a Rwandan journalist who later became a critic of the regime.

I wrote this chapter to fill a gap in the literature on the Habyrimana regime. In order to illustrate this, I refer to two well-known books. The first is Alison Des Forges' *Leave None to Tell the Story* (1999) and the second Peter Uvin's *Aiding Violence: the development enterprise in Rwanda* (1998). The first book offers a very detailed and very rich account of the implementation of genocidal policies in Rwanda from 1990 to 1994. The main thesis of the author is that the political elite in Rwanda chose genocide as a political strategy to remain in power. The second book is a careful analysis of the impact of development aid in Rwanda. It is a harsh critique of the way the Rwandan state, the NGO's and the international donor community organized development projects in Rwanda before the genocide. The main thesis of Uvin is that the developmental process in Rwanda humiliated, frustrated and infantilized the Rwandan peasant. He offers interesting insights and reflections on the relationship between this developmental process and participation in the genocide by the peasants. The arguments that I will develop in this chapter do not question the analysis of the above mentioned authors, but focus on a neglected characteristic of the regime, namely the underlying peasant ideology. Des Forges stresses the intentions of the political elite but does not talk (or not much) about the economic conditions of the country, nor does she discuss Habyarimana's peasant ideology. This is a shortcoming of her book since Habyarimana himself often spoke on the economy and especially the economic-demographic equilibrium in Rwanda. The economic conditions are emphasized by Uvin, but he did not take a look at Habyarimana's speeches either.

I refer to Uvin's book for a discussion on the regime's development policies and how they were misjudged by the donor community. The question of whether or not Habyarimana developed his country depends to a large extent on the definition of development one is using. In order to understand the actions of dictatorial regimes, one should not only look at their 'developmental' outcomes, but also at the intentions of the regime. What particular kind of development did they want to achieve for their country? In order to discover the objectives of the regime, Rwanda is studied as a Developmental State.

2.2 Habyarimana Combined Pronatalism with Malthusian Believes

Rwanda was one of the most densely populated countries in the world, yet developed no family planning policy. In 1973, at the beginning of his dictatorship, Habyarimana told his audience that Rwanda had a demographic problem:

We are aware of the problems caused by the demographic growth of the Rwandan population and they should be getting our permanent and serious attention. We believe however that the people who seem to advocate fast solutions, resulting from a certain literature whose authors do not hide their egotism, should be more reserved. The solution that we are looking for shall be Rwandan, taking our mentalities, our moral values, our culture, our possibilities and human solidarity into account.[2]

During his reign, Habyarimana gave different reasons to explain the absence of family planning. At one point he argues that the Rwandan family wants to have a lot of children. On other occasions he said that his scientists were looking for the best way to prevent population growth and that he is awaiting their answer. At yet another day he appealed to the Church to tolerate family planning. This makes clear that Habyrimana sought excuses to explain the absence of family planning. Local level church initiatives as boarding schools and workshops for young women postponed the age at marriage and thereby, deliberately, the number of children. In fact, as is clear from his speeches, Habyarimana himself was not in favour of family planning. Rwanda had a population bureau, but it was a sham. Prunier (1995, 88–89) writes that the Ministry of Interior allowed Catholic pro-life commandos to attack pharmacies that sold condoms.

I observe a certain evolution in Habyarimana's population thinking: in 1973 he advocated a Rwandan solution, in line with Rwandan culture, to the population growth problem (see previous citation). In 1979, he continues along the lines of Rwandan tradition, stating that

I have already affirmed in other occasions, that the number of inhabitants of our country should not always be presented as excessive, nor always be presented as a constraint on development. That development is exactly the fruit of people's work.[3]

In 1980 he refers to the Rwandan desire to have children

A Rwandan by nature wants to have a lot of children because he considers his children a source of protection, a source of production to secure his living. The Rwandan family wants to have children and it is a disaster when it does not have children.[4]

Such a position on population may not be problematic or exceptional in an African context, many African leaders took it at that time. Rwanda however was the most densely populated country of the continent. The average Rwandan woman had 8 children at the end of the seventies. And there is more to this. In a 1985 publication celebrating the 10th anniversary of the foundation of the MRND, we read—under the section demographic growth—that

---

[2] Habyarimana J., Discours-programme, August 1, 1973.

[3] Habyarimana, J, Discours-programme du 8 Janvier 1979, *Discours et Entretiens de Son Excellence le Général-Major Habyarimana Juvénal Président de la Republique Rwandaise, et Président-Fondateur du Mouvement Révolutionnaire National pour le Développement (MRND)*, ORINFOR, Rwanda, 1979, p. 23.

[4] Habyarimana J., interviewed by Yuki Sato, July 12, 1980, *Discours et Entretiens de Son Excellence le Général-Major Habyarimana Juvénal Président de la Republique Rwandaise, et Président-Fondateur du MRND*, ORINFOR, Rwanda 1980, p. 243.

The population is the first force of a nation, but its large size can become a handicap in particular when the production sector cannot follow the rhythm of population growth. The demographic problem is very real in our country where the annual population growth is 3.7 % and the annual production growth is only 2.7 %, with the risk of an even larger disequilibrium if the proposed strategies do not reach their objectives.[5]

A clearer demonstration of the Malthusian viewpoint is hard to find: according to the MRND, Rwanda has a demographic problem because annual population growth is higher then the growth of production, resulting in disequilibrium. In 1987, Habyarimana said that

We believe there is a real problem. If the population grows faster than the economy, we have a problem. And nevertheless, we must reconcile two things, on the one hand, the more numerous we are, the stronger we are, because we have more arms and more brains, but the more numerous we are, the more we have to produce for that population in order to have enough food, to have education, to have clothes. We must reconcile these two parameters: population and growth.[6]

In 1989 at the inauguration of a potable water project in Kigali, the President stated that Rwanda cannot feed its 7.5 million people.[7] On August 2nd, 1990 Habyarimana said that

Rwanda could, statistically seen, only feed 5 million of the 7.5 million inhabitants adequately[8]

The growth and size of the population is linked with the refugee question (see Chap. 1 of this book and also a 1987 Anniversary publication to be discussed below): in October 1982, when Uganda embarked on a refugee expulsion program, the Rwandan authorities closed the border and refused the entry of several thousand Rwandan refugees. After several months and as result of pressure regarding the inhumane living conditions of the refugees a few thousand refugees were allowed to settle in camps in northern Rwanda. Guichaoau (1997, 20) writes that local politicians and the rural population did not want their presence and were openly xenophobic in their reactions.[9] In 1986, the Central Committee of the MRND decided to refuse the return of the 1959 refugees, stating that the country did not have enough land to accommodate them.[10]

---

[5] Ten years MRND 1985, pp. 342–343.

[6] Habyarimana J, interview given to ZDF, German Television Channel 2, September, 29, 1987, ibidem, ORINFOR, Rwanda, 1987, p. 258.

[7] Jeune Afrique, Rwanda: the fight against overpopulation, 1990, Sept 19–25, pp. 1–7.

[8] De Standaard, 3/10/1990, p. 1, translation by the author.

[9] Guichaoua, André, Antécédents politiques de la crise Rwandaise de 1994. Rapport d'expertise rédigé a la demande du Trbunal Pénal International des Nations Unies sur le Rwanda, Avril 1997.

[10] Nsengiyaremye, Dismas, La Transition Démocratoque au Rwanda (1989–1993), 1995, p. 251. Individual return, decided on a case-by-case basis was allowed and dependent on the financial means of the applicant.

In May 1990, the National Population Office published four volumes titled *The Demographic Problem in Rwanda and the Framework of its Solution* mentioned already in Chap. 1. This publication is a very detailed study of the relationship between population and development in Rwanda and lists a large number of measures to be taken immediately. They include family planning, schooling for women, industrialisation and urbanisation, the creation of off-farm jobs. Measures that were not only costly to the state, but also ran opposite to the regime's ideology and were not beneficial to the regime's hold onto power.

2.3 Food Self-Reliance, Endogenous Development and Political Organisation

Habyarimana was convinced that the Rwandan economy should be agriculturally self-sufficient, making import of food unnecessary. In his speeches, which can be considered official statements, he stresses that the development of Rwanda is the foremost goal of his economic policy, and that auto-development and food self-reliance were the methods to be used to meet that goal.

> If it is true that the first objective of a national economy is to be able to feed the country at the service of the ones it works for and is organized for, and if it is true that the priority of priorities of Rwanda is just to build the national economy around this major imperative, meaning to give it a solid base to allow it to respond to this fundamental demand, one must absolutely be able to identify clearly the key factors our economy needs in order to attain the objective of a well understood food self-reliance.[11]

and

> Auto-development is not a slogan for us, it is not an effort to theorize, it is not a vain aspiration to embrace a doctrine or a school of thought. No, for us, auto-development is our conviction that progress needs to come from our own forces, that we cannot live beyond our means and that the solutions of our problems need to come from us.[12]

Habyarimana's stated policy priority was to make Rwanda food self-sufficient. For many years, Rwandan farmers had been able to increase food production because Rwanda was blessed with fertile soil. At some point, land under cultivation reaches its absolute limits. After reviewing his speeches, one infers that Habyarimana wants agricultural production to increase. In particular, he presents increased production of food crops as the one and only solution to overcome the problems of the Rwandan economy:

> In the coming twenty years, the population of Rwanda will be doubled. We thus have to make sure that we have enough food. Our food strategy gives absolute priority to our peasants and to the production of food crops that are most important to solve our food

---

[11] Habyarimana J., speech 'Youth and Development', May 21st, 1986, p. 49.

[12] Habyarimana J, speech on July 1st, 1987, pp. 205–206.

crisis. The establishment of a policy of increased production demands a profound internal transformation and a continuous effort for a long period.[13]

In 1985, Habyarimana told his audience that culture was the basis of development:

> What was and what is the foundation of our economic policy of development that we have pursued, thanks to the principles and ideas of our National Revolutionary Movement for Development ? Our economic policy, Militants, is one for an auto-development that we really want, endogenous, to wit one whose core can be found in the living forces of the country, in our culture, in the valorisation of our own resources in order for us to satisfy, with our means, our elementary needs, in order for us to survive physically because of our national food production, in order for us to look to the future with confidence because we were able to show that our country, the beautiful Rwanda, holds riches which allow its daughters and sons to find a raison d'être and to prosper for ever more.[14]

In 1988, Ferdinand Nahimana wrote a book conveying and explaining Habyarimana's ideology and the foundation of his policies. Commenting on the 5 July 1985 speech, he writes that culture is not limited to artistic activities, literature and history. Such limitation prevents one to consider it from a global perspective, to wit the whole set of capacities that constitute the national patrimony established over time and still in evolution. He writes that endogenous development and development based on one's own culture is one and the same thing.[15] On page 51 in Nahimana's 1988 book, a photo is published of peasants working in the field with Habyarimana watching from the nearby road. The subscript to this photo reads:

> Gradually but steadily, the Rwandan population has been prepared and accustomed to appreciate its own capacities, to be proud of its own values and to energize itself relying first of all on the forces and realities intrinsic to its society.

Development, Habyarimana explains, is not a stationary state of affairs, but a permanent process, where every day one has to set a step forward in the good direction, as signified in the expression "AMAJYAMBERE, GUTERA IMBERE MU MAJYAMBERE".[16]

The very modest Rwandan efforts towards industrialization were undertaken only after intense outside pressure. The development of small handicraft enterprises for example, was only allowed in 1985 after a campaign by the ILO, the Young Catholic Workers of Rwanda and the special representative of Switzerland.[17]According to Habyarimana and Nahimana, industrial development should

---

[13] Habyarimana J., Speech for July 5th, 1983, p. 220.

[14] Habyarimana J., Discours, Messages et Entretien, 1985, pp. 35–36.

[15] Nahimana F., *Conscience chez-nous, confiance en nous. Notre culture est la base de notre développement harmonieux*, Ruhengeri, 1988, p. 52.

[16] Habyarimana J., Discours, Messages et Entretien, 1986, p. 61. Translation: Development is a process of continued efforts. The core of 'Gutera 'to wit 'tera 'is also found in interahamwe, those who stand together.

[17] Willame J.C, *Au sources de l'hécatombe Rwandaise*, Cahiers Africaines, 1995, p. 154.

always be auto-centered and endogenous. Endogenous development is development based on one's own culture and one's own forces. This resembles the African version of the development model of Communist China and North Korea. Nahimana writes that the ideology of the president was neither capitalist nor communist but was specific to Rwandan culture and traditions and relied on Rwanda's own forces.[18] Remarkably, the president succeeded in maintaining good relations with both western and communist countries. He visited North-Korea and China that helped him with the organisation of the MRND. Importantly, industrial development should be organic:[19]

> Our strategy for industrialization will not have two heads (= formal and informal sector); it will be an organic strategy coming from a global vision of the problems and the needs. Such a strategy will encourage industrial units of national dimension, but who will not be defined separately, or independent, but organic and in line with what is done for the small enterprise, in order for large enterprises to come to support the small ones and not to destroy them.

The use of the word 'organic' normally refers to the anatomy of the human body. In a 1981 speech, we find more evidence for the analogy between the economy and the human body:

> The commune must remain a body constitute of several cells, lively and dynamic. And as every living body, the commune needs several elements to be able to render service to its population. The commune, the basic cell of our development and of our economy, has been restructured in order to fulfil better its mission i.e. to energize the living forces of the country for their well-being.[20]

In this speech, Habyarimana thus viewed the economy as a human body where all organs should function together for the well-being of the whole. This fits perfectly into other parts of his ideology: he frequently repeats that the individual is subordinate to the collective. The 1975 MRND party manifest is very clear on this; it reads: [21]

> Our Movement is a popular movement and it requires unconditional adhesion, in other words, the People and the Society as a whole speak with one mouth, resulting in a unity of vision, harmony, cohesion from the cell up to the top of the pyramid of the 'Movement', in other words the entire Nation. No individual or group can escape the control of the 'Social Body' in motion, meaning the People in search for a better social, economic, political, intellectual and moral life. (capitals in original)

---

[18] Nahimana F., *Conscience chez-nous, confiance en nous, Notre culture est la base de notre developpement harmonieux, Ruhengeri*, 1988, pp. 33–55.

[19] Habyarimana J., Speech 1986, pp. 41–42.

[20] Habyarimana J., Speech on the occasion of the first session of the National Development Council, p. 119, 1981.

[21] Manifeste et Status du MRND, July 5, 1975, preamble, p. 88.

The idea put forward in this Manifest is that the MRND is a Movement to which all Rwandans owe unconditional adhesion. This Movement is seen as a pyramid and it represents the entire Nation, it embodies the will of the People. The idea that the top of the pyramid knows, represents and executes the will of the People will resurge in the period leading up to and during the genocide. In section 3 of Chap. 6 we shall see how top military officers will appeal to this idea. Interestingly, in the same 1975 Manifest the military already is assigned a popular role. The Manifest explains what the objectives of the Movement are and how they can be reached (p. 91). Key is that all sons and daughters of the Nation join forces:

> In order to attack the problems of development and to get rid of the evil forces, we have to rise, march and act as one person and the results will be even more spectacular. The armed forces, for a long time held outside the economic and social activities of the Nation will from now on be integrated in the frame of the general mobilisation of the popular masses. From now on, all patriotic and progressive forces must feel more concerned.

As Prunier writes

> The MRND was a truly totalitarian party: every single Rwandese citizen had to be a member, including babies and old people. All bourgmestres and prefects were chosen from among party cadres. The party was everywhere.[22]

Guichaoau (1997, 18; 2010, 43) agrees with this when we writes that the term 'dictatorship' does not really cover the extent of Habyrimana's regime. Because of the lack of political alternative, the mandatory integration of all Rwandans from birth onwards into the MRND, the promotion of sons and daughters from the rural areas into leading positions, and the multiple levels of authority demanding submission, the term 'totalitarianism' describes better the nature of the regime.[23]

Prunier also writes that the MRND was not supposed to be a 'political' party:

> Indeed, the word 'politics' was almost a dirty word in the virtuous and hard working world of Habyarimanism. Every effort was made to forget- at least officially—that politics existed.[24]

Having one single party was the right choice for Habyarimana given his ideology and his desire to stay in power: he could control the entire population, outlaw political opposition and implement his vision of society. In so-called animation sessions, the population had to glorify Habyarimana. James Gasana (1995, p. 215) adds that the Second Republic used traditional as well as modern methods to control the population, borrowed from the Tutsi monarchy, the Northern Hutu Chiefdoms as well as from North-Korea (Fig. 2.1).

---

[22] Prunier D. *The Rwanda Crisis, History of a Genocide*, 1995, p. 76. The opinion that the MRND was a totalitatian party is shared by other authors, see J.K. Gasana, *La Guerre, la Paix et la Démocratie au Rwanda*, 1995, in A. Guichaoau, Les Crises Politiques de 1993–1994 au Rwanda en Burundi, chapter 14.

[23] Guichaoua A., *Les Antécédents politiques de la crise Rwandaise de* 1994. Rapport d'expertise rédigé a la demande du Trbunal Pénal International des Nations Unies sur le Rwanda, Avril 1997.

[24] Prunier G. ibid, p. 77.

Rwanda is a poor country, we have to unite forces for its development...

Fig. 2.1 *Source* Présidence de MRND, l'Umuganda dans le développement national, Affaires Economiques, Janvier 1990, p.3

In Prunier's words,

> Along the somewhat reminiscent lines of eighteenth century European theories of 'benevolent despotism', President Habyarimana had decided to take upon his shoulders the heavy burden of the state so that his subjects could devote themselves entirely to the business of agriculture.[25]

Prunier also wrote about the ideology of Habyarimana and he believes the system worked at the economic level. He however does not consider the logic of the Developmental State behind the agricultural and peasant ideology (see pages 76–80 of his book). It is possible to see that the policies he adopted were designed to further both the adoption of his ideology by the population *and* his own power. Habyarimana's policies were expressed as 'peasant-friendly', that is, they were presented as helping peasants improve their lives. However, closer examination of several of these policies—including population policy and *umuganda* (see below)—indicates that the peasant-friendly character of these policies was limited. The policies first of all served the political and ideological objectives of the regime as well as its revenue-seeking drive.

---

[25] Prunier G., ibid, p. 77.

2.4 Habyarimana Pictured Himself as a Peasant

2.4.1 Ruralisation

Habyarimana followed a consistent policy to make the peasants stay in the rural areas. They had to remain in an agricultural setting. This anti-urban policy benefited people already living in the cities, the so-called 'elite'. It also explains why in 1973, 95 % of the population lived in the rural areas and in 1993, 90 % still lived in there. Habyrimana considered cities places of immorality, theft and prostitution. This 'moral stand' closely resembled the teaching of the Catholic Church in Rwanda which also considered cities as dangerous places which young people should be kept away from lest they be contaminated by the cities' immorality. Prostitutes or so-called prostitutes (among them Tutsi girlfriends of expatriates) in Kigali were sent to a re-education camp in Nsinda in the prefecture of Kibungo (see below). In an interview in 1980, Habyarimana stated that he had eight children himself and that his character was strongly influenced by his parents and by his life on the farm:[26]

> My parents were cultivators, simple peasants thus, they are dead unfortunately and it is really in this point in life in the countryside, on the hills, in life with the land (soil), that they have influenced me the most, and they were simple peasants, they were not part of the leadership at the time and also the fact that they were Catholic. Many points that one could underline for my parents and that have influenced my character and my own life.

Such statements reveal the inherent populism of the president, who wanted to be considered as a peasant himself, which he clearly was not. His father was a catholic teacher and preacher (a catechist) and his mother descended from the royal lineage of the king of Bushiru, northern-Rwanda (Guichaoua 2010, 102). Habyarimana's rural preference was translated into policies to keep the population in the rural areas. The following excerpt from a Rwandan Ministry of Planning document on communal development, cited in a World Bank report (1987, 10):

> If we are to avoid a situation in which excess rural manpower, mainly the younger generations, begins to pour into the urban centers—a process of spontaneous urbanisation is already starting in Kigali—which could give rise to economic, social and ultimately political problems for the authorities, we must develop the instruments and find the resources needed to limit and control this process of migration to the towns by acting at the commune level[27]

The World Bank adds (p. 11) that the formula *the commune, the basic unit of development* is faithfully reproduced in every official document since the promulgation of the Second Republic. A Communal Action Plan (Plan d'Action Communal) was formulated in 1975 as a sort of "bible presenting a catalogue of the operations to be carried out to facilitate the development of the communes".

---

[26] Habyarimana J, interviewed by Yuki Sato, July 12, 1980, p. 236.

[27] World Bank *The role of the communes in the development of Rwanda*, Washington DC, 1987.

In 1994 report, the World Bank condemned the restrictions on population movement because they impeded the development of market centers essential for developing a market economy. The World Bank added that this policy reduced the potential for economic growth. This means that Habyarimana's migration prohibition policy was considered an impediment to development by one of the world's leading development agencies. Of course, one could disagree with the World Bank on the grounds that it has an ideological bias toward free market economics. In the same document, the World Bank added that these migration restrictions increased poverty by limiting the options of the poor. From the development economics literature we know that migration, and especially temporary employment in cities, is an important strategy to cope with poverty. The Bank does not go as far as saying that this restrictive policy was a means to control the population. When we look at this policy from a dictatorial point of view, the motivation behind the policy becomes clearer, to wit to avoid the rise of political opposition.

The son of 'simple peasants' would first go to study medicine at Louvanium University in Kinshasa, later enroll in the military academy in Rwanda and marry a daughter of the royal lineage of Bushiru. The Cambodian mass murderer Pol Pot also pretended to be a simple peasant. Hitler declared the farmer "the most important participant" in the Nazi revolution. In *Mein Kampf*, Hitler linked German peasant farmland with German racial characteristics.[28] According to Chrétien, several copies of films about Hitler and Nazism were found in Habyarimana's home.[29] In a 1997 book, Large reminds us not to forget rural Germany and especially Bavaria (the NSDAP hot spot) during the rise of Nazism.[30] Other dictatorships favoring ruralization instead of urbanisation have been studied. For instance, on the reason why the Khmer Rouge evacuated the cities, Kiernan writes that it became far easier to control the population.[31] Guichaoua (1997,14) expresses it as follows:

> The social cohesion of this 'overpopulated' peasant-State and the submission of the peasantry to an extremely authoritarian and constraining order was the result of policies that succeeded in maintaining a socially undifferentiated system. The rural populism that unified the Rwandan leaders with 'their' peasantry (the elections only served to confirm a relationship which per definition could not be dissolved) rests on an explicit will to block the emergence of another social order made up of classes, professions and other specific occupations which would remind at the divisions of the old 'feudal' order.[32]

---

[28] Kiernan B., 'Genocide and "ethnic cleansing",' in *The Encyclopedia of Politics and Religion*, ed. Robert Wuthnow, Washington, D.C., Congressional Quarterly, vol. 1, p. 298.

[29] Chrétien J.P., *Les Médias du Genocide*, 1995, p. 256.

[30] Large D. *Where Ghosts Walked : Munich's Road to the Third Reich*, Norton, New York, 1997, taken from a review by Tom Nairn 'Reflections on Nationalist Disasters', p. 151.

[31] Kiernan B., *The Pol Pot Regime, Race, Power and Genocide under the Khmer Rouge 1975–1979*, Yale University Press, 1996, p. 64.

[32] Guichaoua A., *Les Antécédents politiques de la crise Rwandaise de 1994. Rapport d'expertise rédigé a la demande du Tribunal Penal International des Nations Unies sur le Rwanda*, Arusha, Avril 1997.

The anti-urban and conservative character of the regime is exposed in 1983 when it launched a campaign against single women in the capital Kigali. Taylor writes that young urban women, who either dressed too stylishly or had European boy friends were assaulted and intimidated on the streets by police and soldiers.[33] Some women were forced to stand nearly naked until a truck would take them to a detention centre. As such, charged with 'vagabondage' and prostitution, hundreds of women were incarcerated in rural detention centres called 'ingorora muco' (moral re-education centres). Taylor (p. 161) says that most of these women were Tutsi, many were mistreated and some were raped:

> Altough a few may have been prostitutes, the vast majority were not. Most were single women employed in respectable jobs and financially self-supporting; many were highly educated.

According to Taylor, the most enduring consequence of this repression was to plant the idea in the minds of many Rwandans that single Tutsi women were likely to be prostitutes. The women were released after vehement international pressure, but the measures remained in place. Public morality was enforced by agents known popularly as *maneko* and by soldiers who would enter bars and made sure everybody left promptly by midnight. Taylor concludes (1999, 162–163):

> Rwanda was a tightly controlled police state and the marked puritanism of the regime added a moral flavour to its paternalism

2.4.2 Umuganda

Umuganda, the Kinyarwanda word for the wood used to construct a house, was one of Habyarimana's favorite speech topics and one of the regime's most influential policies, both in economic and in ideological terms. On February, 2nd, 1974, the President ordered that every Rwandan perform unpaid collective work one day per week. This was stressed in a speech given by Habyarimana at a seminar for Burgomasters in August 1975, after the creation of the MRND (Mouvement Révolutionaire National pour le Dévelopment):

> The doctrine of our Movement is that Rwanda will only be developed by the sum of the efforts of its own sons and daughters, the product of their efforts belongs to them. That is why it has judged the Collective Works for Development a necessary obligation for all the inhabitants of the country.

The umuganda policy was presented as the re-establishment of an institution that had long existed in Rwandan culture but that had been suppressed by the colonial economy *umuganda* was, according to the MRND, a reaction against the

---

[33] Taylor, C. Sacrifice as Terror, Berg, Oxford International Publishers, Oxford, New York, 1999.

In order to demonstrate the usefulness of manual labour, main occupation of the majority of the Rwandan people, the Second Republic has rehabilitated it in institutionalising Umuganda.

Fig. 2.2 *Source* Présidence de MRND, l'Umuganda dans le décéloppement national, Affaires Economiques, Janvier 1990, p.11 et p.15

Institutionalising Umuganda on 2 February, 1974, His Excellency the President of the Republic has taken agriculture as example, main activity of most Rwandans.

Fig. 2.3 *Source* Présidence de MRND, l'Umuganda dans le décéloppement national, Affaires Economiques, Janvier 1990, p.11 et p.15

monetarisation of the Rwandan economy, the introduction of formal education and the development of off-farm labour under colonialism.[34]

All Rwandans 'had to voluntarily' contribute their labor to the weekly collective works. Economically, *umuganda* was very important for Rwanda since it made an enormous amount of unpaid labor available to the state (for figures, I refer to Chap. 3). During *umuganda*, the Rwandan people built such things as schools, roads, sanitation facilities, health centers and anti-erosion ditches. The latter gained central place in 1986–1987 when a national plan to combat erosion was launched.

Arguably, as Guichaoua writes (1991, 554), the political and ideological functions of *umuganda*, were even more important than its economic benefits. Ideologically, *umuganda* was explicitly designed to make sure that all Rwandans would do manual labor. The local politicians and administrators were responsible for the organization of the weekly *umuganda*, which gave these officials great discretionary power. They could decide who did and who did not have to participate. Not surprisingly, the cronies and friends of the regime escaped *umuganda*.

The Manifesto of the MRND says that *'it is a man's labor that constitutes the essential source of wealth in the country and from there the basis of economic accumulation'*[35] On many public occasions, Habyarimana expressed his low esteem for intellectual work and his high esteem for manual work. He instituted the *umuganda* policy by cultivating a plot of land together with his close friends.

> I admit that I do not understand, that I absolutely do not understand, when listening to certain intellectuals, one is obliged to hear nothing but disobeying remarks and destructive criticism regarding some accomplishments, regarding certain political options taken that are not open for questioning.
>
> I take the example of Umuganda—our collective work for development, thanks to the manual labor of everybody. It is inconceivable that we could do without Umuganda. A country is constructed by hands, not by words! Rwanda will be constructed by the sweat on our face and not by useless speculations!
>
> The results obtained by Umuganda, its remarkable realizations that many countries envy us, constitutes the best proof that it cannot be separated from the progress Rwanda made in the last 10 years, that it is an essential part of that progress and that it corresponds with our ancestral values—to engage oneself—so that everyone, by individual effort, performs better in a collectivity always in progress. Each intelligent and honest Rwandan can see this.
>
> I can only regret, with my last effort, that there still are 'intellectuals' who use their time to criticize, destroy, this institution with their words, instead of telling us how to improve it, making it more performing, adapt it better to our needs.[36]

---

[34] *L'Umuganda dans le dévélopment national*, Présidence de MRND, Affaires Economiques, Janvier 1990, p. 10. In this respect, umuganda is copied from socialist and ommunist-type countries. Also neighbouring countries as Tanzania under Nyerere knew such work parties. The Habyarimana regime explained these policies as if they had always existed and as if they belonged to Rwandan tradition. They were endogenized so to speak.

[35] Manifesto of the MRND, cited from *Umuganda dans le devéloppment national*, 1990, p. 5.

[36] Habyarimana J., "Youth and Development", speech at the occasion of his visit to the National University of Rwanda, May 21, 1986, p. 66.

It is clear that he wants Rwanda's professors to stop criticizing him and to contribute to national development. In other words, the professors should do the same as the general population: do not discuss politics and work hard.

Umuganda gave the local party and state officials knowledge and experience in the mobilization and control of the labour of the peasant population. A skill that will prove deadly during the genocide. In Chap. 5 of the book we will go into detail in the theory of mobilization, it suffices here to show the practise and use of mobilisation:

> Umuganda must be planned in order to reach its objective, developing our country by building the necessary infrastructure for its economy and, allowing the new Rwandan to engage in his work. Because of this, it has to be oriented towards directly productive actions. In order to increase the development projects in the Umuganda framework, the mobilization and awareness of the popular masses is necessary and the MRND offers the appropriate way to do this.[37]

Guichaoua, in a 1991 article, writes that *umuganda* successfully introduced the theme of militant mobilisation with a strong nationalist connotation in the population.[38] The fact that everybody was required to participate, peasants as well as administrators, workers as well as intellectuals, had an important role in the efforts undertaken to reach a general mobilisation. Umuganda is one of the prime examples of a top-down policy with an appealing development image that was designed to use and control peasant labor, to oblige the Rwandan intellectuals to do physical work, to give politicians discretionary power over labor and to indoctrinate the Rwandans with the regime's ideology.[39] Because of abuse, corruption and disbelief, *umuganda* was not popular among the peasant population. As soon as the power of the regime decreased, peasants did not show up for *umuganda* anymore. Uvin (1998), writing on development aid, states that Rwanda is a prime example of state-run, state-controlled, top-down development. Large development projects in Rwanda were controlled by the regime and the MRND party.[40] On top of this, churches, development projects and civil organisations copied the umuganda model and asked peasants to perform unpaid labour on a large scale in their own projects. Guichaoua (1991, 566–568) writes that the peasantry did not really distinguish between the 'official' state-run umuganda and the 'church', 'white' or 'private' umuganda. It were all obligations to participate in unpaid work programs and the officials in charge of these programs were often one and the same person. For example, the targets for umuganda in the coming week,

---

[37] *L'Umuganda dans le Developpement National*, Janvier 1990, p. 39.

[38] Guichaoua A (1991), Les Travaux Communautaires en Afrique Centrale, *Revue Tiers Monde*, XXXII, n 127, Juillet-Septembre, p. 564.

[39] I refer to the 1990 MRND publication on Umuganda p. 20–32 for details on the organisational structure of umuganda. Although Umuganda was forced labor, the majority of the population may have believed in the intrinsic qualities of this policy, at least in the beginning. For an elaborate discussion of the believes and reservations of the population regarding Umuganda, I refer the excellent 1991 article by Guichaoua.

[40] Uvin P., *Aiding violence: the development enterprise in Rwanda*, 1998.

not only for the 'church' umuganda, where announced at the end of the Sunday service.

2.4.3 The Glorification of the Peasantry

In 1986, Habyarimana said on two occasions that the peasants were the real employers of Rwanda, because they allowed the State to function.[41] On the occasion of the 25th Anniversary of the existence of the Rwandan Republic, on July 1st, 1987, Habyarimana devoted his official speech to the glorification of the Rwandan peasant. He said that

> If in the 25 years of our independence Rwanda has known a lot of success in its struggle for progress, if it has been able to take a number of important steps, it is in the first place our farmers who made this happen (…) it is their total devotion to the work, every day (…) their fabulous capacity to adapt, their pragmatism, their genius, their profound knowledge of our eco-systems that allowed them to extract an amazing degree of resources from their plots of land (…)

At the time, a commentator wrote that never before such honor was given to the Rwandan peasants.[42] Four months later, at the occasion of the Government Council of November 13th, 1987, Habyarimana ennobled the Rwandan peasant by extending the term 'peasant' (*umuturage*) to all Rwandans.[43] The term 'umuturage' was commonly used in opposition to the civilised, educated, urban or bourgeois person. Umuturage was the term used in a pejorative sense for the downtrodden, the uncivilised, the rural population. By using and ennobling the term umuturage, Habyarimana wanted to invert the common meaning of the terms. From now on umuturage would be a noble term, all Rwandans should be umuturage (peasants) and they should be proud of that.

In December 1987, Habyarimana will declare the year 1988 "*The year of the protection of the peasant revenue*". These kind of slogans were launched every year and were intended to mobilise the population for a specific activity. Other slogans include "*the year of the increase of production*" (1975), "*the year of the protection of the soil*" (1980), "*the year of the tree*" (1983). These slogans and decisions did not receive much attention from researchers, from western politicians or from the international press. Habyarimana was considered a president who did not fall victim to the urban bias in his policies, he was considered a peasant-friendly president. With the advantage of hindsight however, one can observe that the rhetoric was peasant-friendly, but As Ntamahungiro wrote in 1988,

> To give a medal of honor to each and every peasant. To decorate some peasants as Model Farmers. To give decorations at certain officials considered close to the peasantry. To

---

[41] Habyarimana J., Discours et Entretien, 1986, p. 85 and pp. 143–144.

[42] Ntamahungiro J., Eloge du Paysan Rwandais, *Dialogue*, n.130, Sept–Oct 1988, p. 5.

[43] Ntamahungiro J., Eloge du Paysan Rwandais, *Dialogue*, no 130, Sept–Oct 1988, p. 6.

baptise a street, a place, a hotel, a day in the name of the peasants. To compose a song in their honor. To organise popular parties in each commune or sector. There is no shortage of ideas and we can count on the creativity of certain minds to supply tailor-made expressions (…)

We know however, how much this part, the majority of the population, suffers. The visits of the Minister of Internal Affairs and Communal Development and of the Minister of Justice have shown us some of these injustices. From its side, the national press regularly provides evidence of the poverty in the rural areas and in the cities.[44]

The rhetoric was that of a regime caring for the peasantry. However, as I will show further on in this book [see also Uvin (1998)], the policies where benefiting elite interests, these policies were not advancing the well-being of the peasantry. Whether we take population policy, *umuganda*, tax policy (Chap. 3), coffee policy (Chap. 4), food price policy (Chap. 5), education policy, exchange rate policy or land policy, we consistently find that policy measures favour the importers, wholesale traders, construction companies, state-owned companies.

There is however, more to say about this peasant-friendly rethoric. In his 1998 book, Peter Uvin comments the 1987 decision to ennoble the term "peasant" as follows:

if all Rwandans were peasants, there would be no more classes, no distinctions—except, of course, between Hutu and Tutsi, the only allowed and never forgotten distinction (Uvin 1998, 24)

I believe this interpretation is only partly correct, as I would advance another element in the interpretation: Habyarimana uses the term *'peasant'* in opposition to the terms *'feudal, feudal mentality or feudo-monarchic'*. In Habyarimana's speeches, in MRND documents and in the writings of Rwandan authors and scholars, these terms always refer to the Tutsi monarchy who ruled Rwanda before the 1959–1962 Revolution. In a 1987 Anniversary book commissioned by the President's office (to be discussed below) the 1959–1962 revolution is called a *peasant revolution*. In other works it is called the *Social Revolution* or the *Hutu Revolution*. This means that the term 'peasant' is used for 'Hutu' and the term 'bourgeois' or 'feudal' is used for Tutsi. In other words, in Habyarimana's *ideology* the Tutsi were not peasants, they were considered the bourgeois or feudalists.

This juxtaposition is clearly demonstrated in the writings of Chrétien and Brandstetter. The former is a French historian and the latter a German anthropologist writing on Central Africa:

The government presented itself as République égalitaire and continues to set its hopes on the myth of the egalitarian, peasant society in spite of the growing social and economic tensions. It looks upon itself as rhe inheritance of the 'peasant revolution'…The regime's founding ideology spoke of the sociological majority (la pure démocratie du people majoritaire) which had permanently overcome the 'minority of the feudal Tutsi' (minorité des féodaux tutsi). The Hutu were equated with a democratic majority or 'majority people' (rubanda nyamwinshi) and the Tutsi with an aristocratic and feudal minority….Rwanda

---

[44] Ntamahungiro J., ibidem, p. 8.

was termed 'the Land of the Hutu'....and the opposition between Hutu peasantry and Tutsi feudalism remained central in their discourse.fv [45]

To their reasoning, I add the following arguments:

- From oral history and anthropological field work, we have learned that the term Tutsi was associated with a life-style detached from manual, agricultural labour. Indeed, in popular thinking as well as in the revolutionary Hutu ideology the Tutsi were considered a bourgeois class that lived of cattle and banana beer. (De Lame 1996, 74);
- The term 'Tutsi' in Rwandan history was not a term denoting a racial group of people. Depending on the social and political situation, on personal economic progress or decline, a Hutu family could, over time become Tutsi or visa-versa. It is during colonialism that the terms Hutu and Tutsi were racially interpreted and categorized. Instead of the individual chance of social mobility became a rigid system of ethnic classification (Newbury 1998). Habyarimana vigorously maintained that ethnic identity classification and registration system at the communal and national level. This is not compatible with an inclusive rethoric encompassing all Rwandans.
- Officers of the Rwandan Armed Forces were not allowed to marry Tutsi wives. Taylor (1999, 166) writes that officers suspected of having partial Tutsi ancestry or Tutsi wives were purged from the army. When Taylor was doing field work in Rwanda in 1983-1985 he met such an officer who had been eager to take on the politically favoured ethnicity for himself and his entire family and managed to stay in the army because of that for some time. Again, this policy is not compatible with an inclusive rethoric pertaining that the Second Republic had solved the ethnic question.
- What is the point of calling your entire population 'peasants' and glorifying the cultivation of the soil if you know very well that many Rwandans do not have enough land to make a living? Indeed, most Rwandans, at least for part of their time, have other income generating economic activities besides crop cultivation (see Chaps. 3, 5 and 8). They had to, because land is too scarce to feed the growing population. Instead of acknowledging the variety and diversity of jobs undertaken by Rwandans to earn incomes, the president considers his coun-trymen as peasants. Hence it is clear that it is ideology that is driving this rethoric, not the desire for an adequate representation of Rwandan society.
- The very popular singer Simon Bikindi warned for the return to feudalism in one of his most famous songs 'Bene Sebahinzi' (the descendants of Sebahinzi) a proper name which means the 'Father of the Cultivators' (Human Rights Watch 1999). In a refrain endlessly repeated on RTLM, Bikindi—one of the co-founders of the radio station—sang about the benefits of the 1959 revolution and the need to preserve them. Remark again that it is clear for all listeners that

---

[45] Brandstetter, Anna-Maria, Ethnic or Socio-Economic Conlfict? Political Interpretations of the Rwandan Crisis, *International Journal on Minority and Group Rights*, 1997, pp. 439–440. In her argument she refers to J.P. Chétien (1991, 1992) and Panabel (1995).

'cultivators' equals 'Hutu'. This was not the only such song. Another song, titled 'Wasezereye' (you said goodbye) was composed for the celebration of 25 years of independence in 1987. The lyrics read *'you said goodbye to royal power, the burden of feudalism and colonialism and you obtained democracy'*.

- The regime's peasant rethoric resonated on the ground. Woodward (1996, 16) quotes a respondent to a World Bank poverty survey calling for land availability to be extended to 'real' farmers by taking it away from non-farmers or outsiders. According to Woodward to respondent was a Hutu talking about Tutsi. Mamdami (2001) quotes Hutu who wanted to save a Tutsi girl during the genocide telling her to act and dress *like a peasant* (so she wouldn't be recognised as Tutsi).
- Habyarimana did not shy away from using sophisticated, indirect language to make his point. During an interview for the creation of a national television station, someone pointed out André Sibomana, a journalist critical to the regime. Habyarimana went up to him and said *'I had imagined you taller'*. Sibomana says that what he really meant was *'I thought you were a Tutsi'*.[46]

It is true that, as Uvin says, if all Rwandans are peasants, there are no classes anymore, but, it also means that there is no place for Tutsi anymore. The Hutu-Tutsi distinction is not forgotten in the peasant rhetoric, it is at the core of this rhetoric. Habyarimana's peasant rhetoric masks a racial prejudice behind a class analysis. The danger for pastoralists of an idealized version of peasant cultivation in human history is highlighted by Kiernan (2007, 25–26).

2.5 Habyarimana had a Mission

2.5.1 The Ethnic Cleansing and Coup d'état of 1973

In his 2001 book, Mahmood Mamdani writes that Habyarimana was publicly committed to a policy of reconciliation between Hutu and Tutsi within Rwanda.[47] According to Mamdani, official vocabulary in the Second Republic began to speak of Hutu and Tutsi as 'ethnicities' and no longer as 'races'. The meaning of this, says Mamdani, was clear: "the Tutsi within were there to stay".[48] The new regime, he writes, rejected the 'national Hutuism' of the First Republic and brought the Tutsi back within the political fold. I cannot agree with Mamdani, as one could expect from my analysis of Habyarimana's speeches in this chapter. According to me, Mamdani fails to discuss Habyarimana's peasant ideology.

---

[46] Sibomana A., Hope for Rwanda, Pluto Press, 1999, p. 36.

[47] Mamdani M, *When Victims become Killers, Colonialism, Nativism and the Genocide in Rwanda*, Princeton University Press, 2001.

[48] Mamdani ibidem, citation from p. 140.

The nature of the Second Republic and the political ideology of Habyarimana are at the centre of this debate. In 1973 Habyarimana proclaimed his own coup d'etat a 'Moral Revolution'. Mamdani accepts the good intentions that Habyarimana claimed to have with his 'Moral Revolution'. Mamdani writes that the name given to mark the day of the Revolution namely "a day of peace and reconciliation" which he says, was not just a rhetorical gesture. He gives examples in support of his argument, namely that Habyarimana included one Tutsi minister in his government. This is a weak argument and can easily be countered with the observation that only two members of the Conseil National de Développement (name given to the Rwandan parliament during the Second Republic) were Tutsi.

Mamdami's interpretation of the 'Moral Revolution' is questionable. All Rwandans, especially the peasants, had to participate in the enterprise of development and had to increase their agricultural production. This is revealed in the following excerpt from a speech Habyarimana delivered at the National University in Butare in 1973:

> The coup d'état that we did, was above all a moral coup d'état. And what we want, and we would consider our action as failed if we do not reach this goal, what we want, is to ban once and for all, the spirit of intrigue and feudal mentality. What we want is to give back labor and individual yield its real value. Because, we say it again, the one who refuses to work is harmful to society.[49]

Where Mamdani believes Habyarimana was a president that promoted reconciliation, this 1973 speech advances another interpretation, namely that Habyarimana wanted to go beyond the realizations of the First Republic. *"The spirit of intrigue and feudal mentality"*, *"the valuation of labor"* and *"the harmfulness of the one who refuses to work"* is, we believe, not directed to the Hutu extremists but to the Tutsi. It is exactly the language used to talk about the feudalists, the Tutsi. Additional support for the authors' interpretation of the 1973 coup d'état is found in a 1980 interview with Habyarimana. Asked by Yuki Sato how he judged the economic policy of President Kayibanda, Habyarimana replied:

> One cannot judge a regime that ruled for 13 years in a few minutes time. I think one could search in different official documents to have a correct judgement. What I can say about the First Republic is that I praise its effort to accomplish the Revolution and to devote itself to the development of the popular masses. I have to say that it devoted itself a lot to domestic politics and it is therefore that she has neglected a bit the economic domain and certainly foreign policy. These shortcomings are something we can stress, but they do not diminish the merits of certain leaders of the First Republic. When we have been obliged to take action in 1973, it is because certain groups around the President started to defect from the road that was taken by the 1959 Revolution and by subsequent political activities. That revolution was undertaken to obtain equality between all the ethnic groups, all social levels, and towards 1973 one has raised the ethnic problem again. And that is why we were obliged to intervene to confirm the attainments of the Revolution and to confirm the principle of the equality of all the ethnic groups in our country, and to confirm also the primacy of the interests of the rural collectivity over individual interests. And concerning

---

[49] Habyarimana J, Speech at the occasion of the opening of the academic year in Butare, October 14th, 1973, p. 44.

the economy, one has told you that Rwanda will always be handicapped by its geographical situation...[50]

This interview, suggests that Habyarimana directed his efforts against the leaders of the First Republic to safeguard the attainments of the 1959 Revolution and accused the leaders of the First Republic of jeopardising these attainments. Habyarimana namely suggests that the dignitaries of the First Republic had forgotten the objectives of the Revolution. In this interview Habyarimana says that ethnic problems constituted the reason for his coup d'état. He did not take power because he believed that the leaders of the First Republic were too racist (as one may infer from Mamdami's book), but on the contrary that these leaders had not fully implemented the objectives of the 1959 Revolution. Habyarimana wanted to consolidate the 1959 Revolution and believed that the leaders of the First Republic were off-track.

According to Guichaoau (1997, 2010), it was the head if the Rwandan intelligence service, Alexis Kanyaregwe who developed the strategy to increase ethnic tensions in Rwanda. The aim of this strategy was to make the coup d'état look like a necessary means to resume order. The 1973 removal of Tutsi from schools, administrations and jobs contradicts the assertion that anti-tutsi violence was always a response to an invasion by Tutsi. Indeed, the ethnic cleansing was an internal affair, created to legitimise a coup d'état.[51] This seems to be confirmed in the Yuki Sato interview with Habyarimana discussed above. In contrast to Mamdani, Gasana (1995, 213) sees more continuity than change between the First and Second Republics. Like Prunier, he states that the Second Republic, in 1975, puts in place an even stronger hegemonic structure, to wit the MRND or Party-State. Gasana adds that the opponents to President Kayibanda, afraid of his move to change the constitution and perpetuate his hold onto power, instigated the ethnic tensions to show the failure of his regime and thus legitimise a takeover of power.

From Guichaoua, Gasana and the Yuki Sato interview with Habyrimana, I derive that Mamdami is not correct when he presents Habyarimana as someone who rejected the national Hutuism of the First Republic. He performed a coup d'état to safeguard the attainments of the 1959–1962 Revolution declaring Kayibanda to be off-track and incited ethnic tensions in the country to legitimise his takeover, thereby bringing the northern elite to power and strengthening his powerbase by instituting the MRND as a Party-State. We derive additional support from our interpretation by looking at events at the National University of Butare at the time of the 1973 coup d'état to which we now turn.

---

[50] Sato Y., interview with president J.Habyarimana, July 12, 1980, published in Discours, Messages et Entretiens de Son Excellence le Général-Major Habyarimana Juvénal, Président de la République Rwandaise, Edition 1980, p. 238. Translation by the author.

[51] Guichaoua A., Les Antécédents politiques de la crise Rwandaise de 1994. Rapport d'expertise rédigé a la demande du Tribunal Penal International des Nations Unies sur le Rwanda, Arusha, Avril 1997, p. 12.

One of the problems in the First Republic was that most university students were Tutsi (90 % of university students according to Lemarchand). As Mamdani (2001, 135) correctly points out, the leaders of the First Republic were criticised for not advancing Hutu representation in civil society in general and education and government employment in particular. This caused major disagreement among young Hutu. A 1966 law gave the State the control of the school system and by 1970, 60 % of the students at the National University were Hutu. According to Mamdani the educated but unemployed Hutu ignited the movement to remove Tutsi from schools and public office in 1973. Mamdani (2001, 137) adds: "The context for the crises was created by the massacre of hundreds of thousands of Hutu by the mostly Tutsi army in neighboring Burundi". Vidal (1991, 26–43), who was doing field research in Rwanda in the period leading up to the coup d'etat in 1972–1973, does not mention the Burundese context in her treatement of the 1973 coup d'état. She writes that it was especially the local elites (administrators, teachers and university students, businessmen) who organised the expulsion of Tutsi teachers, Tutsi students, Tutsi administrators from their jobs and from the schools. The so-called *Comités de salut public* published lists of Tutsi who should be expelled from the university or from their jobs. Mamdani then concludes that the inaction of the Kayibanda regime, the agitation in the whole country and the power struggle between Hutu from the north and from the south prompted Habyarimana to take over power. This is the way Habyarimana presented the events: I had to take over to rescue the country. Mamdani does not discuss Habyarimana's involvement or the involvement of any of his aides in the unrest that caused the fall of the First Republic but refers to the 'context' in Burundi. I remark that neither Vidal (1991), nor Guichaoua (1997), nor Gasana (1995) nor Habyarimana himself in the 1980 interview refer to any agitation by Tutsi, attacks by Tutsi or events in Burundi in their explanation of the 1973 campaign of ethnic cleansing which ended with the Habyarimana coup d'état.

Mamdani (2001, 138) accepts that Habyarimana brought peace back to Rwanda: "Thus was born the Second Republic, which immediately declared itself the custodian of the revolution and the protector of all its children, Hutu as well as Tutsi". If this were correct, if Habyarimana was advocating peace and reconciliation as Mamdami believes, why then did Habyarimana not direct his 1973 speech in Butare against Hutu radicals and allow the Tutsi expelled in 1973 to return to their jobs and to their classrooms? Before 1973, these refugees had not joined the 1959 and 1963 refugees in neighbouring countries and were willing to live with and co-operate with a Hutu leadership. The point here is that all these jobs, together with the land belonging to the Tutsi, was already distributed among Hutu, especially Hutu radicals, members of the *Committees of Public Safety*. [52] Importantly, several of the members of the 1973 *Comittees of Public Safety* were to

---

[52] Reyntjens F., Akazu : *Escadrons de la mort et autres 'réseau zéro', un histoire des résistances au changement politiques depuis 1990*, in Guichaoua, A., Les crises politiques de 1993–1994 au Rwanda et Burundi, 1995, p. 271.

become leaders of the 1994 genocide. According to Reyntjens (1995), a historic line can be drawn between the activism of people like Ferdinand Nahimana in 1973 and in 1994. Nahimana, as we have discussed already, is the author of a book titled '*Culture is the basis of our development in harmony*' which is a praise and commentary of Habyarimana's development ideology. Instead of directing his 1973 speech at the university of Butare against these radicals (as one would assume from a president who wants to reconcile), Habyarimana blames '*feudal mentality*', and considers '*the ones who refuse to work is harmful to society*'. In other words, he blames the Tutsi for the unrest, not the Hutu radicals. We encounter here a practise that we will also see in the 1990–1994 period, when Habyarimana tells western journalists what they like to hear, to talk about peace and reconciliation, and that he reserves a different discourse for his domestic audience.[53]

Several other elements should be added to this discussion. One is a biographical one: Habyarimana had been in charge of the army from the start of the First Republic. He graduated as the first and highest ranking officer from the first promotion of the Military Academy in 1962 and was given command of the army right after. Under Kayibanda, he served as Minister of the National Guard and the Police. The single purpose of the army was to defend the country against Tutsi attacks from neighbouring countries. During this period, in which a new leadership had to establish itself, attacks were also directed against Tutsi citizens residing in Rwanda. An example is the massacre of several thousand Tutsi in December 1963 in the prefecture of Gikongoro (see also Chap. 6). In theory, it is possible that a military officer whose entire career-path coincides with the rise to power of the Hutu elite and whose responsibility was to fight the Tutsi rebels, would become a peace-maker and a promotor of reconciliation once he is president. But one should look at the facts. It was the Hutu from the North, who had a history of resistance to colonial and Tutsi dominance, who mounted the 1973 coup d'état. Pottier, referring to food policy and to the land contract (*ubukonde*)[54] writes that:

> When the current (Second Republic) Government of Rwanda took power, their ambition was to restore their own pre-Tutsi culture—a culture dominated by powerful landowners (*abakonde*) who attracted clients (*abagererwa*) through land.[55]

---

[53] Mamdami cites a journalist from Le Monde to support his point.

[54] In contrast to the cattle contract (ubuhake), the land contract was NOT abolished in the aftermath of the 1959 Revolution.

[55] Pottier J., Taking Stock: Food Marketing Reform in Rwanda, 1982-1989, *African Affairs* (1993), p. 29.

2.5.2 A Policy of 'Ethnic Equilibrium'

In 1973, as we just discussed, Tutsi were chased from the university and from jobs in the local and national administration. Throughout his reign, the allocation of secondary and university schooling as well as government jobs to ethnic groups will receive utmost attention from the leaders of the Second Republic. Habyarimana institutionalised a policy of 'ethnic equilibrium' in which all ethnic groups would be alloted places at schools, at the university and in the administration according to their percentage in the population.

According to Guichaoau (1997, pp. 19–21), the effects of this policy were very apparent in schools. When pupils graduated from primary school and wanted to enter secondary school they learned that selection criteria were not based on academic merit, but on ethnic affiliation. As only 8 % of Rwandan children went to secondary school in 1991, one realises the saliency of this policy.[56] Des Forges (1999) writes that

> the MRND regulated access to government-supported high schools supposedly assigning places according to quotas for ethnic and regional groups. These quota, she argues were both inaccurately computed and unfairly applied, favoring children from the northwest or those whose families could pay in money or other benefits for access to education.[57]

When, in the course of multi-party politics in 1991, Agathe Uwilingiyimana (Hutu) became Minister of primary and secondary education, she promptly abolished the quota system and decreed that access to higher education would be decided on merit alone. According to Reyntjens, she immediately was assaulted and beaten by armed men in her home. Thousands of students and mothers turned out to march in support of her new policy.[58] It is not surprisingly then, that under the Habyarimana regime, a sizeable number of Tutsi tried to obtain a Hutu identity card. This is an economic strategy and a strong indication that the Hutu identity was more valuable than the Tutsi identity. Most importantly, a Hutu identity card gave access to government jobs.

Some writers consider the policy of 'ethnic equilibrium' as affirmative action on behalf of a group that has been disfavoured during the monarchy and colonialism. This is exactly the position that the Habyarimana regime took when it was challenged by the African Commission of Human Rights on its policy of ethnic equilibrium in 1991. The Commission did not rule, but two of the three judges considered Rwanda's policy a case of racial discrimination which violated the principles of the African Charter. They stated that the policy violated individual

---

[56] Laurent M., *Panorama succint des Economies de la Région des Grands Lacs Africains*, in Guichaoua, A., Les Crises Politiques de 1993–1994, p. 424.

[57] Des Forges A., *Leave None to Tell the Story*, p. 54.

[58] Reyntjens F., *L' Afrique des Grands Lacs en Crise*, pp. 115–116.

rights. The third judge wanted more information on the policy before making up his mind.[59]

2.5.3 A Remarkable Anniversary Publication in 1987

Further elements are found in a remarkable book published in 1987 by Marchal, a producer of documentaries. The book is an Anniversary Publication celebrating 25 years of Rwanda's Independence.[60] The book is a beautifully illustrated *mythical and romantic history* of Rwanda and was commissioned by President Habyarimana.[61] It was given by Habyarimana to his honorary guests (heads of state, presidents, ministers…) at the 25th Celebration of Independence. The book features many beautiful pictures from the Rwandan landscape, its people, animals and plants. Rwanda is described as a one large village, stating that Rwandans do not like cities (p. 24). The reader is offered a history of Rwanda where the 1959 events are called a *peasant revolution* during which the *predominance of the cow was replaced with the predominance of the hoe*. On p. 44 we read that man is *an eminent product of his soil*. The Abanyiginya dynasty had not respected the land rights of the peasant masses nor recognised their legitimate aspirations to take part in government.

On p. 46, the book tells us that Rwanda is inhabited by *Hutu, Tutsi and Twa*. The first are Bantus, *cultivators* from the great forest of the Sahara. The second are Nilotics, *pastoralists* and great politicians from Egypt and perhaps from India. The Twa finally are Pygmoids, the most frustrated group. At the same time the book honors its leaders, foremost president Habyarimana who is in office since 1973. The president is presented as *the child of God and the Apostle of Life* (p. 96 and p. 56), adding that he is predestined by his name, which literally translates "It is God who gives life".

Marchal (1987, 88) further claims that the president belongs to the *race* of people who cut the forest (the Bahutu). President Habyarimana, the reader learns, brought peace to the country and is not the type of person who would *capture women from the noble classes* (the Batutsi) while contemplating their *extinction* (p. 92). On page 92 one also finds Habyarimana's claim to be a *Muhutu pur sang* (a Muhutu from pure blood) and that his parents were simple peasants.[62] The time

---

[59] The African Commission on Human and People's Rights, Examination of State Reports, 9th Session March 1991: Libya—Rwanda—Tunisia, pp. 61–77.

[60] Marchal O., *Au Rwanda, La Vie Quotidienne au Pays du Nil Rouge*, Didier Hatier, Bruxelles, 1987.

[61] Marchal who thanks the staff in the Presidents' office in the pre-amble of his book, died in 1996. In a telephone interview with the spouse of the Belgian photographer working with Marchal on this book, the spouse told the author that the Anniversary Book was commissioned by President Habyarimana.

[62] Apparently, rumor wanted that the ethnic affiliation of Habyarimana's father was debated, pushing the president to confirm his Hutu identity in public.

he spent in the hills, on the soil has influenced him the most. On page p. 92 it is repeated that the family of Habyarimana belonged to the *race* of people who cut the forest. On p. 97 Habyarimana is called *the greatest adventurer of the end of the millenium*.

When he took power in 1973, we read that Habyarimana said that "the Rwandan will *never spill the blood* of a fellow Rwandan anymore". On p. 100, Habyarimana is honored for *not advocating birth control*, adding that "*live is a gift of God*", which is considered very courageous in a very populous country. On p. 108, the question of the Rwandan refugees in neighboring countries is linked to the demographic situation in Rwanda:

> The Rwandans say: "When Obote has sent us his refugees three or four years ago (a. 1982), if we wouldn't be many, wouldn't he be very eager to send the refugees ?" It is true : the power of a people lies also in their number. Recently, Jacques Chirac (then prime minister), cited the demographic growth of the French population in order to launch the promise to make France the first economic power in Europe. And in Afghanistan, the Russians built their presence on the axiom: "One only needs one million Afghans to build Afghan socialism." In other words, one only needs to make children.

From this quotation, we learn that "The Rwandans" welcome population growth, and moreover consider it as the basis of their political and economic power. In Sect 2.2 of this chapter we already saw how Habyarimana regarded the population as the first force of the nation. Here, the size of the population as a force is linked to the potential return of the Tutsi refugees living in Uganda and indeed as a means to prevent this return.

On p. 174 of the Anniversary Publication, it is claimed that Habyarimana avoided introducing political parties because their rivalries in other parts of Africa had lead to *fratricides*. He set up the MRND to introduce his ideas to the peasant masses.

Of course, one could question the nature of this Anniversary book and dismiss it as the independent opinion of the author in question (Omer Marchal). According to Gauthier De Villiers, a well-known Belgian scholar of Africa, Marchal lived in Rwanda for 35 years and fully subscribed to the Nilo-Hamitic thesis and the resulting ethnic/racist interpretation of Rwanda's history.[63] President Habyarimana must have liked Marchal's writings and opinion because he commissioned the book for what was likely to be the most important celebration of his entire presidency. "*The Rwandans*" from the citation are in fact Marchal's contractors in the Presidential office.

There is more to it however. Marchal is not the founder of Rwandan mythology. As we have seen, what he writes about Habyarimana and "The Rwandans" can be found in other citations of Habyarimana himself. It is therefore highly likely that

---

[63] De Villiers, Gauthier, « L'africanisme belge face aux problèmes d'interprétation de la tragédie Rwandaise »,

p. 117, dans Les racines de la violence dans la region des grands lacs, (ed.) Aelvoet, M. et Les Verts au

parlement européen, 1995.

Marchal only wrote what Habyarimana liked to read. Describing Habyarimana as the child of God resembles the answer the president gave to the question why he was not in favour of a multiparty system. This question was asked in the mid-seventies after establishing the MRND. The answer was: "*You also worship only one God*". In an interview in 1980, the president suggests that he had a mission in life. On the question of how he became president, the answer was:

> …I would like to stress that I have served the First Republic since 1960 and I think of it now. Exactly at the date of Independence, the first of July 1962, was it a symbolic gesture? But I think of it now and you can interpret it the way you want. The first of July 1962, I was part of the March-past and in the troops that composed this March-past, there was a young under-lieutenant. That was me. And it was this under-lieutenant who was given the flag of the army by former President Kayibanda. A flag that we still have now. I think about it and maybe it was a symbolic gesture.[64]

2.6 Concluding Remarks to this Chapter

In this first chapter, the ideological underpinnings of the Habyarimana regime were analysed. From the January 1990 publication on Umuganda, the 1988 book by Ferdinand Nahimana, the 1987 official glorification of the peasantry and the 1987 Anniversary Book on Habyarimana's presidency I conclude that the ideological fervour of the regime did not wane over the years. This ideology, officialised in Habyarimana's speeches from 1973 onwards and institutionalised in the MRND from 1975 onwards remained strong throughout his entire regime.

Consider that (1) the president repeatedly stated that Rwanda has a demographic problem, but he does not install a family planning program; (2) he considers the population as a force; (3) he wants Rwanda to be self-sufficient in food and is very concerned with a disequilibrium between population growth and food production; (4) he said that development should be endogenous, culture-based and organic; (5) he believes that only manual labour is valuable; (6) he had peasants perform collective labour one day a week as an antidote to money, education and off-farm labour; (7) he glorified the peasantry and wanted all Rwandans to be peasants integrated in his Movement, the MRND; (8) his rural preference was expressed in anti-urban, moralising and puritanical policies to which mainly urban Tutsi woman fell victim (9) he believed he had a mission in life, to wit to safeguard the attainments of the Hutu Revolution and to go beyond this with his Moral Revolution; (10) he celebrated the most important day of his presidency (25 years of Independence) with a book and a song that paints a mythical history of Rwanda where the two main ethnic groups are not only presented as holders of different occupations—Hutu as cultivators, Tutsi as pastoralists—but also as two different races. The book portrays Habyarimana as a child of God with a mission.

---

[64] Interview with Yuki Sato, ibid, 1980, p. 237.

I believe that these ten elements are key characteristics of the ideology of the Habyarimana regime and these characteristics help us to understand the regime. The president wanted Rwanda to remain an agrarian nation where a strong and virtuous peasant population tills the soil. A peasant population which devotes all its attention to food crop cultivation, which remains in the rural areas and which is firmly integrated in the unique party MRND. Habyarimana was named '*Father of the Nation*' an expression which personalised and incorporated the relationship between the peasantry, the state and himself.

Chapter 3
The Rwandan Economy 1973–1994: From Macro to Micro

As this book offers a political economy analysis of development and genocide in Rwanda, we devoted this chapter to the structure of the Rwandan economy. I would like to do this here using the schemes that are commonly used in macro and micro-economic textbooks. I start with population figures and macro-economic aggregates, continue with the household level and end this chapter with a discussion of taxes, public goods and political economy.

3.1 Population Figures

One of the most dramatic examples of the power of data collection and their registration is the entry for 'ethnicity' on the identity cards of Rwandans, a practice introduced by Belgium, the colonial power and continued by the Kayibanda en Habyarimana regimes. Although it is not the purpose of this book to study the history of census data in detail, I will be using the figures of the 1991 census on the distribution of Hutu and Tutsi over the prefectures. The 1991 general population census, whose final results were published just before the genocide, is a valuable data base from which we can obtain a general picture of the Rwandan population in the beginning of the 90s.[1] Some of its major findings include

- total population of Rwanda in 1991: 7.1 million (and not 7.6 as the Habyarimana regime had always said) with 91.1 % Hutu, 8.4 % Tutsi and 0.4 % Twa (p. 124)
- annual growth rate of the population in the 80s: 3.1 %, one of the highest in the world (p. 13)
- population working in agriculture: 90 % of which the report adds that only 85.5 % of Tutsi work in agriculture compared to 91.9 % of Hutu. (p. 118)

---

[1] Recensement General de la Population et de l' Habitat au 15 Aout, 1991, Resultats Definitifs, Service National de Recensement, Ministere du Plan, Kigali, April 1994.

P. Verwimp, *Peasants in Power*, DOI: 10.1007/978-94-007-6434-7_3,
© Springer Science+Business Media Dordrecht 2013

The census also gives figures of the distribution of ethnic groups over the prefectures. The report however, does not give that distribution over communes. From Table 3.1 it is clear that the Tutsi population is almost absent in northern Rwanda and concentrated in the prefectures of Kibuye, Butare, Gikongoro, Git-arama and in the capital Kigali.

The report has many demographic statistics, such as the age at the first marriage, the type of marriage (legal, traditional, cohabitation), household size, the number of children per women, the ability to read and write, the level of instruction, the adherence to a religion, child mortality and even the possession of a radio. All these data are also presented in the report according to ethnicity. The authors of the report conclude that

- The number of Tutsi was overestimated in the 1952 survey (p. 125)
- Tutsi women have less children than Hutu women (p. 125 and 241)
- The mortality of children is higher for children where the mother is Hutu (p. 275)
- Tutsi are the principal beneficiaries of the educational system (p. 136)

Alison Des Forges (1999) recognizes that these census data are problematic and advocates a prudent approach:

Even the size of the Tutsi population in Rwanda on April 6, 1994 is debated. Demographer William Seltzer, who has studied the data, estimates the number as 657,000, a figure extrapolated from 1991 census data. Some critics assert that the number of Tutsi was underreported in that census and in the prior census of 1978 because the Habyarimana government wanted to minimize the importance of Tutsi in the population. Although frequently said, no documentation has been presented to support this allegation. The 1991 data show Tutsi as forming 8.4 % of the total population. This figure seems to accord with extrapolations from the generally accepted census data of 1952, taking into account the population loss due to death and flight during the 1960s and the birth rate, which was lower for Tutsi than for Hutu. Whether or not census data were purposely altered to reduce the number of Tutsi, the figures underestimated the Tutsi population because an undetermined number of Tutsi arranged to register as Hutu in order to avoid discrimination and

Table 3.1 Distribution of the population over prefectures and ethnicity

	Hutu	Tutsi	Twa	Other	Total
Butare	82.0	17.3	0.7	0.0	753,868
Byumba	98.2	1.5	0.2	0.0	775,935
Cyangugu	88.7	10.5	0.5	0.3	551,565
Gikongoro	86.3	12.8	0.8	0.1	465,814
Gisenyi	96.8	2.9	0.3	0.1	731,996
Gitarama	90.2	9.2	0.6	0.1	848,027
Kibungo	92.0	7.7	0.2	0.1	648,912
Kibuye	84.8	14.8	0.4	0.0	469,494
Rural Kigali	90.8	8.8	0.4	0.1	905,632
Kigali capital	81.4	17.9	0.3	0.4	221,806
Ruhengeri	99.2	0.5	0.2	0.1	766,795
Total	91.1	8.4	0.4	0.1	7,099,844

Source 1991 Census

Table 3.2 A range of population estimates

% Tutsi in pop.	Source	Number of Tutsi in March 1994[a]	Tutsi deaths in 1994 genocide[b]		Tutsi death in % at midpoint	Hutu deaths 1994–2000 at midpoint estimate[c]	
			Min	Max		Number	%
8.4	Census	630,000	430,000	530,000	76 (480,000)	470,000	6.8
10.7	Comm.	800,000	600,000	700,000	81 (650,000)	300,000	4.4
12	Prunier	900,000	700,000	800,000	83 (750,000)	200,000	3.0

[a] Applying a 3 % annual population growth rate to the August 1991 Census
[b] Applying a minimum of 100,000 and a maximum of 200,000 Tutsi survivors
[c] Using the 950,000 government death count (published in 2002 and collected in 2000)

harassment. Although many Rwandans know of such cases, there is at present no basis for estimating how many persons they represented.[2]

One way to document the underreporting of Tutsi affiliation in the 1991 census is to compare the census data with annual communal registration data. That is what I do in Table 3.2. The communal registration data for December 1983 identify 10.7 % of Rwanda's population as Tutsi. Prunier (1995) regards 12 % as a conservative estimate prior to the genocide. According to the 1991 Census, Tutsi women have less children than Hutu women but also loose less children. The 10.7 % may be underestimated, but the basis for a higher estimate is lacking.

In Table 3.2 I use the 8.4–12 % interval to estimate the number of Tutsi residing in Rwanda in March 1994. At mid-point I arrive at a population of 800,000. Using the mid-point estimate of the number of Tutsi survivors (150,000) I arrive at 650,000 Tutsi killed as my best estimate. Using the widely reported 950,000 government death count (which must include Hutu victims included by the surveyors, see Guichaoua 2010, p. 435 and 437), I arrive at 300,000 Hutu killed in the 1994–2000 period as my best estimate.

3.2 Macro-Economic Outlook

The figures in Table (3.3) give an overview of key macro-economic indicators. They reveal the outlook of the Rwandan economy in the 1973–1993 period: population is growing rapidly, cultivable land per capita decreases with 0.2 ha every few years, there is a structural trade deficit, government expenditure as a percentage of GDP increases over time, export revenue is highly dependable on one crop, income per capita rises until the mid-80s, inflation is under control until the civil war starts in 1990, almost everybody is employed in agriculture. Not in this table, but equally important for a correct picture of the economy is its hilly

---

[2] Des Forges, A., Leave None to tell the Story, Human Rights Watch, New York, 1999, p. 15.

Table 3.3 Macro-economic indicators of Rwanda under Habyarimana

Periodic averages	1974–1980	1981–1986	1987–1990	1991–1993	
Population					
Growth of population	3.5	3.1	2.9	2.9	
Area cultiv. land/capita (ha)	1.4	1.2	1.0	0.8	
% population in agriculture	95.0	94.0	92.8	90.0	
Production					
Growth of real GDP (%)	5.1	3.5	−0.4	−0.2	
Growth of real GDP/capita	1.8	0.4	−2.6	−0.8	
Consumer price index	11.4	5.2	3.0	10.0	
Balance of payments (in % of GDP)					
Export of goods and services	16.5	11.5	7.2	5.0	
of which coffee	57.0	72.0	77.0	55.0	
of which tin	23.0	11.0	0	0	
of which tea	8.0	9.0	15.0	20.0	
Import of goods and services	24.1	22.7	18.1	16.0	
Trade Deficit	−7.6	−11.2	−10.9	−11.0	

Figures for selected years	1973	1981	1987	1991	1993
Population					
Population numbers (in million)	4.0	5.2	6.4	7.1	7.4
nominal GDP (billion US$)	0.41	1.1	2.1	1.8	1.9
GDP per capita (current US$)	130	200	300	253	259
Human development indicator	0.323	0.368	0.411	0.321	0.274
Government budget					
Total Revenue (in billion RWF)	2.4	13.8	23.2	25.0	23.4
Total Revenue (as % of GDP)	5.8	12.7	13.6	11.8	9.2
Grants (as % of GDP)	0	1.3	2.4	6.5	6.4
Total Expenditures (in billion RWF)	3.0	17.0	40.8	53.0	68.7
Total Expenditures (as % of GDP)	7.3	17.4	23.7	25.1	23.6

Sources Berlage L., Eyssen, H., Goedhuys M. Sleuwagen, L., Van den Bulcke D., *Rwanda: Disequilibrium, Reform and the Manufacturing Sector*, World Bank, Country Background Paper April 1993; International Monetary Fund, Rwanda, Statistical Appendices; and Uwezeyimana, L., 1996, Crise du café, faillite de l'Etat et implosion sociale au Rwanda, Serie MOCA Montages et Café, no 4, Université de Toulouse

terrain and the landlocked location, far away from seaports. The hilly terrain increases transportation costs of products to domestic markets and the distance to the ocean constrains the access to world markets as it increases the price of Rwandan products.

In the 70s, average incomes were increasing. This was mainly due to five factors: (1) political stability; (2) all land was taken into cultivation; (3) the price of coffee was high on the international market; (4) the country benefited from sizeable amounts of foreign aid and; (5) all Rwandans were mobilised to work for the country (umuganda). Let us discuss these elements one by one.

Umuganda was responsible for large projects such as road building, school building, tree planting, and anti-erosion measures. The Second Republic had developed an entire accounting system to register and calculate the value of the projects realised during umuganda. A January 1990 report, published by the presidency of the MRND, presents detailed tables for the realisations of umuganda in several economic domains in all communes.[3] The sum of these projects is calculated as 11,546,677,046 RWF for the 1974–1986 period which is about 1 billion RWF per year.[4] Depending on the year under consideration in the designated period, this figure represents 1–2 % of annual GDP. Since umuganda was unpaid communal labour, one cannot only see it in terms of the economic value of realised projects, but also as government tax revenue. To be sure, the Rwandan government never included the value of unpaid communal labour as tax revenue in its national accounts. If it had done so, tax revenue would increase with some 9 billion RWF per year. The average value of one half working day per week before 1990 was 70 RWF.[5] One adult performing umuganda the whole year thus pays a tax of $70 \times 52 = 3,640$ RWF. This tax can be multiplied with 2,500,000 the average number of adults living in Rwanda between 1974 and 1986, yielding 9 billion RWF per year. The annual value of projects realised by umuganda is thus 9 times smaller than the value of tax revenue collected 'in kind' through umuganda. A discrepancy for which I have no clear explanation. I refer to Table (3.4) for the domain specific contributions of umuganda. 60 % of the total value is realised in anti-erosion and tree planting projects.

GDP did not only increase because of umuganda, but also because most of the land that was previously not cultivated, was taken into cultivation. This process already started in the 1960s when, after the Social Revolution, pasture land was converted into farm land. An example of this is the 1966 redistribution of land. Land that formerly belonged to Tutsi chiefs, mostly if not all pasture land, was given to peasants for cultivation.[6] Olson (1990, 146) states that from the end of the 70s onwards, new land was no longer available in rural Kigali or Kibungo prefectures and people started to migrate to Kigali city, hoping to find a job in the informal sector. It is documented that during the Habyarimana regime, many people from the land-scarce western prefectures migrated to the less fertile lands in Bugesera. Olson who studied the migratory movement in Rwanda and writes that

> After independence, increasing population pressure resulted in changing economic circumstances, such as rapid decline in farm sizes and available land per person. One response was a high rate of out-migration from the areas experiencing the most pressure. The destination of these migrants was influenced by political factors; the government was

---

[3] L'umuganda dans le développement national, Janvier 19990, MRND, Kigali.

[4] André Guichaoua also arrives at 1 billion RWF as the annual value of the projects realised by umuganda in this period. Guichaoua (1991), Les Travaux Communautaires en Afrique Centrale, *Revue Tiers Monde*, XXXII, no 127, Juillet-Septembre, p. 563.

[5] The value of an entire labour day was 100 FRW, the sum of a long morning and shorter afternoon.

[6] Gasana, E., Butera, J.B., Byanafashe, D., Karekezi, A., Rwanda, Comprehending and Mastering African Conflicts, 1999, p. 157.

Table 3.4 Umuganda in different economic domains, 1974–1986

Domain	Monetary value (RWF)	Percent
Agriculture	388,431,673	3
Anti-erosion and tree planting	6,950,705,690	60
Water sanitation	282,004,789	2
Road infrastructure	2,160,156,049	19
Cattle raising	131,304,669	1
Construction	1,634,074,176	14
Total	11,546,677,046	100

Source Umuganda dans le développement national, 1990, p. 80

interested in settling land previously used for pastoral activities so it promoted organized settlement schemes in the East.[7]

There were many Tutsi from Gikongoro to Butare among the migrants who ended up in the Bugesera. We come back to this is Chap. 6.

A 1990 report on the position of the government about the refugee question (mentioned already in Sect. 1.4 of Chap. 1 of this book) shows how in the post-colonial period all land was taken into cultivation (see Table 3.5). Since 1958 pasture land dimished by 77 % (from 675,627 to 199,360 ha). This land was converted into land for agriculture.

In the second chapter, I have already discussed the absence of family planning during the Second Republic. Unchecked populated growth, a policy of land redistribution and conversion of pasture land into farm land together with migration to less fertile land, resulted in the closing of the land frontier in Rwanda by the late 70s/early 80s. Habyarimana had always practised a land extensive policy, not a policy of land intensification. The latter, combined with the development of economic activities outside agriculture, however, is the only solution for a land-scarce economy.

Increases in GDP in the 70s were also the result of a higher volume of coffee production accompanied by higher prices. A large part of government revenue was realised through the coffee economy. We come back to this in the third chapter of this book. As we shall see, farmers benefited from a relatively high producer price for several years. Importantly, the high international price for coffee accounted for a large chunk of the increase in government revenue in the 1970s. Marysse (1982) argues that economic growth increased the surplus in the hands of the elite. This surplus was not used for productive investments. This partly explains why Rwanda remained so vulnerable to negative price shocks in the second half of the 1980s. One must add that Marysse wrote this paper even before the economic downturn of the second half of the 80s.

---

[7] Olson, J.M., The impact of changing socio-economic factors on migration patterns in Rwanda, Ph.D Dissertation, Michigan State University, 1990, p. 150.

Table 3.5 Land use (in ha)

Use/year	1970	1980	1986
Pastures	487,884	322,060	199,360
Forest	27,156	57,200	99,500
Fallow land + anti-erosion measures	200,000	154,000	123,000
Agriculture	527,000	710,400	826,500
Total	1,242,700	1,243,660	1,248,360

Source République Rwandaise (1990). Le Rwanda et le problème de ses réfugiés. Contexte historique, analyse et voies de solution, Kigali, Présidence de la République, Commission Spéciale sur les problèmes de émigrés Rwandais, Mai, p. 117

The two remaining reasons for economic growth in the first part of Habyari-mana's reign, political stability and foreign aid, are related. Donors like a country that seems to function smoothly, where the bureaucracy can get things done and is not corrupt. This was indeed the image most if not all donors had of Rwanda. They credited Habyarimana for the political stability he created at home. The attractiveness of this image—and its dangers—are described in detail in Uvin's (1998) book '*Aiding violence*'. In the third chapter, he relates how the development community applauded Rwanda's political stability, the government's concern for the rural population, its effective administration and its prudent, sound, realistic management. The image of a government that had banned 'politics' and devoted all its attention to 'development' was kept intact until the genocide.

In the Table 3.6 and in Fig. 3.1, one can see that per capita income in Rwanda started to decline from the second half of the 80s onwards, with negative growth rates in 1987, 1989, 1990, 1991 and 1993. Per capita income decreased by 20 % between 1985 and 1993.

Table 3.6 The evolution of mean per capita income in Rwanda

	Mean income in 1985 RWF	in 1985 US$[a]	Annual % change
1985	18,670	187	–
1986	19,050	190	+1.6
1987	18,520	185	−2.6
1988	18,566	186	0
1989	17,966	180	−3.2
1990	17,171	172	−4.4
1991	16,289	163	−5.2
1992	16,933	170	+4.2
1993	14,979	150	−11.7
1994	11,542	115	−23.3

[a] 100 RWF = 1 dollar; % change between 1985 and 1993 is −20 %
Source Rwanda Poverty update, World Bank Africa Document, 1998, annex I

Fig. 3.1 Evolution of per capita income (in RWF)

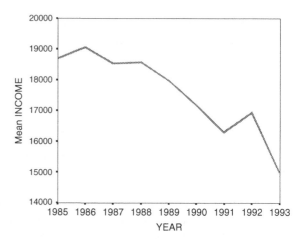

3.3 The Rural Household Economy

At the end of the 80s, 93 % of Rwanda's population lives in rural areas and nearly all rural households are engaged in farming. On average, households cultivate 0.89 ha of land, the vast majority of these landholdings being owner operated. Beans, bananas, sorghum, sweet potatoes and cassava are the main food staples. Bananas and potatoes are also sold for cash. Coffee is a pure cash crop. Farming is labor intensive. Women's labor is particularly important in food crop production. Men's labor is crucial in cash crop production and animal husbandry. Hoes and machetes are the basic farming tools; animal traction is non-existent. Marginal lands once set aside for pasture or left in long fallow are now taken into cultivation. Rural formal and informal credit markets are severely underdeveloped.[8] Between the altitude of 1,500 and 1,700 m, we find the ideal conditions for many crops, explaining the high population densities found on this altitude level.

The Rwandan peasantry has set up an inventive and efficient agricultural system (Bart 1993).[9] This system, that has managed to avoid famine most of the time, is a complex mixture of food and cash crops, cultivated on slopes and in valleys, combined with small livestock (and cattle for the richer peasants) and some income from beer brewing, other business activities and off-farm income. The chosen mix is the result of personal, household, local and climatic characteristics.

Table 3.7 shows that the main sources of cash income are off-farm income and beer sales. On average almost 60 % of income consists of income from subsistence production. Monetary income—the sum of beer sales, crops sales, off-farm income

---

[8] Clay, D., Reardon, T., Kangasniemi, J, Sustainable Intensification in the Highland Tropics: Rwandan Farmers' Investments in Land Conservation and Soil Fertility, *Economic Development and Cultural Change*, 1998, p. 363.

[9] Bart, F., *Montagnes d' Afrique, terres paysannes*, le cas du Rwanda, 1993.

Table 3.7 Household income sources (1990), averages, N = 1,208

Gross income per household (in RWF)	Sources of income at the household level (in %)					
	(1) Subsistence cons. of crops	(2) Crop sales	(3) Beer	(4) Livestock products	(5) Off-farm	(6) Transfers
58,000	58.6	8.3	10.0	5.5	14.7	2.8

(1) crop consumption from own production
(2) sales of all crops (domestic cash crops and export crops)
(3) the sales of artisanal brewed beer (banana and sorghum been)
(4) livestock products (eggs and milk) consumed from own production, livestock sold and received (autoconsumption of livestock, on average 2,000 RWF per household in 1990, is not included)
(5) income from skilled and unskilled off-farm work and from business activities other than beer sales
(6) gifts of food, beer, cash etc. received
Source Author's calculations from data collected by the Department of Agricultural Statistics (DSA). Data are population weighted

and sales of livestock—per household makes up for approximately 40 % of total gross income, some 23,000 RWF per year.[10]

Clay et al. (1995) have calculated that two thirds of the cultivable land in Rwanda is cultivated. The rest consists of fallow land, pasture and woodlots. Half of Rwanda's cultivated fields are intercropped. On 56 % of the cultivated land bananas are grown in association with food crops such as beans, sorghum and sweet potatoes.[11] Intercropping appears to be a response to land scarcity, as it is practised more often by households with relatively few land per person. Less intercropping occurs in high-altitude areas where little or no bananas are grown. In terms of shares of land (in pure stands, accounted for the degree of intercropping), the main crops are bananas (26 %), beans (17 %), sweet potatoes (11 %), cassava (9 %), sorghum (9 %) and mais (7 %).

The effect of population pressure on crop choices and land use in Rwanda has been analysed by Kangasniemi (1998). Using the 1989–1991 nationally representative farm household survey, he finds that Rwandan farmers prefer to keep and even expand their banana holdings. In fact, under population pressure, farmers prefer to grow bananas to brew and sell banana beer. With the money, they buy food crops and finance other expenditures. Food, as we shall see, has to be imported into Rwanda, a reality the Habyarimana regime never acknowledged. Bananas are popular because

---

[10] The sale of livestock, worth on average 3,000 RWF in 1990 is strictly speaking not 'income' but a change in assets or portfolio.

[11] Clay, D., Promoting Food Security in Rwanda through sustainable agricultural productivity: meeting the challenges of Population pressure, Land Degradation and Poverty, International Development Paper no. 17, Michigan State University, Departments of Agricultural Economics and Economics, Chap. 4, p. 16.

they are not only a source of monetary income, but they also provide income the whole year round, a significant difference with e.g. coffee. Banana cultivation is socially very important and provides a protective cover against erosion (Bart 1993). All these factors combine to make bananas the most important and most preferred crop for Rwandan peasants. Clay et al. (1995) add that the farming practises needed for higher yields require more labor than other crops. The brewing activity of course is labor-intensive. Kangasiemi (1998, 133) argues that the exchange strategy (production of banana beer for consumption of beans) is the preferred strategy by the Rwandan farmer to cope with population pressure:

> Multivariate analysis that controls for agroclimatic and other factors shows that in Rwanda's banana zone, households with less land per adult equivalent sell more beer bananas per hectare. In this respect bananas are different from any other major crop, including coffee. This suggests that Rwandan farmers are not substituting food crops for cash crops to cope with land scarcity caused by population growth. While households with less land per person are not making any dramatic transition to cash crops either, they clearly prefer to keep their bananas and to rely on the exchange of banana beer for food. 'Food first' is not their strategy of achieving food security.

The main argument in support of the economic rationale behind the exchange strategy is simple: one can show that the cash revenue from a hectare of beer bananas sold as beer would on average have bought 1,446 kg of beans (Kangasniema, p. 157). This is 72 % more than the estimated average national bean yield. This shows that, at the relative prices and yields that prevailed in 1990, the strategy of exchanging banana beer for beans succeeds in substituting labor for land and improves the food entitlements of those engaged in the exchange strategy. The importance of the brewing of banana beer is such that 80 % of Rwanda's rural households get more cash from bananas than from coffee or any other single crop, and that, for 41 % of the households, bananas are a more important source of cash than all other crops combined.

Clay et al. (1995) report that sweet potatoes are the single most important source of calories for Rwandans. Sweet potatoes have more calories per-kilogram than potatoes or cooking bananas. Except for high-altitude areas, where potatoes grow best, only bananas produce more calories per-hectare than sweet potatoes. Sweet potato production is not labor-intensive, compared to bananas beer production or potatoes and is less demanding for soil quality and moisture. This explain why sweet potatoes are a popular crop in Gikongoro, a region not blessed with fertile soils.

Farms are not only small in Rwanda, but also highly fragmented. Blarel et al. (1992), using 1987–1988 World Bank Survey data of 232 households, found that 40 % of farms have 8 or more plots. In their regressions however, neither farm size nor farm fragmentation seem to have a negative effect on land productivity.[12]

---

[12] Blarel, B., Hazell, P., Place, F., Quiggin, J., The Economics of Farm Fragmentation: Evidence from Ghana and Rwanda, *The World Bank Economic Review*, Vol. 6, no. 2, p. 252.

Table 3.8 Decreasing yields in post-colonial agriculture

Crop	Yield (in kg per ha)		Difference	Difference in %
	1959	1988		
Beans	750	764	+14	+1.9
Peas	800	556	−244	−30.5
Sorghum	1,200	1,188	−12	−0.17
Potatoes	7,000	6,943	−57	−0.8
Sweet potatoes	7,500	6,099	−1401	−18.7
Cassava	13,000	9,162	−3838	−29.5
Bananas	10,800	9,504	−1296	−12

Source as for Table 3.5, p. 112

Place and Hazell (1993), using the same World Bank data, found that Rwandan peasants invest—in short term improvements (continued mulching or manuring) or long term improvements (planting trees, trenching, destumping or green fencing)—more in land when they have secure rights on their land.[13] But this does not mean that yields on these fields are higher. Place and Hazell did not find productivity increasing effects of land rights. They point out that other constraints can be more binding such as technology, credit and fertilizer.

The findings of both Blarel and Place and Hazell are not confirmed in a study by Byiringiro and Reardon (1996) who used a much larger (nationally representative) 1990–1991 data set of 1,248 rural households. They find a strong inverse relationship between farm size and land productivity and a positive relationship between farm size and labor productivity.[14] Small farms invest twice as much per hectare in soil conservation compared to large farms. Byiringiro and Reardon show that erosion severely reduces farm yields in Rwanda.

Several reports published by a research team from Michigan State University find a clear and dramatic decline in yields of all major crops between 1984 and 1991. As a result of this decline and of population growth, per capita food production dropped by 25 %. Half of the farmers in the DSA datas set (used in Table 3.7) report declining productivity. The fact that 1984 was considered to be a modest drought year suggests that the observed decline in production between 1984 and 1989–1991 was real.[15] The report also states that the decline for tubers, the main providers of calories for the poor, is particularly strong. Half of Rwanda's farmland suffers from moderate to severe erosion.

---

[13] Place, F and Hazell, P, Productivity effects of Indigenous Land Tenure Systems in Sub-Saharan Africa, *American Journal of Agricultural Economics*, February 1993, pp. 14–15.

[14] Byiringiro, F. and Reardon, T., Farm Productivity in Rwanda: the effects of farm size, erosion, and soil conservation investments, *Agricultural Economics* 15, 1996, pp. 132–135.

[15] Clay, D. et al., Promoting Food Security in Rwanda, ibidem, Michigan State University, Chap. 3, p. 34.

These dismal statistics on land productivity were well-known by the top MRND political leaders, as the report mentioned in Chap. 1 on the position of the government shows. On page 112 of the report, Table 3.8 documents the decline for all but one crop. The driving force behind declining land productivity, soil erosion and declining per capita income is population growth. Peasants are forced to cultivate marginal unfertile lands, often on steep hill sides. Production increased at the rate of population growth as long as new land was taken into cultivation. Willame (1995, p. 135) writes that *productivity* however, never increased. Boserup (1965) has argued that agricultural innovation is spurred by decreasing productivity. She argues that as land becomes scarcer, peasants will adopt shorter fallow periods, apply more fertilizer and work the land more intensively. This process would allow the peasantry to avoid the Malthusian trap.

From a survey of 14 case studies, Wiggins (1995) concludes that the Boseru-pean model of population-induced agricultural intensification is a correct representation of evolving realities in the African countryside.[16] He argues that farmers have seized opportunities to grow new crops since marketing becomes more attractive as a result of better roads. Platteau (2000) however, considers this picture too optimistic and points to several constraining factors, especially at the technological level.[17] He argues that intensification has proceeded at a very slow pace relative to population growth, in spite of improved access to markets. Interestingly, Platteau considers Rwanda a perfect illustration of this distressing possibility:

> Population growth has reached extremely high levels without giving rise to major technical progress susceptible of providing a decent livelihood to the growing number of people living on the land.

Regional differences are substantial: the Northwest (Gisenyi prefecture) agro-ecological zone produces twice as much output per unit of land as the Southwest (Gikongoro and Cyangugu prefectures). In terms of gross household income, the southern prefectures of Butare and Gikongoro and the western prefectures of Kibuye and Cyangugu are poorer than the northern, central and eastern prefectures. This has not only to do with farm size, which indeed varies a lot over the regions. But differences in household income are also explained by soil fertility and productivity, suitability of the soil for high yielding crops (such as sweet potatoes in the north), access to public infrastructure (such as roads and markets), availability of off-farm jobs, and coffee and tea prices for regions growing these crops. We come back to regional differences in the last section of this chapter (poverty and inequality) and in Chap. 5, where we discuss the food crisis that struck southern Rwanda in 1989.

---

[16] Wiggins, S.Changes in African Farming Systems between the mid-1970s and the mid-1980s, *Journal of International Development*, vol. 7, no 6, 1995, pp. 807–848.

[17] Platteau, J.Ph., Institutions, Social Norms and Economic Development, Harwood, 2000, Chap. 2, p. 26.

Table 3.9 Overview of regional income differences in 1990

Prefecture	Average land size per household	Average gross y per hh	Monetary[a] as % of gross income	Altitude (m)	Rain (mm)	Distance to paved road (km)
Ruhengeri	0.79	73,500	37	2,115	1,124	11
Butare	0.81	42,000	36	1,660	1,120	14
Buymba	1.01	64,000	40	1,888	919	17
Cyangugu	0.66	37,000	38	1,917	1,567	30
Gikongoro	0.89	33,000	37	1,917	1,556	28
Gisenyi	0.45	51,000	44	1,946	1,313	9
Gitarama	0.92	51,000	36	1,630	1,070	15
Kibungo	1.35	109,000	37	1,469	733	18
Kibuye	1.16	33,000	31	2,100	1,275	66
Kigali	0.95	75,000	36	1,581	822	31
Rwanda	0.89	58,000	38	1,802	1,126	22

[a] Monetary income is the sum of income from crop sales, beer sales, off-farm income and the sale of livestock. *Source* Author's calculations frm DSA data, figures are population weighted

In Table 3.9 we present data on all Rwandan prefectures to stress the existence of large discrepancies. Even in a poor economy such as Rwanda, substantial inequalities between regions exist. In Fig. 3.2 data by prefecture are presented. These data include average gross household income, % income earned from off-farm activities, population density and the percentage of Tutsi living in each prefecture.

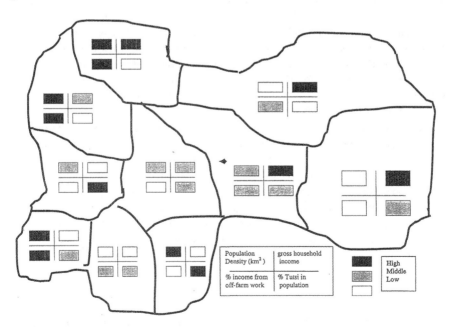

Fig. 3.2 Map of Rwanda in Key figures (1990-1991) per prefecture

We already discussed that the southern prefectures Gikongoro, Butare, Kibuye and Cyangugu were income-poor compared to the Rwandan average before the genocide. Ruhengeri and especially Kibungo were income-rich. The northern prefectures have the highest percentage of monetary income while the southern prefectures have the lowest. Households in Kibuye prefecture have the highest percentage of income from subsistence production. Population density is highest in Ruhengeri, Gisenyi and Butare and lowest in Kibungo. This does not necessarily mean that households in Ruhengeri, Gisenyi and Butare have the smallest land holdings—on average—compared to household in other prefectures, as land could have been allocated for other purposes. In an agricultural economy however, plantations are the only kind of alternative to farming one could think of. Plantations (rural estates) for the cultivation of tea are important in Cyangugu, with the result that households have small land holdings but a relatively high percentage of income earned in off-farm work (working on the tea plantation). In the other prefectures, population density and average land holding correspond very well. After the capital Kigali, the prefectures of Butare and Kibuye have the highest percentage of Tutsi, followed by Gitarama, Gikongoro and rural Kigali prefectures.

3.4 Taxation and Public Goods

Kalinjabo (1984) describes and criticises the dependence of Rwandan tax revenue on international trade. Indeed, throughout the Habyarimana regime, revenue from export and import has provided the bulk of tax revenue.[18] Progressive income taxes, as they are applied in western countries, did not exist in Rwanda. The main feature of the Rwandan tax structure then is its uniformity, its linearity. Most taxes were lump-sum amounts for all Rwandans, rich or poor: 400 RWF per adult, 250 RWF per cow, one half day of communal labour, a fixed producer price for coffee, 100 RWF school fee, to give some examples.

The tax structure was not a real fiscal system, but rather a set of particular taxes, most of them indirect (see Table 3.10). Kalinjabo explains the prevalence of indirect taxes referring to administrative, technical as well as political reasons. Technically, every individual is a consumer and cannot escape consumption taxes (pp. 85–86). This advantage, he argues, is only important when a good proportion of the economy is monetised. This is the case for example for beer consumption and beer trade. However, since a major part of the Rwandan economy is subsistence oriented, indirect taxation has its limits. Administratively, it is easier to tax trade compared to income, especially when the tax administration is not well

---

[18] Kalinjabo, C., (in French) *The role and structure of taxes in Rwanda*, National University of Rwanda, Butare, 1984.

Table 3.10 Different taxes in Rwanda 1973–1994[a]

Direct taxes
- Umuganda is a labour tax, one half day per adult per week
- Head tax is a personal tax, independent of one's income
- Cattle tax is an amount per cow owned
- Health tax is a contribution to the health system
- School fees are a contribution to the education system
- MRND-tax is the membership fee of the unique party

Indirect taxes
- Producer price of coffee different from the international price (this turned into a subsidy after 1987)
- Overvalued exchange rate
- Beer tax on beer consumption
- Water tax for the use of water
- Diverse administrative taxes, contributions and fees for licences

[a] An interesting but brief description of these different taxes can be found in Guichaoua, A., *Destin Paysans et Politiques Agraires en Afrique Centrale*, Tome 1, L' Harmatttan, 1989, pp. 181–183

developed. The main reasons for the importance of indirect taxes as compared to income taxes are political, Kalinjabo argues (1984, 87–88): income taxes hurt wealthy people much more then the poor. Proposals to increase income taxes would be killed immediately by a powerful lobby. Kalinjabo argues that this is not the case with indirect taxes which hurt the poor more than the wealthy. The discontent of the masses will not rise immediately, as everybody will adjust his consumption to soften the effect of the tax. It is only when the tax burden becomes untenable that protest will occur. But,

> in order for the dissatisfaction to be canalised, one needs political action, which is difficult to imagine in a country that is profoundly marked by a political monolith. (Kalinjabo 1984, 88)[19]

It is not easy and maybe even impossible to calculate exactly the overall tax burden on the Rwandan peasantry. But we can start by tracing the burden of taxation over the course of Habyarimana's reign and see how far we can get. When he came to power, he introduced Umuganda, which is tax on labour. He also made the MRND the unique party which had to be supported by a membership fee. Coffee trees had to be maintained carefully and mistreatment was punished by penal law. In the mid-70s, the regime made huge profits from the difference between the producer price for coffee and the international price. Towards the end of the 80s, the regime experienced a lot of difficulties to levy these three taxes (umuganda, MRND fee, coffee) as peasants started to protest against their

---

[19] Original in French: «*pour que le mécontentement soit canalisé, il faut une action politique qui est difficilement concevable dans un pays profondément marqué par le monolithisme politique*».

legitimacy (for umuganda and MRND fee) and as the international price of coffee collapsed. Thus, as far as these three taxes are concerned, the tax burden was higher in the 70s compared to the late 80s. The civil war changes this situation again, but we will come back on this later. Other taxes that were not levied in the 70s added to the overall tax rate in the late 80s. Among these are the health, school and water taxes (Guichaoua 1989). These taxes were very unpopular since the peasantry was already paying several other taxes (umuganda, MRND fee and coffee, cattle and head tax). The introduction of health, school and water taxes however, made the overall tax burden in the 1988–1990 period probably not much different from the tax burden in the 70s. What the regime gives with one hand towards the end of the 80s (coffee subsidies, no MRND contribution or umuganda anymore) it takes with the other hand. If one adds all these taxes, the conclusion of almost constant or slightly increasing tax rates is close to reality.

In his seminal account of the Southeast Asian peasantry, James Scott (1976) argued that a linear tax system is exploitative, because it does not take the variation of peasant income over several years into account.[20] A tax of (example given) 30 % of annual peasant income in a very good year is most likely less exploitative compared to a tax of 15 % in a very bad year. The latter, smaller tax will put survival in danger while the 30 % tax in a very good year will not. Peasants look at the effect of taxes in absolute terms: what will I have after I paid the taxes? In particular, will I be able to remain above the subsistence level? A tax of 10,000 francs which is levied every year independent of (the variation in) peasant income is potentially much more exploitative than a tax which accounts for variation.

In Rwanda, the overall tax burden depends, among other things, on the international coffee price which we will be dealing with in the Chap. 4. If that price is high, peasant producers are heavily taxed under a regime of fixed producer prices. If the price is low, they receive subsidies. Box 3.1 presents an example of the tax burden.

I do not believe that Habyarimana exploited the Rwandan peasantry. The tax burden was considerable, but, as Kalinjabo (1984, 47) argues, the absence of an income tax on agricultural revenue discredits the belief that peasants were exploited. From Table 3.7, it is clear that revenue from agriculture was responsible for 58 % (subsistence only) to 67 % (subsistence + sales) of the income of the average peasant household. Kalinjabo argues that the tax burden on peasants was considerable, not because of the level of an individual tax, but because of the bad distribution of all kinds of taxes. In effect,

---

[20] Scott, J., (1976), The moral economy of the peasant, Yale University Press, New Haven, pp. 29–34.

the rural taxes did not take the real and potential income of the individual tax payer into account. Taxes rather applied in the same way for all citizens, rich and poor alike. (Kalinjabo 47)[21]

Box 3.1: The tax burden for the average farm household in 1985
Household with 2 adults and 4 children; annual gross income is 60,000 RWF; harvested 50 kg of coffee for which it received 6,000 RWF
Implicit coffee tax
Goverment received 200 % of the producer price of coffee on the international market. Subtracting transport, transaction and processing costs, the implicit tax is estimated at 50 % of the sales, or 3,000 RWF
Labour tax paid in kind (umuganda)
2 adults at 70 RWF every week equals 7,280 RWF
Sum of all other taxes
Estimated to be between 2,000 and 5,000 RWF
Total taxes paid 12,000 to 15,000 RWF
When full or pre-tax income is approx. 70,000 RWF (60,000 + 3,000 + 7,000), the tax burden is situated between 17 and 21 %

When, in subsequent years the international price of coffee decreased to 100 % of the producer price, the tax burden dropped to approx. 15 %.

As box 3.1 shows, the labour tax paid in kind through *umuganda* is responsible for the bulk of taxes paid by the average Rwandan farmer. Large coffee farmers paid an implicit tax on coffee in excess of their tax paid through umuganda, but almost all coffee farmers are smallholders. Moreover, from 1987 onwards the coffee farmer continued to receive a fairly high price for the coffee despite the collapse of the international price. From then onwards the Rwandan government subsidized the coffee economy.

My understanding of the absence of income tax is somewhat different from Kalinjabo's. He writes that there was none because a coalition of the wealthy would have stopped it. This may be the case, but since income in the rural areas is mostly income from agricultural produce, a tax on agricultural produce would be unpopular with farmers and impractical to levy. As for indirect taxes, it is correct to argue, as Kalinjabo does, that these hurt the poor more than the rich, but one has to add that this is only the case when both groups have the same consumption pattern. It is likely that farmers will avoid the consumption of taxed goods such as bottled beer that are mostly consumed by the wealthy in the capital Kigali. Thus, the least one can say is that the tax structure did not hurt the wealthy, but it did not hurt farmers either.

---

[21] Original in French: *les impots rureaux ne tiennent pas compte du revenue réel ou potentiel de chaque contribuable pris isolément. Ils l'atteignent plutôt à travers des contributions personnelles et réelles grossières qui frappent de la même façon tous les assujettis, riches et pauvres confondus.*

Thus, one should not only look at the division between direct and indirect taxes, but also ask who is paying what kind of taxes. It seems clear that the Habyarimana regime did not levy taxes on agricultural produce, installs a labour tax in kind, has a series of linear or direct taxes and a series of indirect taxes. Taxation under the Second Republic was a mixed system: a variety of lump sum taxes were levied, such as contributions to the MRND, school fees and the difference between the producer and the international price of coffee. These kinds of taxes were resented by peasants in difficult years, but they did not constitute the bulk of the tax burden.[22] This mixed system cannot be regarded as exploitative as described by James Scott. The salient feature of the tax system under Habyarimana seems to be the absence of tax on agricultural produce, the tax on labour and the coffee tax. These three taxes demonstrate the importance of the peasant economy, and in particular peasant labour. The president wanted to combine two partly incompatible objectives: earn income for the state while maintaining peasant support for himself and his regime. Hence the heavy ideological machinery that was used to legitimate the implementation of Umuganda, as described in the second chapter. Left to themselves to decide, peasants may want to cooperate in collective projects, but only in those projects that yielded a tangible benefit for themselves, their families and there communities.

As the main purpose of taxation is to get revenue for the state, no tax system is entirely friendly to its citizens. The tax system under Habyarimana's regime seems to combine the need for revenue with a lot of attention to the characteristics of the peasant economy and the peasant household as well as being compatible with the regime's peasant ideology.

There is no reason to believe that the tax structure discriminated between the north and the south of Rwanda, or between Hutu and Tutsi. The situation is different when we consider *public goods*. A World Bank 1987 report states that 90 % of all public investment occurred in four prefectures, Kigali, Gisenyi, Ruhengeri and Cyangugu.[23] These are also the provinces with small percentages of Tutsi. This pattern is also observed by Reyntjens (1994, 222) who writes that one third of the 85 most important government positions, as well as almost all important functions in the army and the security apparatus, were held by people from Gisenyi, the presidents' native province. On the basis of household surveys in 1982–1983 Muller (1999) finds that members of households with a Tutsi head have worse nutrition outcomes.[24] Tutsi households, Muller writes, have been generally excluded from political decision circles and may have had worse access to public health and nutrition centres that are spread in the countryside.

---

[22] See also Chap. 5 on crop failure in southern Rwanda in 1989. A local NGO pleaded to free peasants from paying taxes in that year.

[23] World Bank, 1987, *The role of the communes in the development of Rwanda.* p. 12.

[24] Muller, C., The impact of the production composition on the nutrition status of agricultural households in Rwanda, *Applied Economics Letters*, 1999, vol. 6, pp. 125–131.

Table 3.11 Household Income (in ae), poverty and extreme poverty in rural Rwanda in 1990[a]

	Income	Income poverty		Income extreme poverty	
		Head count	Poverty gap	Head count	Poverty gap
All Rural	12,597	69.7	32.0	52.4	19.6
Province					
Butare	9,624	80.5	39.0	65.2	25.0
Buymba	12,949	64.3	29.3	49.7	17.0
Cyangugu	9,217	88.2	46.1	77.1	30.5
Gikongoro	7,804	85.5	50.2	73.9	38.4
Gisenyi	12,937	67.9	29.5	50.0	16.4
Gitarama	11,954	66.2	28.6	47.0	17.2
Kibungo	22,495	35.4	9.1	15.1	2.8
Kibuye	8,857	93.4	46.4	74.8	29.7
RuralKigali	15,151	55.8	21.5	34.4	10.9
Ruhengeri	14,160	69.8	29.7	50.6	16.7
Gender					
Male	12,746	69.0	30.8	50.9	18.3
Female	10,943	73.2	42.4	58.7	24.7
Education					
None	10,516	75.0	36.6	59.2	23.7
Primary	13,320	66.3	27.8	46.6	14.7
>Primary	41,940	17.1	4.8	8.0	0.5
Occupat.					
Farming	11,645	71.5	32.5	53.3	19.7
Agr labour	8,108	90.1	50.2	80.8	35.5
N-agr Lab	22,818	34.1	15.9	23.9	9.7
Business	14,551	55.3	19.7	39.9	11.0
Adm, prof	47,558	0.0	0.0	0.0	0.0

Source DSA 1990, author's calculations

[a] The Food Poverty Line was set at 9,400 RWF per adult equivalent per year, corresponding to the cost of 2,100 kcal. The Poverty Line is constructed by adding a 29.4 % non-food share to arrive at 13,300 RWF

3.5 Poverty and Inequality

In Sect. 3.3, we already discussed average household and regional differences of income. In this section, we want to expand that description by presenting a poverty profile for rural Rwanda. Household income per adult equivalent is used as a measure of welfare. Almost 70 % of Rwandan rural households are poor by this measure. This means they lack the income to buy a standard basket of consumption goods (food and non-food) to attain a standard of living above the poverty line. If we look at food poverty, the percentage declines to just over 50 % of the rural population. Table 3.11 also shows large regional discrepancies, with head count poverty as low as 35 % in the eastern prefecture of Kibungo and as high as 93 % in the western prefecture of Kibuye. The southern and south-western

Table 3.12 Household income and land inequality in rural Rwanda, 1990[a]

	Income		Land	
	Gini	Theil	Gini	Theil
All Rural	0.42	0.32	0.43	0.32
Province				
Butare	0.36	0.22	0.36	0.22
Buymba	0.39	0.26	0.34	0.20
Cyangugu	0.41	0.46	0.43	0.33
Gikongoro	0.43	0.31	0.42	0.32
Gisenyi	0.39	0.26	0.44	0.34
Gitarama	0.34	0.19	0.43	0.32
Kibungo	0.35	0.20	0.40	0.26
Kibuye	0.40	0.49	0.45	0.36
RuralKigali	0.38	0.28	0.44	0.38
Ruhengeri	0.44	0.40	0.43	0.35
Gender				
Male	0.40	0.30	0.42	0.32
Female	0.40	0.28	0.43	0.31
Education				
None	0.38	0.25	0.42	0.29
Primary	0.39	0.27	0.43	0.33
>Primary	0.44	0.32	0.54	0.54
Occupat.				
Farming	0.38	0.26	0.41	0.29
Agr labour	0.41	0.33	0.43	0.31
N-agr Lab	0.42	0.31	0.44	0.35
Business	0.29	0.14	0.67	0.93
Adm, prof	0.37	0.23	0.62	0.74

[a] *Source* DSA 1990, figures are population weighted

prefectures Butare, Gikongoro, Cyangugu and Kibuye are much poorer then the northern and eastern prefectures. The richest prefecture are three times richer then the poorest one.

Households with female heads, with uneducated heads and with heads earning a living as agricultural workers, are poorer compared to households headed by a man, an educated head and a head with a non-agricultural occupation. The poverty gap—the mean distance to the poverty line expressed as a fraction of that line— follows a similar pattern as the poverty head count.

Using the same data, inequality can be described. Table 3.12 presents land and income inequality in rural Rwanda in 1990. As we have no data on urban areas, a comparison between urban and rural Rwanda is not possible. Table 3.12 then only gives the degree of inequality within the prefectures, genders, levels of education and occupation. Two commonly applied measures of inequality are used, the Gini coefficient and the Theil index to measure inequality in household income per adult equivalent and in the size of cultivated land per adult equivalent. Overall income and land inequality in rural Rwanda has a Gini coefficient of 0.42 and

Table 3.13 Ethnic distribution of rural incomes

Ethnic group	No. of households surveyed		Average household income	
	1955	1990	1955 (in BF)	1990 (in RWF per ae)
Tutsi	287	27	4,439	9,893
Hutu	914	304	4,249	9,969
Twa	2	5	1,446	2,664

Theil index of 0.32. This is high, but not different from observations in other African countries. Again, we observe a lot of variation across prefectures, with relatively low levels of income inequality in Gitarama and Kibungo and high levels of income inequality in Ruhengeri, Kibuye and Cyangugu. Inequality is also more outspoken among the educated and non-farmers, especially in terms of land.

3.5.1 Ethnic Income Disparities

Austin (1996), who wrote an overview of the published sources dealing with the distribution of wealth in Rwanda, states that there seems to be no difference in wealth between the two ethnic groups.[25] Objectively, Austin writes, there is no justification for construing the Tutsi as much (if at all) richer than the Hutu. He argues that there is a data problem on the ethnic distribution of income, but reminds us of a rural household survey held under Belgian rule in 1955 which found that the average income of Tutsi households was 4.47 % higher than that of Hutu households. Thus, Austin concludes, the Tutsi in the rural areas shared only slightly in the economic rewards enjoyed by the Tutsi political elite. Although more then 90 % of the population remained in agriculture in the subsequent decades, occupational shifts occurred both inside and outside agriculture. The implications for the ethnic income distribution are difficult to assess. Household surveys during the Hutu Republics rarely published results including ethnic variables. Some of the rare results are presented in Table 3.13.

In 1986, a former minister of agriculture in the Second Republic, Anastase Ntezilyayo, hinted that the number of cattle was decreasing and the area under crops was steadily increasing. This, he said, was partly the result of the political weakness of the pastoralists. The 1959 Revolution had deprived the Tutsi from their formerly dominant position in the control of land in general and pasture land in particular. According to Waller (1993) this does not necessarily mean that per capita income of rural Tutsi households declined as part of the fall in herds is accounted for by refugees taking their cattle with them and Tutsi switching to

---

[25] Austin, G., The effects of government policy on the ethnic distribution of income and wealth in Rwanda: a review of published sources, Department of Economic History, London School of Economics, 1996.

arable farming. But, as Austin argues, is seems highly unlikely that the income of rural Tutsi rose relative to that of Hutu between 1959 and 1994. Two surveys, one from 1983 and one from 1990 seem to confirm this result. In the 1983 Rwandan National Consumption-Budget Survey, the average income of the surveyed Tutsi households is lower than the average Hutu income.[26] Muller indicates that the average income of Tutsi households was lower compared to Hutu households. From my own fieldwork [published in the Journal of Development Economics (2005) and the Journal of Conflict Resolution (2003)], it is shown that the average income of the Hutu households in the sample (1990) is almost equal to that of the Tutsi households (see Table 3.13). Thus, as rural income is concerned, there is no difference between Hutu and Tutsi.

The picture for the public sector is different from the rural economy. Whereas rural incomes are practically the same, jobs in the public sector were mostly reserved for Hutu. Azam (1999) argues that public goods are not a perfect substitute for public sector wages.[27] He says that a dictator uses both public sector wages and public goods as a means to buy loyalty from an ethnic group. Wages, according to Azam, allow better targeting compared to the anonymous provision of a public good. According to Marysse (1982), the disparity of wages in the (urban) private sector was much more pronounced then in the public sector.[28] He adds that jobs in the military are better paid then in the administration—for equal years of schooling—demonstrating the weight of the military in the Second Republic.[29] Concerning the distribution of income over the two ethnic groups, Table 3.14 makes clear that the average public sector employee earned more than the average private sector employee.

Since Tutsi were well-represented in the private sector (Prunier 1995), where they, of course, still remained a minority, it is fair to say that the *average* Hutu with a formal job in Kigali earned more then the *average* Tutsi. Since incomes among private sector jobs were less equal compared to public sector jobs, it is also likely that in the modern economy inequality among Tutsi was larger than among Hutu. The difference however is less important when one takes wages in the army into account. As Storey (1999) argues, public sector employees realise that their job depends on the political power holders.[30] It is exactly therefore that public goods and their provision are not just 'economic' decisions but political economy decisions. According to Marysse (1982) the Rwandan government limited the

---

[26] Muller, C., Transient seasonal and chronic poverty of the peasants: Evidence from Rwanda, CSAE, Oxford University, 1997, p. 28.

[27] Azam, J.-P., The Redistributive State and Conflicts in Africa, keynote address at the annual Conference of the Norwegian Association for Development Research, Oslo, September 1999.

[28] Marysse S., Basic Needs, Income Distribution and the Political Economy of Rwanda, UFSIA, paper 55, 1982.

[29] Presidentiel decrees 3/1/1977 and 28/10/1980. Marysse also adds that the wage increase between 1976 and 1980 for all scales in the army was slightly better than in the administration.

[30] Storey, A., Economics and Ethnic Conflict, *Development Policy Review*, vol. 17, 1999.

Table 3.14 Private and public wage disparities in Rwanda, in RWF

Job	Private		Public	
	1976	1980	1976	1980
Uneducated worker	19,980	28,000	23,500	46,500
Senior manager or highest scale in administration	613,000	840,000	427,000	512,000
Highest scale in the army			651,000	787,000
Average incomes[a]	37,210	56,610	77,860	82,900
Average incomes[b]	52,770	78,580	132,470	151,980

[a] Excluding expatriate wages
[b] Including expatriate wages
Source S. Marysse 1982

disparities in public sector wages deliberately. Using 1976 figures, Marysse finds a Gini-coefficient of 0.38, which ranks Rwanda among countries with low inequality. As we have demonstrated using DSA survey data, by 1990, income inequality had risen substantially with a Gini-coefficient of 0.42 in the rural areas alone.

Chapter 4
The Political Economy of Coffee and Dictatorship

I cannot cultivate the land the whole year while watching merchants drive Mercedes.
Rwandan peasant in 1990 (In *Agriculture African*, no 3, April 1990, authors' translation from French).

4.1 Introduction

In colonial times, Rwanda was already a densely populated country, land was scarce, technology was at a very low level, and human capital was underdeveloped. Labor was the only factor endowment that was abundant and thus cheap. The Belgian colonizer found a way to extract wealth from a labor-abundant economy. He promoted coffee and forced the population to pay taxes[1]. The Belgian elite and later the Rwandan elite realized that this was the only way to introduce the monetary economy in the rural areas. The colonizer had to invest little and bear almost no costs. Habyarimana copied the colonial system and encouraged peasants to grow coffee on their plots. Coffee cultivation was heavily subsidized, so that new plants could be obtained almost free of cost. Some fertilizer was also distributed on the condition it would be used for the coffee trees only. A large administration for coffee monitoring was put in place. Monitors were assigned both advisory and policing tasks (Little and Horowitz 1987), which we will return to in Chap. 10. They advised farmers on coffee cultivation practices and at the same time fined farmers who did not keep up their coffee fields. Uprooting coffee trees was forbidden under the Rwandan penal code (June 1978) and fines were levied.[2]

During the Habyarimana regime (1973–1994) coffee exports accounted for 60–80% of state revenue, depending on annual output and market prices. Tea cultivation on large plantations became increasingly important as the price of coffee declined in the late 1980s. Farmers were driven off the land with little compensation in order to start state-run tea plantations in Gisovu and Mulindi (Bart 1993; Uvin 1998). Leading members of the Akazu (the presidential clan) or personal associates other than family members of the president were always in charge of the coffee and tea agencies (Ocir-café and Ocir-thé). As long as the

---

[1] Uwezeyimana (1996), pp. 51–55.
[2] The Kenyan coffee sector, by way of comparison, was run differently. Kenyan coffee producers were free to chose to cultivate coffee or not and were not subject to government imposed producer prices (Bevan et al. 1989).

international price of these two export crops was high, the Habyarimana regime could afford to pay high producer prices to farmers. The collapse of these prices in 1987 and 1989 caused the regime to lower producer prices and to cut social services by 40 % (Guichaoua 1992). This double loss hit the farmers hard since they were already paying water taxes, health taxes, school fees, and were performing compulsory labor.

In this chapter, I use a political economy approach to dictatorship in order to explain the coffee economy. An economy, such as the Rwandan, that entirely depends on the coffee export, faces severe difficulties when the world market price for coffee collapses. The dictator himself may rely on foreign aid to stay in power, but how can he guarantee the loyalty of coffee-growing farmers? The chapter considers the political salience of the coffee economy from the dictator's perspective. Using the Loyalty-Repression model, set out by Wintrobe (1998), I show how Habyarimana, on the verge of losing power in a single export crop economy, switched to repression and other coercive practices to sustain his power. This stylized model is used to explain features of his regime as well as the genocide.

4.2   A Political Economy Approach

In a recent review essay, Newbury and David Newbury (2000) suggest studying and analysing the connection between state activity and peasant agency in the rural areas, when one wants to understand the history of Rwanda and of the genocide. Relying on research by Leurquin (1960) and Dorsey (1983), they write that the policies of forced crop cultivation (especially coffee) placed the colonial state directly in the production process.[3] It was the colonial state that encouraged and further developed the penetration of state authority in rural areas. The theory of political economy is ideally suited to analyse just this: how do the power of the state and the chosen path of economic development interact? And what exactly is the economic underpinning of the relationship between state and peasantry?

The advantages of a political economy approach are numerous.[4] It allows looking through the dictator's eyes and explaining the decisions the dictator is making. To do that, we have to assume that dictatorial behaviour is rational. Rationality in economics is different from rationality in everyday's parlance. It does not mean thoughtful, smart or nice thinking. Rationality means that the dictator will use resources as well as possible to reach his goal(s). The dictator's first priority is to stay in power.[5] Throughout his reign, in particular by sidelining potential adversaries, Habyarimana has shown that he is very apt at staying in power (Guichaoua 2010, 47–53 and 152–160). Non-economists often define

---

[3] Newbury and Newbury (2000), p. 868

[4] I refer Chap. 1 for the foundation of this approach

[5] Tullock (1987), Autocracy

rationality differently from economists. Horowitz (1976) for example states that rational behavior is a behavior that benefits a country's economy. Political economists believe that people in general, including politicians and especially dictators, care about their own interests first: being re-elected or seeing their power increase. The dictator judges economic policies by the impact they have on his position and not on the welfare of the population. This does not necessarily mean that policies chosen are bad for the population; they can be beneficial as long as the dictator benefits from them. This also means that it can be rational for the dictator to implement policies that do not benefit the population. I refer to the Chap. 1 for a discussion of predatory and developmental behavior of dictators.

Most genocide scholars agree that genocide can be explained by the explicit choices that the regime's elite makes (Kiernan for Cambodia, Hillberg for Nazi-Germany, Vakan'N Dadrian for the Ottoman empire, to name just a few). Genocide scholars argue about the motivations of the regime to implement genocide, about the structure of decision-making among top leaders, about the degree of participation of the population in the killings, and so on, but there is a strong consensus among the scholarly community that genocide requires systematic organization and execution by the top leaders in the regime.

For Rwanda, it has been argued that the group of people in charge of the organization of the country and later the genocide was very small. Des Forges (1999) suggests that only a handful of people organized the genocide.[6] These people, a small group of persons known as the "zero-network", were at the center of power in Rwanda and were responsible for the small-scale mass murders from 1990 onwards (see Chap. 6). This makes it possible to use the unitary actor assumption: in order to use a political economy model of dictatorship I take this zero-network to have acted as a rational unitary agent. If one uses this approach, one can see that political violence and repression, as used by the regime, with special brutality from 1990 to 1994, serves someone's interests. The reason for which the regime uses violence and repression is that it serves the purposes of the regime: to stay in power/increase power. This does not mean that I ignore intra-elite battles for power. We come back to this in Chap. 6. Here it suffices to see that the coffee economy is essential for state revenue as well as peasant loyalty and what we want to do is to model the behaviour of the person/regime who sits at the helmet of this economy.

4.3 The Wintrobe Model of Dictatorship

The Canadian political economist Wintrobe (1998, 46) developed a political economy model of dictatorship,[7] in which repression and loyalty form the input factors in a production function for power. This function is assumed to be well-behaved: the use

---

[6] Personal communication with the author, March 4, 1999.

[7] Wintrobe (1998).

Fig. 4.1 Equilibrium under a
tinpot dictator

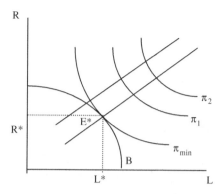

of either instrument alone leads to diminishing returns in the production of power and
there is some complementarity between repression (R) and loyalty (L) in the production of political power.

Not all dictators maximize their power over the population. Some only want
enough power to stay in office and enjoy its benefits. This kind of dictator is called
tinpot. The tinpot wants to have just enough power to stay in office and spend all
resources on personal consumption. His objective function is to minimise the
resource cost of staying in office. This dictator seeks no more power over the
population than that represented by the lowest isopower line in Fig. 4.1.

Wintrobe considers loyalty an asset in the hands of the population, accumulated
to facilitate political exchanges. Citizens and interest groups supply loyalty to the
regime because they expect to receive in return some portion of the gains from
political exchange. Each citizen can be viewed as accumulating an optimum
portfolio of these assets, taking into account the expected rates of return and the
risk. A change in either will lead the investor to change his portfolio and this
change may be broken down into a substitution and an income effect. Citizens who
demonstrate or speak out against the government are essentially offering their
loyalty to someone who offers an alternative policy.

The dictator not only relies on the loyalty of the population, but also uses a
certain amount of repression to stay in power. The supply of loyalty and the level
of repression are related: if repression increases, the risk of dealing with the
opposition increases and the expected rate of return of opposition activities
decreases (see Fig. 4.2). This means that the relative attractiveness of dealing with
the dictator or the autocratic regime increases. The substitution effect implies that
the supply of loyalty to the dictator is positively related to the level of repression.
However, an increase in repression increases the likelihood that the individual will
be the victim pf sanctions, even if he is loyal. This fact reduces his wealth and, as
long as investments in political loyalty are good, reduces all investment in political
loyalty, including to the regime. At low levels of repression, the income effect will
be small for most individuals and, as a consequence, the substitution effect will
dominate the income effect. This effect is important in understanding dictatorial

Fig. 4.2 Equilibrium
repression and loyalty under a
totalitarian dictatorship

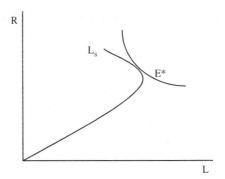

behavior, because it means that a dictator can obtain more loyalty by increasing the level of repression.

The supply of loyalty depends not only on the level of repression, but also on the demand for loyalty by the dictator. Loyal citizens expect a return on their loyalty. Wintrobe describes this as a "price" suppliers receive for each unit of loyalty supplied If the supply of loyalty to the regime is abundant, the "price" each loyal citizen receives is low, making the production of power cheap for the dictator. The regime will try to keep loyalty cheap because it wants to use its resources for other purposes. Many events, exogenous as well as endogenous, however, can increase the price of loyalty. The appearance on the political scene of a political challenger for example, may not only require a higher level of repression, but may also increase the price of loyalty. We assume the supply of loyalty to be positively related to its price.[8]

The third factor that determines the supply of loyalty is the performance of the economy If the rents from political exchange are high, the average citizen will be more inclined to cooperate with the regime. Moreover, a dictator who is able to distribute the rents of a well-performing economy, can buy off even the worst opposition. The opposite is also true. If economic performance declines, the rents from political exchange decline and it is less profitable to be loyal to the regime. Ceteris paribus, the supply of loyalty therefore decreases.

The model can be completed by formally introducing the resource costs to the dictator of repression and loyalty. The costs per unit of repression are the costs of obtaining manpower and capital equipment for the police, prisons, and the court system. It seems reasonable to assume that these per unit costs are not under the tinpot's control, although some dictators may be able to "produce" repression more efficiently than others. We will therefore assume they are fixed (Wintrobe 1998, 49)

---

[8] The price of loyalty received by suppliers of loyalty may differ from the price paid by the dictator for a unit of loyalty. The latter may include all the costs incurred by the dictator to create and maintain loyalty. In the remainder of the text however, we do not make a difference between these two prices, hence we can drop the subscript S (and D for that matter) from the loyalty function.

4.4 Habyarimana and the Coffee Economy

4.4.1 Modelling the Habyarimana Regime

We have seen that the supply of loyalty in Wintrobe's model is influenced by the performance of the economy. In applying the model to the Habyarimana regime, we will specify the link between the political behavior of the dictator and the loyalty of the citizens. We have to do this because Wintrobe's model is generic and needs specificity to describe Nazi-Germany, Stalinist Russia or Apartheid in South Africa. In this section, we undertake a similar exercise for Rwanda. In a coffee economy such as Rwanda, this means that the value of coffee on world markets determines the regime's budget. At the same time, the power of the regime is determined by the loyalty supplied by the population, which in turn depends on the producer price offered to the farmer. Specific for Rwanda is that the coffee price and the volume of coffee produced determine both the dictator's budget and the supply of loyalty of the population. In this section of the paper, I will focus on these characteristics of the Rwandan coffee economy, it is specified as:

$$B = p_m \left[K\left(p_p, R\right)\right] \quad \text{with} \quad \frac{\partial K}{\partial p_p} > 0; \frac{\partial K}{\partial R} > 0$$

where p_m is the world market price, p_p the price paid to the producer, K the volume of coffee sold and B is the regime's budget. Since Rwanda is a price-taker in the international coffee market, Habyarimana *did not* control his budget as much as Wintrobe's dictator. Nevertheless, he could manipulate the producer price of coffee p_p or/and could use non-price incentives to have farmers plant more coffee trees and thus raise the volume K produced, for example by applying penalties. In the model the quantity produced depends on the price paid to the producer and the level of repression R. The regime paid a fixed price to the farmer producer and farmers were forbidden to stop cultivating coffee. From the budget $B = p_m K$, the part $p_p K$ is reserved for the producers. The rest of the budget $p_d K$ (with $p_d = p_m - p_p$) pays for repression.[9]

Habyarimana can thus be portrayed as solving the following problem:

$$Max\, \pi\left(p_p, R\right)$$

$$\text{s.t.} \left(p_m - p_p\right) K\left(p_p, R\right) = p_R R$$

What follows is a mathematical solution to the dictator's problem, which we are not outlining in this book, because we want the text to be readable for

---

[9] In a more complex version of the model, the objective function of the dictator features both power and personal consumption. Although this is certainly more realistic, it is not necessary to study the main characteristics of the political economy of coffee and dictatorship in Rwanda.

non-economists.[10] Of interest for the topic of this chapter is especially the reaction of the dictator to changes in the international price of coffee p_m. The effect of changes of the international price on the price paid to the producers p_p and on the level of repression R can be found by differentiating the first order conditions of the maximisation problem (see the named publications for the derivations). It then follows that

$$\frac{\partial p_p}{\partial p_m} = -z_{11} \frac{\partial K}{\partial p_p} \lambda + \frac{\pi_{p_p R} A_2 - \pi_R^2 A_1}{|B|} K - z_{12} \frac{\partial K}{\partial R} \lambda$$

$$\frac{\partial R}{\partial p_m} = -z_{21} \frac{\partial K}{\partial p_p} \lambda - \frac{\left(\pi_{p_p}^2 A_2 - \pi_{R p_p} A_1 \right)}{|B|} K - z_{22} \frac{\partial K}{\partial R} \lambda$$

This means that an increase (decrease) in the international price of coffee will increase (decrease) the power of the dictator because the increase (decrease) has a positive (negative) effect on the price paid to producers and on the level of repression. The sign of each of the effects on the left hand side depends on the sign of the three effects on the right hand side, to wit the own substitution effect, the income effect and the cross-substitution effect. Since we assume that loyalty and repression are normal goods, a dictator will buy more of one or both goods when he gets richer. This allows us to define three types of dictators: a totalitarian dictator as a dictator who buys (less) more of each when he gets (poorer) richer; a benevolent dictator as a dictator who buys (less) more loyalty and (more) less repression when he gets (poorer) richer; a tyrannic dictator who buys (more) less loyalty and (less) more repression when he gets (poorer) richer.[11] For the correct mathematical description of these behavioral types, we again refer to Capéau and Verwimp (2012).

4.4.2 The Coffee Economy

Figure 4.3 shows the course of the international price (in US$ cents per kg) of other mild arabica coffee and the price that was paid to the Rwandan peasant producers. The end of the 1970s was marked by a coffee boom that generated big revenues for the government and allowed it to increase the price paid to producers from 45 Rwandan Francs (RWF) in 1974 to 65 RWF in 1976 and 120 RWF in 1977. According to Uwezeyimana (1996) it was in this period (1976–1980) that

---

[10] Interested readers are referred to Capéau and Verwimp (2012). A working paper version of the paper is available as Berlage et al. (2003), Dictatorship in a single export crop economy, Discussion Paper, Centre for Economic Studies, Leuven, November. A reduced-from version was previously published in 2001 in *the European Journal of Political Economy*.

[11] The benevolent dictator is similar to the 'developmental dictator' in Olson's or Robinson's term.

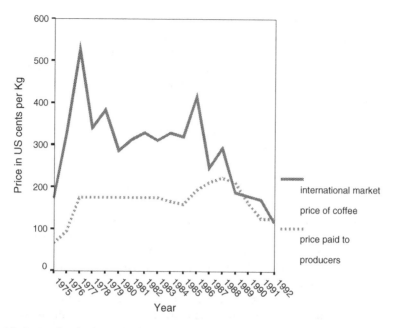

Fig. 4.3 International price and price paid to producers

the Habyarimana regime established itself among the peasant masses. When, towards the end of the 1980s, the international price declined, the regime subsidized producer prices. This is shown in Fig. 4.4 where the percentage of the international price in the hands of the state turns negative.

4.4.3 Political Power and the Coffee Economy

• The Boom of 1976–1979

The first period (1976–1979) coincided with high world market prices for coffee. The difference between the fixed producer price and the world market price was substantial and the dictator derived large amounts of budgetary resources from coffee exports. In 1975, the world market price for coffee increased significantly. Through its dictatorial power, materialized in the monopoly on coffee trade in Rwanda, the Habyarimana regime fixed the producer price for coffee and extracted large revenues from the coffee sector. p_m remained high for several years. In order to continue the highly lucrative coffee policy, the regime implemented two measures. The regime raised the producer price for coffee, giving farmers an incentive to produce more and at the same time it strengthened the monitoring capacity of coffee cultivation. Elements of the latter policy were, to make the neglect of coffee trees punishable by law and to provide every commune with a monitor to advise

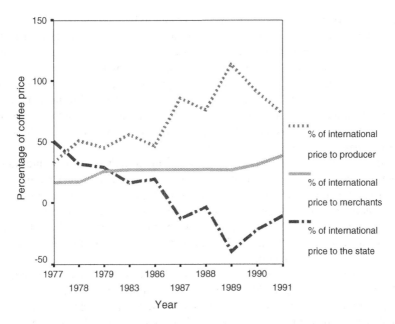

Fig. 4.4 Percentage of the international price paid to producers, to intermediaries and to the state

and control farmers on coffee cultivation. [12] It is not coincidence that these measures were taken in 1978. The very high world market coffee prices allowed the regime's elite to increase both its personal consumption and its power over the population. An increased producer price for coffee (from 60 to 120 RFW) increased the loyalty of the farmer population and at the same time increased coffee production and government coffee revenue.

The state as the monopsony buyer of coffee in Rwanda was not unique in Africa (see Bates 1981). Governments throughout Africa promoted the cultivation of export crops for taxation purposes: a government-run agency buys the coffee (or another cash crop) from the smallholders for a fixed price. The state agency then processes the coffee and sells it on the international market. The justification for this institution is to guarantee the farmer's income. The farmer is protected from shocks in the world market by a fixed price. The aim of the government however is not so much to protect the farmer but to transfer resources from the agricultural sector to the urban sector. The tax revenue from coffee exports is used to pay for the imports that benefit the urban elite. In the official rhetoric of the Habyarimana regime, the farmer was considered important.[13] This glorification of the farmer masked the fact that the farmer was only considered important as a producer. The farmer had to produce coffee for export. In order to secure the loyalty of the farmer

---

[12] Little and Horowitz (1987) and (1988)

[13] I refer to Chap. 2

producer, the price paid to the coffee producer had to be high enough. This means that the dictator is trading of loyalty from farmers against rents. If Habyarimana were a tinpot dictator, the optimal coffee price for the dictator is the price that maximizes the dictator's tax revenue under the constraint that he maintains a minimum level of power (using loyalty and repression). If he were a totalitarian dictator he would maximize his level of power and not care about personal consumption. In the course of this section, we will determine Habyarimana's type by looking at his policy decisions following a budgetary shock. His type does not have to be fixed but can evolve over time.

Profits made through the export of coffee during periods with favorable (high) international coffee prices were supposed to be put in a special fund. This fund was called 'fond d'égalisation' (price stabilization fund) to secure the price paid to the producer in times of low international coffee prices. In Rwanda, however, profits in the coffee trade between 1975 and 1977 were directly transferred to the state budget (Tardiff-Douglin et al. 1993). The coffee sector was therefore directly linked to the core state functions.

In 1975, Habyarimana abolished all political parties and made all Rwandans members of the Republican Movement for Development (MRND), his single party. From then onwards, the MRND would be used as a vehicle for distributing political rents and to build mass loyalty (Guichaoua 2010, 41). Having such a single party to build mass loyalty is, according to Wintrobe, an indicator of a totalitarian type of dictator. In this short period of the coffee-price windfall, we can also observe the workings of the dictator's calculation that turns money into power. When, in 1976 and 1977, the regime's elite were enriched by coffee exports, we notice an increase in repression and loyalty in Rwanda. In 1976, Habyarimana killed dignitaries from the Kayibanda regime by starving them to death. Together with the new coffee laws and the increase in the producer price of coffee, this shows that the increase in the producer price and in the level of repression indeed increased the power of Habyarimana.

If, as I contend in this chapter, the producer price for coffee is not only an important part of the (monetary) income of farmers, but also a key determinant of the political loyalty of the farmers towards the regime, the supply of loyalty from the population to the dictator will increase when the producer price for coffee increases.

• The Period of Decline, 1986–1989

In 1985, the international quota system was abolished. The 1986 international coffee trade was liberalized, but nevertheless, the world market price was very high because Brazil's coffee harvest was lost by unfavorable weather conditions. The price decreased in 1987 only to improve slightly in 1988 with a one-year re-introduction of the quota system. 1989 and 1990 were very bad years with declining international prices and declining domestic coffee production. Government tax revenue from coffee production was halved and never restored in the following years.

Survey research with coffee farmers in 1992 has determined the minimum price required to continue the cultivation of coffee. That minimum price is around 120 RWF/kg. With lower world prices, from 1987 onwards, the government subsidized the coffee agency "to secure the income of the farmer", the regime said. From agricultural research it is known that farmers had other interesting crops, mainly bananas. In his seminal book on Rwandan agriculture, Bart (1993) stresses the importance of bananas and especially banana beer for the peasant income. Compared to coffee, bananas are a source of income the whole year round, with a large domestic market. Bananas can be eaten or used for brewing, its leaves are used to cover the soil, it demands less labor input then coffee and it is important in social life.[14] Habyarimana however, wanted to reduce the area for banana cultivation. According to my analysis, this is not because he believed occult rituals took place on banana plantations (Pottier 1993), but because banana cultivation was the main competitor for coffee in the allocation of land. Bananas were valued on the domestic market and beer was very popular among farmers. The subsidies, I derive, had a political economy nature: to maintain the supply of coffee (raising state revenue) and simultaneously keep the loyalty of the farmers. The total amount of subsidies to the coffee sector was high: 3 billion RWF in 1987, 1.6 billion in 1988, 2 billion in 1989, 4.6 billion in 1990, 1 billion in 1991, 2 billion in 1992, and 1 billion in 1993, indicating the desire of the regime to keep the producer price as high as it could afford. [15]

As Habyarimana's budget began to decline, he tried to find new sources of revenue, from raising new taxes to confiscating property. The best example is the removal of several hundreds of households from their land to allow the regime to grow tea in Northern Rwanda (Mulindi) and in Kibuye (Gisovu). When the world market price for coffee decreased, tea became an important source of foreign exchange for the regime (albeit only for a few years).[16]

In 1990 (before the start of the civil war), the price paid to the producer was dropped from 125 to 100 Rfr. Farmers however, were not interested in growing coffee anymore. Even with a price of 125 Rfr, some farmers preferred to grow other crops. Bananas, for example, yielded a higher return per acre of land and could be sold on the domestic market. Tardiff-Douglin et al. (1993) reports the price level at which farmers said they would destroy their coffee plants (which was forbidden by the regime). At 115 Rfr, 5 % would do it. At 100 Rfr, 10 % would do it. He relies on a 1992 survey by the Ministry of Agriculture. Given the culture of respect (and fear) for authority, the percentage of farmers that would uproot their coffee plants is surely much higher. There is other evidence that supports the dissatisfaction with the government coffee policy. Many authors report that some farmers actually did uproot their coffee trees, in spite of the penalties (Uvin 1998;

---

[14]   Bart (1993), pp. 93–94 and pp. 108–115.

[15]   Tardiff-Douglin et al. (1993), p. 8.

[16]   Human Rights Watch found out that the regime sold the present and future earnings from the tea plantation in Mulindi to buy weapons from Egypt for the value of 6 million US dollars.

Willame 1995). From a survey conducted by Clay in the 1989–1992 period, we learn that 10 % of the farmers who cultivated coffee stopped doing this during Habyarimana's reign.[17] In the 1989–1991 period alone, the survey observed a decline of 5 % in the total number of coffee trees. The only explanation for this is the economic irrationality of the coffee policy from the viewpoint of the farmers. Tardiff-Douglin et al. (1993) writes that a bag of coffee would buy the Rwandan farmer in 1991 only half the goods it bought in 1980. It was especially this real drop in the price of coffee that made its cultivation not interesting anymore to the farmer.[18] Given the evolution of the relative price of coffee versus beans, farmers neglect their coffee trees, quality will go down and eventually farmers abandon coffee altogether.

When an exogenous shock to the dictator's budget occurs, any dictator, even a tinpot type, who uses just enough power to stay in office, would be worried about this decline because he risks to be deposed. Therefore, a dictator will increase repression (because loyalty becomes expensive). This is exactly what Habyarimana did in the late 1980s. With declining coffee prices, he started subsidizing the coffee sector. This subsidy shows that the price paid for loyalty p_p increased sharply and is higher than the world market price, making loyalty more expensive for the dictator. As for the effect of the declining budget on political unrest among the elite, we have the following indirect evidence: in 1988, at the beginning of the coffee crisis, Colonel Mayuya, a top leader in the regime, was murdered.[19] On this, Prunier (1995, 87) writes that,

> in the late 1980s climate, when political competition for the control of the rapidly shrinking economy was becoming fiercer, the succession plans President Habyarimana seemed to entertain concerning Colonel Mayuya were a grave threat to 'le clan de Madame', who might lose control at a time when control was more vital then ever because Mayuya was the President's own man.

Wintrobe argues that a dictator, confronted with a negative budgetary shock has an alternative strategy: a dictator, certainly a totalitarian dictator, can always increase his resources by confiscating property. This is a strategy used by Habyarimana, as shown by the fact that he tried to increase taxes in 1989. This strategy caused much resentment from the farmer population that was already paying all sorts of taxes. At the same time, Habyarimana increased the level of repression or, more accurately, he tried to increase budgetary sources on the one hand and substitute repression for loyalty on the other hand. The latter behaviour reveals the benevolent type in Habyarimana's dictatorship, to wit the type that trades-off

---

[17] Author's own calculation based on the DSA data set.

[18] We can also look at the quality of the coffee as an indication for the decreasing interest of the farmer in the cash crop. In the beginning of Habyarimana's reign, 70 % of Rwanda's coffee was of standard quality with some 4 % reaching superior quality. Towards the end of the 1980s, 70 % was of only ordinary quality. See Uwezeyimana (1996), p. 77.

[19] Revealingly, Colonel Mayuya was replaced by Colonel Bagosora as member of the board of directors of the Bank of Kigali in 1988. Bagosora, now in custody in Arusha, is known as one of the major architects of the 1994 genocide.

loyalty and repression in times of a budgetary shock.[20] The increase in repression is amply documented by the 1993 report of the International Federation of Human Rights Organizations: arbitrary arrest, killing of opposition members by government agents, several massacres against Tutsi, confiscation of property, rape, etc.

- The Institutional Core of the Coffee Policy

If we think a moment about the institutional core (for a definition I refer to Chap. 1) of the coffee policies, one notices immediately the rewards and penalties for "good" behavior. Farmers were not allowed to neglect, abandon or rip out coffee trees under the threat of financial penalties. Annual local contests gave a price to the farmer with the best coffee field. The organisation of the coffee sector made the farmers entirely dependent on the state-run coffee agency, to which they had to sell their coffee. This agency, OCIR-café not only determined the price received by the farmers but also monitored the maintenance of the coffee fields. The overt and covert message to the farmers is clear: your monetary income, and thus the supplement to a households' income from subsistence agriculture, depends on the state. If you do what the state asks you to do, you will be rewarded in times of high international prices for coffee and not penalized in bad times. The relationship between the state and the coffee farmers was especially evident in the *Paysannats*. In these settlement schemes (see also Chap. 6), farmers were given a contract with 2 hectares of land conditional on growing coffee trees on 0.72 hectares. These farmers were highly monitored and deviation from the contract resulted in the land re-taken by the state. In the 1989–1992 agricultural household survey data collected by DSA we can observe that none of the farmers in *Payasannats* rip our or abandon their coffee trees.

4.5 Genocide as a Special Case in the Loyalty-Repression Model

Just before the outbreak of war, in August 1990, the Habyarimana regime decreased the price paid to the coffee producer from 125 to 100 RWF/kg. This sharp drop was the result of the very expensive subsidy policy to the coffee sector, which proved to be unsustainable. The 1990 coffee season was marked by the highest subsidy ever in the history of the coffee economy (4 billion US\$). The history of subsidies from 1986 to 1990 again documents the importance of the coffee economy for the regime, both economically and politically.

---

[20] Using a comparative statics analysis in the article published in the Journal of Theoretical Politics (2012) co-authored by B.Capéau and myself we find more evidence for this 'bad' side of the benevolent dictator.

From a public finance point of view, this cut in subsidies makes sense as it is expensive to maintain the subsidy. However, there is a clear trade-off with farmer political loyalty. The proof of which will be established after the outbreak of war: the government increased the producer price for coffee again from 100 to 115 Rfr in 1991, demonstrating again the desire of the regime to keep up the loyalty of the peasant population. In a political economy analysis, such decisions are not mere coincidence. War not only diminishes the power of the regime (it is proven to be vulnerable), but also increases the need to boost the state budget in order to pay for the army. The price was increased again in 1991 out of fear that the farmers would decrease their loyalty to the regime in the face of the RPF attack and continue to uproot coffee trees. From the dictator's point of view, this increase was necessary to maintain both the loyalty of the farmers AND the level of the state budget. Of course, since the world market price for coffee continued to drop, the cost to the dictator to pay for the supply of loyalty continued to increase. A power maximizing dictator will therefore substitute repression for loyalty. As the budget of the dictator is shrinking, he will look for cheaper ways to increase loyalty and repression. The price paid to the coffee producer was already at its lowest and does not offer cost-saving opportunities. Repression was made cheaper by training and using unemployed youth as militias. This is one of the strategies used from 1991 onwards.

The civil war offered the regime an excellent occasion to increase its popularity, despite declining coffee prices. One can interpret the use of ethnicity as an effort of the Habyarimana regime to cement Hutu solidarity in the context of military confrontation (with the RPF) and internal democratic opposition (with other political parties).[21] A large supply of loyalty by a docile, willing population is the best situation a dictator can have. This keeps the price of loyalty very low. When all Rwandans (and especially the Hutu of course) would feel themselves part of the Habyarimana regime, they would not ask much in return (Prunier 1995). The fact that a Hutu president is in power, according to this ideology, should already be enough for a Hutu farmer to feel proud. As if the Hutu farmer himself was a member of the government. Ethnicity is a cheap mechanism to boost loyalty to the cause.

Even in the late 1980s and early 1990s, when repression increased substantially, most Hutu could reasonably assume that they would not fall victim to the regime's repressive policies. This means that an increase in repression by the Habyarimana regime was positively related to an increase in the *aggregate* supply of loyalty. The loyalty curve of Tutsi is certainly backward bending (as in Fig. 4.2), especially from 1990 onwards. I contend that the Habyarimana regime from 1990 onwards pursued a policy of *immiserization*. Wintrobe (1998, 82–83) believes that a strategy of immiserization may be attractive for the tyrannical type of dictator

---

[21] We are leaving here a political economy of coffee and replace it by a political economy of ethnicity. In both analytical frames it is the quest for loyalty from the leaders point of view that is at the center of attention.

(or, for Rwanda, a dictator that behaves like a tyrant against a specified part of his population): a high level of repression combined with a low level of loyalty. Looting, confiscating, and taxing gives dictators funds to buy off the army and it prevents an impoverished population from spending resources (they no longer have) towards political action. The population will be too poor to oppose him.

From Des Forges (1999) seminal book on the Rwandan genocide, we know that the regime offered a large number of rewards to the Hutu population to incite them to kill the Tutsi. In the stylized framework offered by our political economy model, this can be understood as a governmental policy to increase the price of loyalty in order to get a very large supply of loyalty from the population. The "price" here is not merely the producer price for coffee, but all kinds of material rewards: appropriating land, looting houses, extracting cash from victims, enslaving a Tutsi woman, distributing free beer. In this model, the choice of the regime in Rwanda to use genocide as a political strategy to survive can be characterized as follows:

- The earnings from the export of coffee declined for the last couple of years. Coffee was no longer an interesting crop to the farmer. Together with decreased earnings, especially in real income terms, the loyalty of the farmer to the regime disappeared;
- The regime tried to hold onto power by using ethnic ideology to legitimize its reign. They were able to increase farmer loyalty by frightening them and depicting the rebels as devils and enemies. The regime substituted other rewards for the share of the coffee price to buy loyalty. In this way, the regime was able to hide its own failures (a failed economy and a failed democratization) and put the blame on one group of people (Tutsi);
- The 1994 genocide in Rwanda can be considered as a double corner solution where maximum loyalty is bought from (and supplied by) one group of people (Hutu) and maximum repression is exercised towards another group of people (Tutsi) (Fig. 4.5).

The Habyarimana regime did its utmost best to increase the supply of loyalty by the population. A substantial apparatus of ideological indoctrination was at work, including newspapers, radio broadcasting, and training sessions. The regime made use of its budgetary resources to spread its ideology. Ideological fervour was a cheap instrument to increase the supply of loyalty in times of civil war. Many authors agree that the legitimacy of the Habyarimana regime in the eyes of the farmer population declined at the end of the 1980s. Ideology was a means to boost and secure this legitimacy again. Blaming the Tutsi was instrumental in masking the regime's responsibility for the economic hardship of the population and the political crisis. This ideology became more extreme as the war and the negotiation process went on (1992–1993) and as the coffee price continued to drop. At the same time, we notice a sharp increase in the level of repression used by the regime. And, as we explained before, the repression was mainly conducted against the Tutsi minority of the population, allowing the Habyarimana regime to increase (or at least maintain) its power over the population without losing the loyalty of most Hutu citizens.

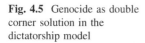

Fig. 4.5 Genocide as double corner solution in the dictatorship model

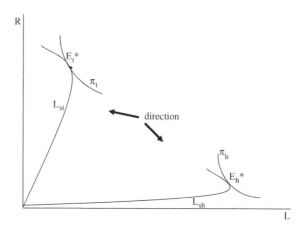

The last element to complete the picture is the level of foreign aid given to the Habyarimana regime. Foreign aid was very important to the regime. From the 1970s to the mid-1980s, foreign aid was roughly equally important as the earnings from the coffee export, but from the mid-1980s to the mid-1990s, the importance of foreign aid relative to export earnings increased dramatically. The continued supply of foreign aid allowed Habyarimana to sustain his budget, even when coffee prices continued to drop. However, foreign aid could not replace the role of the producer price for coffee. Foreign aid helped to keep the dictator in office during the civil war, but it did not help the farmer.

4.6 By Way of Conclusion for this Chapter

Scholars have developed different theories of the political economy of dictatorship. In this chapter, a model developed by Wintrobe was used to account for the political economy of the Habyarimana regime. It is argued that the mechanism used by the dictator to buy loyalty went through the economy. The loyalty of the population vis-à-vis the dictator is transmitted through the producer price of coffee. In a period of economic growth, the producer price of coffee is increased and the power of the dictator increases. Evidence points out that Habyarimana had totalitarian characteristics in the beginning of his reign, but on the whole one can best characterize his dictatorship as benevolent or developmental. Olson would say 'encompassing'. The regime used a carrot-and-stick policy in regard to coffee cultivation: the producer price was high compared to African standards, but coffee farmers were highly monitored and penalized for mistreating trees. When at the end of the 1980s, international coffee prices started to drop dramatically, the regime fell into a political and economic crisis.

When the regime was unable to pay for political loyalty trough the coffee price mechanism, it looked for other mechanisms to keep up its power over the population. Ethnicity was used as a mobilization device and unemployed youth recruited in para-military units. These units targeted Rwanda's Tutsi minority. Genocide is understood in the framework of Wintrobe's model as a double corner solution in which loyalty of one group is bought by allowing and encouraging it to exterminate the other. It is not the fall of the coffee price that caused the genocide, but the desire of the ruling elite to stay in power at all cost.

Chapter 5
Agricultural Policy and the 'Ruriganiza' Famine (1989) in Southern Rwanda

Rwanda is clearly at a crossroads, in that the old strategy is no longer viable: the vision of a nation of self-sufficient peasants, meeting through their labor alone their needs for food and shelter, leading tranquil and meaningful lives centered around the local community, unbeholden to the world without, that vision is no longer sustainable.
World Bank, Rwanda Agricultural Strategy Review, 1991, p. 1.

5.1 Introduction

In the second half of the eighties, Rwanda entered a period of economic decline (see Chap. 3). The period was characterised by a decline in food production per capita, a downward trend of coffee and tea prices, unfavourable weather conditions, unsolved refugee questions, demographic growth and rising corruption and political unrest.

The main objective of the chapter is the study of agricultural policy and the 1989 crop failure in the southern prefecture of Gikongoro and parts of Butare. From the data that we will be discussing, it will become clear that we are not dealing with a famine that killed thousands of people. In terms of mortality, we cannot call it a famine. If however we consider famine as a prolonged period in which a serious food crisis threatens to destroy the fabric of society, the word *'famine'* applies to southern Rwanda in 1989. We are dealing with a creeping agricultural crisis, several years of hardship in which households depleted their resources and could not cope with additional crop failures.

The chapter is structured as follows: In section two we discuss agricultural policy under Habyarimana. Section three describes the 1989 food crisis and the entitlement failure. In section four, we discuss the causes of the famine and relate them to agricultural policies.

5.2 Agricultural Policy Under Habyarimana

5.2.1 Food Self-Sufficiency

Habyarimana wanted Rwandan agriculture to be self-sufficient. Food self-sufficiency was the prime policy objective of the regime. In his speeches, the president paid a lot of attention to increased food production. He believed that the

P. Verwimp, *Peasants in Power*, DOI: 10.1007/978-94-007-6434-7_5,
© Springer Science+Business Media Dordrecht 2013

equilibrium between population growth and food production would be disturbed when the latter cannot follow the pace of the former. The emphasis on food self-reliance is correlated with the adherence to a peasant ideology of the regime. Habyarimana considered the peasants to be the true inhabitants of Rwanda and he wanted all Rwandans to be peasants. In July 1987, at the occasion of the 25th Anniversary of the existence of the Rwandan Republic, Habyarimana devoted his official speech to the glorification of the Rwandan peasant (see Chap. 2).

Habyarimana's argument to focus on agricultural production and his main argument for high food prices was the protection of peasant revenue. While that argument made sense from a producers' point of view, it did not help the majority of the population who were net-buyers (as opposed to net-sellers) of staple food. Because the Habyarimana regime only considered the peasantry as producers of food and of cash crops, it did not recognize that many peasants were net-buyers of beans and of food in general.

In line with Habyarimana's ideology of a hard working and moral peasant population, Habyarimana tried to reduce the production of beer bananas and the consumption of banana beer. It is worth noting that Habyarimana discouraged the cultivation of bananas. In a 1979 speech, he is very explicit about that:

> Despite the opposition and the misunderstanding that I have seen in this question, I remain convinced that the extension of the wine banana and, in certain regions, the appropriation of land for its cultivation, are a great handicap for development and for the food equilibrium of the population. The "myth of the banana tree" must disappear as well as the myth of the "nice corners" and that of the burning of bushes so-called regenerating effect.[1]

Bananas however produce a very high yield per acre and a large domestic banana market existed in Rwanda.[2] The regime considered beer drinking anti-social and beer brewing wasteful (Kangasniemi 1998, 142). For the farmer household however, as we have seen in Chap. 3, beer brewing and selling are very important for food security. Pottier (1992) writes that Habyarimana wanted to reduce the cultivation of bananas because he believed occult rituals were being performed in the banana plantations. A more economic and down-to-earth approach however, suggests that bananas are a direct competitor to coffee, a cash crop that was strongly promoted by the regime.

5.2.2 Import and Export Policy

Although the Habyarimana regime embraced the vision of a self-sufficient agrarian nation, Rwanda was far from self-sufficient. In a June 1989 report, an official of the Ministry of Agriculture published the results of a small survey of informal border trade conducted in April and May 1989. He suggested that Rwanda exported

---

[1] Habyarimana (1979, p. 135).

[2] Little and Horowitz (1987, pp. 254–257).

Table 5.1 Value of food
imports and exports in
million US dollar

	Imports	Exports
1981	37.3	67.4
1982	42.8	69.3
1983	37.4	60.6
1984	48.5	62.9
1985	63.3	68.7
1986	53.4	160.1
1987	38.5	121.5
1988	36.8	91.2
1989	41.0	104.7
1990	46.7	88.6

Source UCTAD Trade Statistics, 1992 yearbook

substantial quantities of manufacturing goods, potatoes, poultry and vegetables to the surrounding countries, and that it is at the same time an important importer of cooking oil, beans, sorghum, bananas, sugar and maize.[3] This survey can be complemented with official trade statistics. Table 5.1 shows that during the eigthies Rwanda imported food for a average annual value of 40 million US dollar during the eighties. Rwanda exported food for on average 90 million dollar annually.

These results indicate that the vision of the Rwandan leadership did not correspond with reality: Rwandan agriculture was not self-sufficient, there was a large volume of cross-border trade. Table 5.1 shows us that the value of food export doubled in the second half of the eighties, compared to the first half. This remarkable upswing in food exports is for the moment unexplained, but coincides with a sharp decline in export earnings from coffee. Food exports could have been used to partly offset the decrease of these coffee export earnings. At the same time, imports of food in the second half of the eighties remained at the same level as in the first half. These import figures show 1988, the year before the crop failure to be the year with the lowest value of food imports in the decade. This has to do with the 'name' that was given to the years 1987 and 1988 by the Habyarimana regime. 1987 was called the year of food self-sufficiency and 1988 the year of the protection of the income of the peasants. Gatete (1996) writes that the Rwandan government had banned all food imports in 1988.[4]

According to the Agricultural Strategy Review (World Bank 1991), it is the informal cross-border trade that is believed to be responsible for the import of beans that eliminated the food shortage in Southern Rwanda.[5] *Informal trade* means that under normal conditions the imports of crops such as beans, sorghum and bananas are officially banned. A division in the Ministry of Commerce was

---

[3] Ngirumwami (1989). No case of re-export was found by the author, indicating that all import was meant for domestic consumption.

[4] Gatete (1996, p. 2.)

[5] World Bank, Ibidem, p. 26.

responsible for assessing the needs for imports based on a projection of national production and consumption. This division only used data on official imports which became available two weeks after arrival in the country. The division did not make any projections on consumption or production and did not have information on unofficial (informal) imports from neighbouring countries.[6] Nevertheless it is estimated that in 1986, a fairly good crop year, unofficial imports accounted for 50 % of the beans and sorghum sold on Rwanda's markets. If the division anticipates food shortages, a complex process of import licensing was set in motion. During the 1989 crop failure, the World Bank writes (1991, 25), the Commerce Ministry decided to authorize ten importers to import beans from Uganda when the price had reached 60 RWF. This was too late to prevent starvation and emigration.

The reduction and surely the banning of imports of course is detrimental to a farming population that, under the pressure of population growth, concentrates efforts on high value crops. The exchange strategy (banana beer for beans) that we have discussed in Chap. 3, is only viable when beans are in effect imported into Rwanda. In the absence of imports, the exchange strategy is useless and farmers have to grow all subsistence crops themselves.

As with licensing in general and under famine conditions in particular, large profits and speculation from the side of the traders and from the side of the license giving authority are possible. Import policy in Rwanda under the Habyarimana regime was managed by Séraphin Rwabukumba, member of the Akazu and half-brother of Agathe Kanziga, the wife of the president. He headed the powerful company 'La Centrale' which was in charge of official import into Rwanda. At the same time this person was in charge of the foreign currency division of the National Bank. Since import cannot occur without foreign currency, Rwabukumba sat in a key position. La Centrale did not import basic foods needed by the Rwandan population, but imported high quality products for the Rwandan elite. Well-informed people knew that La Centrale did not pay import or export taxes.[7] Both the non-food and food imports for the elite took up a large part of the foreign currency. As Bézy argues, the food that was imported was destined for[8]:

- the expatriates from industrialized countries, to allow them to continue their food habits
- the growing number of tourists
- interns in schools who benefited from non-traditional food
- the national elite who lived a european-style of live
- the whole of the urban population (5 %) who had introduced milk powder, tomato concentrate, imported cooking oil, sugar and rice (whose domestic production remained too low) into its eating habits.

---

[6] World Bank, Ibidem, p. 25.

[7] Reyntjens (2001)

[8] Bézy (1990, p. 13). The author also refers to J. Nzisabira, dans Bulletin des Séances, ARSOM, XXXIV, n° 4, 1987, p. 641.

Reading the 1987 speech of Habyarimana in which he pleaded for import restriction, one gets the impression that the Rwandan peasantry had to produce more food to limit imports, while the elite continued to import luxury products, both food and non-food. Indeed, each dollar that is saved on import of basic foods can be used for something else. Additional information, found in numerous articles of the journal *Kinyamateka*, seems to validate this statement: between June 1989 and December 1989, Kinyamateka published several articles in which they revealed that government authorities embezzled public funds on a large scale. André Sibomana, priest and editor of *Kinyamateka* put it this way:

> Rwanda was a country which still had the reputation of being well run, ruled by a sort of 'enlightened despot', Juvénal Habyarimana. But you don't become an honest man just by knowing how to quote French poetry to President Mitterrand. Juvénal Habyarimana and his people were plundering the country while the peasants were starving. We had evidence that he or his wife were diverting funds allocated to buying food for the population to import luxury items instead, for example televisions which were sold at vastly inflated prices. We also had information on drug trafficking.[9]

This is one such example of the economic rents that the clan around Habyarimana and his wife, the Akazu, accumulated through their political patronage of the Rwandan economy. Guichaoua (2010, 101–106) describes the functioning of the clientilist system: all important decisions in the country, from nominations in the administration, promotions in the army, directorships of state-run companies and so on were decided by Habyrimana and the Akazu. They made sure that only persons loyal to them were rewarded and allowed to profit themselves.

5.2.3 *Lack of Inputs*

Although peasants contributed vasts amounts of savings to the well-known Banques Populaires, very few loans were given to peasants. Half of the loans were given to traders and businessmen whereas this group only made up 14 % of the people with deposits at these banks.[10] Under Habyarimana, Rwanda was the country in the world that used the lowest amount of fertilizer per capita.[11] This has to do with the deliberate restriction of import but also with the distribution of the available fertilizer. The regime wanted to restrict its use for industrial crops only (tea and coffee). The absence of fertilizer is cited by a peasant in an IWACU documentary as one reason for the incapacity to cope with the crop failure (see the Appendix of this chapter for details).

---

[9] Sibomana (1996, p. 25).

[10] I refer to "Aiding Violence" by P. Uvin and to a 1991 report by IFAD for details on the Banques Populaires.

[11] World Bank, Rwanda, *Agricultural Strategy Review*, 1991.

The Habyarimana regime undertook a massive and nation-wide anti-erosion effort. The regime obliged all peasants to dig ditches on their plots. Ditches were considered the best means of combating erosion. Peasants who refused to do this were fined, just as in the case of neglect of the coffee trees. Guichaoua (1991) who interviewed farmers in 1989, reports that farmers resented the harsh labour requested in the nationwide anti-erosion policy of digging ditches. No doubt erosion was one of the main problems of the country given that peasants have to cultivate the slopes of hills. However, as Kangasniemi (1998, 174) writes, Rwanda's anti-erosion campaign was rigid and simplistic, leaving no room for local physical conditions (rainfall, soil type, slope) indigenous practices, and household specific economic circumstances (crops, livestock).

A Belgian brother in the north of Rwanda, specializing in agriculture had developed an alternative way of combating erosion. He taught the peasants to construct radical terraces. When the author visited the brother in Byumba in August 2000, a very large area was covered with radical terraces. The brother did not have to oblige the peasants to adopt radical terracing, they came to him to learn the technique by themselves.[12] The contrast with the mandatory anti-erosion techniques decreed by the regime could not be greater: upon the beginning of the democratisation process (1989–1990) and the decrease in power of the MRND, peasants neglected the maintenance of the anti-erosion ditches or destroyed the ditches.[13] This resembles the treatment of their coffee trees (see Chap. 4). Peasants started to rip them out, even before 1991, although this was prohibited by law.

While the absence of credit and fertilizer, the mandatory coffee cultivation, the umuganda policy and the anti-erosion measures where not confined to the prefecture of Gikongoro (indeed they were nation-wide policies), their cumulated effect exhaust a population that is on average poorer than in other prefectures. While peasants all over Rwanda suffer from mismanagement and bad policies, it are the poor who are hit most. Under normal weather conditions, a poor population may just be able to survive despite bad government policies. The occurance of a drought unveils their vulnerability to crop failure and famine.

5.3 The Food Crisis and the Entitlement Failure of 1989

5.3.1 The Entitlement to Food

Farmers use part of their production of food crops for own consumption. Sen calls this the *direct entitlement* of food the farmer has. When the farmer also earns a

---

[12] This means that, according to the Belgian Brother, farmers in Byumba adopted radical terracing. Nduwayezu (1990) in contrast, writes that no Rwandan farmer adopted radical terracing. For several reasons, the brothers' testimony is much more credible than Nduwayezu's affirmation.

[13] Ntezilyayo, ibidem, p. 324.

wage, produces cash crops, receives transfers or has another source of income which he can use to buy food, the farmer has an *exchange entitlement* in Sen's terms. Most farmers have a combination of direct and exchange entitlements to food. A farmer producing beans has a direct entitlement to beans. An increase in the price of beans will not endanger the direct entitlement of the bean producer. Farmers who are not producing beans will see their exchange entitlement to beans decreased when, ceteris paribus, the price of beans increases. This allows us to stress the importance of relative prices in the conservation of a farmer's exchange entitlements. As 80 % of Rwandan peasant households are net buyers of beans, the price of beans is very important.

Taking a look at direct entitlements first, we note that beans, bananas, potatoes and sweet potatoes are the major food crops for Rwandans. Bananas are often used to brew beer and thus give access to exchange entitlements. Coffee is an export crop and also gives access to exchange entitlements. In 1989, production of beans and sweet potatoes declined sharply in Gikongoro. Since sweet potatoes are the most important crop in Gikongoro (in contrast to Rwanda as a whole were bananas are the most important crop), this decline caused *a severe loss of direct entitlement to food*. Figure 5.1 shows that the production decline in 1989 was a local and not a country-wide phenomenon.

In contrast to direct entitlment failures, which can occur as a result of bad weather, rain, crop disease, drought or other calamnities, exchange entitlement failures depend on relative prices and thus on market forces. The entitlement approach focusses on *starvation* and not on famine mortality. People starve when they cannot command enough food. As Sen indicates, many famine deaths are the result of epidemics, but this is not of our interest here. People will more easily become victim of sickness or disease when they lack adequate food consumption. The command over food a peasant has, by means of his direct and his exchange entitlements over food is thus at the centre of our attention.

The production decline in seasons 1989a and especially 1989b in Gikongoro (and parts of Butare) prefecture (see Fig. 5.1) are evidence of direct entitlement failures. This affects consumption if households are not able to compensate for this through purchases of food on the market. In the next sections we will see whether exchange entitlement failures were also part of the peasant situation.

In order to detail the relative importance of different food items consumed by Rwandan households, we look at Table 5.2. It is shown that, in terms of value, beans, bananas and sweet potatoes were the most important crops in the Rwandan diet in 1990. Together they constitued 67 % of the average crop consumption per month in the 1990a season. Very few meat is consumed, wheras large quantities of banana beer were consumed. The later took 20 % of total consumption in Rwanda and 15 % in Gikongoro. Table 5.2 also shows other regional differences, in particular the importance of sweet potatoes in Gikongoro.

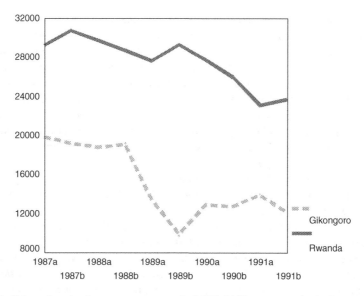

Fig. 5.1 Value of production over ten seasons in RWF (1987 a season prices). *Source* author's calculations from DSA datase. *Legend* full line _____ for Rwanda, dotted line ------ for Gikongoro. **a** stands for the first agricultural season (October–March); **b** for the second season (April–September)

Table 5.2 Food consumption data per household per month (season 1990a)

Crops	Rwanda			Gikongoro		
	kg	Value	%	kg	Value	%
Beans	21.96	869.62	26	8.54	354.59	22
Potatoes	16.85	282.74	8	8.89	155.71	9
Peas	0.99	49.50	1	1.33	66.56	4
Mais	12.69	288.82	9	4.07	92.67	6
Manioc	16.43	281.45	8	3.70	67.32	4
Bananas	42.14	715.54	21	2.17	39.87	2
Sweet potatoes	46.70	683.22	20	51.27	726.33	44
Sorghum	6.37	190.54	6	4.84	141.40	9
Total of 8 crops		3,360.9			1644.4	
Meat		181.3			69.76	
		(48.7)[b]			(67.7)[a]	
Banana beer (liter)	28.22	889.05		9.73	311.38	
		(15.6)[c]			(20.9)[b]	
Adult equivalents (ae)		4.90			4.59	
Consumption of 8 crops, meat and beer per ae per month		904.33			441.29	

Data source Agricultural Household Survey, Department of Agricultural Statistics (DSA 1989–1992)
[a] Quantities are the sum of production in season 1990a minus kg sold and given to others plus kg bought and received from others. Prices are average market prices in RWF per kg in season 1990a for Rwanda and in the prefecture of Gikongoro. Percentages is the percent of the total value of 8 crops
[b] % households with no meat consumption
[c] % households with no consumption of banana beer

5.3.2 *Some Exchange Entitlements*[14]

• Coffee Versus Beans

Export crops are another way to secure one's living in a peasant economy. Table 5.3 shows the evolution of coffee cultivation over several years. For the whole of Rwanda, about half of the peasants were cultivating coffee in 1989. On average, they held about 150 coffee trees. Over three years, this number stayed about the same, but the income from coffee dropped by one-third. The regional differences (not in the table) are sharp: households in Gikongoro increased their number of trees between 1989 and 1991 only to end up in 1991 with half of the coffee income compared to 1989. Although peasant investment behaviour is not the main topic of this chapter, we need to look at the value of coffee in relation to other crops. The hopes of 'a good coffee harvest' expressed by farmers in discussions with NGOs on the crisis, however have not come true. In Butare, coffee income also dropped sharply over three years time, but peasants did not invest in new coffee trees.

Coffee was Rwanda's most important export crop and was responsible for high state revenue in. For the farmer, coffee is a source of monetary income. As long as the producer price of coffee is high, the farmer has an economic incentive to grow coffee. When that price decreases, he may want to replace coffee with other crops. Bananas and beans are the major competitors of coffee for land allocation in the peasant household. By decree, coffee trees may not be intercropped, neglected, abandoned or destroyed. As can be observed from Fig. 5.2, the price of coffee was fixed by the government, first at 122.5, then 125, then 100 and later at 115. The relative price of coffee versus beans however has shown a severe decline between 1986 and 1993. Where 1 kg of coffee would buy the farmer 1 kg of beans in 1986, the farmer needed 3 kg of coffee for 1 kg of beans at the end of 1993. It is not surprising then, that towards the end of the eighties, farmers started ripping out coffee trees, an act forbidden by penal law. Table 5.3 on coffee production already showed that the average coffee income in Rwanda decreased by 1/3 in the course of three years (1989–1991). This general decline was due to decreased production per tree, but masked big differences between prefectures. Gikongoro prefecture is a case in point: average coffee income decreased by almost 50 %, while the number of trees had increased by 15 % in the 1989–1991 period. This means that Gikongoro farmers had invested heavily in new trees, which only bear fruit after three years. From the scarce but relevant literature on hunger in Gikongoro in

---

[14] We deal with coffee and livestock in this section. For Rwanda as a whole, the exchange entitlement of banana beer is important as well, but coffee and livestock are more important than bananas in Gikongoro. In addition, famine researchers also study the exchange entitlement of the agricultural wage. However, I only have data on wages from the 1990 and 1991 seasons and thus not during the crop failure season. Wage data from 1990 and 1991 do not show entitlement failures for wage earners.

Table 5.3 Coffee production and income at the household level 1989–1991

	1989	1990	1991	1989–1991 %
Rwanda				
% households doing coffee	46.7			
Number of coffee trees	149	155	154	+3.3
kg sold	48.3	48.4	34.1	−29.3
Coffee income (RWF)	6,038	4,846	3,932	−34.8
Gikongoro				
% households doing coffee	48.4			
Number of coffee trees	195	195	224	+14.8
kg sold	44	32	26	−40.9
Coffee income (RWF)	5,548	3,250	2,980	−46.3

Source Authors calculations from DSA data

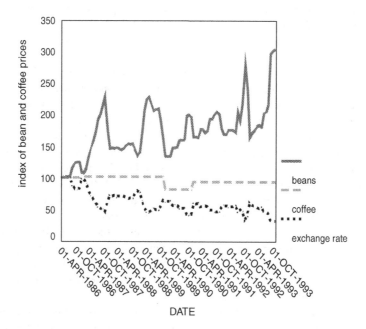

Fig. 5.2 The price and the exchange entitlement of coffee

1989, we retain that peasants tell investigators that they would starve next season when the next coffee harvest fails:

> Everybody's eyes are focussed on the coming coffee season. When it is good, they can survive, when not, they will die.[15]

---

[15] Les Retombées de la Famine dans les Préfectures de Butare et de Gikongoro, 1990, p. 17.

Table 5.4 Average livestock holdings over several years, in TLU's

				% change	% households without livestock		
	1989	1990	1991	1989–1991	1989	1990	1991
Gikongoro	0.84	0.78	0.65	−22.6	24.7	39.3	43.8
Rwanda	0.91	0.86	0.86	−5.4	32.0	35.1	38.4

Tropical livestock units for Rwanda are calculated as cattle 1; pig 0.25; goat 0.17; sheep 0.17; 1140 other hh were surveyed in three rounds 1989–1991
Data Source Agricultural Household Survey, Department of Agricultural Statistics (DSA 1989–1992)

As for the famine months of the 1989b season, coffee farmers in Gikongoro and in the whole of Rwanda experienced a sharp exchange entitlement failure versus beans. The 1989b price shock of beans and the (subsequent) loss of exchange entitlement however was only the beginning of a more serious decline of exchange entitlements in the 1991a season and thereafter The price of coffee remained at the 115 level till the beginning of the genocide (April 1994).

• **Livestock Versus Beans**

Table 5.4 shows that Rwandan households, on average, have decreased their livestock holdings during the three years of the survey. During this period, household livestock holdings (in tlu's) declined on average by 5.4 %. The decline in the southern prefecture of Gikongoro was much larger than the Rwandan average. Gikongoro prefecture has the highest percentage of households who lost all livestock between 1989 and 1991, an increase by 77 % of households without livestock (the Rwandan average being 20 % increase). Several other prefectures (Kibungo, Kibuye and Kigali) have seen an increase in the number of households holding livestock over this period.

With incomplete risk markets—entailing interdependence of production and consumption decisions—livestock is an important asset which helps protect the consumption of poor people (Ravalllion 1997, 1223). It is known from other countries that the value of livestock decreases in periods of famines. Sen for example, writing on the Ethiopian famine (1972–1974) says that the economic distress of the pastoralists was not confined only to the loss of animals (by drought or displacement from traditional grazing land),

> The exchange entitlement associated with any given stock of animals vis-à-vis grains also fell sharply. It is sometimes overlooked that a pastoralist does not live only by eating animals or consuming animal products like milk. He also exchanges animals for other means of sustenance, chiefly grains.[16]

---

[16] Sen (1981, p. 105).

We only have observations on the price of sheep and goats from October 1989 to September 1991, thus missing the high point of the famine in Gikongoro. As we have stated before, the 1989–1991 period is a time of prolonged agricultural crisis in Gikongoro and the livestock data are an indication of this. As crops fail because of drought, lack of inputs or plant diseases, peasants are forced to eat or sell (parts of) their livestock in order to survive. When crop failure is a covariate shock (as opposed to an ideosyncratic one), many households sell livestock at the same time, thereby causing a sharp decline in the market price of livestock (Ravaillion 1997, 1223). From the national-level livestock price data, we cannot say that livestock owners experienced a sharp exchange entitlement loss verus beans.

We conclude from this section that coffee producers experienced an exchange entitlement failure relative to beans in the period of the food crisis. This came on top of a direct entitlement failure. The price of coffee continued to decline after 1989, making the exchange rate of beans versus coffee not particularly low in 1989 compared to other years. In general, what we observe is in fact very close to Sen's observations on the Ethiopian famine (1972–1973). Sen observed that the peasant population in Wollo starved to death without substantial rise in food prices.[17] The peasants experienced a direct entitlement failure and could not command food in the market by lack of purchasing power. As Sen (1981, 101) writes:

> The biggest group of destitutes in the Wollo famine came from the agricultural background, and indeed were farmers—both tenants and small land-owning cultivators. The entitlement decline here took the form of *direct* entitlement failure without involving the market in the immediate context. The output—typically of foodgrains—was severely reduced, and this led to starvation in a direct way. In so far as the Ethiopian farmer eats the food grown by the family without becoming involved in exchange to acquire food, the immediate influence affecting starvation is the decline of the food grown and owned by the family, rather than the fall in the total food output in the region as a whole. The distinction is important, since the Food-Availability-Decline-approach would focus on the latter variable. The hunger of the Wollo peasant had a more direct origin.
>
> But, of course, once his own crop had failed, the Wollo peasant would have tried to get hold of food trough the market *in so far* as he could have exercised market command. But since the agricultural failure also amounts to a collapse of his *source* of market command (namely his income), he was not in a position to supplement his reduced food output by market purchase. The Wollo agriculturalist could not provide much effective demand for food in the market, and despite widespread starvation the food prices in Dessie and elsewhere recorded very little increase.

Peasants in Gikongoro, already the poorest in Rwanda, experienced a sharp decline in coffee income and livestock holdings during a period of food crop failure. Only off-farm labour (which is in short supply) and the sale of livestock products are sources of purchasing power that are independent of agricultural output. The sale of beer (which depends on the supply of bananas and sorghum) and crops on the market is not independent of agricultural output. High bean prices in the beginning of the 1989b season (April–June 1989), can therefore be an indication that households still had some cash to command food in the market. The absence of

---

[17] Sen, p. 69.

(very) high bean prices in subsequent seasons (1990–1994) therefore may then be an indication that households on the one hand produced more beans themselves and on the other hand had no resources anymore to command beans in the market.

5.4 Crop Failure and Non-response to Famine

5.4.1 A Malfunctioning Food Marketing System

Accroding to Pottier (1993), OPROVIA, the leading Rwandan agency for food marketing, intervened only to a limited scale in food markets.[18] It was OPRO-VIA's task to assure price stability, especially for beans and sorghum. The Rwandan government however expected that OPROVIA could be run as a profitable business, which was not possible when OPROVIA had to buy surpluses in the post-harvest period above the market price and sell from its stocks below the market price in periods of shortage.

> The impact of the 1988 harvest failures, caused by excessive rainfall, was unusually harsh since the authorities had banned all food imports that year; 1988 being Rwanda's Année de l' Autosuffisance ![19]

According to Pottier, it was the policy of food import minimization that made it impossible for Rwanda to re-supply its food stocks at the time of the 1988 bad harvest. This is one reason why, one year later in 1989, food stocks where almost empty. Official inquiries revealed that the Rwandan Government was setting OPROVIA an impossible task. OPROVIA's impasse, Pottier writes, was proof that no real progress had been made since the drawing up of agreements with the EC in 1982. The second report of the Interservice Commission warned, with regard to Rwanda's internal food trade:

> It has been noted that even when food is abundant, the shops and silos belonging to the cooperatives and communes remain poorly stocked, even though these structures are theoretically the most appropriate for supplying all of the country's communes. It is therefor a matter of urgency that all the serivices concerned (ministeries, OPROVIA and agricultural projects) decide how the decentralized stockage system could be activated in the interest of a nationwide distribution of foodstuffs[20]

The government of Rwanda nevertheless continued to believe that OPROVIA would take the initiative for inter-regional food commerce (Rapport 1989, 23) The expectation, Pottier argues, that OPROVIA could raise the funds required for

---

[18] Pottier, J., Taking stock, Food Marketing reform in Rwanda 1982–1989, *African Affairs*, p. 6 and p. 15.

[19] Pottier, ibidem, p. 15. During the Habyarimana regime, every year was given a slogan. 1988 was called the year of food self-sufficiency.

[20] Republic of Rwanda, Rapport sur la Situation Alimentaire de notre Pays, Ministry of Agriculture, Octobre 1989, translation by J. Pottier, ibidem, 1993, p. 20.

effective inter-regional distribution of surpluses in times of crisis was unrealistic. In fact, the contrary was true, there were signs of gross neglect towards the very apparatus for state-controlled marketing:

> The Rwandan governement still needs to reimburse OPROVIA the promised 28,000,000 RwF it lost in 1988 after selling at artificially low prices the sorghum it had bought too dearly in 1986.[21]
> And,
> The Rwandan government should reajust the agricultural prices at which it bought from OPROVIA in 1989 to ensure that this organisation in future can reduce the losses it must incure.[22]

There is also an information problem in the game: one can argue that the population, through the speeches of Habayrimana (restriction of import), can start believing that future public stocks of grains or other crops will be low and that the government will not be able to intervene in the case of a crop failure. This information problem may lead to high expected prices.[23]

Relying on this discussion of OPROVIA, we argue that the Rwandan elite never really cared to set up a functioning food marketing system. Pottier (1993, 27) is right on the mark when he writes that

> It may even be fair to suggest that the slow progress—in food marketing—was yet another illustration of how policy makers tend to regard improved nutritional status as the by-product of agricultural strategies rather than a goal in its own right.[24]

This is exactly what we have been saying when discussing the peasant ideology of the Habyarimana regime in the first chapter: the regime considered the peasants as producers (of food and coffee), not as consumers. The leadership did not equip OPROVIA with the means to succesfully secure access to food for the destitute; it did not pay back debts; it banned food imports and increased food exports; it professed to secure the income of the peasants and considered the application of more labor to agriculture as the solution.

5.4.2 The Non-response of the Habyarimana Regime

The crop failure that struck several communes in Butare and Gikongoro prefectures in 1989 was the result of a five year period of drought (starting in 1984) from which the region never really recovered. The drought was so severe in 1989 that the roots of crops turned into ash. Crop failure however does not necessarily lead

---

[21] Republic of Rwanda, Compte-rendu de la Réunion tenue au Minagri en date du 02/05/1989 sur la situation alimentaire du Rwanda en Avril 1989, Ministry of Agriculture, p. 4.

[22] Republic of Rwanda, Compte-rendu, p. 4.

[23] I refer to Ravallion, M., Markets and Famines, 1987 for an exploration of the price effects of information.

[24] Pottier, ibidem, p. 27.

to famine. Several circumstances can avert famine. If a population has other sources of income outside farming, famine can be averted by using market mechanisms. The population affected by crop failure will buy the necessary food items on the market. Policy measures averting famine are well-kwown. The government can temporarily employ people in public works (as e.g. in India), the government can hand out food aid to vulnerable people, the government can allow aid organisations to hand out food, to name just a few policy measures. The literature on famines also suggests that the government stop taxing poor people struck by crop failure. Governments are also advised to stop requiring mandatory labour dues and school fees. These measures will not avert shortages, but will help to ease the burden of a crop failure. None of the aformentioned measures were taken by the Habyarimana government in 1989.[25]

Devereux (1993) writes that non-response to famine (not giving food aid nor taking other measures to avoid famine) is to allow a 'Malthusian final solution' to happen, namely to equilibrate population with resources. For an analysis of Habyarimana's Malthusian concerns, I refer to the Chap. 2. When he visited the famine struck region in March 1990 the president not only said that he didn't know what was going on in this region—that he was not informed of this—but he also describes the situation as a production problem (*«une manque de production»*). The causes of the famine according to the president were the following: not enough rain in certain regions, too much rain in other regions and insects. He said that there is a shortage of land because of population growth and that the communes that are most struck are those who are most densely inhabited.

The president pleads for a solution that will conquer this problem for the future to come.[26] In his speech, the president also offers a number of solutions to the problem: food aid distribution, means to increase production, agrarian reform, a better knowledge of the problem of population growth and rural development policies.

Do the Malthusian believes of president Habyarimana explain his non-response to the famine? He indeed refers to land shortage and population growth as one of the causes of the famine. But there were also other motivations. For as we have seen, man-made famine can be intentional or non-intentional. Whereas the direct cause of the crop failure in Southern Rwanda was a long lasting drought, the relationship between crop failure and famine is far more complex. The underlying reasons for a crop failure to develop into a famine are identified by a political

---

[25] The 1990 report of the Caritas Social Bureau states that (p. 26) it would be useful to suppress several mandatory taxes such as the personal tax, the tax on cattle, diverse contributions to the MRND, to the communal projects,…and voluntary contributions to the Red Cross, the Church and so on. The fact that this NGO is giving this advice, is a serious indication that these taxes continued to be levied during the period of the famine. I refer to Chap. 2 for my treatment of taxation under Habyarimana.

[26] Habyarimana, J, Speech on Famine in Rwanda, Mars 22, 1990, published in Kinyamateka, N° 1319, Mars II, 1990, pp. 10-11.

economy analysis. When actual starvation occurs on a more or less grand scale, immediate measures can be taken to relief the starving population. I will now discuss the non-intervention and the reasons behind this.

The Rwandan government did not react to the crop failure, it did not provide food or other aid (only 9 months after the peak in June 1989) and thus allowed a crop failure to develop into famine. The height of the famine occurred in June 1989, when the price of beans rose to 60 RWF per kilo. The regime did not mention the famine, no government agency or ministry reacted to it. In February 1990, the Belgian newspaper «La Libre Belgique» reports that Rwandans are fleeing to Tanzania because of famine. The Rwandan Ambassador in Belgian denied this saying that they are migrating because of lack of cultivable land in Rwanda. Only from mid-March 1990, after the publication of a documentary film about the famine, the government started providing food aid. Although famine conditions became evident from March 1989 onwards, government disbursed aid only one year later. IWACU, a non-governmental co-operative organisation, made a documentary film explicitly to prove that famine existed in the country.[27] The government was indeed denying that famine existed. Other sources that documented famine are mentioned in the Appendix to this chapter.

The refusal to accept that famine struck Southern Rwanda had everything to do with the ruling principle of food self-sufficiency. Acknowledging that famine existed would have been the same as saying that Rwanda could not feed itself, the latter being the flagship policy objective of the Habyarimana's regime. Famine was the ultimate proof that a policy of food-self-sufficiency at the household, communal and national level did not protect households and regions from famine. The government thus refused to acknowledge that its policy had failed.[28] In order to prevent the outside world from getting information about the famine, the government tried to prevent journalists from entering the famine region and writing about it. A Belgian journalist was told by security chief Augustin Nduwayezu not to write articles which irritated the highest authorities.[29] The government did not accept aid from foreign governments or international organisations.[30] This strategy may have been adopted to avoid disruption of domestic production. But then it should have provided relief from domestic sources, by organising food transport from food surplus to food deficit regions. As we have shown earlier in this chapter, by the time of the famine in Southern Rwanda, Northern and Eastern Rwanda were not experiencing a decline in food production. Nevertheless, no transport of food was organised.

---

[27] Iwacu, personal conversation, Kigali, August 12, 2000.

[28] During one interview, a respondent told the author that the Rwandan bureaucrats under Habyarimana were used to tell their superiors only the things that pleased them, hiding real problems. While this attitude may have retarded the reaction of the regime, one cannot conclude from this that the president was uninformed about the famine.

[29] Prunier (1995, pp. 87–88).

[30] Iwacu, personal conversation, Kigali, August 12, 2000.

Besides not wanting to admit policy failures in the face of the stated self-sufficiency objectives, the non-response of the Habyarimana government also had other reasons. A second reason for the regime to passively allow the population to starve was that the people living in the famine struck region had never been in favour of Habyarimana. The president was considered as a man from the North who had shown no interest in the improvement of the living conditions of the population in Southern Rwanda including Butare and Gikongoro. In the presidential elections held in December 1988, in which officially 99 % of the population voted in favor of the sole candidate, Habyarimana, the population of Gikongoro had voted en masse against the president.[31] According to one of our interviewees, a long term and well-informed resident of Gikongoro, this result awoke the anger of the president. Nsengiyaremye (1992) writes that the elections were rigged: in Gikongoro, the préfet did not even count the votes, but declared that Habyarimana got 100 % of the vote, which was the target set by Habyarimana's supporters.[32]

In addition, it is known that during his regime people from the south (Hutu as well as Tutsi) did not get promoted in the administration. All senior posts went to people from Habyarimana's own region. Fr. Nzamurambaho for example, a popular politician from Gikongoro and a former minister of Agriculture wanted to present himself in the November 1988 legislative elections. He was removed from the list of candidates without any explanation. The president, everybody knew, only wanted people who depended on him and who were completely loyal to him.[33]

Thirdly, the famine-struck prefectures, Gikongoro and parts of Butare, and especially the part of both these prefectures that was used to be called Nyaruguru, had a large Tutsi population. Several sources indicate that, by 1989 or even earlier, president Habyarimana was informed of the probability of a military invasion of Rwanda by the RPF. This can be documented as follows. In May 1989, at the summit of Nyagatare, the president of Uganda, Museveni, told Habyarimana that he had better solve the refugee problem if he wanted to avoid a military attack.[34] People all over Uganda were talking of a possible attack. One can assume that Habyarimana's secret service also monitored the build up of the rebel movement. In 1988, Tutsi in the diaspora had held a major conference in Washington DC. One of the conclusions of this conference was the desire and the right to return. As early as 1987, Tutsi leaders in the diaspora were fundraising for an invasion.[35] The embassies of Rwanda in Kampala, Nairobi, Addis-Abeba and Washington had

---

[31]   Interview, Kigali, August 13, 2000. Unofficial results say that in 1988, 78–90% of the population voted against Habyarimana in December 1988. Another informant told us that the Gikongoro population already voted against the president in the 1978 election.

[32]   Nsengiyaremye (1995, p. 242).

[33]   Nsengiyaremye, ibidem, p. 242.

[34]   Nsengiyaremye, ibidem p.247 and interview, Kigali, August 14, 2000.

[35]   Adelman and Suhrke (1999).

warned the Rwandan government of the preparations for an invasion.[36] In 1989, at the high point of the famine in Southern Rwanda, a fraction of the RPF made an abortive attack in north Rwanda. Ogetunnu writes that Habyarimana's intelligence service had several officers from the RPF on its payroll in order to sow division inside the RPF. This means that even before the famine was under way, Habyarimana knew of the build up of RPF forces in Uganda.

Therefore, the question is whether information on an upcoming civil war influenced the decision not to intervene in Gikongoro in 1989. Had the presidential clan already made up its mind in 1989, to consider the Tutsi inside Rwanda as accomplices of the RPF and thus as enemies of his regime? In the event of an RPF attack, Habyarimana may have anticipated that young Tutsi from Rwanda would join the RPF forces (which eventually happened). The author interviewed several survivors from the genocide in Gikongoro who confirmed that a number of young men from Gikongoro joined the RPF before the 1990 attack.[37] Moreover, the regime's leadership considered Gikongoro prefecture quasi-lost to the RPF as it would be very easy to penetrate the prefecture from Burundian territory through Nyungwe forest. There is an extra reason related to this war strategy. If Habyarimana anticipated an upcoming civil war, he could preserve the country's food stocks (however small they may have been) for his own soldiers.

A.1 Appendix 1

Figure 5.3

A.2 Appendix 2

Published sources documenting famine in Southern Rwanda

One of the most interesting examples of the documentation of the food crisis in southern Rwanda is a film. In February 1990, a group of researchers working with IWACU, a cooperative organisation working in the rural areas, produced a film, "Haguma Amagara" which means "you only live once". The film was a response of this grass-roots organisation to the silence of the Habyarimana regime. Since the regime refused to acknowledge the famine, which in February 1990 was already going on for more then eight months, IWACU decided to film the evidence. The film shows poor peasants in southern Rwanda having nothing to eat, showing markets without products, peasants deconstructing their houses to sell the parts for food, peasants migrating to other parts of Rwanda and to Burundi, hungry children

---

[36] Nsengiyaremye, ibidem, p. 247.

[37] Interview, Kigali, October 12, 2000.

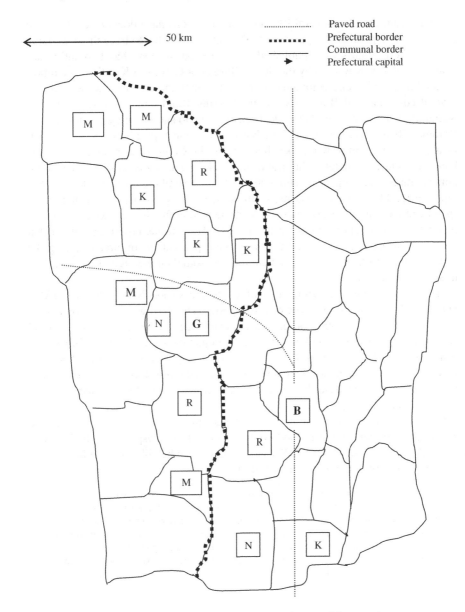

Fig. 5.3 Famine struck region in Butare en Gikongoro prefectures. Most struck communes are indicated with their first letter: in Gikongoro:Mubuga, Rwamiko, Nyamagabe, Kinyamakara, Mudasomwa, Karama,Karambo, Rukondo, Musango, Muko; in Butare : Nyakizu, Runyinya, Kigembe

and mothers, adult males who are telling the film-maker that they are to weak to work. The film indeed documents hunger in southern Rwanda in the 1989–1990 period.

Apart from the film, several Rwandan organisations have documented the food crisis and have published reports on it. The author was able to trace three valuable reports. These reports were published over a period of more than two and a half years. The first was written by the Social Bureau of Caritas in Kigali.[38] The report cites administrative and communal sources documenting hunger and starvation in several communes of Butare (Nyakizu, Runyinya) and Gikongoro (Nyamagabe, Karama). It counts the number of death people due to starvation by commune: 5 in Karama, 30 in Nyakizu and 107 in Nyamagabe. On top, 2,316 people had left Nyakizu to find food or work elsewhere (p. 3) . In Runyinya commune, about one hundred children had left school and 500 in Karama. Many husbands had temporarily migrated. Crops were stolen at night and several cases of suicide had been reported (p. 11). Peasants also report the absence of solidarity among neigbours (p. 19). In Gikongoro, peasants hoped that the next coffee harvest would be good, if not they would starve to death (p. 16–17). The Caritas report concluded that there was nothing to eat anymore in the south, peasants were already eating the leaves and the roots of their plants. Peasants had sold their belongings at low prices to secure some cash.

The second report was written by staff of the grass-roots NGO called CCOAIB, but the author could not get hold of this report.[39] The third was a report on a local agricultural survey of 300 households in several communes by the Agricultural Development Project in Gikongoro. This project was run by the Ministry of Agriculture.[40] This report stated that 25 % of the surveyed households were indigent and that female headed households suffered more. Two of the reports used the word 'famine' to describe the food crisis in Southern Rwanda and the third spoke of starvation.

Kinyamateka, the most important independent newspaper in Rwanda, also published information on the food crisis in 1989. The newspaper's articles infact made the famine known to the Rwandan public. André Sibomana, editor of the newspaper in 1989, expressed it as follows:

> In 1989, a terrible famine struck the south of the country. There was a natural explanation for this phenomenon, but the authorities did nothing to improve the situation. Worse still, I had evidence that part of the government's assistance which was intended for the population at risk had been diverted. It was a scandal. I decided to publish this information. We were threatened and we were called liars, until I published photographs which were overwhelming. This had an immediate effect. Readers wrote into express their satisfaction: at last the truth was being told.[41]

---

[38] *Les Retombées de la Famine dans les Préfectures de Butare et de Gikongoro*, Bureau Social Urbain-Caritas, Kigali, Février 1990, 26 p.

[39] Twizeyimana and Uwimana (1989, 43 p).

[40] Gascon (1992, 62 p)

[41] Sibomana (1999, p. 22.)

	87a		87b		88a		88b		89a	
	prod	%p	prod	%p	prod	%p	prod	%p	prod	%p
Ruhengeri	26775	40	23020	43.2	29377	32.7	21164	50.9	27770	44.5
Butare	31285	35.6	30707	37.9	27111	39.4	30168	41.2	24627	46.3
Buymba	29323	40	35121	28.6	28142	37.8	30474	36.0	26012	50.5
Cyangugu	24833	45.8	25240	36.9	25447	36.1	24550	39.8	21699	60.0
Gikongoro	19796	62.7	19137	64.3	18744	65.5	19043	59.5	13347	81.3
Gisenyi	23710	59.1	20137	71.2	26934	53.6	17799	73.6	22771	60.2
Gitarama	33396	25.4	38733	21.4	33271	25.9	34245	27.5	33639	25.8
Kibungo	35617	15.7	39722	14.5	34305	19.0	39361	11.9	38661	24.2
Kibuye	25803	55.4	15584	78.6	29583	48.2	14906	75.6	20064	63.5
Kigali	35419	26.8	47539	22.9	38964	23.0	44777	30.9	40727	21.7
Rwanda	29171	39.3	30702	40.1	29684	37.1	28693	43.5	27589	45.8
N	1073		1089		1076		1075		1211	

	89b		90a		90b		91a		91b	
	prod	%p	prod	%p	prod	%p	prod	%p	prod	%p
Ruhengeri	22030	66.9	26636	57.0	24089	56.3	28499	48.8	21937	59.7
Butare	27612	48.7	22760	55.5	24484	55.2	16399	66.9	20697	59.6
Buymba	31073	42.9	31003	44.9	33185	42.2	-	-	-	-
Cyangugu	22910	57.3	19492	63.2	17604	69.5	19571	71.4	17299	68.9
Gikongoro	9853	86.2	10014	86.2	12699	81.9	13848	83.5	12102	80.7
Gisenyi	14036	80.0	22855	64.1	15839	73.4	17761	69.8	14215	76.9
Gitarama	38299	25.9	32070	29.3	32879	29.1	25845	45.1	31268	40.3
Kibungo	52659	22.1	44268	27.1	39231	22.1	34216	34.1	32380	32.3
Kibuye	11123	82.3	17866	64.1	11846	89.4	16855	73.3	11624	85.9
Kigali	52922	18.2	41386	24.7	37629	28.8	30635	38.5	37186	30.7
Rwanda	29247	50.9	27691	49.5	25935	52.4	23072	57.1	23687	56.3
N	1202		1230		1230		1038		1022	

Fig. 5.4 Value of production in 10 seasons

A.3 Appendix 3

Production for these 10 seasons is the value of total production of 8 crops: bananas, potatoes, sweet potatoes, beans, mais, peas, sorghum and manoic. %p is the percentage of households that has a value of production lower then 2/3 of the mean value of production in Rwanda in 1987a. This mean value was 19.447 RWF (Fig. 5.4).

Chapter 6
The 1990–1992 Massacres: A Case of Spatial and Social Engineering?

6.1 Introduction

Between 1990 and 1992, around 2,000 Tutsi civilians were killed in a number of massacres that were perpetrated in Rwanda—mainly in the north-west of the country, but also in the south-eastern region of Bugesera. These massacres, while denied at the time by the local and national authorities, have been well documented and are now considered a part of our body of knowledge concerning the 1990–1992 period of Rwandan history. Thanks to several high-profile publications on human-rights violations in Rwanda, there is no doubt that these massacres indeed took place.[1] According to reports by diplomats and human rights organisations, the anti-Tutsi pogroms of 1990, 1991 and 1992 were in fact organized by the national and local authorities. These pogroms, which occurred in several different communes, took place in locations that had been carefully chosen by the national leaders. The leadership mobilized the Hutu peasants by spreading rumours (fabricated stories) in order to install fear and incite Hutu hatred. One report, dated

Verwimp, Philip (2011), The 1990–92 Massacres in Rwanda: a case of spatial and social engineering? Journal of Agrarian Change, Vol. 11, n. 3, July, pp. 396–419.
© Blackwell Publishing Ltd 2011

[1] The four most cited reports on human-rights violations that focus on, and were published during, this period are: (1) International Commission on Human Rights Violations in Rwanda since October 1990 (FIDH, March 1993), which implicates the country's highest-level authorities in the organisation of the killing of 2,000 Tutsi in several locations throughout Rwanda; (2) the report published by the US Department of State in February 1993 which describes the massacres of the Bagogwe (January 1991) and of the Tutsi in Bugesera (March 1992) (in March 1991, the US Department of State had already published a report on the January 1991 massacre); (3) two reports published by the Rwandan human-rights group ADL in December 1992 and December 1993, respectively, which describe in detail several massacres and instances of human rights violations against the Tutsi; and (4) the report by the UN special rapporteur on Rwanda that was released in August 1993, which maintains that these massacres comply with the international definition of genocide.

March 1993, has discussed the applicability of the term 'genocide' to the killings that had already taken place prior to that date, while another, published in August 1993, argues that the killings comply with the international definition of genocide.

With regard to the interpretation of the massacres, particularly their *cause(s)*, the scholarly community is in disagreement. Generally speaking, two main sets of arguments have been put forth in order to explain the massacres that were committed in Rwanda in the period between October 1st, 1990 and April 6th, 1994. The first one, formulated in slightly different versions by René Lemarchand, Filip Reyntjens and Scott Strauss (among others) maintains that these massacres were linked to the war (Reyntjens 1994); constituted a rational response to attacks by the Rwandan Patriotic Front (RPF) on the part of a population that felt threatened (Lemarchand 2002); or constituted a response to RPF attacks by the government and the local authorities in a context of war, insecurity and political uncertainty (Strauss 2006).

All these authors have in common the fact that they place the war in the centre of their explanations of the massacres—whether this is presented as having been exacerbated by fear on the part of the population, in some versions, or driven by a response on the part of the leadership with a view to re-establishing order, in other versions. Lemarchand adds that the response on the part of the peasant population had a spontaneous character: 'They had no other choice but to kill in order not to be killed'. Strauss applies this line of reasoning not only to the 1994 genocide and the 1990–1992 massacres, but also to those that were perpetrated in late December 1962—at which time between 5,000 and 10,000 Tutsi civilians were brutally put to death in the province of Gikongoro. According to Strauss (2006, 184–188) this latter massacre took place in reaction to an attack on Kigali via Bugesera (in the province of Rural Kigali) by armed Tutsi.

The second set of arguments regards these massacres as trial runs in preparation for the 1994 genocide. In her seminal book on the Rwandan genocide, Alison Des Forges writes that '[t]o execute a campaign against Tutsi effectively took practice. Before the grim background of war, economic distress, violent political competition, insecurity and impunity, and to the accompaniment of virulent propaganda, radicals staged the practice for the catastrophe to come. The rehearsals took place in more than a dozen communities' (1999, 87).

With the benefit of hindsight, these massacres may seem like pilot runs or rehearsals leading up to the 1994 genocide, but this latter event cannot be considered a satisfactory explanation for events that preceded it. Rather, the explanation for the 1990–1992 events needs to be sought in facts and events that either took place at the same time as these massacres or preceded them. Des Forges (1999, 87–88) argues that the massacres were organized by Habyarimana and his supporters, and adds that the regime used ethnic violence to its advantage. At a time when Habyarimana was facing military and political threats, these massacres strengthened his position, fostered Hutu solidarity and rallied the Hutu behind a united cause. This author's analysis portrays these massacres as having been perpetrated for instrumental reasons (in order to consolidate power, heighten ethnic tensions and polarize society), which is in stark contrast to the proponents of the 'war argument', for whom the massacres were a desperate expedient, a price that had to be paid and a response to prior attacks that had disturbed peace and order.

In order to understand why it was that the regime organized attacks on Tutsi citizens from the very beginning of the civil war, it is necessary to look at the details of the massacres that were perpetrated prior to 1994. For this, it is useful to draw on the report published in March 1993 by the International Commission of Human Rights Investigators—a group of experts who investigated several of the massacres that took place in Rwanda in January of that year. This report provides a wealth of detail on these massacres and, in this paper, special attention is given to the sequence of events in each of these early massacres.

It is probably futile to look for one *single* objective or explanation behind the massacre policy of 1990–1992. It is highly likely that several different factors played significant roles at the time—including the threat posed by the RPF and the governments' wish to show its resolve, consolidate its power and foster Hutu solidarity. In view of the arguments put forth in the literature, however, one major factor is arguably missing in the discussion: the peasant ideology professed and practiced by the Habyarimana regime. Taking the latter into account allows for an alternative explanation of the massacres, or at least for a richer interpretation of the motivation behind the massacres. This third interpretation is as follows: the Habyarimana regime had adopted a policy of agricultural extensification—turning all available land, such as pastures, marshes and forests, into cultivable land—as opposed to a policy of intensification. In Rwanda, this policy came up against the land frontier in the late 1980s, i.e. all the land had by then been converted to agricultural activity. In their turn, pastoralist groups like the Hima and the Bagogwe used land as pastures for their cattle, living off the cattle itself and the trade in meat and dairy products. They did not cultivate and were therefore considered a non-agricultural group. Under the predominant ideology of the Second Republic, which portrayed itself as a Peasant-State, pastoral groups were marginalized, and pastoral lands were converted into land for cultivation and into *paysannats*—the prime agrarian settlement scheme. Pastoralism as a way of life did not fit within the agrarian order of the Second Republic, which was built on a vision of hard-working smallholder peasants.[2] The regime used the opportunities provided by the civil war in order to claim the last remaining parcels of land by finishing off the remnants of pastoralism in Rwanda. Therefore, these massacres can be described as instances of ethnic cleansing. The point was not that the Hima, the Bagogwe and the Tutsi owned cattle (for many rich Hutu and the dignitaries of the Habyarimana regime did so, too), but that their pastoralist livelihood did not fit in the Peasant-State. One can romanticize peasant cultivation, but when such an ideology is combined with racism towards ethnic groups regarded as non-peasant, such as the Tutsi, it can assume an extremely violent character.[3] This interpretation is supported by the socio-economic

---

[2] For an institutionalist and political economy perspective to conflict between agriculture and pastoralism I refer to Platteau (2001) and to Salih et al. (2001).

[3] For a discussion of the link between romanticism and violence I refer to Kiernan (2007).

geography of the massacres, and for that reason this chapter seeks to draw attention to the spatial dimensions of violent conflict.[4]

A.M. Brandstetter is one of the few scholars that have analysed the peasant ideology of the regime. In her 2001 article on purity and violence in Rwanda, she puts forth the argument that the 1994 genocide was an act of purification of the body politic whereby the sons of the soil (the peasants) sought to clear the bush. Although this author did not address the 1990–1992 massacres, nor examined the agrarian re-settlement schemes, my own analysis has many aspects in common with hers. For example, she argues that 'the genocide, through its violence, was meant to implement the exclusion of the pastoralists from the project to constitute an agrarian society' (Brandstetter 2001, 68, author's translation from the German text). In their turn, Bézy (1990) and Newbury (1992), writing on rural development in Rwanda, have highlighted the limitations of the extensive land policy: agricultural production was increased only because more land was taken into cultivation, not due to agricultural innovations or intensification. By the end of the 1980s, the physical land frontier had been reached: there was no more land available to be taken into cultivation (Bézy 1990; Newbury 1992).

6.2 Population, Space and Settlements

Rwanda's history can be traced through the management and settlement of land, driven by political power on the one hand and population growth on the other. As long as Tutsi held political power, they earmarked land for pastures. When that power disappeared, the land was turned into agricultural land. Habyarimana was not against cattle, presumably he recognized the value of having a cow for dung as fertilizer. The point made by Bart (1993, 185) is that he disfavoured the traditional way of holding cattle, meaning herding a lot of cattle that grazed on pastures. For him this was an inefficient use of the land.

The reorganization of agrarian space, land settlement in the *paysannats* (organized settlement schemes), *umuganda* (mandatory communal labour), the development of the five-year plans as well as the nationwide anti-erosion campaign are part of the agrarian developmental state that Rwanda became under the Second Republic. The developmental state was organized much in the same way as mapped out by James Scott in his 1998 book *Seeing Like a State*. Scott characterizes four elements constituting disastrous social engineering: the administrative ordering of nature and society, or its 'legibility'; a high modernist ideology; an authoritarian state; and a prostrate civil society (described in the Chap. 1). Ethnic cleansing may be considered as an especially extreme form of social

---

[4] See, for example, Raleigh et al. (2010); also see Nathan (2005).

engineering.[5] This occurs when the social engineers not only regard space, land, cattle and settlements as malleable factors, but the size and the composition of the population itself.

The power of the state was used to remodel agrarian space, register and control the population and replace politics by development. But it did not stop there. Social planners considered the size and the composition of the population as malleable factors, both at the local level and the national level. This is best illustrated by the rural to rural migration and resettlement into *paysannats* settlement schemes.

The Habyarimana regime promoted internal rural-to-rural migration and resettlement from densely populated to less densely populated areas. In this way, newly colonized land as well as land previously earmarked for pasture was transformed into agricultural land. Olson (1990, 150) who studied migration patterns in Rwanda, writes that:

> After independence, increasing population pressure resulted in changing economic circumstances, such as rapid decline in farm sizes and available land per person. One response was a high rate of out-migration from the areas experiencing the most pressure. The destination of these migrants was influenced by political factors; the government was interested in settling land previously used for pastoral activities so it promoted organized settlement schemes in the East.

A specific agricultural settlement scheme, the *paysannat*, was part of this resettlement plan. Farm households were given a plot of land which they could cultivate on condition that part of the plot, specified in a contract, was allocated to an export crop such as coffee or pyrethrum. The latter was grown in the province of Ruhengeri on land in Mukingo commune previously used as pastures by the Bagogwe (see below). The contract stipulated that division, fractionalisation or renting out of the plot was not allowed (art. 4) and that upon signing the contract and at the latest six months after, the holder renounces his rights to previously held land and pastures (Bart 1993, 406, author's translation). While the farmers in the *paysannats* were in general better equipped (water tanks, pipes, mills, silos) and monitored (1 agricultural monitor per 120 instead of 750 households), this kind of contract was not compatible with the traditional way of living of Rwanda's farmers, in particular in terms of marriage and inheritance. As a consequence Bart found married couples still living with their parents. He also found many absentee owners (traders, army officers, civil servants) benefiting from the settlement scheme without residing in it.[6]

The First and Second Republics vastly expanded the area devoted to the *paysannats* and the people living in them, allowing Bart (1993, 91) to write that 1/

---

[5] We refer to Michael Mann (2005) for a treatment of the common ethnic cleansing roots of many advanced democracies and to Mark Mazower (1998) on mass population movements and forms of ethnic cleansing in Europe in the 20th century.

[6] The Belgian administration for development cooperation, assessed that the costs of the paysannats are out of proportion with the benefits (Bart 1993, 405).

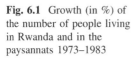 **Fig. 6.1** Growth (in %) of the number of people living in Rwanda and in the paysannats 1973–1983

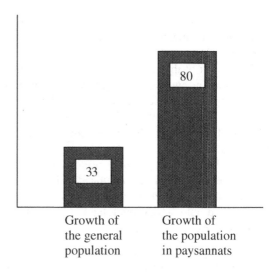

Growth of   Growth of
the general   the population
population   in paysannats

20 farmers now live in such a settlement scheme. The authorities used the scheme to put in place a coherent policy of land colonisation and control of internal migration. At the regional level the *paysannats* dominate the landscape and the communes in which they are implemented. During the first 10 years of Habyarimana's presidency (1973–1983), the number of households living in *paysannats* increased from 30,000 to 54,000 (250,000 people, see Fig. 6.1 below, Bart 1993, 393), with the bulk of the increase in the first 5 years and with a new *paysannat* in Mutara (Byumba province). Jean-Claude Willame (1995, p. 136) writes that the authorities associated the *paysannat* schemes and the projects for integrated rural development with the Hutu Revolution. This was a short cut from the side of the authorities because the *paysannat* settlement schemes already existed before independence and were a product of the colonial regime. It does show, however, how much the First and Second Republics continued these schemes and considered them *their* policy.

   The population that came to live in the *paysannats* originated from the most densely populated or poorest areas of Rwanda (Gisenyi and Ruhengeri in the north and Butare and Gikongoro in the south). They left their ancestral rural land to become modern farmers in a new environment prepared and managed by the state. Map 6.1 gives the example for the region of Bugesera. Francois Bart (1993, p. 395), in his seminal book on the geography of Rwandan agriculture, writes that farm households from densely populated areas in Rwanda came to live in the *paysannats*, sometimes mixed with locals. All those residing in the *paysannats*, however had to adapt their way of living to the new settlement scheme. This meant:

> In Masaka, in the paysannat of Icyanya; most of the 92 pastoralist households stayed and accepted the new conditions thereby changing progressively their way of living. In the paysannat in Ntongwe, in Mayaya, 11 out of 20 interviewed households declared to be originating from the hill where from 1966 onwards the paysannat was established. They

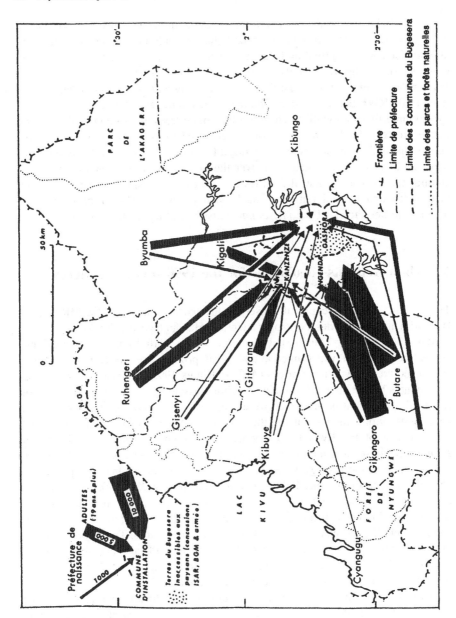

Map 6.1 Internal migration paths and the colonisation of the Bugesera, *source* Bart (1993)

said that the authorities obliged them to move their house alongside the new road. In this case, the paysannat presents itself as an enterprise for the remodelling of the pre-existing agrarian structure. Essentially, it proceeds with the colonisation of new land more than the reshaping of existing land structures.

During fieldwork on the origins of the genocide in the province of Gitarama in 2004 (see Chaps. 9 and 10), we found that the administration appointed an agronomist and an agricultural surveyor per commune as well as agricultural monitors (i.e. extension agents) who were assigned to three cells at a time.[7] Farmers who did not follow careful maintenance practices were punished with a fine of 100 RWF per coffee tree. The agronomist and agricultural monitors came two to three times a month to check on the coffee trees and to punish delinquent coffee growers. In the area we visited there used to be a *paysannat* where the agronomist and the monitors also organized the weekly *umuganda*. Consequently, they had a lot of sway and power over the people in the *paysannat*. The agricultural surveyor had a list of families to visit each season to collect data about their fields and to find out how much each produced. This information was recorded to keep track of the *paysannat* statistics and agricultural records.

6.3 Main Activists-Ideologues for the 1990–1992 Massacres

The activities of three people, all closely connected with the top of the MRND and Habyarimana himself, deserve closer attention: Hassan Ngeze, Léon Mugesera and Ferdinand Nahimana. The journal *Kangura*, which started publishing anti-Tutsi articles in May 1990, was printed at a state-run printing press in Kigali, receiving subsidized credit or reduced prices (African Rights 1995). In its June 1990 issue, four months before the start of the war, editor Hassan Ngeze claimed that 70 % of Rwanda's prominent businessmen were Tutsi. He also wrote that these rich Tutsi collaborate with refugees outside the country.[8] The theme of Tutsi wealth and Tutsi control of the Rwandan economy would come up in many editions of *Kangura* in subsequent months and years. In December 1990, two months before the massacre of the Bagogwe (see below), the 'Ten Commandments' (part of an 'Appel à la conscience des Bahutu') were published in *Kangura*. The text is a racist anti-Tutsi statement, prescribing rules of behaviour for all Hutu in their interaction with Tutsi. It argues that all Hutu who have Tutsi wives, Tutsi concubines and all Hutu who do business with Tutsi are traitors. The *Appel* says that the Tutsi inside Rwanda are the accomplices of the RPF and that the enemy is among us. These messages were very effective in arousing fear of the Tutsi and brought home the message that 'the enemy is among us'.

Ferdinand Nahimana was a university professor of history before he became director of ORINFOR, the state agency for information. He was already 'active' in 1973 on the Butare campus *Committee du Salut Public* which implemented the

---

[7] A cell was the smallest administrative unit in Rwanda consisting of between 50 and 100 families. For an analysis of the results of the field work we refer to Pinchotti and Verwimp (2007).

[8] Kangura June 1990, No. 3, p. 3.

expulsion of Tutsi students and professors from the university. In 1988 he published a book on Rwandan culture and development in which he explained and glorified Habyarimana's approach to development and to the peasantry. In his book, *umuganda* is described as a virtuous practice deeply ingrained in Rwandan culture and tradition.[9] Under his leadership Radio Rwanda was openly racist. In February 1993 Nahimana advocated a civilian defence force made up of young people. He stressed the usefulness of such a popular force to safeguard the peace inside the country.[10] In August 1993 Nahimana became head of RTLM, the notorious hate radio.

Léon Mugesera was vice-president of the MRND in Gisenyi. In November 1992 he gave a speech in Gaseke commune that would resonate nationally because of its racist content.[11] In the speech he rhetorically asked whether the Hutu were waiting for the *Inyenzi* (cockroaches) to come and kill them. We made a fatal mistake in 1959, he said, by allowing the Tutsi to leave. If the judicial authorities do not act against RPF accomplices, he said, the population must take matters in their own hand. He asked whether his audience knew that the Falasha (Ethiopia's Jewish population) returned to Israel and suggested that the Tutsi should be sent to their homeland Ethiopia via the Nyabarongo river. He started and ended his speech with a salute to president Habyarimana who never disavowed the content or the speaker. He also attacked Hutu of other parties who were negotiating with the RPF and called them *Inyenzi* talking with other *Inyenzi*. He blamed the Hutu of other parties for the loss of Byumba to the RPF. Hutu should not allow themselves 'to be invaded'. Mugesera ended his speech with a call for unity: 'we must all rise, act as one person'. Strauss (2006, 197) interprets this speech as a call for retaliation, self-defence and deterrence.

That Mugesera's speech was understood as a 'program' is confirmed by the words of the burgomaster of Kibilira (see below) who said that that the program announced by Mugesera would be continued. Ngeze, Mugesera and Nahimana were seen by everybody as acting on behalf of Rwanda's leadership. They owed their jobs to their MRND mentors and were die-hard ideologues of the cause. They incited hatred among the population with impunity, which could only mean that they were protected from above.

---

[9] Nahimana, F., 1988, *Conscience chez-nous, Confiance en nous: notre culture est la base de notre development harmonieux*, Ruhengeri, Presse National du Rwanda. The author states that the book has been published with the support of the presidency of the MRND and the Ministry of Education and Scientific Research. In 1990, an official MRND publication even goes a step further when it deplores that the value of umuganda was lost through contact with the coloniser and in particular because of the introduction of money, the generalisation of education and salaried employment. Translated from the French version in *Umuganda dans le developpement National*, MRND, Kigali, 1990, p. 10. (see Chap. 1).

[10] Human Rights Watch 1999, *Leave None to tell the Story*, p. 110.

[11] Speech by Léon Mugesera before the militants of the MRND, sous-préfecture de Kabaya, Gisenyi, 22 November 1992, mimeo, translation from the French version to English by the author.

6.4 The Massacres Committed Between October 1990 and Mid-1992

6.4.1 Mass Imprisonment Right After the Start of the War in October 1990

It is highly likely that Rwanda's intelligence service informed Habyarimana of the upcoming attack by the RPF (Adelman and Suhrke 1996, 20). Already in May 1989, at the summit of Nyagatare, the Ugandan president Museveni had warned Habyarimana of a potential invasion.[12] This means that the regime could prepare itself for the attack. The 'preparation', however, was not a military one, as one would expect. Des Forges (1999, 49) writes that the Rwandan commander at the border, aware of the pending invasion, demanded reinforcements from head-quarters. He got none, leading him and others to speculate that Habyarimana wanted the invasion. Apart from soliciting French military support (and thus drawing in foreign powers in the conflict) few military preparations were made. Asked by the author why the regime did not fight the rebels more forcefully (it is well-known that the war between the RPF and the FAR was a low-intensity war with a limited number of battles and a limited number of casualties), a person close to Habyarimana answered 'I believe Habyarimana counted on the population'.[13] We encounter here the notion that 'the population or the people' will at one point come to the rescue of the Nation, embodied in the figure of the president. We will come back to this below when we discuss ideology.

Only three days after the attack, the regime launched a faked attack on the capital Kigali which allowed it, under the veil of assuring security, to round-up 8,000–10,000 people and put them in prison.[14] Many of them were Tutsi businessmen and intellectuals. They were held without charge in deplorable conditions for several months, they were tortured and several dozen died in prison.[15] It was not the first time that the regime rounded up many people in Kigali. In the mid-eighties it launched a campaign against 'loose women' by taking young girls from the street who were accused of being prostitutes and transported them to a re-education camp (Jefremovas 1991).

---

[12] Nsengiyaremye, D., La Transition Démocratique au Rwanda (1989–1993), in Guichaoua, A., ibidem, p. 247.

[13] Interview, Kigali, November 2000.

[14] Strauss (2006, 192) doubts that the faked attack was intentional and argues that it may have been caused by panicky soldier firing.

[15] De Standard, 1990, 15 october 1990; Reyntjens (1994, 95); Desforges (1999, 49).

6.4.2 The Hima of Mutara (Savannah in North–East Byumba)

Until 1972 several groups of pastoralists, the Hima, lived as a nomadic people with their herds of cattle in the savannah of Mutara, in the north of the prefecture of Byumba, in the communes of Muvumba and Ngarama. In August and September 1973, 4,762 Burundian refugees were installed in Mutara, near the church of Rukomo (Bart 1993, 397). Their settlement site was known as the *paysannat* of the Barundi and it marked the beginning of the colonisation of the Mutara region. From 1974 onwards Office pour la Valorisation Pastorale et Agricole du Mutara (OVAPAM), a large integrated project installed 11,850 families in an area of 37,000 ha (Bart 1993, 526). The pasture land was organized into ranches where the cattle owners were taught modern livestock techniques. In order to benefit from these services, the pastoralists had to sign a contract in which they renounced their rights to other land and agreed to follow the instructions given by OVAPAM staff for the treatment of the cattle.

On October 8, 1990, one week after the beginning of hostilities between the RPF and the FAR, soldiers from the FAR murder *at least* 65 Hima in Mutara.[16] A journalist from *De Standaard* (Belgium's leading newspaper) visited Rukomo several days after the massacre. He wrote that it was clear that the Hutu from the *paysannat* were implicated in the killings and in the looting of the Hima ranches. The journalist added that his interviews with people in the area contradicted official statements denying that there was a bloodbath (president Habyarimana) or blaming the Tutsi for the killings (the Rwandan Embassy in Washington, DC). He also wrote that people in Rukomo believed that the killing was planned ahead and they considered it as punishment for the Hima because they were believed to have aided the RPF.[17] Prunier (1995, 138) writes that these killings were preceded by a radio message from the Minister of Defence demanding that the population 'trace and arrest those who infiltrate'. An officer of the FAR, interviewed by FIDH, said that several FAR companies were given the order *to clean the zone* between Nyagatare and Kagitumba of all its inhabitants (FIDH 1993, 62).

6.4.3 The Tutsi of Kibilira Commune (Gisenyi)

In the second act of mass murder in mid-October 1990, 348 civilians were killed in 48 h in Kibilira commune in Gisenyi province (FIDH 1993, 20). The report is very clear on the role of the communal authorities. They incited the population under the

---

[16] Association Rwandaise pour la Défense des Droits de la Personne et des Libertés Publiques, *Rapport sur les droits de l'homme au Rwanda*, Kigali; décembre 1992, pp. 83–85. The report mentions many other names, but without exact date of death, reason why I write *at least* 65. In Hope for Rwanda (1997, 41–42), André Sibomana put the figure at several hundred, a number also used by FIDH (1993, 62) and Des Forges (1999, 50).

[17] De Standard, October 13–14, 1990, p. 2.

fabricated story that Tutsi had come to exterminate Hutu. The burgomaster who was taken to prison (and released several weeks later) for his role in the mass murder declared that people should '*continue working*'. Independent witness accounts confirm the role played behind the scenes by Léon Mugesera who would two years later deliver racist speeches in Kibilira and neighbouring Gaseke commune. One of the local government agents (*conseiller*) directing the slaughter declared to the investigators that he followed the attackers to guarantee their security. The same Tutsi families in the same commune would fall under attack again in March 1992, at the same time as the massacre in Bugesera (see below) and again in December 1992. On January 10, 1993, the burgomaster of Kibilira said that the program announced by Mugesera had not changed and would resume when the international investigators (who were in Rwanda in January 1993) had left.

The massacre in Kibilira happened one week after 8,000–10,000 people were taken from the streets and imprisoned in Kigali in the first week of October 1990. Thus, already from the very beginning of the civil war, in the rounding up of many people in the capital and in the two massacres committed in October 1990, we encounter several ingredients that were to characterize subsequent massacres. First, attacks were fabricated and stories were spread to allow the regime to rally support, undertake an operation and incite the population to kill Tutsi civilians; second, the authorities (national or local) took the lead; third, these same authorities lied about the nature of the operation and denied that one ethnic group was targeted; fourth, the operation was legitimated under the veil of assuring security; fifth, the metaphor of 'work' was used to describe the killing; and, sixth, national level figures or ideologues monitored the local campaign.

Only at a later stage, towards the end of 1992 and in 1993 would so-called Hutu moderates also be killed in targeted attacks. This sequence is important because some scholars argue that, because right after April 6th 1994 Hutu moderates were the first to be killed, the regime did not in particular targeted Tutsi. The examination of what took place prior to 1994, however, shows that that is not the case.

6.4.4 The Bagogwe of the North–West (Gisenyi and Ruhengeri)

Between 25 January 1991 and 4 February 1991 (three years before the genocide) a massacre was carried out against a group of Tutsi known as Bagogwe. They used to be—and for the most part still were in 1991—pastoralists. The Bagogwe preferred to live in the high mountainous regions with good pastures for their cattle. Only recently, with the reduction of pasture land, had they begun to cultivate. Bill Weber and Amy Vedder, co-founders of the Mountain Gorilla Project, wrote that the northern elite of the Habyarimana regime had dispossessed the Bagogwe already in the mideighties from their land and cattle. This occurred through the Giswati Agro-Sylvo-Pastoral Project financed by the World Bank. The northern elite captured this project and sidelined its intended beneficiaries. Weber and Vedder (2001, p.231) write that

"The Hutu regarded the Bagogwe as a barely tolerated minority in their midst. They could be driven away, squeezed into the remnant natural forest, or forced across the border into Congo for that matter. Families loyal to the Hutu leaders'clan would take their place".

At least 300 people (and maximum 1,000, FIDH 1993, 37) were killed in a series of brutal attacks in several sectors of the north-west of the country, in the prefectures of Gisenyi and Ruhengeri. According to the 1993 report, president Habyarimana himself presided over the meeting that organized the massacre of the Bagogwe. I cite from the FIDH report, p. 38:

The journalist Janvier Africa worked as an agent for the Central Information Service until the beginning of the war, after which he worked directly for the Presidency. He confirms that he assisted in reunions held be a group known as 'Death Squads' (Escadrons de la Mort). He recalls a reunion at 2.00 a.m. in January 1991 before the attack on Ruhengeri by the FPR. Participating in this reunion were Joseph Nzirorera (then Minister of Mines and Handycraft), Charles Nzabagerageza (then préfet of Ruhengeri), Côme Bizimungu (then préfet of Gisenyi) and Casimir Bizimungu (then Minister of Foreign Affairs). After the liberation of the city, they decided to kill the Bagogwe. Colonel Sagatwe, Protais Zigiranyirazo (brother-in-law of the president), member of parliament (député) Rucagu and préfet Nzabageraza all agreed on that point.[18] Préfet Nzabagerageza should instruct burgomasters to find trustworthy people to do the job. Janvier Africa confirms that it was a big operation that cost 15 million Rwandan francs. The role of Janvier was to verify the results of the operation, to make sure that those who had to be killed really were dead. He showed credible evidence of his participation in the operation.

The reunion that prepared the massacre of the Bagogwe was presided by Juvenal Habyrimana himself, his wife was also present, as well as Colonel Sagatwa and his wife and a traditional truth-teller (sorcier) invited by Sagatwa. Minister Joseph Nzirorera was charged with the delivery of the money to préfet Nzabagerageza.

It was Colonel Elie Sagatwa who proposed the massacre of the Bagogwe and President Habyarimana agreed by nicking his head. Nzirorera, Nzabagerageza and Côme Bizimungu had to look for trustworthy Burgomasters. Once the operation started, one had to make sure that the police participated in order to get the job done. (author's translation from French text).

When reading about the preparation of the massacre, it is clear that this massacre was not a spontaneous outburst by an anxious population. It was planned and organized by the national leadership. The fear of the RPF was twisted and manipulated by the leadership into an immediate threat to Hutu livelihoods, thereby inducing the Hutu population 'to act first'. A fake assault—fabricated to legitimize the campaign—worked so well that the immediate reaction of the Hutu population was to flee. The burgomaster had to persuade them to stay and attack their Bagogwe neighbours (Des Forges 1999, 88). Since the massacre of the Bagogwe was executed right after an attack by the RPF on the centre of Ruhengeri, it seems easy to infer that the massacre was an act of retribution (or revenge) by the Habyarimana regime. However, the advocates of the revenge interpretation fail

---

[18] The names of these persons, of which several belong to the inner circle of the Akazu, will come back later and are found among the chief organisers of the genocide. The fact that the FIDH team managed to unveil the murderous intentions and the names of these people already in early 1993 signals the high quality of their report.

to explain why the revenge took the form it did, i.e. the massacre of unarmed civilians. Revenge could have taken several other forms, such as killing Tutsi who were still in prison after the October 1990 raids in Kigali or launching an offensive against the RPF. Throughout the civil war the regime spent a lot of energy attacking and killing the unarmed Tutsi civilian population inside Rwanda. This is what needs to be explained and 'revenge' is far from accomplishing that. The civil war indeed accounts for the timing of the massacre, but it does not explain why these massacres took the form of ethnic cleansing.

6.4.5 The Tutsi of Bugesera (South-Central Rwanda)

In March 1992, authorities organized the killing of several hundred Tutsi in Bugesera, a region located to the south of Kigali where Hutu (from the north-west) and Tutsi (from the south-west), both from densely populated areas in Rwanda, had recently migrated and settled. Map 6.1 shows how Hutu and Tutsi from the north, but in particular from the south of Rwanda migrated to the new to-be-colonised lands in Bugesera (communes of Ngenda, Kanzenze and Gashora).

Hassan Ngeze, editor of *Kangura* (see above), visited the area several times prior to the massacre and spread tracts and rumours about the danger of the *Inyenzi* (Des Forges 1999, 89). On March 3, Radio Rwanda issued a warning that Tutsi were going to kill Hutu, in particular Hutu leaders in Bugesera. At that time, Ferdinand Nahimana (see below) was director of the Rwandan Office for Information (ORINFOR) where he supervized Radio Rwanda. The burgomaster of Kanzenze, Mr. Fidèle Rwambuka who played a leading role in the massacre was a member of the Central Committee of the MRND. Rwambuka, who denied knowing about the massacre when interviewed by the FIDH, could count on the support of *interahamwe* (at that time the name for the youth militia of the MRND) dispatched from Kigali and on soldiers from the nearby Gako camp. In Nyamata in Bugesera one can visit the grave of Sister Locatelli, an Italian Nun who was living there at the time of the massacre. She warned embassies in Kigali that the massacre was taking place and was subsequently killed by the perpetrators.

An experienced observer of Rwanda's history, David Newbury, described the period as follows:

> With the pretence for looking for internal enemies, from late 1990 and early 1991, there were small-scale killings (of several hundred people) and wider roundups of "suspects" within Rwanda. The military leaders learned two principal lessons from this exercise: that such tactics were feasible, and that they generated no meaningful response by outside powers.[19]

---

[19] Newbury, D., Understanding Genocide, *African Studies Review*, Vol. 41, No. 1, 1998, p. 79.

6.5 The Political Geography of the Massacres

A clear pattern characterises the massacres in Kibilira, of the Bagogwe and in Bugesera: Fabricated stories are spread stating that Tutsi killed or planned to kill Hutu; ideologues are present at massacre sites to give speeches or animate meetings; 'trustworthy' burgomasters are enlisted to call meetings with the conseillers; young people and *interahamwe* are dispatched to hunt, pillage and kill. Each time, FIDH and ADL establish a personal and organisational link with the national leadership in Kigali making these massacres all but spontaneous outbursts of violence. Most of these massacres took place in the north-west of the country, where the MRND was strongly supported by the local administrators and the population.[20] Habyarimana's home province Gisenyi and neighbouring Ruherngeri had received by far the largest amounts of government subsidies and benefited from the greatest number of government jobs. Several top leaders of the MRND and the Akazu (Juvénal Habyarimana, Joseph Nzirorera, Protais Zigiranyirazo) originated from the communes where these early massacres took place. The other area where a massacre took place was Bugesera, in the province of rural Kigali, a region that had only recently been populated by Hutu from Gisenyi and Ruhengeri, as well as by Tutsi from Gikongoro and Butare.

The strong support for the MRND is not the only element that distinguishes these provinces and communes. Gisenyi and Ruhengeri are by far the most densely populated provinces in Rwanda. In 1991, accounting for the forested areas in both provinces, Gisenyi counted 735,000 people on 1,350 km^2 of cultivable land which is 560 persons per square km and Ruhengeri 532 persons per square km. This is almost twice the average of the other provinces.[21] The average size of a farm in Gisenyi (0.45 ha) was by far the smallest compared to the other provinces. The communes in Gisenyi where the violence against Tutsi was orchestrated, Kibilira, and in later instances of violence also the commune of Mutura, have the highest percentages of Tutsi (8.6 and 9.7 % of the population respectively) in the province. For the province of Ruhengeri, the communes of Kinigi (3.7 %) and Mukingo (2.1 %), where Bagogwe were killed, had the highest percentage of Tutsi in Ruhengeri. Kanzenze commune in recently settled Bugesera had the highest percent of Tutsi of the entire province of Rural Kigali (31 %).[22] Several thousand Tutsi who had been internally displaced in the wake of the 1959 Hutu Revolution had resettled in Nyamata, Bugesera. Recall that the Hima of the savannah in northern

---

[20] Out of 17 incidents of serious violence in the 1990–1993 period, 14 took place in Gisenyi or Ruhengeri (Des Forges 1999, 87)

[21] Only urban centres had an even higher density, but urban people do not live of the land. Gisenyi is also the location of the fieldwork undertaken by André in 1988 and 1993. She found an extreme pressure on land which even deteriorated in just 5 years. The resulted in many conflicts over land and a large number of landless or quasi-landless peasants whose farm size was too small to make a living, to feed the family and to offer land to sons who wanted to marry.

[22] The source of these percent is the 1983 count of the population by ethnicity in the administrative records kept at the commune level.

Byumba were a pastoral people who were recently settled into ranches as part of a large land re-settlement program. Thus, these first massacres occurred in places combining the following features:

– strong MRND support among local authorities and/or population
– the most densely populated areas in rural Rwanda or recently (re)settled area
– communes chosen had highest percentage of Tutsi in the province.

In other parts of Rwanda, a smaller number of Tutsi were killed (compared to the four massacres described above) in the 1990–1992 period. At those places, we find evidence of the same logic as in the massacres sites above:

• Communes of Rwamatamu and Gishyita in Kibuye province: higher than average population density and very high percentage of Tutsi;
• the region of Nasho in commune Rusumo (Kibungo province): pastoralist population settled after 1982 expulsion from Uganda. Pastoralists killed by FAR soldiers and members of the local *paysannat* (see Map 6.2);
• Sector Rwanbuka in commune Murambi, Byumba province: MRND stronghold with burgomaster originating from the sector where the killings occur and;
• Commune Mugina, Gitarama province: the killing of a Tutsi specifically to occupy his pastoral land.[23]

What is evident is that immediately after the beginning of the October 1990 civil war, Tutsi are targeted and killed in local massacres. More specifically, the places where these massacres of the Hima, Bagogwe and Tutsi were committed in the 1990–1992 period are located on the land frontier, in recently settled areas or in *paysannat* settlement schemes. Several of the places where the early massacres occurred such as in Mutara (northern Byumba), Kinigi, Mukingo, Bugesera and Rusumo were places where *paysannats* had been established. In fact, 10 out of the 19 communes where massacres occurred in the period 1990–1992 were communes with a *paysannat* settlement schemes (see Table 6.1 and Map 6.3). As Rwanda had 17 communes with *paysannats*, which is 12 % of all 145 communes, this means that 59 % (10/17) of the communes having such a settlement scheme were hit by a massacre. This figure needs to be compared with the probability of a massacre in communes without *paysannats*, which was 7 % (9/128), an enormous difference.[24] In Gashora—a commune neighbouring Kanzenze in Bugesera—where part of the March 1992 massacre occurred, a model-village was established for model farmers with rectangular houses built in a grid of straight roads, the only such one in Rwanda at that time.

---

[23] Association Rwandaise pour la Défense des Droits de la Personne et des Libertés Publiques, *Rapport sur les droits de l'homme au Rwanda*, Kigali; décember 1992, p. 353. This report uses the word 'genocide' at several occasions to describe the massacres. Also FIDH (1993, 52–55).

[24] The comparison becomes 45 % (10/22) compared to 7.3 % (9/123) when including the very small paysannats located in the province capitals. The Chi-square statistic is 35.35 with 1 ° of freedom and a p-value of 0, meaning that the result cannot be ascribed to chance.

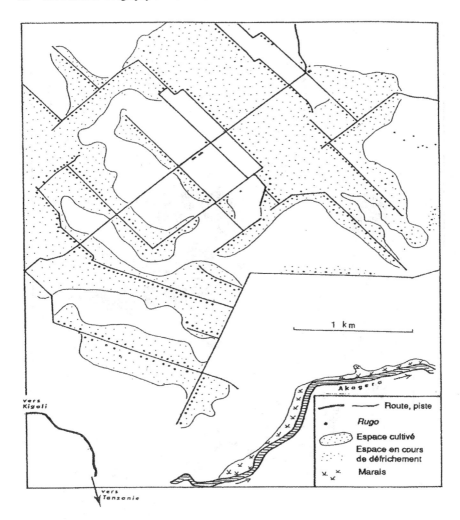

Map 6.2 The Paysannat of Rusumo, province of Kibungo *source* Bart (1993)

Table 6.1 Number of communes (N = 145), communes with a paysannat and with a massacre 1990–1992

Communes with a Paysannat	Communes with a Massacre 1990–1993	Communes with a Paysannat and a massacre
17/145[a]	19/145[b]	10/17[c]

[a] Bart (1993, p. 394) with at least 1,000 h
[b] Des Forges (1999, p. 87); Reyntjens (1994, p. 186) and ADL (1992)
[c] These 10 communes are: Muvumba in northern Byumba; Mukingo, Nkuli and Kinigi in Ruhengeri; Mutura and Karago in Gisenyi; Kanzenze, Gashora and Ngenda in Rural Kigali and Rusumo in Kibungo. *Pearson Chi square test* (1) = 35.35 *with p* = 0.000

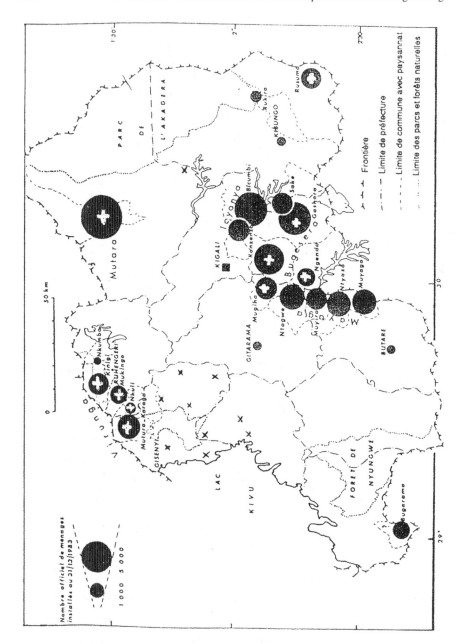

Map 6.3 Paysannat and massacre sites in Rwanda (1990–1992). A circle represents a Paysannat, *source* Bart (1993). A cross represents a massacre, sources as under Table 6.1

In Kanzenze (Bugesera), the commune most touched by the March 1992 massacre, two thirds of the population lived in a *paysannat* (Bart 1993, 382). The early massacres inscribe themselves in a logic of land colonisation, re-settlement, depredation and deprivation of cattle and land in areas where the land constraint was biting the most and where peasant society was being re-modelled in a rational, geometric way.[25] These early massacres can thus be described and understood as acts of spatial and social engineering through ethnic cleansing: the removal of pastoralist groups from the land in order to occupy the land for food cultivation, *paysannats* settlement schemes and export crop production. In times of civil war, the Tutsi need not be re-settled, there is no space for them anyway, they can be killed.

Just as there was no space anymore for pastoralism after the 1959 revolution and no space for Tutsi refugees in the seventies and eighties, there was now no space anymore for Tutsi inside Rwanda. Delicate operations such as massacres could, at that time, only be executed in MRND strongholds. The massacres occurred in strongholds with very high population pressure, high percentages of Tutsi compared to the provincial level and in areas with previous experience of land colonisation and resettlement such as the *paysannats*. They were executed as *umuganda*, the obligatory communal labour. The policy of communal labour was introduced by Habyarimana in 1975 to re-establish the value of manual labour. It gave local authorities a lot of sway over the peasant population, which they used to mobilize for the killings.

6.6 Intermediate Conclusion

I have put forth a third, alternative or at least complementary interpretation of the massacres that were perpetrated in Rwanda prior to the 1994 genocide. This interpretation, which is based on the desire of the leaders of the Peasant-State to exclude the pastoralist groups from the realm of the state, to remodel agrarian space and colonise new land, challenges, or at least complements, the two pre-vailing interpretations in the literature.

The Bahima and the Bagogwe had not sought to take on positions of power in the state; indeed, they had sought to stay away from the influence of state power. Prunier (1995, 169) writes that, in the context of Rwanda, the Bagogwe were poorer than average. They lived off their cattle on the little pastoral land that was left. However, the state would not leave them alone. In the commune of Mukingo, in the northwest of the country, a *paysannat* was established on their land, whereby contracts were signed with farmers with a view to the growing of pyrethrum for export. In the northeast, ranches were created for their cattle as part of a large-scale rural development program. Whatever the specific form in which case was, the point is that no one could escape the Second Republic's drive to register, handle, monitor and develop its people. The 1990–1992 massacres took place in communes where there was already a substantial experience of spatial and social

---

[25] Just how tough the effects of the land constraint were can best be understood in a paper by André and Platteau (1998). The field work for their paper was undertaken in 1988 and 1993 on a hill in Gisenyi province. Verwimp (2005) presents an economic profile of perpetrators.

engineering on the part of the Second Republic, and where agrarian space had been significantly remodelled from above. Then, in the context of the civil war, spatial and social engineering went a step further, meaning that the pastoralists were killed rather than re-settled. The fate of Rwanda's Bahima and Bagogwe pastoralists illustrates the nature of the developmental state: 'seeing like a state', the regime decided that these pastoralists should be removed from the body politic. The cover of the civil war was thus used to rid specific areas of their pastoral inhabitants. The regime denied that any massacres had taken place and instead described the events as either spontaneous outbursts of violence (when far from the battle front) or as war operations (when close to the front).

The Habyarimana regime used up all the available land in Rwanda. The regime got to this point by way of an extensive land strategy—turning land that was used for pastures into agricultural land and colonising new (often marginal) land, mainly through the *paysannats* settlement scheme. The primacy of agriculture over pastoralism was a key outcome of the Hutu Revolution, as shown by the abolishing of Ibikingi rights and the subsequent cultivation of pastoral lands. The Rwandan State intervened strongly in land management, not least through the establishment of *paysannats* and the expropriation of households with a view to the creation of tea plantations. This policy was met with resentment, given that farmers on the land frontier were forced to move and ended up with smaller parcels. In 1986, the Central Committee of the MRND refused the return of Tutsi refugees from Uganda, arguing there was no space for them. In 1989 and 1990, Habyarimana maintained that many of the country's problems, such as famine, were the result of population growth.

The Habyarimana regime adopted a policy of agricultural extensification, as opposed to intensification. This meant turning all available land (such as pastures, marches and forests) into cultivable land. In Rwanda, this policy came up against its limits in the late 1980s, as all the land had by then been taken over. It is therefore important to note that, by 1991, most Bagogwe were still pastoralists. They preferred to live in the high mountainous regions, where there were good pastures for their cattle. Only more recently, with the reduction in pastoral land, did they begin to cultivate. Pastoralists such as the Hima and the Bagogwe live off cattle and the trade in cattle products. They do not cultivate and are therefore considered a non-agricultural group. Pastoralism as a way of life did not fit in the agrarian order of the Second Republic, which was based on hard-working smallholder peasants. The regime used the opportunity provided by the civil war in order to claim the last remaining parcels of land by removing the last remnants of pastoralism in Rwanda. This was perfectly in line with the prevailing ideology of the Second Republic, i.e. that Rwanda was and would always remain an agrarian nation of hard-working peasants. The point was not that the Hima, the Bagogwe and the Tutsi owned cattle (for many rich Hutu and the dignitaries of the Habyarimana regime did so, too), but that their pastoralist livelihood did not fit in the Peasant-State. Peasant cultivation and rural life can be romanticized, but when this ideology is combined with racism towards ethnic groups regarded as non-peasant, such as the Tutsi, this ideology can take on a vicious character.[26] Thus, in view of all of the above, these massacres can be adequately described as instances of ethnic cleansing.

The international commission that wrote the FIDH report of March 1993 discussed the applicability of the term 'genocide' in the case of the massacres that it described in detail. Then, in a report dated August 1993, the United Nations Special Rapporteur on Summary, Arbitrary and Extrajudicial Executions concluded that the killings did indeed constitute an instance of genocide according to the terms of the 1948 Convention on Genocide.

I argue that the intention to kill a group of people for who they are (the core element of the definition of genocide according to the 1948 Convention) was clearly present from the beginning of the civil war: the Bahima, the Bagogwe, and the Tutsi were targeted because of their pastoralist character and because they were regarded as belonging to a different (Nilo-Hamitic) race. The leaders of the Second Republic espoused a racial ideology and the acts of mass murder that they perpetrated cannot be properly understood outside this racist paradigm.

President Habyarimana denied that any massacres had taken place in the case of both the Hima (in October 1990) and the Bagogwe (in August 1991), just as a year earlier he had denied that there had been a famine in Gikongoro.[27] This denial of harm, suffering or killing is a part of the classic repertoire of the perpetrators of genocide. Genocide is the result of a gradual policy involving identification, hate propaganda, the militarisation of society, resource allocation and so on. The 1993 FIDH report revealed the existence of a high-level committee behind the mass murders. This group met on several occasions, enabling its members to address a number of issues and organize the subsequent events. The meeting in which the massacre of the Bagogwe was decided also discussed the means that were to be used in the operation (FIDH 1993, 38). These means consisted of trustworthy burgomasters, 15 million RWF and the help of police officers. By the time that the leaders of the regime took the decision to go ahead and execute the mass murders, they already had a pretty good idea of how to do it.

My analysis has sought to highlight the social and geographical features of the massacres that were perpetrated in Rwanda in the early 1990s. These features, along with the available evidence on the motives and organisation behind the violence, are clearly indicative of an agrarian logic underlying the massacres, which cannot be satisfactorily explained as a defensive reaction to imminent invasion or as preparation for a wider genocidal project. Rather, to a significant extent these massacres were rooted in the crisis of an ideological programme and

---

[26] A strong example of the ideology in the mind of the organisers of genocide is found in an essay written by Colonel T. Bagosora after the genocide (Yaoundé 1995). He writes that the civil war was an ethnic war of Hutu against Tutsi and that the Tutsi are a nilothic people of immigrants without a country of their own. They have tried to impose their supremacy on the rightful original inhabitants.

[27] De Standaard, 1990, October 13–14, p. 2 for the denial of the massacre of the Hima and Des Forges 1999, pp. 90–91 for the denial of the massacre of the Bagogwe.

its associated policies. The massacres took place in locations chosen for their particular characteristics, the strong level of support enjoyed by the MRND, their very high population density, the fact that there was a relatively high percentage of Tutsi and their recent history of land colonisation or of remodelling of the agrarian space into *paysannat* settlement schemes. Under the cover of the civil war, it was here that the regime unveiled its darker side: that of a Peasant-State unleashing its full violent potential against people considered to be non-peasants.

Chapter 7
Civil War, Multipartism, Coup d'etat and Genocide

7.1 The April 1992 to March 1994 Period

This period is characterised by parallel development on three levels, developments that are interrelated and often steered by the same group of people. We distinguish political developments, discontent in the army and the organisation of civilian self-defense.

7.1.1 Political Developments[1]

From April 1992 to the end of 1993 we enter a phase with important new political developments: the hate speech by Léon Mugesera in Gisenyi, the signing of the peace agreements in Arusha (and their disavowel by Habyarimana three months after signing), the surprise attack by the RPF, the publication of the FIDH report, the murder of president Ndadaye in Burundi, the split of the Mouvement Démocratique Républicain (reincarnation of the Kayibanda era Parmehutu party) in a 'moderate' and a 'power' faction, targeted assassinations of well-known politicians and the arrival of UNAMIR. These developments show that Habyarimana and the leaders of the Second Republic only have partial control over events. With the adevent of multipartism, the MDR had to be reckoned with and the RPF is using targeted killings of political leaders to install more fear and heighten insecurity. In disagreement with the ongoing Arusha talks, MRND extremists had set up their own party, the CDR.

---

[1] I refer to Alison Des Forges (1999) and André Guichaooua (2010) for a very detailed analysis of the facts of this period. I am responsible for the combination of arguments and interpretation offered here.

P. Verwimp, *Peasants in Power*, DOI: 10.1007/978-94-007-6434-7_7,
© Springer Science+Business Media Dordrecht 2013

In this period, new killings are reported in several communes of Gisenyi, in Nkuli (Ruhengeri), Mbogo (north of Kigali) and in Murambi (Byumba), as reported in the second volume of the ADL reports (published in December 1993), but these killings do not have the magnitude of the previous massacres. Given the multiple attacks on the hegemony of the MRND, its leadership not only targets Tutsi (as in the massacres described in Chap. 6), but also Hutu who are considered opponents to Habyarimana. These two new facts, to wit the halting of large scale massacres of Tutsi and the killing of Hutu opponents are the result of adaptive behaviour of the regime towards pressing new developments mentioned above.

First, in this period the regime was fighting for its survival. Apart from the RPF, it had to deal with Hutu opponents because it was afraid that they would collude with the RPF. According to Alison Des Forges (1999, p. 83), this possibility, known as the 'Kanyarengwe effect', explains the virulence of the attacks against Hutu.[2] The targeting of Hutu opponents and the accusation that these Hutu are jeopardizing the Hutu cause are measures taken to maintain Hutu unity. The singer Simon Bikindi (see also Chap. 2) spread this message in a song titled 'I hate Hutu'. In one version, he particularly targets the Hutu of Butare[3]:

> Let us start in the region of Butare where they like feudalism, who would blame me for that? I hate them and I don't apologisze for that. I hate them and I don't apologize for that. Lucky for us that they are so few in number…Those who have ears, let them hear!

As the MRND needed to be 'reinvented' and adapted to the new situation of multipartism, three people are placed at the helm of the party. Habyarimana had promised not to cumulate anymore the fourfold position of Head of State, head of the army, Minister of Defense and president of the MRND. It are three skilled politicians and party leaders who will, after the death of Habyarimana, manoeuvre the MNRD back into its leading position similar to the one of the Party-State before 1991 (Guichaoua 2010, 330, 457 and 489). Their actions, in collaboration with those of Colonel Theoneste Bagosora (see below) will be crucial for the implementation of the policy of genocide later on. Habyarimana skilfully managed to remain above the battles between political dignitaries and weakened them when he felt that they became too powerful or too popular. The party was renamed the Revolutionary Mouvement for Development and Democracy (MRNDD).

In line with the style of leadership he has adopted from the beginning of his reign (see Chap. 2), Habyarimana continued with his direct appeal to the masses. In a speech in Ruhengeri on November 15, 1992 he urges the militants of the party to listen to the farmers who he said are the roots of the party.[4] In this speech, in

---

[2] Named after Colonel Kanyarengwe who fled Rwanda in 1980 after accusations that he was plotting against Habayrimana. He joined the RPF and was serving as its president. His participation in the RPF, being a Hutu, represented the unwanted cooperation between dissatisfied Hutu and the RPF.

[3] Recorded from RTML broadcasts, October 17–31, 1993, cited from Des Forges, p. 83.

[4] The president used the same words at the occasion of the MRND conference of April 28, 1992 in Kigali: "The farmers are the roots of our Movement. Party leaders should not stay in their

contrast to the diplomatic wording of his official declarations, he said that he counts on the mobilisation of the MRND militants and in particular on the Interahamwe (see below). He invites the army and the interahamwe to accompany him on his electoral campaign (Guichaoua 2010, 145–147). According to James Gasana—former prominent member of the MRND and Minister of Defense in the multiparty government until his resignation under pressure of the extremists— president Habyarimana counted on the demographic majority and considered the Arusha negotiations subordinate to the will of the people. It is his permanent outreach to the masses and his call for the mobilisation of the peasantry in support of the MRND that strikes me as one of the defining characteristics of the president. It is really that that makes him the *Father of the Nation*.

In his book Guichaoua (2010) presents in great detail the strategies developed by the three leading MRND personalities to safeguard their own positions while at the same time forging a coalition with the leaders of other parties: (1) Mathieu Ngirumpatse, who succeeded Habyarimana in July 1993 as president of the MRND, did not originate from northern Rwanda and was therefore not considered to be part of the inner cercle of the Akazu (presidential clan). Habyarimana counted on him to appeal to southern Hutu. Ngirimpatse managed to forge relations with the MDR and in particular its president Twagiramungu; (2) Joseph Nzirorera, who was from Ruhergeri and trusted by the Akazu, became national secretary of the MRND in 1993 and in this capacity in charge of the MRND apparatus. He was a favourite of the president but the latter realised he could not appeal to the southern Hutu. He also lacked the charm of the president, a powerful asset in a competitive political environment. Nzirorera was close with P. Zigiranyirazo, brother of Agatha Kanziga and as such closely involved with the clientilist network around the presidential clan; (3) Edouard Karemera, vice-president of the MRND, had served the Second Republic since 1976 in different capacities (councillor in Ministry of the Interior, in the office of the president, Minister himself and member of the Central Committee of the MRND). Because of his training as a lawyer and his different positions he was well-acquainted with the internal functioning of Rwanda's administration. He was however not a technocrat, but a skillful politician charged with complex and politically sensitive tasks throughout his career.

Second, in March 1993, a group of Human Rights organisations (FIDH) published the report on the massacres perpetrated since October 1990 discussed in Chap. 6. Alison Des Forges (1999, 94) writes that in the months after the

---

(Footnote 4 continued)

offices… but go out and approach the farmers." (My translation from the French transcript of his speech). The words used in Kinyarwanda 'abahinzi borozi' by the president translates to 'farmers' in English and to 'agriculteurs-éleveurs' in French and in includes cultivators who have one or a few cows or livestock, as many farmers do. The president considered this an efficient use of the land. It does not include 'pastoralists' meaning people for which herding cattle was a livelihood. As I have described in Chap. 2, the appeal to the farmer or the cultivator is understood by Habayarimana's audience as an appeal to the Hutu.

publication of the report, no more massacres of Tutsi were committed. The report was widely distributed among donor nations and even handed out by the UN Department of Humanitarian Affairs to representatives meeting to discuss assistance to Rwanda. Habyarimana responded to the charges in the report in a formal statement, declaring that the government had failed to assure the security of citizens, but denying that officials had taken the initiatives in any of the abuses.

As a result of the above mentioned political developments, the Hutu-'Power' coalition emerges in the second half of 1993. It consists of MRND, the MDR Power fraction, the CDR, the youth wings and militia of these parties together with the military officers who were against the Arusha Agreement. RTLM became the voice of this coalition. The political, military and ideological leaders of this coalition—often seen together at meetings—will implement a policy of genocide after the death of Habyarimana. In Sect. 7.3 we will describe how they implemented this policy.

7.1.2 Discontent in the Army

In December 1991, a commission of ten officers, set-up by Habyarimana and chaired by Colonel Théoneste Bagosora prepared a secret report on how to defeat the enemy in the military, media and political domains. The enemy was defined as the Tutsi inside or outside the country who were nostalgic for power and never recognized the realities of the 1959 social revolution.[5] This does not mean necessarily that the commission defined all Tutsi as the enemies, its aim was rather to define the social milieu in which the RPF recruited. Indeed, as Bagosora said during his interrogation before the ICTR, there were also Tutsi who did not oppose Habyarimana, and thus they were not part of the enemy. However, it does present the conflict in ethnic terms (one of the milieus in which recruitment takes place is mentioned as the 'Nilo-Hamitic people of the region').[6] In its judgement, the ICTR recognised that the definition does not target all Tutsi.[7] I am not surprised that the commission defined the enemy in military and social terms: all of the members where military officers, not politicians and some of them were not considered as extremists, Augustin Cyiza being one of them. However, because of its ethnic connotation, the definition will later be (ab)used by military and political hardliners. For now, Habyarimana did not allow its distribution and even ordered

---

[5] Des Forges, A. (2006), The Rwandan Genocide: How it was prepared, Briefing Paper, Human Rights Watch, April, p. 6.

[6] Bagosora stated several times that the war is another version of the age-old struggle between "The Hutu people" and the Tutsi, not between political parties. See Colonel BEMS Bagosora, T., (1995), *L'assassinat du Président Habyarimana ou l'ultime opération du Tutsi pour sa reconquête du pouvoir par la force au Rwanda*, Yaoundé, October 30, p. 7.

[7] See the transcripts of the interrogation of Bagosora on October 26–27, 2005 at the ICTR and the decision on the Tribunal on the Bagosora case of December 18, 2008.

remaining copies to be destroyed. The two only copies were handed to the new Minister of Defense in January 1992, Augustin Ndidilyama. According to Guichaoua (2010, 81) this non-distribution occurred because the document deplored the absence of renewal in the top echelons of the army and its bad management of the war with the RPF.

What seems to me at least as important as the ethnic element in the definition is the reference to the 1959 Social Revolution. The definition in the original report stressed with capital letters that the enemy, extremist and nostalgic for power, has NEVER recognised and HAS NOT YET recognised the realities of the 1959 Social Revolution. This indicates I believe the defensive nature of the statement: we have to defend the accomplishments of the revolution against an enemy that does not recognise them. It is this line of thinking that comes back time and again in the discourse of extremist politicians throughout the period 1990–1994.

On September 21, 1992 the Army Chief of Staff Déogratias Nsabimana directed the commanders of all units to ensure that their men understood the definition of the enemy, quoted above, that had been produced by the 1991 commission.[8] The dissemination of this report and the definition at this time showed how much Nsabimana and other military authorities feared the loss of common purpose among the rank and file and how they consciously used the idea of Tutsi as enemy in an effort to bond the contending parts of the armed forces together. Immediately thereafter, Nsabimana proposed a course of 'civic and psychological preparation'. In the course, which Nsabimana proposed to be designed and taught by Ferdinand Nahimana (professor of history and Hutu extremist, see above), soldiers should be able to understand and absorb the following information: the misdeeds of the Tutsi monarchy; the causes and consequences of the 1959 Social Revolution; the operation and advantages of the institutions that resulted from the revolution; the refusal of the Inyenzi to accept these institutions in launching repeated attacks against Rwanda, the control of the media by the RPF and their refusal to ever share power. In fact the constant use of the word 'Inyenzi' or cockroaches to describe the RPF referred to the use of the term in the 1960 for the armed group that wanted to re-install the monarchy. Again we find very explicit fears to loose the accomplishments of the 1959 Revolution, expressed in a language of venom.

In July 1992, Colonel Nsengiyumva, head of military intelligence addressed a letter to Nsabimana and Habyarimana in which he openly wrote that discontent in the army was so great that the country risk a coup d'état. Claiming that "the people" were asking the army to act and save the nation, Nsengiyumva warned Habyarimana and proposed that the coalition government, responsible for negotiations with the RPF as well as for changes inside the administration and the armed forces, be removed (Des Forges, HRW Briefing Paper, 2006, 5–6). It is worth citing the letter from the top intelligence officer because it shows what was really going on in his mind:

---

[8] Colonel Nsabimana, D., (1992), to Liste A, Cmdt Sect OPS (Tous) No 1437/G2.2.4, September 21. Cited from the 2006 Human Rights Watch Briefing Paper.

Discontented soldiers may be forced to flee before the RPF and that before they do so, officers 'will settle their account with those of our leaders who would have been at the root of that disaster in naively accepting all the claims of the ENI (enemy) who is fighting us'.

Elsewhere in the same letter he writes

the people 'fear the RPF and would flee their advance and that' before fleeing, they are first going to massacre the Tutsi.

In addition to these specific warnings, Nsengiyumva added a more general prediction that insisting on fusing the RPF with the Rwandan army (proposed in the negotiations) would result in a civil war even more murderous the war until then. He also added that unless the opposition parties, and particularly the Liberal Party—that generally identified with Tutsi—changed their behaviour,

there was a danger that the people themselves would act.
And, he cautioned, "action by popular masses can be hard to keep under control."[9]

The dissatisfaction with the current state of affairs, the desire for ethnic solidarity and the prophesy of action by the popular masses are the three compelling ingredients of this warning by a top intelligence officer. As if he knew what 'the people' were going to do, Nsengiyumva writes that, before fleeing, the people are first going to massacre the Tutsi.

He was not the only one predicting the engagement of 'the people' in the war. On September 22, 1992 (one day after the release of the 'definition of the enemy' by Nsabimana) the CDR issued a press release where it warned of the dangers from enemies inside Rwanda: "the CDR party calls upon the government and the president to deal with this problem. If it does not, the great mass (rubanda nyamwinshi) cannot stand by and do nothing. An enemy is an enemy. Anyone who cooperates with the enemy is a traitor to Rwanda".[10]

As with the three leading MRND politicians, Guichaoua (2010) does an excellent job in portraying Colonel Theoneste Bagosora in the politico-military context of the early nineties. This personality was a strong alley of the president and the Akazu, but at the same time discontent because he had not made it to the rank of General. In his own words he belonged to the Akazu, but not 'inside the house', only in the 'enclos' (the garden surrounding the house). One the eve of the genocide he was retired together with several other high-ranking officers from Gisenyi province but Habyarimana had managed to appoint him as the director of the cabinet of the Minister of Defense James Gasana. From that key position he was able to maintain his politico-military network.

---

[9] Lt.Col.Anatole Nsengiyumva, (1992), Note au Chef EM AR, «Etat d'esprit des militaires et de la population civile, Kigali, July 27», the Linda Melvern archive.

[10] Itangazo, no. 5, ry'ishyaka CDR, 22 September, 1992.

7.1.3 The Organisation of Civilian Self-Defense[11]

As part of the recently released pieces from a Rwandan government archive, several documents reveal an evolving plan of a nationwide civil defence force.[12] Already in December 1990, a group of university faculty including the vice-rector proposed that the minister of defense establish a self-defense program for all adult men. They suggested that men be trained locally, within the commune, under the command of soldiers and that they should learn to fight with traditional weapons because they were cheaper than firearms.[13] In July 1991, Habyarimana was advised by Ndindiliyimana, then minister of defence and security, of the benefits of creating a trained militia in all of Rwanda's communes.[14] Ndindiliyimana told army officers that there were not enough resources to pay for compulsory military service and to provide weapons to every person. However, a civilian militia could be established alongside the professional army. This was possible given Rwanda's young population, he said.[15]

In September 1991, Colonel Nsabimana, proposed training and arming one person from each unit of ten households. They would ideally be between 25 and 40 years old, married, patriotic and of high moral character. They would be trained locally and continue to live at home.[16] On January 20, 1993, a group calling themselves Amasasu (bullet) and purporting to be soldiers wrote to Habyarimana asking that at least one battalion of 'robust young men' be established in each commune. Trained on the spot, the recruits would live at home and from a 'popular army' to support the regular army.

In February 1993 Bagosora wrote in his agenda that recruits of a self-defense force would live at home and be trained locally, either by communal police or by former soldiers or military reservists. They were to be organised by sector with coordination done by sector councillors and police (HRW Briefing Paper, 2006, 8). I cite from HRW:

> Where possible some recruits would be armed with Kalashnikovs or grenades, but he noted that participants should be trained to use spears and bows and arrows. He mentioned the importance of using the radio effectively and noted the name of Simon Bikindi, whose anti-Tutsi songs were broadcast repeatedly during the genocide to heighten fear and hatred of the Tutsi.

---

[11] This section is based on Alison Des Forges (2006), HRW Briefing Paper.

[12] Melvern, L., 2004, *Conspiracy to murder: The Rwandan Genocide*, Verso, London, New York, p. 20.

[13] Jean-Berchmans Nshimyumuremyi; Vice-Rector of the UNR, Butare Campus, to the Minister of National Defense, P2-18/813/90, December 26, 1990, Butare Prefecture.

[14] Rwanda Republic. Note to his Excellency the President. Subject: study of the means necessary for defence and to allow the population to counter any attack from inside or outside the country. Undated. Colonel Augustin Ndindiliyimana. Linda Melvern archive.

[15] Rwanda Republic. To the President and Minister in charge of Defence and Security. Subject: Minutes of Meeting. Rapporteur: Lt.Gregoire Rutakamize, 9 July 1991. Linda Melvern archive.

[16] Col.Déogratias Nsabimana to Monsieur Ministre de la Défense Nationale, no.181/G5.3.0, September 29, 1991.

A week after the Hutu Power rally in late October 1993, a commission of army officers met to organise the long-discussed program. A document "Organisation de l'Auto-Défense Civile", seized from Jean Kambanda upon his arrest in 1997 reveals the organisational structure of the program. Kambanda said in a statement before the ICTR Appeals Chamber that the document predated April 1994 and that is was regarded as highly confidential. Des Forges situates the undated document in mid-February to March 1994. The document specifies that "popular resistance" should be organised by officers of the national police, by retired soldiers and reservists—particularly by those living in civilian areas instead of in military camps—as well as by supporters of political parties that 'defend the principle of the republic and democracy'. At the time and during the genocide these were the parties in the Hutu Power coalition. The plan assigned the chairmanship to the ministries of the interior and defense and a variety of tasks from the level of the presidency and the army general staff down to the level of the administrative sector. Participants were to lead the population in self-defense against the RPF and obtain information on the presence of the enemy locally and denounce 'infiltrators' and enemy 'accomplices'. It calculated the need for firearms and mentioned that people should bring traditional weapons like bows, arrows and spears. The program was also meant to defend against these 'accomplices' and 'disguised RPF'. From the start of the civil war in 1990 this was language used to mean Tutsi civilians.

On March 29, 1994 army officers met again to plan the 'defense of neighbourhoods in Kigali and the tracking down and neutralisation of infiltrators in different parts of the city'. Reporting on the meeting to the minister of defense, Chief of Staff Nsabimana said that soldiers living outside military camps would command the civilians. Groups were to be organised within administrative units. The military commander for Kigali, present at the meeting, indicated that some parts of the city were already organised and were waiting for arms. The commander and the prefect respectively where asked to supply list of members of the armed forces living in residential areas and reservists and reliable civilians.[17] The next day the prefect sent the chief of staff lists of several hundred people, by cell, sector and commune.[18]

7.2 The Murder of President Habyarimana and Its Aftermath

7.2.1 Revenge or Coup d'état?

Returning from Dar-es-Salaam where he agreed to implement key aspects of the Arusha Agreements (after several months of institutional deadlock) the Falcon

---

[17] Déogratias Nsabimana, Général-Major, Chef EM AR, to the Minister of Defense, No. 0599/G3.9.2, Kigali, March 30, 1994. The Linda Melvern Archive, University of Wales.

[18] Le préfet de Kigali, Renzaho Tharcisse, Col.I.G. to Monsieur le Chef d'Etat-Major, no. 14/04.07, Kigali, March 31, 1994. The Linda Melvern Archive, University of Wales.

airplane carrying president Habayrimana was shot down over Kigali when approaching the airport. With him, several high ranking members of his staff, notably Colonel Elie Sagatwe as well as the president of Burundi and all passengers aboard including the French pilots of the aircraft were killed. Table 7.1 lists arguments why either the RPF or the politico-military extremists could have done it. I do not know who did it and therefore focus on the hours and days following the attack. This section recounts to power struggle in the top political and military echelons after the death of the president. Unfortunately, not much information on the whereabouts and the actions of top RPF commanders is available and this section is thus one-sided. For a complete understanding of the actions that led to the murder of president Habyarimana, a two-sided approach is necessary. I do not offer that here. The killing of the president is one thing, the subsequent massacres however is another. While either side could have shot down the plane, the actions to kill moderate Hutu leaders and many Tutsi citizens immediately after can be attributed to one side only, to wit the Akazu, its military associates and political leaders of the Hutu-power factions of political parties. If it was the RPF who shot down the plane, then they bare the responsibility for having created the opportunity for these extremists within the regime to seize power.

During the hours following the attack the High Command of the FAR tries to establish control over the situation. The highest ranked members of the FAR meet for several hours, these meetings are documented, we know who attended and we have transcripts of the decisions made in the meetings. We know that the first meeting started around 9 p.m. and ended around 2 a.m. and we also know that General Dalaire and Luc Marechal attended the meeting for about 1 h, from 10 p.m. to 11 p.m. During that meeting, Colonel Bagosora tried to be named as Chair of a military Crisis Committee. The other officers where not in favour of him presiding and proposed that the highest ranking officer, major-general Augustin Ndidilyama be named as Chair. The latter however, not keen to take the position, neither assumed the leadership nor declined it. All witness accounts confirm that it was Bagosora who was de facto calling the shots. Realising that his fellow officers not want him to be the Chair, he proposed that Augustin Bizimungu—the highest ranked commander of any operational sector—an officer promoted to the rank of Colonel just recently and originating from the north—be promoted to become the new Chief of Staff of the FAR (following up General Nsabimana). In turned out however that Colonel Marcel Gatsinzi was the oldest and highest ranked, because Bagosora had overlooked that the sector Butare-Gikongoro was (recently) also made an operational sector. Thus, Bagosora first tried to impose himself through an 'official' or at least formal process, to wit an appointment by his peers. When that did not work, he tried to have a close associate elected, and failed there too. Thus, Bagosora reveals himself here as a man who knows what he wants and goes after it, but fails because he does not find enough support.

But that is just the 'official', documented, or 'FAR side' of the story. More important then the above—at least in terms of decision making in matters of live and death—is what is going on behind the scenes. During the meeting, it is now clear, Bagosora used his Motorola radio to be in direct contact with the officer in

Table 7.1 Arguments on both sides: reasons why either could have done it derived from their behaviour before and right after the attack

The group of extremist or discontent political-military leaders ('T. Bagosora')	The RPF ('P. Kagame')
• The geometric-ballistic research report by the French judges Trévedic and Poux says that the rockets were fired from Kanombe military base, a base occupied by the Presidential Guard	• The work of the French judge de Bruguière holds a small group of commando's acting under orders from General Paul Kagame responsible for the attack(*)
• Key actors Protais Zigiranyirazo and Mathieu Ngirumpatse lie about there whereabouts in the night of 6–7 April	• Right after the attack, the RPF mobilised its troops
• Bagosora is seen to be in control of events. According to General Daillaire he was even the only person with authority in the night of 6–7 April	• Several key witnesses who have implicated the FPR in the shooting down of the aircraft, have been killed
• Bagosora was using one or more private, direct walkie-talkie lines (Motorola) with the Presidential Guard that did not run via the General Staff of the Army	• From the beginning of the war the stated aim of the RPF was to overthrow the Habyarimana regime
• Bagosora was on the phone with key leaders of the Akazu on April 6–7 (Agathe Kanziga, Protais Zigiranyirazo)	• The highest UN diplomat in Kigali, Jacques-Roger Booh–Booh, told Habyarimana that Kagame may attempt to kill him
• Bagosora was overheard saying 'eleminate them all' (Muhere ruhande)	• In the months before April 6, 1994, the RPF had killed other top political leaders in Rwanda
• Akazu members were overheard saying that the Belgians killed the president	• After they have taken power in Rwanda, the RPF-lead government has taken no action and no interest in setting up an investigation into the shooting down of the plane
• Presidential guard starts killing politicians opposed to the MRND in the night of April 6-7, starting with those whose position would legally or constitutionally entitle them to take charge of the government after the death of the president	• The RPF had the military capabilities to carry out such an attack
• Bagosora was discontent because he had to retire from the army and did not attain the grade of General	
• Bagosora proposes to install a military comité instead of a civilian government, but was rebuked by his fellow officers	
• Extremist political and military leaders were discontent with the concessions made by Habyarimana in the Arusha Agreement	
• There was a precedent in neigbouring Burundi: Tutsi military officers killed Hutu president Ndadaye in October 1993	

(*)In their documentary "Rwanda, a manipulated investigation", Catherine and Philippe Lorsignol (2013) deconstruct the investigation by Bruguière and implicate French Captain Barrill in the attack on the plane

charge of the presidential guard. He also left the meeting room several times to talk on the phone in private (Guichaoua 2010, 254–258). Most likely these private conversations were with Agathe Kanziga, Protais Zigiranyirazo and other members of the Akazu. Witnesses present in the room with Agathe Kanziga have testified that she asked them a few times to leave the room that night, i.e. to have the chance to have a private telephone conversation. We also know that the head of the Paratroopers, visited the residence where Agatha Kanziga was staying several times that night. And it is the Presidential Guard and the Paratroopers that will cause havoc in the city that night. They kill people who had been put on a list by Protais Zigiranyirazo. They include Agathe Uwilingiyimana (Prime Minister), Joseph Kavaruganda (president of the constitutional court), Boniface Ngulinzira (Arusha negociator), Fréderic Nzamurambaho and Faustin Rucogoza (Ministers and members of the opposition to the MRND) and Félicien Ngango and Vénantie Kabageni (president and vice-president of the Transitional Parlement). Every time news came in that one of the listed people was killed, the members of the Akazu would applaud and rejoyce (Guichaoau 2010, 255 and 258).

Thus, while the High Command of the FAR tried to control the situation, the best armed and best trained unit was killing Rwanda's moderate political elite in the city, Hutu as well as Tutsi. The evidence clearly shows that we are dealing with parallel decision making channels. The FAR officers would tell their units to calm the situation, but the presidential guard—under direct command of the Akazu—was conducting targeted murders in Kigali.

During the night Bagosora, the Akazu and the officers in charge of the presidential guard are creating facts on the ground in which the top military officers of the FAR have no say. The Akazu and its associated military officers prevent the Prime Minister, Agathe Uwilingiyimana to make a declaration on the radio by killing her together with her husband.[19] What does that all mean? How to make sense of it? If it was shere revenge from the side of the Akazu to wreck the death of its most prominent members, then the consequences of that revenge created a powervacuüm at the helm of the state. One could argue that the shooting down of the plane already created such a vacuüm, but that is not really correct: there is a legal and constitutional way to appoint a successor for Habyarimana. That is what Dallaire, Marchal and Jacques-Roger Booh–Booh have been telling Bagosora and the other military officers all night. And that is also the road that the large majority of FAR officers wanted to follow (Guichaoua 2010, 252). By killing the people who are most entitled to assure the continuity of the state, because of the position they currently occupy or because they are named in the Arusha Agreement, Bagosora and the Akazu forestall a legal transfer of power. The question is than whether it was pure revenge from the side of the Akazu to kill the Prime Minister or did they intentionally wanted to avoid a legal transfer of power? We know—and

---

[19] In order to kill the Prime Minister, the Presidential Guard had to incapacitate ten Belgian Minuar soldiers and several Rwandan soldiers who were supposed to protect her. These ten Belgians were disarmed and brought to Camp Kigali were they were killed subsequently.

the Akazu knew—that the Prime Minister wanted to make a declaration on the radio in the morning of April 7, 1994. The 'pure revenge' thesis considers the creation of a political vacuüm at the helm of the state as a mere consequence or by-product of the desire to wreck the killing of president Habyarimana and Elie Sagatwe, not as its objective. The 'coup d'état' thesis on the other hand considers these killings, under the veil of 'revenge' as an opportunity to install a new government composed exclusively of MRND or Hutu Power political leaders.

Even when we allow for a desire the wreck the death of one's husband, brother or boss, shouldn't we assume that the de facto decision makers at that very moment (Agathe Kanziga, Protais Zigiranyirazo and Theoneste Bagosora) astute, capable and efficient as they have proven themselves during that night, knew very well that, by killing Rwanda's moderate political leaders (Hutu as well as Tutsi) they would leave the power vacuüm for the extremists to fill? This question has wide-ranging consequences, because the advocates of the 'pure revenge' thesis implicitly believe that the subsequent massacre of Tutsi population of Kigali is the second by-product of the revenge of the death of the president. In that reasoning, this second by-product follows the first by-product being the filling of the political vacuüm by the extremists.

There are several indications that the by-product thesis is not correct and that Prime Minister Agathe Uwilingiyimana and the other moderate leaders were killed deliberately to install and new government that is solely composed of Hutu extremists:

1. Jean Kambanda, new Prime Minister of the Interim Government who will implement a nationwide policy of genocide several days later (see below) has declared before the ICTR (T2-K7-66, May 19, 1998) that:

   Froduald Karamira, vice-president of the MDR, told me, and I remember very well, when he came to my house in Kacyiru [he accompanied Bagosora]: "Ibya Agahta byabaye ngombwa ko tubirangiza ngo tubone uko dushyiraho guverinoma", translated as "it was necessary to kill Agathe Uwilingiyimana in order to be able to put our government in place". He told me that because he believed this was good news for me as I could finally become Prime Minister (translated into English from French by the author, from Guichaoua (2010 303);

2. On June 5, 2007, before the Brussels Court d'Assises judging major Ntuyahaga (for killing the 10 Belgian Minuar soldiers) Colonel Balthazar Ndengeyinka declared that he woke up at 5 a.m. on April 7 because of gunshots—after attending the Crisis Committee meeting till 4 am—and telephoned lieutenant-colonel Cyprien Kayumba (who was on guard at the headquarters of the FAR[20]) and that the latter told him: "it are our troops who want to prevent the Prime Minister going to the radio". (translated from French into English by the author, Chronique judiciare Assises Rwanda, 2007, nr. 7, Brussels, p. 3);

---

[20] In the meeting of the High Command several hours earlier he was seen to leave the room for a phonecall and, when he returned, he declared himself in favour of a military Crisis Committee to take over power (Guichaoau, 2010, 271). .

3. Colonel Rusatira (Chief of Cabinet of the Minister of Defense, J. Habyarimana, till 1992) has declared that in the second meeting of the High Command, which started at 10 a.m. on April 7 at the Military Academy (Ecole Supérieur Militaire) two officers from Gisenyi, lieutenant-colonel Nkundiye, former head of the Presidential Guard and Ntabakuze, the commander of the Paratroopers, both situated in Bagosora's camp, told the meeting that he agreed with the course of action decreed by the previous meeting, meaning to establish calm and order in the city (Rusatira, TPIR, March 4, 1999, pp. 7–8). Rusatira later realized that these two officers put up a smoke screen and were only acting *as if* they wanted a return to calm. At the very moment of this second meeting, the presidential guard was searching the Prime Minister in order to kill her, which occurred around 11 a.m. that day[21];

4. When talking about the new government, Bagosora called it 'his' government. In fact, he was the one putting the new government in place, as stated above, composed solely of Hutu Power extremists. Some Ministers, even from the MRND, only found out very late that they were supposed to be Minister in the new government (see below);

5. When one believes that revenge is the driving force in the night of April 6–7, how does that square with the fact that the the MRND ministers and leaders considered as extremists and/or close with the Akazu were picked up by the presidential guard and transported to safety (Guichaoua 2010, 303). Such actions more resemble a coordinated action than a wave of revenge.[22]

Before continuing with the next phase of Rwanda's drama, I want to comment on the interpretation of André Guichaoau. From a very detailed analysis of the whereabouts, the meetings and the actions of the key decision makers, this eminent scholar seems to support the by-product thesis, at least that is my understanding of Chap. 8 of his book.

7.2.2 The Interpretation by André Guichaoua (2010): Comments and Critique

In his 2010 book, professor Guichaoua, one of the foremost experts on the Second Republic, pays a lot of attention to the behaviour of the most important actors, on an hour-by-hour basis. His main sources are interviews with several of the actors

---

[21] The smoke screen interpretation is not shared by everyone. Augustin Cyiza for example believes that Nkundiye wanted civilians from the south to take responsibilities in the government, because the burden of the war was carried too much by the north (Guichoaua, 2010, 276).

[22] Colonel Gatsinzi, the newly appointed Chief of Staff of the FAR also believes that there were two parallel actions going on: one military, of which he was in command and a second, secret, of which Bagosora was in command. The latter were executing a 'pre-established plan'. (Colonel M. Gatsinzi, Ministry of Justice, Kigali, PV 0142, June 16, 1995).

as well as the depositions before the ICTR of several ministers of the Interim Government and military officers. I admire the meticulous work produced by this scholar of Rwanda. The descriptions he presents in his book however allow me to question some of his interpretations.

Guichaoua regards to killing of adversaries of the (hard-line wing) of the MRND as revenge from the side of the presidential clan (Akazu), executed upon orders from Agathe Kanziga, Protais Zigiranyirazo and Theoneste Bagosora by the presidential guard.

My *first* point of critique is that, if it were revenge, then the targets of that revenge were chosen strategically and the course of action by the presidential guard was systematic, efficient and deliberate, as I have stated above. Some of that behaviour may be compatible with a 'revenge' interpretation, but certainly not all of it. The *second* point is that Guichaoua considers it a 'mistake' by the Akazu (p. 249) not to have realised that the removal of James Gasana from the Ministry of Defense (in July 1993) would badly affect the moral of the army as well as its combativity. I would agree with Guichaoua if the Akazu relied on the army to win the war (to beat the RPF on the battlefield). There are several reasons to doubt that they did:

1. from mid-1992 onwards the Akazu realised that the FAR could not beat the FPR on the battlefield (opinion shared by Augustin Cyiza, see Guichaoua 2010, 276);
2. they also realised that they would loose their privileged position in Rwandan society under a new government after the implementation of the Arusha Agreement. This brings us back to Chap. 1 of this book, where I have written that the choices of an elite should not be regarded as optimising general welfare, but rather as optimising its own welfare. If they realised that the FAR was not able to win the war and thus guarantee their welfare and their privileged position, then the morale of the FAR (and thus the person of James Gasana) was subordinate to the interest of the Akazu. In particular when Gasana ordered the retirement of several high ranking officers loyal to the Akazu. One could argue that that is very short-term reasoning, because in the longer term their own privileged position could only be safeguarded when the war would be won. Correct, but that means that the war has to be won 'by other means'. And that brings us to the creation of the extremist group of military and political leaders who will foment hatred, create RTML, train interahamwe, buy weapons abroad, create civilian self-défense forces and rely on 'the population' using institutions inside the Party-State and if necessary outside of it. Indeed, when one recognises that Habyarimana and the presidential clan counted on the demographic majority of the Hutu population, then there is no reason anymore to judge the removal of James Gasana as a 'mistake.'

My *third* point is that Guichaoau (2010, 249) also considers it a mistake by the Akazu to believe that they could task the army not only with fighting the RPF but also with the extermination of Hutu moderates and Tutsi civilians without soliciting opposition from senior officers, large sections of the population as well as the international community. Here again, one would agree with Guichaoua only if the priority of the Akazu was to rely on the FAR to win the war. Then indeed that double task would be a strategic mistake. Several senior officers (not part of or allied with the Akazu) of the FAR were opposed to the massacres and the FAR three months later indeed lost the war. But, as I just said, at this stage (April 6, 1994) it is doubtful that the Akazu's priority was to rely on the army to win the war. They may indeed have reasoned differently: our only chance to safeguard our own privileged position in Rwandan society, in the short as well as in the longer term, is by using unconvential ways to win the war, to wit by the extermination of all our enemies. The presidential guard's—which operated under direct command of the Akazu and on which they could rely for a 100 %—main and only task then was to kill these enemies, rather than fighting the RPF.

Guichaoua (2010, 281–282) goes a step further when he writes that Bagosora kills the leading members of the political opposition in the morning of April 7 to show his force and determination to his fellow FAR officers who do not grant him the presidency of the Crisis Committee. Does this imply that there would have been no targeted killings of political leaders had Bagosora been granted the presidency of the Crisis Committee? We will never know the outcome of this counterfactual, but it seems unlikely for ar least two reasons:

1. Bagosora needs to kill the political opponents to forestall a legal solution and a transfer of power in line with the Arusha Agreements. With Agahte Uwilingiyimana and others alive, there would have been no need for a Crisis Committee (as the other officers recognized);
2. Such causal interpretation also gives a lot of weight to the discontent and power hunger of one man. While the latter certainly typifies him, he was not the only one making decisions. In fact, just before the second meeting of the High Command (April 7 at 10 am), Bagosora had a meeting with the three leading politicians of the MRND (M. Ngirumpatse, E. Karamira and J. Nzirorera) at 8.00 a.m. in which it became clear that none of them wanted to step forward to succeed President Habyarimana. As a result they decided to promote Théodore Sindikubwabo (president of the CND) to interim president. Thus, already at that time Bagosora can be confident that he and the three MRND leaders will install a puppet government, what he called 'his' government. While he preferred the 'military' option and be named Chair of the Crisis Committee, by 10.00 a.m. he already knew that the 'civilian' option would work if he would not be named Chair. Guichaoua (2010, 301–302) recognizes this when he writes that Bagosora at that point had two options to reach his goal, via the Crisis Committee or either via an MRND-approved and installed Interim Government.

To conclude this section: whether it was the RPF or the Akazu who shot down the presidential aircraft, the facts on the ground show that

1. Bagosora takes charge and, in close communication with the Akazu takes the decisions that matter on the ground;

2. the High Command of the FAR is sidelined in decision making;
3. Hutu moderates and Tutsi, in particular high ranking political opponents of the Akazu are killed.

We have seen that the presidential guard (commanded by Protais Mpiranya), with the help of the Paratroopers (commanded by Aloys Ntabakuze) executed these murders upon direct order from the Akazu. If it was the RPF that shot down the aircraft then the Akazu members, the officers in charge of the presidential guard as well as Theoneste Bagosora reacted in a highly efficient manner. They had just lost their president together with two of the most important men in Rwanda, Colonel Elie Sagatwe and General Nsabimana, but nevertheless managed to be in control that evening. In this case the RPF would be responsible for the creation of the political vacuüm. In contrast, if it was Bagosora and/or the Akazu itself that organised the shooting down of the plane, then these and the subsequent killings need to be considered as part of a coup d'état that brought the extremists to power. This would further discredit the by-product thesis in favour of an intentional interpretation. There is also a third, 'intermediate' position possible: if it was the RPF who shot down the plane, then the 'pure revenge' thesis does not have to follow automatically. One could imagine that Bagosora seizes the opportunity to install either himself as the leader of a Crisis Committee or install a new civilian government composed solely of Hutu Power extremists. He in effect tried both options and succeeded with the second one. As I will develop further below (7.4) it is not necessary to assume that all key actors share the same motivation to embark on a joint course of action. When Agathe Kanziga rejoyces when one of her husband's political enemies is killed, Theoneste Bagosora could seize the opportunity to install an extremist government. These motivations are compatible with one another.

Schematising the two theses:

(1) *By-product thesis: Shooting by the FPR→revenge→political vacuüm→killings*
(2) *Intentional thesis: Shooting by Hutu extremists→Coup d'etat→genocidal government*

7.3 The Interim Government and the Organisation and Implementation of Genocide

On April 8, Theoneste Bagosora and Jospeh Nzirorera install the Interim Government (IG), composed of the Hutu Power wing of each party (except the RPF) that was supposed to be represented in a new government according to the Arusha Agreement. This composition had the advantage that they could claim that they respect the Arusha Agreement and that the Hutu of the southern prefectures were well-represented.

Jean Kambanda, MDR leader from Butare and Prime Minister of the Interim Government, realised very well that his government was a puppet-on-a-string put in place by the military and political leaders of the MRND who themselves stayed behind the scenes (Guichaoua 2010, 300–301). When the Council of Ministers met, the presidents of the party as well as the military leaders sat around the table with the Ministers and 'guided' the decision making. This had to do with the inexperience of the MDR, PSD and PL Ministers, but also with the control of information by the MRND politicians and their military associates. With many years of experience in government and in the unique party, the MRND Ministers, and in particular the three leading MRND politicians, were showing the others how to govern. The MRND Party-State was back and the other politicians were considered apprentices in government. It is this Interim Government that will implement a nationwide policy of genocide.

Guichaoua attributes the push towards genocide solely to the duo Bagosora/Nzirorera. On their choice to implement a nationwide policy of genocide, he gives the following arguments (for which he relies mostly on Augustin Cyiza):

- They risked to become marginalized in the event that the IG would halt the interahamwe, stop the killing in Kigali and thus create the conditions for talks between the FAR and the RPF. So they needed to make everyone share responsibility for crimes (p. 337);
- If it would stop now they were afraid that they would be the blame for the killings of the past few days (p. 415);
- After the death of Habyarimana the accomplices of the enemy needed to be destroyed. (p. 336). Clearly, the 'internal' enemy is now considered to be the Tutsi population of Rwanda;
- The extermination of the Tutsi is considered a price to be paid to Bagosora in order for him to accept not to become Habyariman's successor (p. 336);
- An extermination will prevent the enemies of Habyarimana to beneft from an RPF victory (p. 343);
- The lives of Tutsi civilians can be traded for peace in talks with the RPF (p. 337);
- The escalation towards nationwide extermination allows them to safeguard their own position and the interests of the Akazu (p. 339);
- An extermination makes sure that the Akazu and the nordist-extremist politicians and military officers win the struggle for power and cement their control over the state (p. 442).

These explanations have in common that they regard the implementation of a nationwide policy of genocide as a struggle for the political survival of Rwanda's northern elite. Guichaoau considers the push towards genocide as a strategically chosen escalation of the conflict in order to safeguard one's own political future. While I agree that Rwanda's nordist politico-military elite organised the genocide, some comments need to be made on this argument. My comments her follow Guichaoua's interpretation of the events right after April 6, described in Sect. 7.2.2. His interpretation has the advantage of clarity: personal interests of political survival are the key driver of the implementation of genocide. But is the self-interest of these two leaders sufficient to explain the outcome of events? On the one hand, as I will argue in Sect. 7.4, there are at least three other motivational clusters that drive the genocide, with each cluster inhabited by a specific type of perpetrator/organiser. One the other hand, there have been many struggles for political power in other African countries that did not end in genocide. Hence one needs to explain why and how a struggle for political survival turned *genocidal*, became a campaign to exterminate all Tutsi in Rwanda.

While I believe that Guichaoua is right to focus on the importance of a very small but powerful extremist elite who pushes the genocidal policy forward, I do not agree with him when he writes that this elite does not implement the genocide to save the Republic (2010, 442). In fact, the position of the MRND in the State, of its top political leaders and of the nordist military establishment was so intertwined with the survival of the Second Republic that these two interests (personal versus survival of the Republic) cannot be separated. More in particular: the nordist Hutu elite believed that these two could not be separated. That is why they emphazised time and again in the propaganda that the RPF will take away the accomplishments of the 1959 Revolution, that the Second Republic needs to be saved from the return of the feudo-monarchists and that the population has to rise in the defense of the Nation. This propaganda allowed the people who did the dirty work (the actual killing operations) to genuinely believe that they were working for the benefit of their country.

This fusion of personal and group interest was a cornerstone of the Second Republic under Habyarimana from the start. I refer to Chap. 2 where I described that—from the beginning of the Moral Revolution in 1973—Habyarimana wanted to mobilise everyone, the farmers as well the agents and institutions of the state. He repeated this on 15 November, 1992 in his speech in Ruhengeri (see Sect. 7.1.1). Instead of a political party, the MRND was a Movement in which every Rwandan was engaged from birth. Ordinary citizens could not escape the authority of the Party-State and they did not need to escape because the president was an enlightened despot or an encompassing dictator (see Chap. 1). Guichaoua (2010, 40–44) argues that the term 'educational totalitarianism' may best describe the relations between the rulers and the ruled in the Second Republic: the masses had to be educated, animated and sanctioned by the elite because the latter knew what was good for them. Everyone spoke with one voice, the voice of the MRND. It is this desire for this type of alliance or even fusion of the interests of the elite and the masses that we find back in the organisation of the genocide. A few examples:

1. On April 12, Edouard Karemera wrote a letter to the population (and had it printed at the military print office) in which

   - he asked that the population saves the Republic and Democracy;
   - he stated that the Inkotanyi have come to reverse the acquierements of the 'people's revolution' of 1959 and re-conduct you to servitude;
   - he asked councillors of the communes and members of the cells to organise themselves and warn the population;

- he asked the population to put their differences aside and unite forces to confront the grand-children of the UNAR who have decided to reconduct you to servitude;
- he asked to population to organise security ronds and set-up check-points to cut-of the road for the enemy.

As Habyarimana had done throughout his reign, Karemera appeals directly to the peasant masses asking for complete mobilisation (see Guichaoua 2010, 145–146 and 481). He is also as skilled as his former boss in using the tricks of the trade of populism, which can be derived from his speech on May 3, 1994, where

- he reminded that the government, on April 10, 1994, had accepted to pay the salaries of all the responsables of the cells (lowest administrative unit), but that as a counterpart the latter have to do their job and assure security[23];
- he asked the population to generate ideas that can help the authorities manage the land and the assets left behind by the victims in such a way as to benefit the people.

2. The leaders of the (extremist wings) of the political parties assisted in the meetings of the Interim Government. One of the Ministers has testified that in one of these meetings Donat Murego (leader of the MDR) talked about the killings and the war as "a means of completing the 1959 revolution" and as "a way to position his party for future elections". (Guichaoua 2010, 486).
3. Several Ministers and many high-ranking officials personally assisted in killing operations, i.e. being physically present. The Interim Government dispatched its members to the different prefectures and communes from which they originated in order to mobilise and motivate the population and to supervise 'security'. This corresponds with the example that Habyarimana had set from the beginning of his reign, to wit that the dignitaries of the regime participate in *umuganda* (weekly manual labour) themselves. He gave the good example (see Chap. 2 as well as Figs. 2.1–2.3 in this book) by rolling up his sleeves, taking a hoe and cultivate together with the local population in *umuganda*. One could term this *the politics of proximity*. This proximity to the masses was a factor determining the success of the genocide, because ordinary perpetrators believed that their actions were legitimate, supported by the Interim Government whose ministers and politicians were 'working' with them on the spot.

This brings us to the ideology that first, in its 'light' version as peasant ideology, cemented the hold onto power of the nordist elite and later, in the extreme version of Hutu Power, guided the killing campaign. I distinguish three elements in this extreme ideology: (1) it had a clear anti-Tutsi, *racial component*. The perpetrators identified Tutsi on the basis of some stereotypical physical

---

[23] This action resembles very much the increase in the price of coffee paid to the producer after the start of the civil war , which, in my analysis (see Chap. 4) is a strategy to buy political loyalty, just as the Interim Government demonstrates with its payment of the salaries on April 10, 1994.

characteristics, Tutsi women were depicted as prostitutes of Minuar officers,[24] tens of thousands of women were raped and held as sex slaves, many of them had their breast or genitals mutilated before they were killed, the children of Tutsi were killed while the perpetrators shouted that one has to cut the roots of the tree to prevent its return. Tutsi men had to watch their women being raped and were then told to kill them themselves. Not only adult Tutsi had to be killed but also their descendants and even the biological capacity to reproduce; and (2) it had a *group welfare component*. The genocide was framed as self-defense to secure the attainments of the 1959 Revolution for which all Hutu had to unite. This component appealed to the welfare of the Hutu as a group. They had to 'work' in defense of the Nation and their strength lies in their number; and (3) it also had an *egalitarian component*, a desire for a classless society, anti-urban and anti-intellectual. De Walque and Verwimp (2010) document this component with an empirical analysis of survey data from the Demographic and Health surveys (1992, 2000). They show that people from educated families and families living in urban areas had a higher probability to be killed. This pattern is in line with the peasant ideology and the anti-intellectualism of the Second Republic. In my earlier work (Verwimp 2003, 2005) as well as that of others (André and Platteau 1998), on the economic profiles of victims and perpetrators it is shown that the landed elites formed a coalition with the poor to kill the Tutsi population. Wealthier Hutu were also targeted, especially in areas with few Tutsi or in the aftermath of the killing of Tutsi.

In my opinion, Guichaoua's approach needs to be reconciled with the presence and importance of other motivations, in particular the group welfare aspect of it. This does not mean that ideology was the most important motivation for each and every of the top decision makers. It does mean that this small nordist elite believed that the elimination of the Tutsi would preserve the order of the Second Republic and thus their own privileged position. This reconciliation of narrowly defined self-interest (one's own political future) and common interest (the preservation of the Second Republic) can be achieved when we understand ideology as 'group welfare', a definition that I will adopt in Sect. 8.3.1.

The rationale for invoking the preservation of the Social Revolution (and thus the group welfare of the Hutu) and relying on the population—instructed, monitored and lead by the MRND—for the execution of the genocide is as simple as it is horrific: as Rwanda has no mineral resources, the elite needs to use, organise and manage the labour of the rural masses as good as possible. Thus, an elite, presidential clan or Party-State that wants to benefit from power (increase or safeguard its own revenue) AND at the same time wants to stay in power (see Acemoglu and Robinson in the Chap. 1) has to choose a model of development that will not change the political status quo. The elite can only do this through an efficient

---

[24] Remark that in 1986 the regime rounded-up 'loose women' in Kigali who had to stand half-naked on the street before being transported to a re-education camp. Most of these women were Tutsi, of which several the girlfriends of expatriates. See Chap. 2.

organisation of a rural economy of peasant producers. Hence, just as in the development model, they are going to rely on the peasant masses to execute the genocide. The mobilisation of the masses for genocide is undertaken in the same way as the organisation of development, to wit through the pyramidal organisation of the Party-State under the legitimacy of the Interim Government and with the use of propaganda. Its success is overwhelming because there is a great demand for action in particular from unemployed youth.

On April 21, ten days after the Hutu Power government took office, the authorities directed recruitment for civilian self-defense in Butare and Gikongoro, exactly as described in the March documents: the local military commander cooperated with administrative officials, the burgomasters and the communal councilors to recruit young men who were to be selected by administrative unit in which they lived, to remain there and to be trained in the use of arms by communal police officers or reservists.[25]

To rely on the population for the execution of the genocide is not the same as saying that popular action cannot be controlled and that the genocide takes on a life of its own (Guichaoua 2010, 445). I agree that people have taken actions in their own hand, that there was score settling and that the authorities could not control everything. But the authorities were clearly in control of the main actions and could have stopped the interahamwe and the population if they wanted. But as an interahmwe leader stated, these authorities chose the opposite, they encouraged the interahamwe and supplied them with weapons.

7.4 Some Reflections on Intentionalist Versus Functionalist and Ideological Versus Instrumental Interpretations of the Implementation of Genocide by Way of Conclusion and Transition to Chap. 8

The question how to characterise the implementation of a policy of genocide is often framed in the choice between an intentional versus functional interpretation on the one hand and an ideological versus an instrumental interpretation on the other hand. The first couple debates the question to what extent the genocide was planned. An *intentionalist* interpretation would mean that the perpetrators planned the massacres and the killing of man, women and children ahead of its actual implementation and, since the conception of the plan, took conscious steps towards its execution or implementation. A *functional* interpretation does not deny that at some point, a group of perpetrators decided to kill as much Tutsi as possible (and thus implement genocide), but they argue that decisions were made along the way,

---

[25] Lt. Col.Tharcisse Muvunyi, Comd. Place BUT-GIK, to Mons. Le Bourgmestre, no. 0085/MSC 1.1 April 21, 1994.

that there was no plan and that the choices and preferences of people who later would become the organisers of the genocide were formed during the process.

The second couple debates the prime motivation driving the execution of a policy of genocide. An *ideological* point of view would mean that the key organisers were die-hard anti-Tutsi extremists who killed the Tutsi because they were considered to be another ethnic group, race or class. These were people who wanted to purify the body politic from its bourgeois elements so that only the real peasants would remain. An *instrumental* interpretation points the finger at the interest of the politico-military group that implemented the genocide, such as personal thirst for power, blocking reforms that would entail loss of power, influence and wealth, settling personal scores.

In the power circle surrounding Habyarimana, including his wife Agathe Kanziga, her bother Protais Zigiranyirazo and half-brother Séraphin Rwabukumba; the children Habyarimana, the military officers from Gisenyi who had been in charge of the army and the presidential guard throughout the Second Republic, the top-MRND politicians and the university trained intellectuals and propaganda specialists we find representatives of each of the four quadrants of Graph 7.1. In the upper-left quadrant (I) we find people such as Fernand Nahimana, Léon Mugesera and Hassan Ngeze. These propagandists of the Hutu cause were die-hard anti-Tutsi extremists who spread hate propaganda in speeches, journals, pamphlets and on the radio. They called for the Tutsi to be killed and send back to Ethiopia. There motivation was ideological and there actions intentionally contributed to the implementation of genocide. In the upper-right quadrant (II) we find the defenders of the attainments of the 1959 Social Revolution. They wanted to preserve the benefits that the Hutu in general (access to land) and the Hutu elite in particular (power and wealth) had gained from that revolution. Their logic to engage in genocide was instrumental. They clearly had strong and outspoken preferences to kill the Tutsi, because for them this was they only way to preserve what they had. I place the nordist military officers such as T. Bagosora in this quadrant. In the lower-left quadrant (III), we find people who have an ideological point of view, in essence anti-Tutsi preferences, but who do not take conscience steps with the intention to implement a genocide. They are not active in propaganda or do not train or command interahamwe. They are not first movers. They agree with a policy of genocide when they see that the odds are turned against the Tutsi and they agree because of ideological reasons. I place several Ministers in the Interim Government in this quadrant, including its Prime Minister Jean Kambanda. And last but not least, we have the opportunist quadrant (IV), these are persons who turn against the Tutsi to enrich themselves, to settle scores, maybe to save their own skin. They did not intent to kill Tutsi before and do not hold anti-Tutsi preferences. A large part of the rank-and-file Hutu who executed the genocide could be placed in this quadrant. We come back on this in Chap. 8 when discussing the behaviour of the Hutu population.

What is key is that the preferences and interests of the ideologues, intentionalists, the instrumentalists and functionalists converge in the days after April 6. Among the organisers and executioners of the genocide we find representatives of

Graph 7.1 Framing the
decision to implement a
policy of genocide

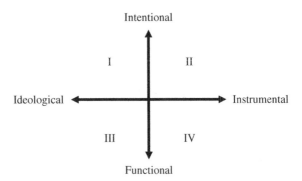

all four quadrants. In effect, one and the same outcome, the extermination of the Tutsi, is found to be the result of several motivations which converge at a given point.

The elements mentioned in 7.2 and 7.3 are prime evidence showing how top military and political leaders were searching for the most adequate way to 'defend' the country. Given the growth of Rwanda's young, underemployed and poor population, these leaders used labour—Rwanda's only abundant factor of production—instead of capital and technology as the main ingredient of their strategy. These leaders speak of 'robust young men to be trained', undoubtedly because they are not in short supply, and they want them to be trained in the use if traditional weapons, because these are cheap. In addition, they want the program to be overseen and implemented via the administrative organisation of the Second Republic, to with the presidency, the ministries, the burgomasters down to the sectors. These elements, the reliance on abundant labor, cheap weapons and the state administrative apparatus allow me to conclude that the design of this program is *endogenous* to the Second Republic, meaning that its design does not come out of the blue but that it can be explained by Rwanda's institutions, created by the revolutionary zeal of the Party-State and by Rwanda's endowments, to with the very high population density, the high percentage of young and poor people in the population.

Remark that the term 'defense' or 'self-defense' was frequently invoked in the 1990–1993 period by the Hutu ideologues in the journal *Kangura*, in speeches and on RTLM. Casting the civil war as an attack on the attainments of the Hutu Revolution in general and as a direct mortal threat to Hutu livelihoods in particular, Hutu had the obligation to defend themselves. In his 1992 speech, Mugesera said that "Time has come for us to defend ourselves" and he asked the crowd "Why do we not arrest the parents who have send their children away and why do we not exterminate them". Since not all Hutu equated 'self-defense' with killing one's Tutsi neighbour, the regime would have to make sure that all mechanisms— from incitement to promises and from threats to sanctions—were put in place to convince the hesitating part of the population to become active killers. It is to these mechanisms we turn to in Chap. 8.

Chapter 8
Collective Action, Norms and Peasant Participation in Genocide

8.1 Review of Selected Literature: The Explanation of Participation by Peter Uvin

I will focus on theoretical insights from social science research on the participation of human beings in collective violence. Peter Uvin's well-known book on the genocide is a good starting point for this. In his book, Uvin devotes an entire chapter to the question why (parts of) the population participated in the genocide. The mainstream story that the elite manipulated ethnicity in order to stay in power, is not satisfactory to Uvin. He asks the (difficult) question as why did (parts of) the population accept and believe the manipulated stories? In the chapter on participation, Uvin pleads to stop regarding peasants as passive executors of official orders. Here as well as elsewhere in his book, he writes that Rwandans are not passive recipients who automatically follow the wishes of their beloved leaders.

> People, even those living in poverty, have a capacity to choose the messages they will respect and to modify them according to their own preferences.[1]

There are indeed many examples showing that Rwandan peasants often disobeyed official orders, neglected them or found strategies to avoid the effects of orders when these orders went against their own interests. These instances include the refusal to pay taxes, not showing up for the compulsory community labor (umuganda), ripping out coffee trees (prohibited by penal law), intercropping or neglecting coffee trees or using fake identity cards.

> Thus, contrary to a widespread vision of Rwandese peasants as obedient executors of orders from above—even if these orders involved killing their neighbours—they should be seen, like all people, as independent actors, facing constraints, to be sure, but capable of making decisions. (Uvin 1998, 67)

There are also documented cases, Uvin writes, of active resistance on the part of the peasants before the genocide. Farmers destroyed development projects realisations that were supposed to benefit them, such as wells, electricity generators,

---

[1] Uvin P., *Aiding Violence*, p. 67.

P. Verwimp, *Peasants in Power*, DOI: 10.1007/978-94-007-6434-7_8,
© Springer Science+Business Media Dordrecht 2013

reforestation areas and other project-created infrastructure (Nshimiyunurenyi 1993, 21). Other documents report farmers invading uncultivated lands owned by churches or dignitaries of the regime (Seruvumba 1992, 12). Uvin reports stories by some technical assistants of stones being thrown at their vehicles by angry farmers. These instances of peasant behavior will multiply tenfold during the three months of the genocide, but it is important to note here that, before the genocide, farmers were perfectly able to take matters in their own hands, even when they had to oppose authority for it. As it happened, peasants followed or opposed official orders depending on their own perceived interest. At one point, in an event described by Longman (1995), farmers locked up the Burgomaster (the highest local authority) in his own office.

As a political economist, the author agrees with Uvin in considering peasants not as passive recipients of orders, but independent actors making choices under constraints. In advancing his explanation of peasant participation in the genocide, Uvin rejects most political, sociological, psychological and economic theories. From these different disciplines however, he retains three concepts: (1) The overall framework and the leading concept in Uvin's explanation is structural violence. It was Galtung (1969) who first wrote on the condition of structural violence. In the literature, the term describes situations of inequality, repression and racism that prevent people living their full potential (Uvin 1998, 103–104). Examples of such living conditions, Uvin writes, are found in apartheid South Africa, Brazil or inner-city America. According to Uvin, frustration, humiliation and the feeling of inferiority were part of the daily experiences of Rwandan peasants. Uvin devotes many pages of his book to describe how the state machinery, local elites and the development projects treated the peasants as underdeveloped, ignorant and poor people. This condition of structural violence, together with the widespread prejudice of anti-Tutsi discrimination and racism, facilitated acute violence against the Tutsi. Disempowered, infantilized people who are made to lose their self-esteem, become frustrated and develop a strong need to regain their dignity. Official anti-Tutsi racism provided a convenient scape-goat (Uvin 1998, 134–138 and 216–218).

Uvin thus also uses two other concepts. These are (2) relative deprivation, drawn from political science research and (3) the theory of scape-goating, drawn from social psychology. It is not very clear from Uvin's book how structural violence and relative deprivation relate to each other. However, maybe the best way to put it is to say that structural violence is the overall concept and relative deprivation and scape-goating are two sub-concepts in Uvin's book. Uvin needs these two sub-concepts to link structural violence with acute violence. Arguing with Merton (Social Structure theory) and Gurr (relative deprivation), Uvin (1998, 136) writes that gaps between what one has and what one expects to have (should have) lead to frustration and resentment and, through that, to violence. He is not the only one using these theories. Willame for example writes that.

the population, who slid unnoticed from poverty to misery, is easily manipulable by forms of ethnicity in which the 'other', 'stranger', or the 'invader' becomes the scapegoat (cited from Uvin 1998, 136).

We will now take a closer look at the explanatory power of each of the three concepts that together make up Uvin's approach. We have to proceed in this way, concept by concept, because, as stated before, Uvin does not rely on one theory, but draws from theoretical concepts from different disciplines. For reasons of expositional clarity, I will start with the two 'sub-concepts' and then move on to the overall concept of structural violence.

Granted that Uvin also considers elements beyond relative deprivation (upon which we will touch soon) he does rely strongly on frustration as (part of) his explanation of participation in collective violence (Uvin 1998, 210–211 and 136–138). This frustration should be understood as the result of the gap that the peasants observe between what they have and what they expect. Uvin considers the development community as a prime cause responsible for the peasant's frustration. To quote Uvin (1998, 210–211) :

> It can be argued that the whole development enterprise, with its ideas of material progress, its well-paid employees (whatever the color of their skin) with the four-wheel-drive vehicles, villas, foreign travel, and hundreds of small, daily status symbols, created a permanent reminder of the life that could be but that never would be for the majority of the population.

The problem with Uvin's approach and with the theoretical concepts he used is that a large body of social science research has found that relative deprivation or the frustration-aggression hypothesis does not explain the participation of people in collective violence. This is documented in a paper by Brush (1996) on the dynamics of theory change in the social sciences.[2] Let us take a look at the evidence and arguments put forward by Brush. According to Brush, the theory of relative deprivation was developed in the late 1960s by Gurr. Gurr argued that the potential for collective violence depends on the discontent of members of a society; discontent is a result of a perceived gap between what they have and what they think they should have. It is in fact a concept linking (some would say reducing) sociology and psychology, where the Observation of the (social) gap between one's position and one's expectations provides the motive for action through the psychological frustration-aggression mechanism. It was tested by a number of empirical studies, especially in the 1970s and mostly refuted. The theory was abandoned or substantially modified by Gurr and others who had supported it; relative deprivation is no longer considered the primary cause of collective violence, although it may be a considerable contributing factor under some circumstances (Brush, 1996, 524). Brush considers this rise and decline of the relative deprivation theory a good example of the practice of science.

---

[2] Brush S.G., Dynamics of Theory Change in the Social Sciences, Relative Deprivation and Collective Violence, *Journal of Conflict Resolution*, vol. 40, No. 4, December 1996.

Hypothesis are put forward and tested after which the research community decides whether they hold or not.

After relative deprivation theory in sociology and political science had been abandoned and replaced by other theories, Brush writes, the theory became a flourishing topic among social psychologists. This was possible because some scientists in social psychology continued to refer to publications from sociology and political science favourable to the relative deprivation theory (mostly from the earlier period) and paid less attention to publications that refuted the theory.

For our purpose, I believe that Uvin is making a similar mistake, he is still relying on a theory that has been abandoned and refuted in social science research on participation in collective violence. More particularly, one does not find an explanation in Uvin's approach, and in relative deprivation theory in general, how *individual* feelings of discontent and frustration can be translated into *collective* action. Indeed, it is not enough to state that structural violence leads to acute violence as Uvin does, but one also has to trace and explain the mechanism by which structural conditions (resulting in individual feelings) influence or determine individual decisions (resulting in participation in collective action). Since this problem is not limited to relative deprivation theory, but questions the validity of the correctness of the link between the concept of structural violence and participation in the genocide, we come back to this later on.

Among the alternative theories that replaced relative deprivation theory, Brush mentions resource mobilisation theory as the most important. Tilly (1969, 1975, and 1978), the most well-known advocate of this theory, argued that collective violence is a normal part of the struggle for power among contending groups in a society; it does not occur when groups are especially discontented but when they calculate that action will be successful with benefits that exceed costs (Brush 1996, 527). This brings us again to the question on how collective action occurs.

The second sub-concept on which Uvin relies, scape-goating, is also necessary for his theory to hold. In this, he relies on Staub (1990): under difficult living conditions, scape-goating can diminish feelings of personal and group responsibility for problems, protecting the self-concept. (Uvin 1998, 137). Or, insecure or frustrated people have a high probability for prejudice. To quote Uvin after Staub (1990, 137):

> The benefits of scape-goating include renewed comprehension of the world, hope and feelings of purpose and (138).
> Structural violence provoked a need for scape-goating among ordinary people.

It is however questionable whether you need a theory of scape-goating to explain peasant participation in genocide. According to Valentino (2000, 15) the scapegoat theory suggests that mass killing serves to alleviate the psychological frustration and fear generated by national crisis in society at large. If this claim is correct, we should find that mass killing is usually a popular undertaking among members of dominant social groups. Members of these groups should demonstrate spontaneous support for the killings. Valentino argues that history provides little confirming evidence for these propositions. Mass killing is often carried out with little public support, even from members of dominant social groups. Mass killing in countries such as Cambodia, El Salvador, Uganda, Guatemala, Mozambique or Algeria were not driven by bottom-up public discontent or a popular desire to blame others, but rather by powerful political and military interests working from the top down (Valentino 2000, 16). The weight of scholarly opinion also opposes Goldhagen's conclusion that the Germans wished to see the Jews exterminated. Hitler, the Nazi regime and many of the limited anti-Jewish measures they promoted before the war were broadly popular, but forced deportation and systematic extermination received much less support.

Is the Rwandan genocide a case of broad popular participation? Looking at an absolute figure of about 100,000 perpetrators (approx. 10 % of the adult male Hutu population), one ought to answer 'yes' to this question. However, this would also mean that 90 % of potential adult Hutu male perpetrators did not participate. Des Forges (1999, 260–262) argues as follows:

> When the national authorities ordered the extermination of Tutsi, tens of thousands of Hutu responded quickly, ruthlessly and persistently. They killed without scruple and sometimes with pleasure. They jogged through the streets of Kigali chanting, "let's exterminate them all." They marched through the streets of Butare town shouting "Power, Power." They returned from raids in Kibuye singing that the only enemy was the Tutsi. They boasted about their murders to each other and to the people whom they intended to kill next....Some Rwandans, previously scorned in their communities, seized on the genocide as an opportunity to gain stature and wealth....Not all killers were poor and living in misery. The authorities who directed the genocide constituted a substantial part of the Rwandan elite, vastly richer and better established than the masses—whether participants or victims. Nor were all the poor killers. Some refused to attack Tutsi, even when offered the prospect of pillage or the chance to acquire land that might provide security for their families. The people of Butare, arguably the poorest and most over-populated prefecture, were the last to join the killing campaign.

At least, we believe, there is a case to consider Rwanda one of the most 'popular' genocides ever. However, when we do observe broad popular participation, as in the Rwandan genocide, is this then explained by a theory of scapegoating? Here again, the problem of causation arises: how do you explain the link between the desire for scape-goating and participation in the genocide? Such a link, when it exists, should explain how peasants who have racist feelings and prejudices against the Tutsi engage in collective action. Clearly, we need an explanation of 'popular' participation.

As we have seen, Uvin believes that unfulfilled expectations and frustration were necessary for the genocide to occur. He also believes that Rwandan peasants needed a scapegoat. We agree with Uvin that frustration, prejudice and the conditions of structural violence were widespread among the Rwandan peasantry. Nevertheless, we are trying to show why we do not agree with the link Uvin makes between structural conditions, prejudice, racism on the one hand and participation in collective violence on the other hand. In fact, we are not convinced that we need a theory of frustration nor a theory of scape-goating to explain participation. Instead, we are looking for a theory where we do not need these concepts.

As for Uvin's main point, that structural violence leads to acute violence (participation in genocide), we think that he makes a mistake found in other social science research. As Cohen (1994, 128) puts it, structural explanations must show, rather than assume, that structures do in fact cause the action that leads to the outcome being explained. Showing how a collective outcome results from the choices and constraints of actors, is far from a trivial exercise. For to answer *why* structural conditions produce a certain outcome, is to explain *why* the actors involved in producing that outcome *chose to act* in the ways they did and *how* their choices produced the collective action being explained (Cohen 1994, 19). In other words, structuralists have no other choice than then to analyse the peasant's choice problem in their effort to explain participation in genocide. It is this element of choice analysis that is lacking from Uvin's approach. Following Gupta (1990, 60), we add that relative deprivation has nothing to say about the kind of violence individuals are likely to be engaged in.

Uvin (1998, 213) writes that the genocide was the result of pre-planned, freely chosen actions of leaders and ordinary people alike. In fact, when Uvin uses "independent actors", "preferences" and "constraints" he is in fact on his way to adopt a rational choice explanation of participation in genocide. We come back to this later; all I do here is to show that Uvin's own arguments and his own reasoning could have taken him to adopt a rational choice approach.

When several scholars studying peasant participation in the Rwandan genocide refer to peasants as independent actors and to the choices they made under constraints, then, we believe, the theory most suited to analyse these choices (to participate yes or no and to which degree) is rational choice theory. It was Mancur Olson who in 1965 explained why even the most frustrated individuals usually *do not* engage in collective action. This brings us to the next section in this chapter.

8.2 Rational Choice and Collective Action

8.2.1 Peasants as Rational Actors

In a recent review essay, Catherine and Newbury (2000, 857–858) write that scholars of Rwanda before and during colonialism almost exclusively focussed on the central state, neglecting the world of the peasants in their studies. In postcolonial writings, the narrow character of earlier studies was recognized and research on the peasantry was undertaken along two (different) paths. One school studied the history of the rural areas. Their focus on the past, the Newburys argue, could not bridge the separation between rural life and central politics. Displacing the focus of their work to earlier periods, they removed peasants from power. Another school specialized in technical studies of rural development.[3] By examining the

---

[3] The well-known 1984 National Agricultural Survey is a good example of this school.

technical aspects of rural crisis without considering politics, this school also removed power from rural residents. They considered the peasants as objects, as victims, as recipients of state power and not as actors in their own right.

Recently, several authors working on Rwanda are convinced that peasants should be viewed as consciously acting agents. They place the connection between state power and peasant agency at the centre of their studies. Catherine and David Newbury, Danielle De Lame, Peter Uvin, André Guichaoua, Gérard Prunier and Claudine Vidal are among these authors. None of them however have approached peasant participation in the genocide by means of rational choice theory. In the scrutiny of Uvin's approach in the previous section, however, we have tried to show that the logic of his explanation could have brought him to consider a rational choice approach.

A purely economic approach to participation in acts of collective violence sees itself confronted with the well-known problem of free-rider ship: since collective goods benefit everyone, regardless of the degree of participation, the lure of common goods cannot be the motivating factor for a rational economic man (Tullock 1971). According to Gupta, this approach explains why people *should not* take part in collective action, but fails to explain why people actually *do*. Sociologists and social psychologists on the other hand explain why men *should* rebel in the face of systemic frustration, but fail to explain why they frequently *choose not to*.

Before we argue why we have opted for a (broadly defined) rational choice approach, we will illustrate the approach with an example from the literature. The example confronts important research findings using a structuralist approach to explain peasant rebellions (Skocpol 1979) with a new explanation of the same phenomenon using a rational choice approach (Taylor 1988).

According to Skocpol, peasant rebellions play an important role in bringing about social revolutions. The collapse of the coercive capacity of the state opens the door to peasant rebellions, while *strong community relations* among the peasants increases the likelihood of successful revolutionary collective action.[4] Cohen (1994) argues that Skocpol only makes vague remarks about peasant communities forming the social and organisational basis for peasant revolt. Skocpol never elaborates on how the degree of community in peasant villages affects the behaviour of peasants. As a structuralist, she does not pay attention to the motivations of peasants and therefore stops short of a genuine explanation, offering instead a *correlational* statement. She links a structural variable to a form of collective action: the stronger the community, the higher the probability of a peasant rebellion.

Michael Taylor has shown how Skocpol's argument can be improved, by resorting to an intentional type of explanation. Taylor argues that Skocpol is essentially correct concerning community and rebellion, but she fails to provide

---

[4] Skocpol T. *States and Social Revolutions: a Comparative Analysis of France, Russia and China*, Cambridge University Press, 1979.

the intervening links showing the effect of social structure (community) on the individuals (peasants) and the interaction between those individuals. Taylor shows that strong communities were more likely to generate peasant rebellions because strong community made it rational for a peasant to rebel (Cohen 1994, 20). He notes that a strong community facilitates co-operation among peasants, and therefore makes participation rational, *not just because individual behaviour can more easily be monitored, but because a strong community has at its disposal an array of powerful, positive and negative social sanctions*, sanctions that *can be used as selective incentives, not only to induce individuals simply to contribute or participate, but also to bolster conditional co-operation—which is always a precarious business.* In the absence of community, the villager has a much greater incentive *not* to participate in collective action. Since weaker communities do not have the means to punish free riders, or to reward participation, the individual peasant has an incentive to let the other peasants rebel; he will get the benefits of rebellion anyway. As a consequence, no one will have an incentive to rebel and a rebellion will not take place.

Cohen argues that the rational choice theory of collective action tells us, *why*, in strong communities, revolt becomes a feasible option and tells us, *why*, in such communities, a rational peasant chooses that option. Taylor's explanation is perfectly compatible with Skocpol's structural explanation (or better correlation), Cohen argues, but Taylor does a far better job. Skocpol argues that people do not 'make' revolutions; these are largely the unintended consequences of people acting under structural circumstances which were not of their choosing. Structural circumstances may be important, Cohen writes, but they do not reveal the causal mechanism linking structure with peasant action. Taylor just does this, he explains revolts as a result of the choices of rational agents.

8.2.2 Rational Behaviour in Economics and Political Science

With Tsebelis (1990), we argue that the rational choice approach is very well suited to studying political behaviour, for the following reasons. Tsebelis uses *five arguments in defence of a rational choice approach to political decision-making*. I will follow his reasoning here and argue why his arguments can be applied to Rwanda:

1. *Salience of issues and information*: depending on the issues at stake, people prefer to conform with the behaviour prescribed by rational choice theory. Otherwise, they pay a price. If very important matters are at stake, people will try to make good decisions, they will gather information, they will weigh the different options very carefully. Moreover, when information is available, people will be able to approximate the calculations required by rational choice better than when payoffs are not well known. As far as Rwanda is concerned,

the issue of whether or not a person participates in acts of killing one's neighbors, attacking Tutsi who are sheltering in a church, or any other kind of violent behaviour, are very important issues. Since a lot is at stake, it is safe to assume that an individual will do his/her utmost best to take an optimal decision, one that conforms to or approximates the conditions of utility maximisation under uncertainty.

2. *Learning*: the properties of the rational-choice model suggest that people engaging in repeated activities approximate optimal behaviour through trial and error. In fact, subjective probabilities will converge to objective frequencies as additional information becomes available through iteration. Consequently, Tsebelis argues, the final outcome becomes almost indistinguishable from rational-choice calculations. Learning is not independent of the salience of issues and information. One would expect a correlation between the speed of learning and the salience of the issue. Convergence to optimal behaviour is faster as the frequency of the decision-making problem increases. In Rwanda, in a period of three and half years (October 1990–March 1994), peasants have learned that violence is part of daily life, that violence is directed against Tutsi and Hutu who oppose the Habyarimana regime, that the perpetrators of violence are not punished and that these perpetrators are shielded from prosecution by the regime itself. This means that ordinary peasants learn that violence against Tutsi is not sanctioned and even encouraged. This learning experience will influence decision-making at the time of the genocide, in April 1994.

3. *Heterogeneity of individuals*: in order for rational choice theory to be realistic, it is not necessary that all individuals make rational choice calculations. Haltiwanger and Waldman (1985) have shown that equilibria where only some individuals confirm to the calculations of rational choice, will tend towards equilibria where all individuals behave rationally. This is because the rational individuals will anticipate and compensate the behaviour of non-rational individuals. For the study of peasant participation in the Rwandan genocide, it is therefor not necessary to assume that all peasants confirm to rational choice theory. Peasants or other individuals with—let us say—high stakes, will foresee that other peasants will not behave rationally and will anticipate this behaviour. If very well-informed individuals believe that less-informed individuals will refuse to attack Tutsi hiding in a local school, they will spread the rumor that these Tutsi have just killed the Hutu schoolmaster. Such a rumor will increase the readiness of the "less-informed" Hutu to participate in the attack on the school.

4. *Natural selection*: when members of a population are defined by their different reactions when faced with the same situation, the same behavioral outcomes (equilibria) can be reached when an evolutionary path is followed. In the long run, the most successful individuals will be rewarded and their behaviour reinforced. The outcome will then approximate optimal choice without any conscious means/end calculation by those involved. Since an evolutionary approach adopts weak assumptions about individuals' motivation and attributes selection to environmental factors, evolutionary arguments can be used to support the optimality of behaviour only after eliminating alternative

explanations. The reason for one's selection namely may not have been the behaviour under investigation. In Rwanda, people who participated in the 1959 Revolution, in the 1963 massacres and in the 1973 coup d'état have seen themselves rewarded with influential positions in business and politics. After the Revolution, Hutu peasants clearly experienced that land that was previous earmarked for pasture was now open to cultivation. This means that many Hutu households, both in the administration, the business community, the schools as well as the peasantry experienced tangible benefits from ethnic cleansing and expulsion of Tutsi, many years prior to the genocide.

5. *Statistics*: this argument involves the properties of the population mean. Assume, that rationality is a small but systematic component of any individual, and all other influences are distributed at random. The systematic component has a magnitude of x, and the random element is distributed with variance s^2. Under these assumptions, each individual of the population will execute a decision in the interval [x − (2s), x + (2s)] 95 % of the time. If, however, we consider a sample of a million individuals, the average individual will make a decision in the interval [x − (2s/1000), x + (2s/1000)] 95 % of the time. This can be verified by the statistical properties of the mean : the rational decision assumed to be only a "systematic although very small component" was approximated by the average individual of the sample at a factor of one thousand times that of the random individual (Tsebelis 1990, 36).

8.3 Mechanism Explaining Participation in Rwanda's Genocide

In this section we will investigate several mechanisms explaining participation of human beings in collective violence. We follow Bardhan's (1997) approach and apply his and other insights to the Rwandan situation.

8.3.1 Individual and Group Welfare

Although economists generally believe that actors are self-interested and as a consequence maximise private expected utility, the rational choice approach does not require that an actor is purely self-interested. As Sen (1987, 15) has put it.

Why should it be uniquely rational to pursue one's own self-interest to the exclusion of everything else? It may not, of course, be all that absurd to claim that maximization of self interest is not irrational, at least not necessarily so, but to argue that anything other than maximizing self-interest must be irrational seems altogether extraordinary.

Following Sen, we argue that the assumption of a perfect correspondence between selfishness and rationality prevents many economists (and others) to explain a large chunk of human interaction. In a pure Olsonian logic of the free rider, no public work in a democracy will ever be funded, no call for social change will ever be followed by action, no battle will ever be won. As a consequence, we accept that an individual is not only self-interested, he is also a social human being.[5] An important part of our identity consists of our relation with the collectivity. We are happy to work not only for our own interests, but also contribute to the well-being of our collective identity, be it a national, religious, political, ethnic or cultural collectivity. We thus recognize that an individual is interested in his own welfare and in the welfare of the group with whom he identifies. The bridge between these dual motivations is what Gupta (1990) calls 'ideology'. Ideology determines the relative strength of an individual's interest in his personal welfare and in group welfare. The importance of group welfare in the real world is beyond any doubt. In the name of our collective identity, wars have been fought, barriers have been overcome, enormous buildings have been constructed, and last but not least, massacres have been committed. The importance of the collectivity or ideological factors is slowly being accepted in economics (Arrow 1972; Stigler 1981), or at least it has been recognized that the existence of such factors is not inconsistent with the economic view of human behaviour (Becker 1974, 1976; Hirshleifer 1977, 1985).

If we accept the proposition that rational behaviour *can* include factors of group welfare or ideology, then there are several reasons to believe that they are likely to be more prevalent in the political domain than in the pure economic domain (Kalt and Zupan, 1984):

- Altruistic behavior contains a clear component of improving the conditions of the members of a group. This collective good attribute makes the demand for collective goods susceptible to the free-rider problem within the market system. The actions taken by the government (through its coercive capabilities) offer a solution to the free rider problem in the marketplace;
- In much political activities, an individual has little control over the outcomes or to promote his own investment effectively. Therefore, an individual is more apt to choose on the basis of tastes, preference or ideology;
- Since the exact costs and benefits of public goods remain undetermined in the minds of the ordinary citizens, the opportunity costs of ideology (in terms of forgone pecuniary returns) may appear to be lower in the political arena than what they may be in the marketplace.

We stress that we are considering 'ideology' in a rational choice framework. By no means do we want to state that ideology (group interest) is the only or even the most important motivation behind individual behavior. The author is too much an economist to believe that ideology alone drives ordinary people. It is however clear to me that while criminal activities are committed for the personal profit of the criminal, political activities bear some element of group welfare.

---

[5] Gupta 1990, p. 114.

- **Application: The 'Majority People' Becomes the 'Great Mass (Rubanda Nyamwinshi)'**

In Rwanda, "group welfare" was not an abstract concept, it was applied in day to day business. The ethnic identity cards are probably the best known policy that demonstrates that the Rwandan state wanted every Rwandan to know and *to identify* with the category mentioned on his or her identity card. In peaceful times, in the hills of Rwanda, ethnicity was not very important in a peasant's day to day activities. In contact with the state and with state agencies however, every Rwandan felt the influence of the ethnic identity card. Every cell, sector and commune held detailed list of the ethnic composition of the population. In schools, at the start of the new school year, children were asked what their ethnic affiliation was. In times of troubles, division along ethnic lines soon gained importance. Lame (1996) recounts how relations between Hutu and Tutsi in the area of her field work (commune of Bwakira, prefecture of Kibuye) became tense after Hutu from Burundi took refuge in southern Rwanda in 1988.[6]

As I have shown in the first chapter, the Habyarimana regime used overpopulation as an argument to ban the return of Tutsi refugees, even when they were expelled from Uganda. As soon as the RPF invaded the country, the Habyarimana regime appealed to *"the majority people"* to unite for the Hutu cause. Remark that the regime again relies on the demographic composition of the Rwandan population to make its point. It clearly counted on the idea of group identity and group welfare to unite behind the Hutu leadership. In the course of the civil war, everything was undertaken to replace loyalties to political parties with purely ethnic loyalty. This is evident from the documents on the organisation of civilian self-defense discussed in Chap. 7. During the genocide, the members of the militia and the peasants that joined these militia believed they were working for the common good. They shouted that they were the "Hutu people" and that they were not afraid of the Tutsi.

8.3.2 Fear, Trust and Social Cohesion

- **The Explanation by Réne Lemarchand**

Lemarchand (2002) considers the "fear factor mechanism" to be the prime cause of participation in the genocide. He argues that the Hutu masses were so afraid of the re-installation of a Tutsi monarchy that they *"had to act first"* before they would be killed themselves.[7] According to Lemarchand, the Rwandan genocide

---

[6] De Lame D. (1996), Une Colline entre mille ou me calme avant la tempete, Transformations et Blocages du Rwanda Rural, Musée Royale de l' Afrique Centrale, Tervuren, postface p. 295.

[7] Lemarchand, R., Reconsidering Rwanda and the Holocaust, *Journal of Genocide Research*, September 2002.

then was a *"retributive"* genocide, as distinguished from an "ideologically motivated" genocide. Lemarchand regards fear caused by the civil war responsible for the genocide.

There is certainly evidence of fear caused by the 1990 invasion, but there is very few evidence that this fear was the prime mover in the killing behaviour of Hutu peasants prior to the killing of president Habyarimana (April 1994). Violence against Tutsi not "erupted" as Lemarchand (2002, p. 505) writes, it was organised at a few carefully chosen places, as I described in Chap. 6. The "cause" then of the killing is not the fear, but the deliberate and targeted campaign implemented by the national and local leadership.

Lemarchand pays a lot of attention to the context in which the killings took place (namely the civil war), but he fails to discuss the organisation behind the massacres as well as the fabricated stories spread just before each attack. One must have a complete disregard for the facts mentioned in the FIDH and ADL reports to attribute these killings to fear for the RPF. Had the authorities not organised, incited and called for murder, these massacres would not have taken place.

When I argue that the fear factor mechanism in the way it is described by Lemarchand is not the mechanism driving Hutu peasants to participate in the violence, I do not mean that there was not fear. The point is to qualify the source, the existence and the functioning of this fear. In fact, this approach stems from research in the rational choice tradition by Weingast (1994) and Bardhan (1997). The first argues with a game-theoretic example applied to the process of disintegration of Yugoslavia that the damage from victim-hood is often so large that even a small probability that the other group will act aggressively can induce the first group to initiate violence, even when the latter would have preferred to live in peaceful coexistence. When democratic institutions and credible mechanisms of commitment and arbitration collapse, the ethnic composition of different regions may be such that there is reciprocal vulnerability to violence. In such situations each group is afraid of being victimized (Bardhan 1997).

Was this mechanism at work in Rwanda? And if so, to which degree? We can consider the non-implementation of the Arusha peace-agreement and the continuation of the civil war as a breakdown of commitment and arbitration in Bardhan's sense? The Hutu population regarded (a large part of) their Tutsi compatriots sympathetic to the invading force, either this sympathy was implicitly believed to be there or it was demonstrated explicitly. The attack caused resentment among the Hutu population and their leaders. Ordinary peasants together with local and national elites believed they would loose the benefits brought by the 1959 Revolution in case of an RPF victory. Ordinary people were afraid of losing their land and administrators were afraid of losing their privileged position in society. The perspective of losing one's assets, one's opportunities or even one's life can drive people to strike pre-emptively. Interviews with perpetrators suggest that fear played a role in their actions: *"If we did not act first, the Tutsi would kill us all"* is an often heard expression in prisons.

Importantly, the strategic recourse to violence is the result of missing institutions of arbitration, trust and commitment. Three examples from the 1992–1993 period may illustrate the breakdown of institutions of trust in Rwandan society:

1. The February 1993 surprise attack by the RPF which gave them a strategic advantage in northern Rwanda and opened up the way for an attack on Kigali. In a time when RPF is in full negotiation with the government (by then a multi party one) in Arusha, such an attack is devastating for trust building.
2. The declaration by Habyarimana himself in Nov 1992 that the agreements with the RPF are only "*a scrap of paper*". Such a declaration strengthens the believes of the opposing party that only a military solution can solve the issue. Regime supporters can interprete such declaration as a refusal to solve the issue peacefully and that they should be prepared for further fighting.
3. The coup d'état in Burundi in Nov 1993 where the Tutsi army killed the elected president Ndadaye (Hutu). According to Lemarchand,[8] this event caused widespread distrust among the Rwandan Hutu leaders. According to Reyntjens,[9] this putsch radicalised the Rwandan Hutu.[10]

Weingast's model is one of institutional failure: when there is a breakdown in trust and commitment, members of a group re-evaluate the probability of facing aggression from an opposing party, and when that probability exceeds a critical value (below which peace is maintained), fears of becoming a victim will induce the former group to initiate violence.

From the moment Habyarimana's plane was shot down, the situation on the ground becomes increasingly tense, what may best be described as a roller-coaster upon which the whole of Rwanda takes a ride. Fear among the Rwandan population is at a maximum level, both among Hutu as well as among Tutsi. Tutsi know for sure that many of them will die and many Hutu are afraid of the acts fellow Hutu will want them to commit to show their adherence to the Hutu-cause. The shooting down of the plane offers a window of opportunity for the extremists.

Lemarchand (2002, 507–508) is convinced that it is the fear factor that drives people to participate in the murder of their neighbours. Given such fear, he believes it is rational for a Hutu person to kill Tutsi. According to Lemarchand, the shooting down of Habayarimana's plane required an immediate response of the Hutu extremists to secure their survival (p. 512):

---

[8] Lemarchand R., Reconsidering Rwanda and the Holocaust, *Journal of Genocide Research*, September 2002.

[9] Reyntjens F., *l'Afrique des Grands Lacs en crise*, 1994, p. 301–302.

[10] We remark that the November 1993 coup d'état in Burundi was followed by large scale killing of Hutu and Tutsi, occuring without interference of the international community. Several scholars deduce from this that the Habyarimana regime learned from this that 'Tutsi' (remark the generalisation) could not be trusted. Other scholars remark that they may have learned something else: that the killing of large numbers of people could take place without firm international response. We remind that by the time of the coup d'état the Habyarimana regime had already organised the killing of 2,000 Tutsi in several Rwandan communes.

> The decision to apply the full force of genocidal violence against all Tutsi as well as every Hutu suspected of Tutsi sympathies stemmed from straigthforward rational choice proposition: either we kill them first, or else we'll be killed. Thus framed, the logic of the 'security dilemma' left no alternative to annihilate the enemies of the nation.

I believe it is interesting to bring the rational choice perspective in the discussion, as Lemarchand does, but I do not agree with his understanding of the mechanisms at work. Other mechanisms seem to be at work, mechanisms we will turn too. With Bardhan (1997), we argue that, after discussing ideology, war and fear, we still need to understand the decision making process of the individual member of a group to join a rampaging campaign. This is what we will do in the subsequent sections. First however, I refer to social capital theory to show that the breakdown of trust (bridging social capital) between two groups is one thing, but the increase in intra-group trust or bonding social capital is at least as important.

• Social Capital, Social Cohesion and Collective Violence

Social capital helps to solve the mobilization/coordination problem. It predisposes peasants to mobilize for group activities and collective action: activities such as attending association meetings, working together, gathering in places of worship, building and maintaining public infrastructures and cooperating for a common purpose create fertile ground for collective outputs. In villages with active groups and associations, households' participation is likely to be high and monitoring mechanisms are more likely to be in place. Households are accustomed to working together, and social ties deter free-riding. Social capital provides examples of positive patterns of cooperation that can be used for purposes different from the one usually pursued. Networks and associations facilitate collective action and decision-making by increasing benefits of compliance with expected behavior or by increasing the costs of non-compliance. Social capital manifests itself in obligations, expectations, information sharing, norms/sanctions, that influence group behavior.

Social Capital also facilitates social control. In the hills of Rwanda everybody knows everybody. There exists a strong tradition of social control by the authorities: tight administrative control with ability to monitor the population. Information is diffused more quickly within a cohesive group (or community) than between groups. It facilitates the transmission of knowledge about the behavior of others: reputation, expectations about their behavior. As an enforcement mechanism, it increases the efficiency of groups. It also facilitates the spread of knowledge, information, rumors, threats (see Lederman et al. 2000). Janky and Takacs express it as follows:

> Collective action aims at the provision of certain public goods for a community. If narrow self-interest does not provide incentives for the private provision of public goods, collective action may fail. However, some forms of social control might help to overcome the social dilemma that stems from the lack of incentives for voluntary contribution. Social control operates as a constraint on individual decision posed by the influence, as well as by

the behavior, opinion and expectations of relevant other individuals. Interpersonal ties are one of the key mobilizing forces in collective action, because they transmit different forms of social control that would be less present in anonymous communities. Intensive interpersonal ties, closed and dense social networks can produce a strong social capital that maintains group norms, fosters cooperation and triggers the expected individual behavior.[11]

Graph: Social Capital, Social Cohesion, Collective Action and Violent Conflict

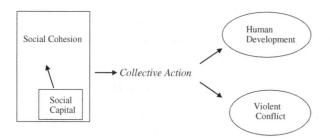

Social capital forms a subset of the notion of social cohesion. According to Berkman and Kawachi (2000), social cohesion refers to two broader intertwined features of society: (1) the absence of latent conflict (inequalities, tensions, division, disparities); (2) the presence of strong social bonds (trust, norms of reciprocity, abundance of associations that bridge social divisions, presence of institutions of conflict management). Social cohesion is the key intervening variable between social capital and violent conflict. A cohesive society possesses inclusive mechanisms necessary for managing conflict before it turns violent. The weaker the social cohesion, the weaker the reinforcing channels of socialization and social control (compliance mechanisms). Weak societal cohesion increases the risk of fragmentation and exclusion, potentially manifesting itself in violent conflict. Social capital can be readily perverted to undermine social cohesion and fragment society for individual and group gain. We refer the chap. 8 to see bonding social capital at work.

8.3.3 Norms, Social Sanctions and Selective Incentives

Participants and potential participants in the attacks on Tutsi civilians received selective benefits or were promised these benefits. The organizers of the genocide provided all kinds of incentives to increase the number of participants and their degree of participation: administrators, political leaders, military leaders and

---

[11] Janky B. and Takacs K., Social Control, Participation in Collective Action and Network Stability.

wealthy businessmen distributed free beer, paid wages, promised land and jobs, and allowed and encouraged rape. All these incentives can be considered as rewards, as payments that are directly received by the participants and that cannot be consumed by non-participants. If one or a few members of a group have a considerable interest in the success of collective action, they will do their utmost best to increase the contribution of group members. In other words, they minimise the number of free riders by offering selective incentives. As Olson has described, these incentives can be positive (rewards) or negative (punishments). *These selective incentives induce peasants to participate, in other words: they make participation rational.* Des Forges (1999, 236–237)—who is an historian, not a rational choice scientist—gives perfect examples of the power of these selective incentives:

> They (Burgomasters) directed or permitted communal police, militia, or simply other citizens to burn down houses and to threaten the lives of those who refused to join in the violence. They also offered powerful incentives to draw the hesitant into killing. They or others solicited by them provided cash payments, food, drinks and, in some cases, marijuana to assailants. They encouraged the looting of Tutsi property, even to the point of having the pillage supervised by the communal police...In several places police reprimanded those people who wanted only to pillage and not to kill. ...One of the most important resources for the burgomaster in enlisting participants was his authority to control the distribution of land, a much desired and scarce source of wealth for the largely agricultural population. Hutu who had attacked Tutsi in the 1960s had acquired the fields of the victims. A generation later, people again hoped to get more land by killing or driving Tutsi away. As Pasteur Kumubuga commented in a meeting in Bwakira commune: "Those who killed say that the properties of the victims belong to them." At a later meeting, another participant commented that people were cultivating lands taken from victims "to reward themselves for the work they had done." As usual, "work" meant "killings."

Next to positive incentives for participation, we also have to consider sanctions (disincentives to refuse or lower participation). *We have models in economics that show how a Nash equilibrium of individual conformity to unpleasant group behaviour can be reached and sustained when there exists a mutually sustaining network of social sanctions against disobedience.* The model Akerlof presented in 1984 may be the most well-known: in his model, a norm, once established, will persist, provided that disobedience of the norm results in sufficient loss of reputation, and provided that the cost of disobedience is sufficiently high (Akerlof 1984, 71). This means that, when the right sanctions or in place and can be executed, a social norm may be obeyed even though it is to everyone's individual economic disadvantage to obey it.

In Rwanda, evidence suggests that Hutu *complied with the norm 'to kill Tutsi'* not only or not merely out of fear for the RPF, but out of fear for their fellow Hutu who were actively engaged in the killing campaign. As Forges writes (1999, 388).

> To turn pillagers into killers and resisters into participants, Ntaganzwa decided to eliminate several moderate Hutu leaders who were providing a model and a cover for others who would not kill. The most important was Jean-Marie Vianney Gasingwa, the PSD leader in the commune and Ntaganzwa's rival for political control since more then a year

before. ...He had refused to disarm the Tutsi the day before the massacre, thus encouraging a similar refusal from others.

The death of this influential Hutu moderate and other moderates was very important in shaping popular thinking (p. 389).

When party leaders got killed, that scared the lesser PSD people. As in so many places in Rwanda, people who had begun just by fearing the RPF now had reason to fear their own officials and political leaders. Because Ntaganzwa had already demonstrated his ruthlessness before April 6, people could easily believe that he would use force against any who opposed the genocide.

Lemarchand (2002, 508) turns this around, writing that it were the MRND extremists who feared the Hutu opposition. If this bears some truth, at least we are talking about another kind of fear, namely the fear to loose power. Hutu moderates and Tutsi did not fear to loose power, they feared that Hutu extremists would kill them.

As Akerlof says, the punishment for disobedience (non-participation) should be sufficiently high in order to maintain the norm. For many Hutu, who were rounded up to join the killing campaign, there was no way back (at least in their perception): either you demonstrated your commitment to the cause or either you were considered a traitor. Evidence suggests that many Hutu went to great lengths to avoid this dilemma: they stayed at home, they hid themselves, they pretended they were participating in the killing when they were only stealing goods, and so on. If fear for the RPF was the prime motivating factor to join the killing campaign, Hutu would not face these dilemma's.

It should be stressed that we are not looking for a unique type of participant. People indeed have participated at different levels and for different reasons. There were killers who were highly motivated by ideology (a small but very active minority) and who hated the Tutsi, there were opportunist who joined in for personal profit, there may be other types of behaviour, but a large part of the Hutu population was neither motivated by ideology nor by personal profit, they just wanted to get through this dreadful period. Doing as others were doing (obedience to a new norm) was one way to overcome that period. Gupta (1990) distinguishes three types of participants: ideologists, opportunists and captive participants. Reading the literature on massacres committed during the Nazi-period, we believe that these three types of perpetrators, considered in a collective action framework, go a long way in explaining perpetrator behavior. In his seminal book on police batallion 101 (normale Männer 1999), Christopher Browning describes the complexity of the behavior of the members of a batallion that massacred thousands of Jews in their own villages. Among the perpetrators, Browning counts a small number of real ideologues, committed Nazis (1999, 67–68). He also gives evidence of opportunist behavior, policemen enriching themselves during the massacres by taking the property of the Jews (1999, 33 and 44). Career thinking also played a role, as a number of people stayed with the police even after the war (1999, 222). The majority of the members of the batallion however can be labelled as "captive participants" in the killing campaign. They namely experienced great difficulties in the execution of their murderous task. Many of them in fact did not want to participate, hid themselves in the wood during the massacres, asked their superiors for another job or deliberately saved their victim by misaiming their guns (1999, 94–104). The very fact that most members nevertheless carried out the murders can be explained by Akerlof's norm abiding mechanism and Axelrod's theory on the dominance and sustenance of norms (see below).

We remark that our discussion of the obedience to a norm is not the same as the traditional *"obedience to authority"* that is invoked by some scholars to explain peasant participation. In that line of thinking, peasants are considered passive recipients of orders and they do what the local leaders tell them to do. The Akerlof model is something different. This model explains why a rational individual would choose to obey a norm even when obeying it is not in his individual interest.

The presence of such a killing norm would also explain why Tutsi believed that the entire Hutu population joined the killing campaign. This was not the case, but one can imagine that victims must have experienced it in that way: the dominant mode of behaviour of gangs or groups of Hutu was to attack and kill Tutsi. When this norm is sustained and does not encounter much resistance from non-murderous Hutu, or when this resistance is overruled, a victim would soon get the impression that all Hutu are killers. In order to find an answer on the development of such a norm, we proceed to the next mechanism.

8.3.4 A "Tipping" Equilibrium, Bandwagons, Legitimate Authority, Rumors and Informational Cascades

According to Gupta (1990, 131), the mobilisation of participants acts as a cumulative factor in a collective movement, as potential participants upgrade the perception of the probability of their getting apprehended for non-participation. Members of rampaging crowds find comfort in numbers. This *"bandwagon effect"*, as more people join in, causes the equilibrium or the peace norm to turn over or tip into a killing norm (the idea of a "tipping" equilibrium is coined by Schelling 1960). This means that their exists a point at which a population tips over from a non-aggressive behavioral norm to a norm of extreme aggression depending on the perceptions of the probabilities of population members which of the two norms is going to dominate. Kuran (1995, 247–260, see below) describes this bandwagon effect as a process where the private preferences of individuals are influenced by the public discourse. If a critical value in the public discourse on violence or peace is reached (by one or the other event), a number of people who hitherto behaved peacefully will stop supporting peace and turn become supporters of violence. Their behavior will in turn influence the public discourse (that has by now become more violent) and thus lower the threshold for new participants. If the support for peace among a population is equally distributed from 0 to 100 among a population, Kuran argues, a few violent people can set such a bandwagon in motion.

The organisers of genocide not only used selective incentives to increase peasant participation, they also did everything they could to make all Hutu believe and perceive that the killing norm was going to rule and become the dominant norm. Using radio propaganda, demonstrating their power in the streets, punishing and killing people who resisted the genocide, they send the message to every Hutu that it was his and her duty to participate. What we encounter here is the effect of (*supposedly*) *legitimate authority* in setting a norm. Potential participants hesitated in the beginning of the genocide to pillage and kill. When however they saw that the local and national authorities encouraged the pillaging and the killing, ordinary people went along (Des Forges, 262). Organisers of the genocide used their authority in the hills to make a whole group complicit in the killing process. As Brandstetter (1999, 177), writes, they wanted to develop a new Rwandan Nation, consisting of people who were complicit in genocide.

Axelrod (1997, 63), who has studied the emergence and promotion of norms, writes that it is easier to get a norm started when it serves the interests of the powerful few. This exactly applies to the Rwandan situation where, as we have seen in Chap. 7, a powerful elite of politico-military leaders pushed the genocidal policy forward. If a powerful group promotes a certain pattern of behavior, their punishments alone can often be sufficient to establish it. Persons who resisted the genocidal policy where either killed or replaced.

Bardhan (1997, 1391) argues that there is an additional element of fragility in the information processed by members of crowds or masses. He argues that *rumors* play a very important role in sparking communal riots in a hitherto quiet neighbourhood. Such rumours often spread a message of violence perpetrated by members of an opposed community. In the dynamics of imitative decision making processes, also called *informational cascades*, rumours play a particularly destructive role. Bikhchandani et al. (1992) describe an informational cascade as a situation in which it is optimal for an individual, having observed the actions of those ahead of him, to follow the behaviour of the preceding individual without regard to his own information.

> a Hindu or a Serb will ignore his private information about his friendly Muslim neighbor and go by what others have told him about the aggressive propensities of Muslims. (Bardhan 1997, 1392)

An informational cascade aggregates the information of only a few early sources. Contrary thus to the bandwagon effect (where members find comfort in their number), a cascade can be broken when new and credible information turns up denying the early rumor or other source of information.

In the 1990–1993 period as well as in the genocide itself, we have watched the devastating impact of rumours. Consider for example the killing of ten Belgian peace keepers on 7th April 1994. During the hours that preceded these murders, the rumour was spread that it were the Belgians who shot Habyarimana's plane (Senate's report of Inquiry on Rwanda 1997). This shows the double effect of a rumour. It is spread intentionally to obtain a certain goal (to ruin one's name, making the Belgians leave Rwanda) and to convince Rwandans of the enmity of the Belgians, making it easier for them to attack former partners.

Testimonies gathered by Des Forges (1999, 372) also illuminate the power of rumors:

> A witness from Rutobwe linked the anti-Tutsi propaganda directly to Ntaganzwa's meetings with his circle:
> At these meetings, every sector was represented by one or more people, friends of the burgomaster...Those people trusted by the burgomaster came out of the meetings and they spoke to others. They went to the leaders of the party, saying:"Be careful, those Tutsi are going to kill us. They are RPF all over. They have hidden arms."
> In this way, by spreading these rumors, they made a large part of the population afraid of the RPF. I remember once I was speaking with one of my students and I told him: "You are crazy to say that all Tutsi are armed RPF." Even though he said these things, I really didn't believe that he was serious. "Did you ever see an RPF soldier?" I asked him. But he was serious. They cultivated fear.

Other messages could and would have reduced fear. But certain people had decided that hate and fear and not other messages should be spread.

8.3.5   Timur Kuran and the Theory of the Formation of Public Opinion

Timur Kuran developed a theory of the interaction between private and public opinion. His theory explains why and under which circumstances people will follow prevailing behavioural norms. We outline this theory in detail since we believe if offers substantial insight in the 'success' of the Rwandan genocide. Kuran's theory is in essence a model of social pressure to conform to group norms, or to public opinion. It goes as follows:

An individual has a private preference towards a policy on a scale from 0 to 100 where 0 means complete opposition towards the policy and 100 means full agreement. The maximisation of his private preference, e.g. at $x = 20$ yields *intrinsic utility*. The choice of 20 means that privately he would like society to set the policy at 20.[12] Other options, below and above 20, are ranked in accordance with their distance to 20. This does not mean that our individual will reveal his choice of 20 in public. Apart from the mentioned intrinsic utility, his total utility is also composed of *reputational utility* and *expressive utility*. The former are the rewards and punishments associated with his publicly declared preference and the latter are the benefits he derives from truthful self-expression. With his concept of reputational utility Kuran (1995, 26–27) namely recognises that humans feel stress when they are isolated, that they care about the opinion of others and that they want to be seen as accepting society's basic institutions out of fear to loose social

---

[12] For simplicity we assume the intrinsic utility function has a single peak.

recognition.[13] Individuals however also resist some of the demands placed on them, occasionally at substantial personal risk. Not everybody submits to social pressure. This need to have self-esteem from resisting social pressures and establish ourselves as people to be reckoned with is captured by the concept of expressive utility.

Now, when he declares his *public preference*, *y*, as different from his private preference $x = 20$, he engages in *preference falsification*. This is the practice of misrepresenting one's genuine wants under perceived social pressures. In large groups, our individual's impact on the group decision will be negligible and thus he will consider society's decision (and thus his intrinsic utility) as given.[14] Therefore, in revealing his public preference, he will trade-off reputational and expressive utility. An individual cultivating his individuality to a maximum would set *y* equal to *x*, meaning supporting publicly what he prefers in private. In setting *y* different from *x*, the individual sacrifices this kind of utility, but makes gains in reputational utility. The greater the degree of preference falsification (*y* widely different from *x*), the larger the sacrifice in terms of expressive utility and the larger the gains in reputational utility.[15]

Kuran argues that there is a lot of variation between people inside one country or culture and across countries in the desire for self-esteem and their readiness to bow to social pressure. In the Asch and Milgram experiments, subjects facing identical social pressures differed in their readiness to conform to the majority. Variation in people's responses to prevailing social pressures implies that individuals differ in terms of the incentives needed to make them abandon one publicly declared preference for another. Kuran calls this switchover point one's *political threshold*. This is the percentage of the population that has to declare himself in favour of a policy before the individual changes his publicly declared opinion.

Kuran writes that the Olsonian logic of collective action does not provide an adequate explanation of the emergence of new political movements or pressure groups for a specific policy. According to his theory, such pressure groups can best be explained by pointing out that they are initiated by *activists*. These activists, in opposition to non-activists have unusually intense wants on particular matters, coupled with great expressive needs. They gain high satisfaction of truthful self-expression and are therefore insensitive to reputational incentives. While the support of the activists to the cause is unconditional, that of the far more numerous non-activists is conditional on the prevailing public opinion.

Consider our individual's public preference declaration on an issue of great sensitivity. Her private preference happens to be x = 20. There are two pressure groups each supporting a stance on the extremes of the distribution, 0 and 100.

---

[13] Kuran mentions the Asch and Milgram experiments to support his view that people fear isolation in groups.

[14] But see below for the influence well-placed people can have on group-decisions.

[15] In this threefold conception, Kuran recognises the economic, social and psychological sources of utility.

If the pressure from both groups is equal, our individual will publicly support 0. If the pressure from the group advocating 100 would be very large, our individual, as a non-activist would trade-off expressive utility for reputational concerns.[16] This implies that there is a level of social pressure at which he is indifferent between publicly declaring his support for 0 or 100. This level is his political threshold.

As individuals have different private preferences, expressive needs and fears of disapproval, their political thresholds will vary. We can then plot a cumulative distribution of thresholds that shows for each policy between 0 and 100 the percentage of society with thresholds at or below that level. As this cumulative distribution determines the propagation of preference falsification; Kuran names it the *propagation curve*.

In this model, non-activists will adapt their public statements depending on the size of the majority. At any particular time, each member of the society will have some expectation of mean public opinion in the period just ahead. Kuran assumes that *expected public opinion* Ye is the same for everybody. Given Ye, the prevailing propagation curve will yield a realisation of public opinion.

In Fig. 8.1, public opinion over an issue is divided in two camps supporting either 0 or 100. At the start we assume Ye = 20. The propagation curve indicates that 35 % of the population has a political threshold at or below 20. This share of the population will give its public support to 100 and the other 65 % to 0. In the figure, any expectation below 40 will fall short of the corresponding realisation and generate upward revisions till a public opinion *equilibrium* is reached at Ye = 40.

Figure 8.2 depicts a case with multiple equilibria, one at 20, the second at 50 and the third at 90. The equilibrium at 50 is unstable as nearby expectations will generate a movement in the direction of one of the two other equilibria. Public opinion will go to one or the other, depending on whether their expectations are below or above 50. Assume again that at the start Ye = 20. Various factors could make an individual's threshold move. We already mentioned very effective pressure from one group. Another possibility could be a change of private preference, say to x = 30 or x = 40. Such a change, possibly caused by an event external to the model, would reduce the expressive disadvantage from supporting 100 and would thus lower his political threshold.

Such change will raise the propagation curve from the solid curve to the broken curve in Fig. 8.2. The shift destroys the initial equilibrium at 20 and forms a *bandwagon* that only stops when 90 % of the population is on board. This bandwagon develops because some people with lowered thresholds are now switching sides on the issue. This is enough to elicit change from others. This process is self-augmenting till a new equilibrium is reached at 90.

Let us now apply this model to the Rwandan case to investigate how it can help us understand the participation of individuals in the genocide. For this purpose we

---

[16] Kuran (1995, 64) models reputational utility as a function of mean all public preferences or *mean public opinion*.

Fig. 8.1 Public opinion over an issue is divided in two camps

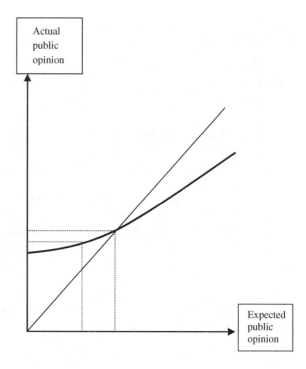

Fig. 8.2 Depicts a case with multiple equilibria

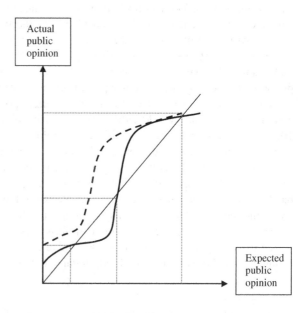

describe the entire Rwandan Hutu population as a set of ten individuals with different private preferences towards the implementation of a policy of genocide against the Rwandan Tutsi population. At the two extremes of the distribution we find two persons who are insensitive towards changes in the public opinion. Person A, the Hutu extremist is in favour of genocide and person J, the human rights activist is completely against it. Both A and J each represent 10 % of the population, small minorities thus. As leaders in their field, they believe they can influence public opinion and they derive high expressive utility from advocating their private preference in public. The private preferences of the 8 other persons B to I (representing 80 % of the Rwandan hutu population) are not observable, because they are not declared in public. We can only assume that there is a wide variety of privately held preferences occupying the space between 0 and 100. Some individuals, B and C may have private preferences close to those of the extremists, whereas others, H and I may hold private preferences close to those of the human rights activists. Important is that the publicly declared preference of these 8 is sensitive to the expected sizes of the groups that advocate for or against genocide. Table 8.1 presents a pre-genocide public opinion and a distribution of genocidal thresholds.

Before the genocide, a large majority of Rwanda's Hutu population—and thus the mean of public opinion—was publicly against genocide. This situation is compatible with different distributions of unknown private preference towards genocide. A likely distribution is that of a large majority of Hutu (e.g. persons D to J) were against genocide in private, resulting in low expressive and reputational costs when stating their public preference against it. This group does not have to practice preference falsification. A few non-activists (B and C) who in private prefer a policy of genocide keep this opinion for themselves, and, given the weight of public opinion against genocide, practice preference falsification. They do this because of reputational incentives, because as non-activists they do not care much about their expressive needs. In this pre-genocide setting, we have A (10 % of the Hutu) that is in favour of genocide and declare it in public, 20 % (B and C) that are also in favour but keep quiet about it and 70 % that is against it.

Now, as a result of a first series of events in 1990–1991, such as the attack by the RPF, the fake attack on Kigali, the imprisonment of some 10,000 Tutsi and opponents of the regime, local massacres in the north, the publication of the Hutu manifesto and so on, one individual (B) will lower his political threshold from 25 to 20 (see Table 8.2). This can result from different factors. One could be that B lives in the north of Rwanda, is badly treated by the RPF and flees to a refugee camp in the centre of the country. His private preference towards genocide has

Table 8.1 Pre-genocide public opinion and genocidal thresholds

Individuals	A	B	C	D	E	F	G	H	I	J
Cumulative % of population	10	20	30	40	50	60	70	80	90	100
Public preference	100	0	0	0	0	0	0	0	0	0
Genocidal threshold	0	25	30	35	40	50	60	70	80	–

Table 8.2 Change in genocidal thresholds after series of events

Individuals	A	B	C	D	E	F	G	H	I	J
First series	0	20	30	35	40	50	60	70	80	–
Second series	0	15	25	35	40	50	60	70	80	–
Third series	0	10	20	30	40	50	60	70	80	–

changed and he has become more extreme. This lowering of his genocidal threshold can also be the result of increased social pressure by extremist A living in his neighbourhood, thereby changing B's reputational incentive. Importantly, the preferences of the rest of the Hutu population (80 %) towards a policy of genocide against the Tutsi remain untouched by these events and their thresholds are not changed. This is compatible with what we have discussed before, that people vary in their private preferences and in the way they react to social pressure. Actual public opinion thus remains at 0 (against genocide).

A subsequent series of events such as racist speeches by political leaders, new attacks by the RPF, local massacres, the formation of youth militia and the killing of the Burundese president in the 1992–1993 period may have the same effect as above. Some individuals (C joins B this time) change their private preferences and/or are susceptible to social pressure from the extremists, resulting in the lowering of their genocidal threshold.[17] Again, the genocidal bandwagon is not set in motion because thresholds have not lowered enough and public opinion remains at 0.

After a third event, the assassination of president Habyarimana, some individuals (B, C and D) now have private preferences in favour of genocide and/or bow for the social pressure of the extremists which results again in lower genocidal thresholds. This time, a genocidal bandwagon is set in motion because the publicly declared preference of each individual is enough to draw the next individual on board (because the threshold of the next individual is reached). The bandwagon only stops when 90 % of the population is in favour of the genocidal policy. Only individual J, the human rights activist whose publicly stated opinion remains untouched by actual public opinion does not jump on the genocidal bandwagon.

It should be pointed out that in the example fully 60 % of the population (E–J) never changed their private preference nor bowed to social pressure from the extremists. Its genocidal thresholds thus never changed as a result of any of the series of events. These events have only influenced a minority (B, then C and ultimately D). Nevertheless, these small changes (15 points for B; 10 for C and 5 for D) set a bandwagon in motion that will ultimately engulf 90 % of the population to declare themselves in favour of the genocide.

---

[17] Guichaoua (2010, 124–125) for example describes how the extremist radio RTLM reported vividly on the death of the Burundese president and interpreted the meaning of his assassination for Rwanda.

8.3.5.1 The Interpretation by Scott Strauss

Strauss (2006, 172–173) finds that war, race and power were the three central dynamics that drove the genocide. He arrives at this conclusion by an analysis of the rationales that the perpetrators gave during interviews. Scott concludes that the assassination of Habyarimana and the fear for the RPF were critical:

> In narrative after narrative, the perpetrators describe how the president's death crystallized an abstract fear, which in turn gave wartime propaganda a new resonance and saliency. Tutsi neighbours rapidly transformed into nascent threats, into rebel supporters whose ultimate goal was Hutu extermination. The Hutu's task became very basic: attack first. There is a cluster of emotions at work here. They include fear, anger, revenge, self-defense and security. Men killed because they thought they were in combat. They killed to win the war, the avenge the death of their leader, and to protect themselves. The aim was 'security' in a context of acute insecurity.

We can apply the theory of the formation of public opinion to Scott's findings to investigate under which conditions the assassination of Habyarimana and the fear for the RPF were critical for the unfolding of the genocide. This theory has demonstrated that a small but articulate minority can set a bandwagon in motion resulting in a change in public opinion from one stable equilibrium to another. This change has everything to do with the expectations of the public which norm is going to prevail.

For Strauss's model to work, to wit that Habyarimana's assassination together with race and power set the genocidal dynamic at work, the distribution of political thresholds among the Hutu population is distributed as presented in Tables 8.3, 8.4 or 8.5. In Table (8.3) a sudden shock causes a decline in the thresholds of individuals B to F. This results in a bandwagon that at the end takes 90 % of the hutu population on board. Individuals G–I also join this bandwagon because the 60 % threshold they need is reached. In Table 8.4, the thresholds of all Hutu are affected in the same way (namely a decrease of 10) and, given the distribution of the thresholds over the population prior to April 1994, this decline will also set a bandwagon in motion that will stop only when 90 % of the Hutu are on board.[18] In Table 8.5, thresholds before April 1994 are high making that the assassination of Habyarimana must cause a very large drop in the threshold of B; a large drop for C and a drop of 10 for D to set the genocidal bandwagon in motion.

When one considers the assassination of Habyarimana as critical to set the genocidal bandwagon in motion, then one of the following two conditions has to be satisfied: (1) one either has to assume that the distribution of thresholds before the assassination was such that large segments of the population (groups B–F in 8.3

---

[18] This does not mean that 90% of the population become active killers, it suffices that they accept the new norm.

Table 8.3 Shock that lowers the genocidal threshold of individuals B–F

Name of the group		A	B	C	D	E	F	G	H	I	J
Cumulative % of population		10	20	30	40	50	60	70	80	90	100
Thres hold	Till April 1994	0	20	20	20	20	20	60	60	60	–
	After assassination	0	10	10	10	10	10	60	60	60	

Table 8.4 Shock that lowers the genocidal thresholds of individuals B–I

Name of the group		A	B	C	D	E	F	G	H	I	J
Cumulative % of population		10	20	30	40	50	60	70	80	90	100
Thres hold	Till April 1994	0	20	30	40	50	60	70	80	90	–
	After assassination	0	10	20	30	40	50	60	70	80	

Table 8.5 Shock that lowers the genocidal threshold of B by 30, C by 20 and D by 10

Name of the group		A	B	C	D	E	F	G	H	I	J
Cumulative % of population		10	20	30	40	50	60	70	80	90	100
Thres hold	Till April 1994	0	40	40	40	40	50	60	70	80	–
	After assasination	0	10	20	30	40	50	60	70	80	

and B–D in 8.4) already had very low thresholds towards supporting the genocide before the assassination; or (2) large segments of the population did not have these low thresholds before April 1994 (as in Table 8.5) and the drop as result of the shock was very large for some groups (B–D).

If condition (1) is assumed, then one has to explain why these thresholds were already that low before the assassination. The most logical interpretation would be that three and a half years of civil war, anti-Tutsi propaganda, emergence of the Hutu Power movement, local level massacres, assassinations of political leaders, distribution of weapons, and increased levels of misery are responsible for these low thresholds before April 1994, as in Tables 8.1 and 8.2. If this is the case, then the assassination of Habyarimana is the extra push needed to lower the threshold and set the bandwagon in motion. The assassination then becomes the final event (one in a long series of events) needed to start the bandwagon and not the critical event as in Strauss. Strauss (2006, 172) is aware of the effect of propaganda, when he writes that "the assassination...gave wartime propaganda a new resonance and saliency". This can be interpreted—in my present set-up—such that, in the absence of propaganda, the death of the president would not have caused the lowering of thresholds required to set the genocidal bandwagon in motion. Is it then his death which is crucial or the three year long racist propaganda which framed the meaning of his death?

If condition (2) is assumed, then one has to explain why the assassination is so different from all other events that happened in the 1990–1994 period. Several important political leaders were namely killed in 1993, killings that did not unleash a genocidal bandwagon. One interpretation is that Habyarimana was considered the 'Father of the Nation' and as such had an almost divine status among many Hutu. The loss of their beloved 'Father' would then explain why individuals B–D had a sharp drop in their thresholds, allowing for the genocidal bandwagon to develop. Is it then his death which is crucial or is it the organisation, since 1974 of weekly animation sessions in honor of the president by the MRND apparatus, which ascribed almost divine status to Habyarimana?

Thus, both the models in Tables 8.2 (gradual decline of thresholds over 3.5 year period) or 8.5 (sudden sharp decline in April 1994) can explain the motion of the genocidal bandwagon. Conditions (1) for Tables 8.3 and 8.4 and (2) for Table 8.5 are both plausible, but only condition (2) corresponds with the description in Strauss (2006). In the latter case it is the status of Habyarimana among important segments of the Hutu population that explains the reactions of these segments.[19] Strauss finds that the death of Habyarimana was critical. His sudden shock model is represented in Table 8.5.

Even for the threshold levels in Table 8.5 one needs a core of extremists who voice their opinion so loud and brutal that other sections of the population believe that the genocidal norm will prevail. When, on the hills, non-activist sections of Rwanda's Hutu population saw that the genocidal norm was going to prevail, they acquiesced with it. Some grasped the opportunity to actively join the extremist in the genocidal campaign, others bowed to the social pressure from those extremists. Strauss (2006, 173) recognises this when he writes that his interviewees participated because they received the authorisation to do so:

Many ordinary men believed that 'the law' required that they participate in the extermination of the Tutsis.

In areas where the extremists of Hutu Power already obtained a powerful position before April 1994 the genocide broke out immediately after the death of Habyarimana, such as in the capital Kigali, in several communes in Rural Kigali, Gikongoro and Kibungo. There, the new norm to kill the Tutsi was quickly established. But in other communes, notably in Butare and Gitarama, it took two weeks for the genocidal norm to prevail. This means that the death of Habyarimana was not an automatic mechanism that set the genocidal bandwagon in motion. It shows that on the ground, hutu extremists had to exert tremendous pressure to gain the upper hand in these provinces. This delay cannot be explained by the death of Habyarimana nor by fear for the RPF. Guichaoua (2010) and Forges (1999) are very clear about that. The genocidal bandwagon in these communes was set in motion after the ministers of the Interim Government visited these provinces and urged the burgomasters to do their 'work'. These meetings occurred in Giterama on April 12 and in Butare on April 19. The switchover of these burgomasters after this visit of the interim government or the start of the

---

[19] For a description of the ideological, political and economic mechanism used by Habyarimana to cement his power I refer to chapters 1–4.

killing campaign after the death of burgomasters opposed to the genocide shows that we are dealing with a battle for public opinion (and thus over the norms to prevail) as described by Kuran. This battle was won by the extremists who in some communes met few resistance but in other communes had to overcome strong resistance against the genocide. In addition, André Sibomana, priest, editor and human rights activist, years before April 1994, understood that the clan around Habyarimana poisoned the debate via manipulation of public opinion, most notably via the extremist RTLM radio. He and his fellow journalists published 2 volumes on human rights violations (in Dec 1992 and 1993) and held many speeches during those years complaining about and criticising this manipulation. In a series of long interviews published after the genocide Sibomana (1996, 49) said that one had to be blind not the see what was being prepared. I consider the voice of this Hutu intellectual as additional evidence that models 8.2, 8.3 or 8.4, to wit the gradual development of a genocidal norm, better represents the facts compared to the shock model in Table 8.5.

Chapter 9
Fieldwork in Gitarama Introduction, Setting and Methods

9.1 Gitarama Prefecture: General Introduction

9.1.1 Situating Gitarama in Rwandan History

The prefecture of Gitarama is situated in the heart of Rwanda, in the agro-ecological zone of the Central Plateau. The altitudes, temperature and rainfall in this zone proxy the Rwandan average. The plateau has less altitude compared to the Congo-Nile Watershed covering parts of Kibuye and Gikongoro but it is higher and receives more rainfall than the Bugesera or the Eastern plateau in Kibungo.[1] The Central Plateau stretches from Butare in the south, over Gitarama to Ruhengeri in the north. Because of its moderate climate this stretch has been the most populated in Rwandan history.

The area covered by the prefecture of Gitarama has played an important role in Rwandan history. Its southern town centre Nyanza was the seat of the monarchy before and during the colonial period. Since the King of Rwanda exerted absolute power over his subjects, Nyanza was the centre of power of the nascent Rwandan state. Tutsi as well as Hutu living in this part of Rwanda did not experience the monarchy as an alien institution occupying their territory and demanding tax payments. Such resentment is often found in areas peripheral to central Rwanda such as in Ruhengeri and Cyangugu which were brought under royal rule in subsequent expansions of the Rwandan State, in particular in the 19th century.[2] In the 1950s and 1960s scholars presented a unified Rwandan historiography. It focussed almost exclusively on royal ascendancy and consolidated administrative, court and missionary perspectives to create a single narrative of 'Rwandan' history

Co-authored by Jacob Boersema and Philip Verwimp

[1] Verdoodt and Van Ranst (2003), p. 80.
[2] Newbury (1988).

which portrayed Rwanda as a unitary society. Newbury and Newbury (2000, p. 848) write that this contradicted much of the earlier written and oral historiography.[3] In reviewing the scholarship on the relation between the Rwandan State and the peasantry, these scholars write that:

> There was a great deal more individual mobility and interchange than any static model of some collective "Rwandan past" can account for. The State was not'created' by a single culture hero or even by a single group. Power and ethnicity did not coincide originally; they took shape and salience in relationship to each other, not in confrontation with each other. Before the mid-eighteenth century – and in some contexts, long after – region was more important than royalty in defining identity, and ecology more influential than ethnicity in moldings people's lives.[4]

In their co-authored article, Newbury and Newbury (2000, 843) criticise research that present a homogenized image of Rwandan history. They write that this image is the product of colonial scholarship that focussed too much on the central state and neglected the agency of rural people. Relying on foundational research conducted in the beginning of the 20th century and based on oral accounts, they stress the existence of regional heterogeneity:

> From these accounts, it is clear that local dynamics were often local as well as dynamic, and that regional particularities were often more important than broader cultural generalizations extended to the entire society. The German writings make this especially clear; in the early years of colonial rule, for example, Jan Czekanowski underscored the importance of regional particularities, especially contrasting the north and the north-west of the country with the royal court norms that characterised the central and southern regions.[5]

The same authors refer to a whole body of work which has demonstrated the existence and political autonomy of several polities inside the territory of present day Rwanda, from kingdoms in the east (such as Gisaka, Ndormwa, Bugesera and Mutara) to independent polities in the west (Busozo, Bukunzi, Kingogo and Bushiru) and in the north.[6] The royal court never succeeded in winning the hearts of the populations of present day Gisenyi, Ruhengeri and Cyangugu, no matter how hard it tried to present a unifying and thus homogenous image of the Rwandan State. Whereas Hutu living in these areas never really felt part of the Rwandan monarchy, this was quite different for the Hutu of Gitarama and Butare. Feeling part of the Rwandan State or Nation, with the King as their monarch was not difficult for them. In territory that was not part of central Rwanda, the monarchy sought to establish alliances with local leaders and chiefs to gain influence.

In the 1950s and 1960s, the regional division in Rwandan politics was trumped by the ethnic issue. Intransigent attitudes of the royal Tutsi elite combined with popular desire for a better life allowed the nascent Hutu elite to make a Social Revolution in 1959–1962. The city of Gitarama, some 30 km north of Nyanza,

---

[3] Newbury and Newbury (2000), p. 848.

[4] Newbury and Newbury, ibidem, p. 840.

[5] Ibidem, p. 843.

[6] Ibidem, pp. 850–851, we refer in particular to footnote 46 for the references.

home to Kabgayi, the centre of the Catholic Church in Rwanda would become the new locus of power. Grégoire Kayibanda, himself from Gitarama, became the first president of Rwanda. He was educated in a catholic seminary and was the assistant of the Bishop of Kabgayi before he became president. In 1962, Rwandan independence was declared in Gitarama and the new regime derived its power base largely from popular and church support in Gitarama. Having his base in the same region as the monarchy, Kayibanda played the ethnic card as well as the regional one to gain the loyalty of the population.

This would also become the Achilles heel of the First Republic when Hutu leaders from northern Rwanda felt that political power only benefited to people from Gitarama. In 1973, Kayibanda was removed from power in a coup d'etat by Juvénal Habyarima. The arrival of Juvénal Habyarimana to power signified a new watershed change in Rwandan history. For the first time, a man from the north would wield power over the whole of Rwanda. This ascent to power was welcomed by the population of northern Rwanda, Habyarimana's home region, who now felt part of the Rwandan Nation. Given the fact that very few Tutsi lived in Gisenyi and Ruhengeri after 1973, Habyarimana could play the regional card again with great confidence. It was clear who would benefit from his regime. Reyntjens (1994) writes that almost all military officers came from the north. One study (World Bank 1987) claimed that almost all public investment was send to Habyarimana's favourite region (see Chap. 3). Under Habyarimana's regime, Gitarama and Butare Prefectures in the centre of the country saw the least government support; with about 20 % of the country's population, they received about 1 % of government funding.[7] It should be no surprise then that the people from Gitarama and Butare, Hutu as well as Tutsi, were less enthusiast about Habyarimana and the MRND.

9.1.2   Situating Gitarama in the Rwandan Household Economy

By many accounts, climatic, historic, political, ethnic or economic, Gitarama is a mini-Rwanda. Comparing income, ethnic composition, farm size or poverty for the different prefectures, the results for Gitarama are very close to the Rwandan average. Kibungo by contrast was much richer then Gitarama before the genocide, Gikongoro much poorer. Butare and Kibuye had a much greater percentage of Tutsi compared to Gitarama and the northern prefectures of Gisenyi and Ruhengeri had a much lower percentage of Tutsi. The population density in Ruhengeri and Butare prefectures exceeded the one in Gitarama, but Gitarama was more densely populated then average. Several communes in Gitarama had a *Paysannat*, a scheme we described earlier in Chap. 6.

---

[7] Newbury and Newbury, ibidem, p.873.

Table 9.1 presents a summary of indicators. In 1993, the population of Gitarama counted 900,000 people (850,000 from the 1991 census multiplied by $(1.03)^2$). Between 9 and 12 % of the population, or 81,000–108,000 people, were registered as Tutsi. Farmers, which counted for 90 % of the population, had an average farm size of less than one hectare. One-third of farmers, in Rwanda as well as in Gitarama had less then half a hectare. This farm size is too small to sustain a living from one's farm only, necessitating other sources of revenue for the farm household. When we use income as our indicator for poverty, two-thirds of the population is poor, meaning that their income is too low to command a standard basket of food and non-food items that are considered a minimum. About half of the population is extremely poor, they lack adequate income to command even enough food. In terms of poverty, extreme poverty and inequality, Gitarama is doing slightly better then the Rwandan average. The southern prefectures Butare, Gikongoro and also Kibuye performed worse than Gitarama. More households in Gitarama compared to Rwanda have cattle, grow coffee and have a head of the household that can read and write. In general, Gitarama, more then any other province has values for the used indicators that are very close to the Rwandan average.

9.2 The Political Scene in Gitarama 1990–1993

As long as the entire population, by birth, belongs to one party or movement, it is difficult to assess the strength of political opposition. The arrival of multipartism in

Table 9.1 Gitarama prefecture compared to Rwanda in 1990

Indicator	Gitarama	Rwanda
Population density per km^2	389	271
Percentage Tutsi in census/registration[a]	9.2/11.6	8.4/10.6
Average farm size in hectares	0.91	0.91
Percentage farmers with <0.5 h. farm size	37	36
Percentage farmers without cattle	63	76
Percentage heads of households literate	50	46
Percentage farmers growing coffee	66	53
Average income per household in RwF	54,800	58,400
FGT poverty measures, income based[b]	66.2/28.6/16.0	69.7/32.0/18.1
FGT extreme poverty, income based	47.0/17.2/8.7	52.4/19.7/9.9
Gini/Theil inequality, income based	0.34/0.19	0.42/0.32
Gini/Theil inequality, farm size based	0.43/0.32	0.43/0.32

Sources 1991 population census, communal registration data, 1989–1991 DSA survey, author's calculations. [a] The census data were collected in 1991 and are the outcome of one visit by an enumerator. The registration data is a commune based permanent system registering all births, deaths, marriages and migration in the commune on a rolling basis. [b] Foster-Green-Thorbeke (1986) measures: headcount poverty/poverty gap/severity of poverty. Income is gross income and is composed of consumption from own production, crop sales, beer sales, off-farm income, livestock sales and transfers. For the FGT measures, it is expressed in adult equivalents

Rwanda allowed the opposition to manifest itself, in the press, in the church, in human rights organisations and in the form of political parties. Gitarama, with its history of the *Parmehutu*, would become the stronghold of the MDR, the Democratic Republican Movement. At the national level, as described earlier, the years 1992 and 1993 are marked by intense struggles (see Chap. 7).

There was an MDR committee in each of the 17 communes, composed of four members per committee. However, not every commune fell in the hands of the MDR. The communes of Runda, Taba, Musambira and Masango had a lot of MRND supporters. According to the préfet of Gitarama, Fidèle Uwizeye, several Burgomasters never changed to MDR, and remained MRND. Many others changed to MDR, but in their heart they stayed MRND. "They changed to be able to govern the MDR public."[8] The Burgomaster of Runda for example was MRND and was friends with the Minister of Internal Affairs. The préfet of Gitarama, Fidèle Uwizeye, member of the MDR, told us that he had no authority over him. The Burgomaster depended directly on the Minister.

Claver Kamana, vice-president of the MRND in Gitarama, was a direct opponent of the préfet. He was a member of the national committee of the MRND and very rich man. When Fidèle Uwizeye became préfet, Kamana moved to Kigali. In the summer of 1992, Kamana had already obtained guns, and his band of about ten or twenty members of the MRND youth, the Interahamwe, always accompanied him, wherever he went. These young people were not trained at his house but at GAKO, the military camp in the Prefecture of Rural Kigali. That summer, there was a national meeting of the MRND. After that meeting, he received all the people from Gitarama in his bar in Kamuhanda, and then later in Gihara. They drank a lot and started to insult people and throw stones. Some people called the préfet. He came with the procureur, the president of the tribunal and they took all the Interahamwe with guns to Gitarama prison. A few days later the préfet told us that he got a call from the National committee of the MRND to release them.[9] Kamana financed the MRND and participated in national meetings. In 1993, the préfet had organized a meeting with all the important persons of Gitarama to banish Kamana. The parquet issued an arrest warrant against him. In 1994, he was in a military costume and with a gun and came to the préfet's office to insult him.

After the national 'Power' meeting, in November 1993, there were no more meetings of MDR in Gitarama. For a political meeting, they needed the permission of the préfet, and he did not give any permissions anymore. Officials in Gitarama, lead by the préfet decided to write a letter, which forty people signed, to the national MDR bureau in which they told them, that they disagreed with Hutu power. The wife of Twagiramungu, leader of the moderate wing of the MDR, was the daughter of Grégoire Kayibanda. According to Fidèle Uwiyezu, this explains why the population of Gitarama did not like MDR-Power.[10]

---

[8]   Interview with Fidèle Uwizeye, September 2004.

[9]   Ibidem.

[10]   Ibidem.

9.3 The Unfolding of Genocide in Gitarama[11]

9.3.1 Three Meetings

After the shooting down of Habyarimana's plane, the préfet of Gitarama conducted three meetings. The first took place on April 8th and all burgomasters were
there. They discussed the security situation and concluded that it was calm. It was
decided to follow the following strategy:

- All burgomasters had to collect information on MRND-members that wanted to
  sensitize the population;
- Any activities of these persons needed to be repressed to show that the authority
  was present and had control.

The second meeting was held on April 11th. The burgomaster of Taba, Jean-Paul
Akayesu, told the attendees that Gerolf, Kamana, and Désiré were driving around,
everyday, that they were armed and organizing the local Interahamwe. They told
the local Interahamwe to be vigilant and ready. They also had ordered them to list
all the Tutsi's.[12] According to the préfet, he told Akeyesu that he had asked him at
the first meeting to repress such behaviour. "If you are now not able to repress them,
you can look for cars and transport and bring the 'cibles' (targeted) persons to
Kabgayi, that is what he bourgomaster of Munenge has done." In that second
meeting the decision was taken that the préfet would visit all the communes to talk
to the population and to support the burgomasters. He visited 12 communes.
       The préfet continues:

> In the beginning there were no roadblocks. But after a while that became a problem. When
> I passed one, I would ask who put up that roadblock, but they said that I was a dog (a
> traitor –very low in Kinyarwanda), and asked me if I thought I was more important then
> Callixte. They meant Callixte Nzabonimana, the Minister of Youth, Culture and Sport and
> president of the MRND in Gitarama. He wanted to take over Gitarama. The Burgomaster
> from Ntongwe refused to invite the population.[13]

He continued to visit the communes till the 18th of April, the day of the third
meeting.

> In Taba, there was a problem, the Interahamwe went to the nurses in the medical center. I
> came with some soldiers and they stopped. When I returned from Rutobwe commune, they
> shot at my car. My tier went flat. The gendarmerie by then had refused to accompany me.
> From Kamonyi, a nun called me for help when the Interahamwe attacked, and I could stop
> the attack.[14]

---

[11] This section is based on an interview with the préfet of Gitarama at the time of the genocide,
Fidèle Uwizeye, conducted by team member Jacob Boersema in September 2004.

[12] Ibidem.

[13] Ibidem.

[14] Ibidem.

On the 18th, the third meeting took place. The préfet invited all burgomasters and all political party representatives. The objective was to write a 'memorandum' to the government to say that the local authorities were incapable to protect the local population. They also claimed that the government was involved in criminal acts ('acts mauvais') and held them responsible. The invited persons all came, but when they started the meeting, they were interrupted by the secretary of the prime-minister Kambanda. He told them the meeting should take place at Murambi, the place where the interim government had moved its headquarters to on April 12th. The préfet recounts:

> When we arrived at Murambi there was a gendarmerie there who remarked that all the Tutsi's that were present could not come in. I protested, I told them that if they would forbid them to come in, I would also not go in. We all went in. Inside the Prime Minister asked us: 'What kind of problems do you have?' I answered him that I was responsible for all the population, but that I saw some people among his company that wanted to burn the prefecture. Then I pointed to Callixte, who was sitting at the table, he was sitting along with all the heads of the political parties. I also told him that I could not continue working with people with whom I do not have the 'same word' (Kinyarwanda expression). After me, some Burgomasters repeated more or less the same, among them the one from Mugina. Then Callixte got up and spoke. He insulted me, called me an 'imbécile'.[15]

After that, one by one, the presidents of the political parties spoke. Matthieu Ngirumpatse, the president of the MRND said: 'The Interahamwe are fighting on the side of the army. They are not like the préfet and his burgomasters. They are like Inkotanyi'. Next spoke Mugenzi, the new PL-president. He used to be leader of the power fraction of PL. He said: 'We are loosing time here with discussing. It is better that they leave.'[16] But préfet Uwizeye refused and asked the prime minister what his position was. The prime minister, instead of answering, read some pages from his inaugural speech. Thereafter, he said: 'we are not here to kill Tutsi' and ended the meeting.

9.3.2 Resistance Worked

In the beginning the préfet advised the burgomasters to stop the killing, to organize meetings to calm the population. "I asked them to organize the resistance, like we did in 1991. At that time they were killing the Bagogwe in Gisenyi. Some of them escaped to the province of Gitarama. The killers pursued them, but the local population of Gitarama resisted them, and killed in the end seventeen attackers. I gave them that example and told them to do the same."[17] The préfet recounts that résistance was effective in several communes: "Some Burgomasters followed my orders. The one in Mugina was a demobilized soldier, he organized himself.

---

[15] Ibidem.

[16] Ibidem.

[17] Ibidem.

In three other places there was good organization: Nyakabanda, Masango and Mushubati. The latter is near Kibuye, nearby is Nyange church. When the Inter-ahamwe destroyed that church, some escaped to Mushubati. There, the second-man of the commune was in charge. The burgomaster was at that time in a foreign country. He called me and I send some gendarmerie in one of my own minibuses. That officer, captain Mugabu, lead eight gendarmes, armed with firearms, against the Interahamwe and killed eleven Interahamwe. In Mugina, the burgomaster called me, and we send some trucks of the bishop to carry 176 wounded people to Kabgayi. The Interahamwe came three times to Mugina. The first time they came, the burgomaster resisted. The second time, they also resisted Tebira and his man. But the third time they were over run, they came with so many people."[18]

Together with the bishop, the préfet had set up an eleven members committee to organize and distribute food among refugees taken to Kabgayi. At the height of the genocide there were 43,000 refugees, the préfet said."[19] Tutsi from all communes of Gitarama and beyond, fled to Kabgayi, hoping to find a safe heaven. If the préfets figure is correct—and we do not have grounds to dispute it—the number of refugees at Kabgayi is almost half the number of the entire Tutsi population of Gitarama. Kabgayi remained one of the few safe heavens till the end of the genocide.

9.3.3 Challenges to Authority from Above and Below

The resistance against the genocide in Gitarama was challenged from below as well as from above. In the interview, the préfet says that Callixte Nzabonimana, the Minister of youth, sport and culture distributed guns. "He was a big chief during the genocide. Callixte was born in Nyabikenke commune, but his wife was from Mushubati commune. When the government moved to Gitarama-ville (on April 12th), he started living with his step-parents. He wanted to be liked by fear and force." Callixte Nzabonimana also ordered the killing of moderate Hutu's in Gitarama. Guido Ruhondo, the secretary general of the chamber of commerce, a MDR moderate, was murdered. Kalinda, a journalist, was also murdered. "They killed fifty-three of my family members."[20] Karamira, MDR-Power leader exhorted MDR supporters to collaborate with the MRND and the CDR in fighting the common enemy. Callixte freed men arrested by the burgomaster of Rutobwe for having slaughtered Tutsi cattle and publicly slapped the burgomaster for not joining the killing campaign.[21]

---

[18] Ibidem.

[19] Ibidem.

[20] Ibidem.

[21] Des Forges (1999) p. 272.

There was a woman officer, by the name of Marianne who came to Gitarama-ville, shot her gun in the air and started to shout at people that they should pillage, but she was chased by the commander of the gendarmerie. There was also colonel Mudacumura. He organized the pillaging in Ruhango center. When he came to other parts of Gitarama-ville and saw all the shops open, he became very angry and started to pillage. The population in Gitarama has been intoxicated. All the roadblocks were put up by people from Kigali. They kept asking everybody: 'What are you doing? Haven't you started killing?' The MRND said I was RPF. On the 18th of April I arrived at the roadblock and they accused me. They told me to go away.[22]

Soldiers and members of the Interahamwe did not regard the préfet anymore as a leader or a person that carried authority. They felt strengthened to contest his authority by messages they received from Kigali and from RTML. With the presence of the interim government in Gitarama, the militia and soldiers they brought from Kigali, the préfet and the burgomasters were loosing the fight against the implementation of a policy of genocide.

According to préfet Uwizeye, Gitarama is the only prefecture were the genocide was not organised by the local authorities. This intriguing point from his interview needs to be qualified. *Firstly*, several of the personalities with high political office in the interim government, such as Callixte Nzabonimana, were from Gitarama. *Secondly*, several of the local authorities did not anymore resist the implementation of genocide or became perpetrators of genocide themselves after the April 18th meeting with the interim government in Murambi. *Thirdly*, several of the direct subordinates of the préfet, e.g. the sous-préfet, were active or passive supporters of the genocide. When however, the préfet means that the local or prefectural authorities in Gitarama did not, by themselves, organise or spearhead the genocide in Gitarama, he has a valid point: the push for genocide, with the well-known attributes of the genocidal policy such as arms, vehicles, money, beer and militias, came from Kigali.

9.4   Qualitative Research in Seven Communes in Gitarama

In the Fall semester of 2003, the author was lecturing at the Catholic University of Leuven in Belgium on the political economy of development. After finishing my PhD I wanted to do in-dept research into the particularities of the genocide in individual communities, a topic understudied thus far. Together with a group of eight graduate students we set out to study what we called 'the local dynamics of the genocide'. Every student would research one particular location during the three months in the field, and I would function as a coordinator. Another idea was to triangulate this local research with interviews with prisoners from the different research sites. Therefore, one of the eight students selected to participate was a criminologist. Having ideas on how to undertake such research in mind, extensive

---

[22] Interview with préfet F.Uwizeye.

consultations with the students took place in order to develop this into as a common project. Fieldwork in Rwanda is a perilous undertaking with a large group, so I recruited the eight students through personal interviews that assured me of their personal and academic capabilities necessary for the project.[23] The graduate students and co-researchers are co-authors of this Chap. 9 and Chap. 10.

The team comprised Jacob Boersema, a graduate in Geography who was pursuing a Masters degree in Holocaust and Genocide Studies at the University of Amsterdam at the time of the field work. Arlette Brone, a graduate in political science from Louvain-La-Neuve, the French speaking university affiliated with my own university; Bert Ingelaere, at the time of the selection a teaching assistent in Philosophy at the Law department of the KU Leuven and a graduate in philosophy and anthropology; Jerome Chaplier who studied political science in Louvain-La Neuve; Shanley Pinchotti, who completed her undergraduate degree in Psychology at Wesley College and who was pursuing a Masters degree in Development and Cultures at KU Leuven; Cecelle Meyer, a graduate in Organisation Studies, Policy and Communication from the University of Amsterdam. She was completing post-graduate study in International Relations at KU Leuven; Inge Thiry an advanced undergraduate in criminology at the KU Leuven and Marij Spiesschaart, who was pursuing a degree in commercial engineering at KU Leuven.

In the spring of 2003, the preparation consisted of reading a lot of literature on the Rwandan genocide, participate in several workshop sessions dealing with these reading, and all students had to write a paper of the Rwandan genocide from various perspectives building on their disciplinary expertise. By May 2004, the team of eight students was complete. The team comprised of eight Belgian (French and Flemish speaking), Dutch and American students, from seven different academic disciplines, male as well as female. It promised to be a highly skilled, very motivated and interdisciplinary group of people. From previous fieldwork experience in Rwanda, I knew that one had to prepare well in advance of such an ambitious project. The most important issues to be dealt with were the selection of the Rwandan research assistants, the securing of the permission from Rwandan authorities to do research in the rural areas, and the logistics of the field work. This all had to be done in the first weeks of our presence in Rwanda.

9.4.1 Preparations in Rwanda

In order to get acquainted with Rwandan culture and the current living conditions of Rwandan families, students were staying with Rwandan families in the first two weeks of their stay. It proved an ideal way to become familiarized with Rwandan

---

[23] They were: be a graduate student in one of the social sciences, have obtained good results at exams, demonstrate strong motivation for field work in Rwanda, demonstrate to be able to live and work in a stressful environment with minimum facilities, be a team player, be available between June and September 2004, able to find financial resources to pay for one's participation.

life. After that a house was rented to have a central point for the entire group in which to prepare our fieldtrips, debrief during weekends, organise study sessions, invite or interview people, to have discussion sessions and also a place to rest, to email and to take a hot shower. In the first weeks, research sessions were held on anthropological techniques of doing interviews, a role play was played with the research assistants, visits to several NGO's that were working in the field, and numerous group sessions were held to draw up an interview protocol, a list of possible questions, work ethics and how to deal with difficulties encountered in the field. Throughout the three months of the research project feedback sessions were organized to share emotional experiences, compare the findings, and develop new research strategies to tackle particular problems like uncooperative authorities, unwilling interview subject, threats and all the other problems associated with the complexity of doing research on genocide at the local level.

9.4.2 Research Question

The research plan at the beginning of the fieldwork period was finalized as follows: Each group member would concentrate on a number of cells within a particular sector and interview people from those areas. These areas were selected as the research coordinator had previously collected data on these sites, both socioeconomic data and information about the genocide. We would particular look at the social and economic organization in the sectors and the cells before the genocide and find out whether or not there was a link between that organization and the dynamics of participation in the (local) genocide. The rationale behind this approach was that the social and economic organization of the cells in the community might have influenced the development of the genocide, specifically the nature of popular participation.

   It is impossible for a researcher to enter the field without predispositions or beliefs of how things work, but we made a strong effort to maintain an open attitude towards the data. The research was not about looking for a confirmation of the previous findings of the research coordinator. The focus was on finding alternative and additional explanations not thought of before, which would reveal the social and political complexity of genocide at the local level. The students went into the field with an overview of Rwandan history in mind and with an understanding of a series of theoretical approaches from the social sciences.

9.4.3 Oral History

To reconstruct the history of the genocide in the local community's one could rely on two possible sources: oral history and archival research. Best would be to combine the two sources. Yet the second source is difficult to obtain because of the political reality in Rwanda of today. The Rwandan government is extremely protective of the archives of the former regime. Reasons for this remain vague but have much to do with the general suspicious attitude towards foreign research and investigations into what they regard as Rwandan affairs. Not even the official ICTR investigators had access to many files of the former regime at the time of our fieldwork (2004). This is less so for the local archives. In some communities, unfortunately, the local archives were destroyed at the end of the genocide either by the former Rwandan army or by RPF forces. Through contacts the archives at the prefecture office were searched and also the files at the parquet, but none of the records of our communes and sectors were found or disclosed to us. At the Ministry no access was given to the archives.

The history of the seven communities in Gitarama reconstructed in Chap. 10 is thus entirely based on oral history. That is, the story is based on oral recollections of past events by individuals who live, or have lived, in the communities under research. Doing oral history involves paying attention to the use of language, the moment of interviewing and the interaction between interviewer and interviewee. For many reasons, this study was not able to follow many of the 'rules' for doing oral history, nor could the rich material be acquired that would able the use of the full pallet of oral history techniques.[24] There can be stated three reasons for this: first, during the interviews there had to be made use of a translator Kinyarwanda-French. A translator was selected who knew the current and past realities of Rwanda well, and was competent in Kinyarwanda and French.[25] Second, we could not use a tape-recorder. Because of the sensitivity of the subject and the community-approach of the research we opted instead to make notes on the spot of the translation of the translator. We have given specific instructions to our translators to overcome this problem, but nevertheless some information might have been lost in the process. Third, we spend approximately three month in the field. While that is a considerable time, traditional ethnographic studies focusing on oral history involve a longer period. One shortcoming for instance was the fact that to obtain the maximum of information many interviews lasted only between two and three hours, and most interviewees were interviewed only once, a relative short time to built trust and get acquainted with the interviewee. An advantage of our approach was that each student was doing research in one sector only and was able to get acquainted with the specific local dynamics of the genocide relatively fast.

We used semi-structured interviews to gather information in a total of 400 interviews. Some key informants were interviewed a number of times. On purpose, there was a wide variety of interviewees: both Hutu and Tutsi, farmers, unemployed, as well as educated persons like teachers and priests, both victims and perpetrators, both eyewitnesses and active participants. Such a variety was

---

[24] See for detailed guides on doing oral history: Caunce (1994); Thompson (1988); Tonkin (1992); Leydesdorff (2004).

[25] One of the research assistants was fired in the first week after showing little interest in performing the job. One of the assistants spoke English as a third language with one of the graduate students.

chosen, not only to gather most of the facts about what had happened, but also to acquire a layered account of the genocide.

Every eyewitness has different observations included in his story of the geno-cide. In general, as oral historian Elizabeth Tonkin quote's Marc Bloch, it is important to observe that "there is nothing direct and simple about observation, even when, perhaps especially when, one is a participator."[26] She goes on to argue that the eyewitness not only sees only fragmentarily, he or she may also not know enough of the background to understand what is going on (though his experience is none the less vivid!).[27] To get the full picture, or better, the fullest picture, one has to incorporate many different viewpoints and statements. For recording people's recollections it is important to keep in mind the teller's 'point of view' in relation to other participants in the events described—people's situatedness. This relates not only to the actual situation but in the case of Rwanda, also to peoples position during the genocide. We need to go in more detail on how people witness, and how and what they remember of their witnessing. This is different for the various groups during the genocide: the perpetrators, the victims and the bystanders.

9.4.4 Memory and Research

In general human beings do not have perfect recall of past events. But in the case of such disastrous and traumatic event like a genocide, the relation between the actual event, the memory of the event and possible induced trauma's is fairly complicated. Memory is for instance influenced by the level of stress experienced during the event and also by competing events during the time of memory storage. In wartimes people often fall victim to a series of quick dramatic and life changing events, which are difficult to memorialize correctly all at the same time—often it takes years to work through events like death that happened in seconds.[28] Intense levels of stress can lead to trauma's in later life. Trauma's can be defined as shocking events that influence later life permanently and can lead to various forms of deregulated emotional life.[29] While trauma is most widespread among victims, also former perpetrators can suffer from it and its consequences.

For many interviewees it was the first time to be asked to recollect the events leading up to the genocide. This demanded more caution in the approach towards the interviewees. Exposing victims and eyewitnesses for the first time to an interview, it requires taking the role of a 'supportive listeners.' The interviewer has

---

[26] Tonkin, p. 41.

[27] The comment proved invaluable for the research. There was an amazing variety in describing certain events but also recollecting things only fragmentarily and naming proved always difficult.

[28] Jon (1999) pp. 77–92.

[29] Leydesdorf (2004), p. 204.

to deal with the fact of being first time witness to their testimonies and has to cope with everything that telling ones story can bring to the table.[30]

All individual memories are unique and stand on their own but that does not mean there are no patterns in the various narratives told. There are regularities in the way particular groups remember the past. Vagueness, amnesia or selective remembering reoccurs in certain patterns and sometimes it is simply feigned by particular groups. The Rwandan context makes talking about issues related to the genocide both politically and socially highly demanding for the interviewee. Regret, shame or avoidance might may drive a person not to speak about the events with a stranger. We experienced that the general value of politeness in Rwanda 'forces' everyone to participate.[31] It is interesting to note that none of the respondents refused to be interviewed. We were nevertheless very prudent not to press for participation or continuation when the person felt uneasy about it.

9.4.5 Survivor Testimony

There is a difference between being an eyewitness to the genocide and the testimonies of survivors. For one, survivors have survived by virtue of their ability to escape the killers. They went into hiding, fled or were saved by others. Hence, their picture of the genocide is a limited one; limited to the extent their way of survival made it possible to observe up to a certain point or place what was happening to them and to others. But also what they did observe should be treated with caution. Steering the interviews with survivors proved difficult as they wanted to tell a lot and did not know where to start. At the same time our research ethics obliged us to hear their stories in full. Trying to be as good as you could a supportive and an empathetic listener might have conflicted with primary research goals. But the well-being of the victims took always precedence over possible research aims. At other times also shame was over won, and the anxiety not to be heard, all stemming from self censorship.

Yet genocide survivor testimonies vary widely. This can be attributed to a number of factors. Memories of exposure to stressful or traumatic events are not stable and reliable over the months and years immediately following the trauma exposure.[32] There is also evidence that emotions went through after the event ('reliving the event') influence the memory of the actual event.[33] Hatzfeld notes how some survivors continuously changed the details of those fatal days, as to change the question of guilt and luck. One of the survivors interviewed by him

---

[30] See Laub (1995), pp. 61–75.

[31] See Leydesdorf (2004), p. 107.

[32] Barbara L. Niles et al. Stability and fluctuation of veterans' reports of combat exposure p. 311. Jon (1999), pp. 311–318.

[33] See Wagenaar and Groeneweg (1990), pp. 77–87.

explains how some of his memories of the genocide are made perfect, while others are being neglected.[34]

9.4.6 Perpetrators

Perpetrator testimonies are in a different way selective and incoherent, and the same is true for testimonies of their family members. Unsurprising, as the reliability of self-report varies according to the behavior being reported—or asked after—and the social approval associated with that behavior.[35] During the research there were many instances were witnesses, particular suspected perpetrators or people have social connections with them, would be extremely vague, and seem to suffer from, or fain, the existence of amnesia or repression, or mix up their memories almost too obviously. But as research has shown, the realization that memories are contradictory and internally inconsistent do not stop people from believing and enacting them.[36] Vagueness allows for generalized accusations. It protects the speaker from potentially nasty probing questions about individual responsibility and knowledge, and it prevents from speaking up about issues bringing one into a socially sensitive position. Vagueness, therefore, is a crucial instrument of self-protection. Forgetfulness remains part of the common accepted trauma cliché's. In reality there is little research that supports the existence of repression, and equally not for traumatic amnesia and dissociated memory.[37]

As a consequence of these mechanisms perpetrators, even confessed, will not report on the acts they have committed—even if confessions would not incriminate them given the confidentiality of the interview or because they have already been sentenced.[38] Instead, the criminologists Sykes and Matza have suggested that next to vagueness, they use a set of neutralization techniques to temporarily or permanently neutralize the moral connection between them and the law.[39] They try to deny their responsibility, they try to deny the damage done or they counterattack any inquisition into their behavior with judging the judger.[40] In an interview setting the last would naturally be the interviewer. Stanley Cohen, an English

---

[34] Hatzfeld in Leydesdorf, p. 112, my translation.

[35] Haynes, S.N. (1978) Principles of behavioral assessment. New York: Gardner.

[36] Page 264–5, 284) Myerhoff (1986) pp. 261–286.

[37] See Jon (1999), pp. 77–92.

[38] In Rwanda confessed perpetrators often make a 'deal' with the justice department through the 'guilty plea procedure'. In exchange for a (single) confession they get sentence reduction. There is only little control from the judiciary system to what extent this confession are really true, or whether that are all the crimes they have committed. With Gacaca however, this perpetrators might face new acquisitions and witnesses of hidden crimes.

[39] Sykes and Matza (1957), pp. 206–213.

[40] The result of the work of the criminologist team member is published in the Dutch language criminology journal *Panopticon*. We refer to Thiry and Verwimp (2008).

professor of sociology, argued that both persons and communities go a long way to deny information that is too shocking, threatening or unique to be recognized in whole.[41] He categorized thee ways in which this is done: through literal denial, (something simply has not happened),[42] interpretive denial (something has happened but is given a more neutral meaning either through technical jargon or euphemisms) or implicatory denial (neither the event or its interpretation is denied, just the possible psychological, political or moral consequences). But denial or lying does not make an interview completely meaningless. In his portrayal of a group of killers the French journalist Hatzfeld convincingly shows how perpetrators lie in many ways, but still disclose parts of the truth.[43] As Tonkin notes:

> The finding of error in an account… does not necessarily invalidate the account, or the medium through which it is purveyed. It may also be very revealing. In what purports to be reminiscence, it is well known that all sorts of errors, foreshortenings and forgettings occur which need not mean that key information is absent.[44]

What it does mean is that personal involvement or guilt is often hard to establish with the interviewed perpetrators. They often were extremely knowledgeable of what had happened during the genocide (the organization of the events, people's participation) because of their access to information, lack of trauma, and overview of the event. They might share that information during an interview, but they will still argue for their absence in the events described and their involvement. Instead of asking after their direct involvement and participation, a lot of information was gathered therefore through questioning in a more general way.

9.4.7 Research in a Community Setting

History in Rwanda is extremely contested. This is true for the nation as a whole but also for individual communities. During the Gacaca, the grassroots lay-courts that

---

[41] Cohen (2001) States of denial, knowing about atrocities and suffering. Cambridge: Polity Press.

[42] Janssen in his account on remembering the past post-war villages in Croatia gives some striking accounts how communities reinterpret local history through selective amnesia. See Janssen (2002), pp. 77–94. Janssen notes that for the Serbs still living in Croatia if any crime by Serbs was mentioned at all, responsibility was put squarely on the shoulders of 'people from outside', militant Serbs from Serbia and from other parts of Croatia.(Jansen, p. 84). This was precisely the same in Rwanda. If you asked if someone was killed in the cell, it would be outside the cell. If you asked in the sector, it would have happened in the neighboring sector. If you asked about the commune, the killings would have been done in the next commune. This types of denial were done through changing place and people.

[43] Jean Hatzfeld (2003) Seizoen van de machetes. Het verhaal van de daders. Amsterdam: de Bezige Bij.

[44] Tonkin, p. 114.

are set up to judge the tremendous amount of perpetrators in their own community, this will be an explosive issue. There are many versions of the events during the genocide in communities. Something as big as the truth with capital T about the genocide in Rwanda will never be known.

According to oral historian Selma Leydesdorf, the ability to speak out, depends not only on people's personal histories, but also on the cultural setting of the interviewee. Indeed cultural factors influence the way emotions are communicated in a society. In general, one could say that in Rwanda, emotions and feelings are difficult to talk about. One must also take into account that the approx. 150,000 Tutsi survivors formed a minority in post-genocide Rwanda. They held other believes about the dynamics of the genocide and other preferences about justice than Hutu, but also than the RPF.

The openness of communities and its individual members about the traumatic events of the genocide various widely across Rwanda. Even communities neighboring each other varied widely in the way the genocide was being discussed. Their could be a conspiracy of silence where nobody said barely anything if you asked about specific details of the genocide, or one could be very open about it.[45] Memory is strongly influenced by how and how much the memories are talked about. In that sense the collective memory is intimately connected to the individual. If communities speak (more) openly about their past, either publicly or among smaller social groups, this will influence the individual collected testimonies. In *Dans le nu de la vie*, Jean Hatzfeld shows how the survivors of Nyamata have been silent for years but that when he came, they felt the necessity to talk. He also shows how they tried to forget what had happened to them. Continuously they talked with each other about what had happened, at the same time doing everything to make a history without guilt. These efforts also changed the stories being told.

Narratives of the past play a central role in the positioning of self. In that sense, as Elizabeth Tonkin argues, "individuals may be supported or threatened by public representations of pastness that seem either to guarantee their identity or to deny its significance"[46] Or to put it another way, the way people remember or think about their own past is strongly influenced by public memory in the community. Hence, in a community where there is a conspiracy of silence, even individual recollections will be influenced by it.

Based on his research after the war in Croatia, Stef Jansen argued that most local narratives of the past were not half as striking in their explicit content as in their systematic gaps and silences.[47] Also other research shows how drastic change

---

[45] It remains speculative why this differs so much but some possible reasons could be: One, the number of perpetrators originating from the community. Two, the number of perpetrators still at large and living in the community. Three, the number of surviving Tutsi's and their position in the community. Four, the number of refugees that settled in the community. Fith, the leadership of the community.

[46] Tonkin (1992), p. 10.

[47] See Janssen (2002), pp. 77–94.

often precipitates a disambiguation of the past in order to understand a ruptured present.[48] On the other hand, if there is a strong public narrative about the events, this can dominate the personal experience and its recollection. Even to such an extent that people can borrow certain experiences of which they have no individual recollection, and incorporate them into their personal narratives.[49]

9.4.8 Doing Interviews

So far the study has only dealt with what might be encountered during the research, and not so much with the positioning and the role of the interviewer himself. Clearly, as a documenter and listener he or she has a central role. Best know is the Hawthorne effects: subjects tend to tell researchers what they think investigators want to hear. There is a substantial body of laboratory research and some field research that suggests that human subjects' report of events can be altered or influenced by factors such as post-event questioning or suggestion.[50] Part of this trap has been circumvented through several precautionary methods; fact checking through multiple witnesses, triangulation through the combination of village interviews, prison interviews, and thorough study of the literature, posting as open questions as possible, building trust through multiple visits and interviews, discretion in use of knowledge. But suggestibility is a naturally occurring trait that varies across individuals, and no precautionary method can fully prevent it from happening.

On average every interview lasted between two and three hours. Mostly the first hour devoted to gain trust and ask general non-threatening questions about the situation before the genocide, the second hour existing of more detailed questions on what happened always taking care that questions were not intruding. Sometimes, when particular interviews were knowledgeable and willing to share more, numerous visits were being made. This was also done to double check facts. Interviewers lived and stayed in the villages and shared communal live. They went to church, participated in marriages and in broader social life.

9.4.9 Selection of Interviewees

While every effort has been made to include the most diverse and largest population of interviewees, the final sample is not a completely unbiased sample. For reasons of security clearance and authorization all researchers started their work

---

[48] Page 31 Ganguly (1992), pp. 27–50 and also p. 274. Myerhoff (1986), pp. 261–86.

[49] Ganguly (1992), pp. 29–31 and also p. 274. Myerhoff (1986), pp. 261–86.

[50] Page 78. Jon (1999), pp. 77–92.

with getting acquainted with the local authorities, and from there, 'snowball' their way through the community. We approached the local authorities to get the necessary permissions, but avoided to be seen together in public with them as this would compromise our independence.

The availability of interview subjects, the willingness to talk and the extent to which they really were open to sharing their histories was influenced by the relationship between what happened during the genocide and the current composition of the community. In some communities, most of the perpetrators were killed after the genocide or had fled the country, in those cases the community was more open to talk. At times also the number of survivors, and their position in the community, seems to have influenced their ability/willingness to talk. In some communities for instance, they were very well organized and occupying important post in the administration. In other cases, the killing bands had come almost surely—and not, as was often claimed, *said* to come from the outside—from outside the community, and people were also willing to talk.

In other words, our experiences showed that not only the current authoritarian climate in Rwanda influences the outcome of the research, but also the connection of the present with the historic particulars of what we were after in the first place: the local history of the genocide. In other words, whether the actual genocidaires were still at large, in Rwanda or abroad, still living in the community or dead seemed to matter greatly to the willingness of the respondents to talk. Also there seemed to be a connection between the way the different groups in the community were connected. It also mattered whether real or accused perpetrators were connected through kinship or economic ties.

None of the respondent refused to be interviewed. Some would not show up at an appointment or arrive considerable late, but none of them simply refused. Maybe because of the authorization, maybe because non-participation looked even more suspicious is hard to tell. But participating is different from cooperating. Uncooperative interviewees simply did not share much.

Chapter 10
The Developmental State at Work: Agricultural Monitors Becoming Political Entrepreneurs

10.1 The Sector of Ngali in Tongawe Commune[1]

We performed in-depth qualitative field work in seven communes in Gitarama. Goal of this field work was to collect information on the dynamics of the genocide at the local level through in-dept face-to-face interviews. Leading questions for the field work were:

- How was economic and political life organised at the cell and sector level before the genocide?
- Who were the major figures at the local level and how did they relate to each other?
- How was the genocide implemented ar the local level?
- Which role was played by each of the leading figures?
- What is the relation between the organisation of economic and political life before the genocide and the implementation of the genocide?

We start by treating the case of the sector of Ngali in detail after which we discuss the situation in other sectors and communes. We focussed our field work on two cells in sector of Ngali, to wit Akatwa and Nyagasera.

Co-authored by Jacob Boersema, Arlette Brone, Jerome Charlier, Bert Ingelaere, Shanley Pinchotti, Inge Thiry, Cecelle Meijer, Marij Spiesschaert and Philip Verwimp

---

[1] This section is based on Pinchotti and Verwimp (2007), Social Capital and the Rwandan Genocide: a micro-level analysis, HiCN Working Paper 30, Brighton. Given the level of detail on personal histories in this and the next section, all names were changed expect those of well-known perpetrators.

P. Verwimp, *Peasants in Power*, DOI: 10.1007/978-94-007-6434-7_10,
© Springer Science+Business Media Dordrecht 2013

10.1.1 Before the Genocide

Before April 6, 1994 there were approximately 650 people in Akatwa, of which 370 were Hutu, 200 Tutsi, and 80 Twa. The Twa were only one percent of Rwanda's population and did not play a specific role in the genocide in Akatwa. Most of the Twa in Akatwa kept to themselves and were considered "stupid" by a majority of the Hutu and Tutsi interviewees. Nyagasera's population was less ethnically balanced. With a population of 1,000 there were zero Twa, 27 Tutsi, 973 Hutu. Of the 27 Tutsi, 25 of them belonged to the two Tutsi families living in Nyagasera and the other remaining two had moved to the cell for marriage. Only a handful of people held non-farming jobs, such as a teacher or store owner. Among the farmers, many worked together in agricultural associations in order to gain more money. There were mixed marriages between Hutu and Tutsi. It was nearly impossible for teenagers to attend secondary school since none existed in all of Ngali sector. There were only two primary schools in Ngali, neither one in Akatwa nor Nyagasera, so children from differing cells went to the same school. The same was true for churches, where people of the various cells were able to meet one another at a common church.

The social organization of Ngali provided potential for bridging social capital among the people of Akatwa and Nyagasera (see Chap. 8, Sect. 8.3.2 for social capital theory). This potential existed primarily in agricultural associations and *tontines*. Agricultural associations were groups of farmers who culled their own resources to harvest a field together. Most of these agricultural associations obtained their communal land from the government. Each member paid a fee to join and had to work on the association's field one to two times a week. Then they took the association's harvest to the market and sold it as a collective. With the profit from the market and money from the membership fees, they deposited a portion in a rural bank and reinvested another portion back into the association in the form of farming equipment, a storage facility, or even a party for the members. *Tontines*, known to Rwandans as *icybinas*, were different from agricultural associations in that they dealt solely with money. A group of ten to twelve people got together and each paid 1,000 to 1,500 Rwandan Francs (RWF) each month to one member. Then each month another member of the *icybina* received the money. Over half of the interviewees had been or were currently involved in one or more forms of these organizations. In Akatwa and Nyagasera, there were eight agricultural associations and more than 20 *icybinas* comprised of people from various cells in Ngali. These offered many chances for contact and cooperation among the people of Ngali. By all accounts, membership in both of these groups always was ethnically mixed and no one reported any exclusionary tactics before 1990.

There was an elected counselor for the sector, and each cell had a responsible who headed a committee of four members. Those who were elected were usually the few who were educated.[2] The activities of the sector and cell administrations were well organized and integrated. Each week the counselor of Ngali held meetings with the responsibles and the cell committees to discuss events in the sector, problems, and tasks needed for the commune, namely the *umuganda*. In Ngali during the meetings with the counselor, responsibles and cell committees, the counselor himself made the final decisions regarding the *umuganda* for the week. On Tuesdays, all youth reported to the sector office for the *umuganda*; on Wednesdays all the men came; and the women were assigned to Thursdays. The counselor himself told the people what their duties were for that day.

An important aspect of Ngali's interaction with higher-up levels in the administration was that a *paysannat* was established in the cells (see Chap. 5). Each family was allotted two hectares of land on which they had to grow coffee trees, maintaining them according to a standard set by the government. When the people collected the coffee beans from their trees, they had to sell it to OCIR, the national coffee agency of Rwanda, at a fixed price per kilogram. Those who did not follow the careful maintenance were punished with a fine of 100 RWF per tree. The *agronomist* and agricultural monitors came two to three times a month to check on the coffee trees and to punish delinquent coffee growers. Consequently, the *agronomist* and agricultural monitors had a lot of sway and power over the people in Ngali. They were chosen based on their ability to read and having had at least a primary education, which made them admired within their communities. The *agronomist* and agricultural monitors traveled between cells and interacted with all people throughout the region.

The agricultural associations could be seen as a burgeoning of civil society in the cells, but they were completely dependent on the government to allot them a piece of communal land and could have their land taken away at any time. During the *umuganda*, the cell members were all working together, regardless of ethnicity, but the state was always the mediator, demanding that everyone come and do his/her part. As with *umuganda* and the *paysannat*, the government instituted punishments in the way of fines. This only further entrenched the state's involvement in their daily lives, thereby giving the (vertical) government the ability to direct and control the (horizontal) networks that existed between the people. In this way, we will see how social capital is able to be manipulated through politicization stemming from these vertical integrations.

---

[2] The counselor of Ngali sector Francois Gohinga was a Hutu who was a former teacher and came from a powerful family in Akatwa. The dead of the Akatwa, Responsible Fidele Rudabo, was a Tutsi farmer and his cell committee was mixed with one Tutsi and three Hutu representatives. In Nyagasera, however, Responsible Egide Mawiza and all the cell committee members were all Hutu.

10.1.2 The Coming of Political Parties

When the decision to allow other political parties was announced, organization of opposition parties and meetings quickly began. People identified themselves according to which party they belonged. The MDR, an updated version of the 1959 Parmehutu party, gained the largest following in all of Ngali sector, quickly becoming the most important party in both Nyagasera and Akatwa. Referring back to this revolutionary period, the Parmehutu had been the party of Kayibanda and had its stronghold in Gitarama Province, promoting an anti-Tutsi ideology. It was therefore only natural that so many people in Ngali joined this party again in 1991 and it became labeled as the Hutu party. Other parties were formed, such as the *Parti Social Democrate* (PSD), *Coalition pour la Defense de la Republique* (CDR), and *Parti Liberal* (PL). The PL was referred to as the Tutsi party that had ties to the RPF. In addition to these new parties, the MRND continued its existence as well, and carried a small but powerful contingency in Ngali, including the Counselor of the sector Gohinga.

In 1991, we see the politicization of social capital beginning. The MDR's message wasn't initially focused solely on Hutu dominance. Instead, the organization of bonding social capital culminated in those Hutu who adamantly supported the removal of Habyarimana from the presidency. The country had become increasingly poor and it was difficult to make ends meet. "Habyarimana and the MRND were said to give all development money to their own region", said the current Responsible of Nyagasera, who admitted to having been at some MDR meetings as a teenager.[3] As a result, the MDR gave hope to the people that they could bring great change in the way of wealth and higher living standards. Joseph, a *commercant* in Ngali, explained the MDR in terms of *mandazi*, which are fried sweet dough balls frequently eaten in Rwanda:

> The MDR's objective was to show people only the good things to get them to join and to hide the bad. For example, if I make one ball of *mandazi* with eggs, fresh milk, and lots of sugar, and let some people have a piece, then they will tell everyone that I have the best *mandazi*. In reality, I am making all the rest with just flour and water, but everyone will come to buy it and it won't be true. This is how the MDR worked. They promised running water, electricity, hospitals, and new schools when they won the election. They even took the people to the place to show them where the water would run. It was all lies.[4]

The MDR held meetings within the cells, at the Ngali sector office, the commune office in Bikele, and even in Gitarama ville. When the meetings were in Gitarama or Bikele, sometimes the *commercants* or wealthier leaders who had cars would transport some of the people to these meetings. During meetings in Akatwa or Nyagasera, people would gather outside in the center of the cells, carrying flags, wearing their party hats and t-shirts, marching through the streets singing, dancing, and chanting that they would throw Habyarimana out of government. Leaders

---

[3] Interview August 24, 2004, Nyagasera.

[4] Interview September 2, 2004, Akatwa.

from the commune and even prefecture level came to some of the sector and cell meetings to instruct the local leaders on how to conduct the meetings and to give even greater sensitization to the people in the party. Each week there was a meeting at the sector office for the MRND and MDR, but they had to have their meetings on different days or else fighting would break out between members of the two parties. As the ex-responsible of Nyagasera noted, "Many people joined political parties here in 1991, and it was like teams. It changed their personalities and they could not get along with people in other parties. People who used to be good friends and drank together fought against each other and became enemies when they joined opposite parties."[5] Members of the MDR had to wear clothes that were black and red, so they could identify each other easily. During the MDR's weekly marches in Akatwa and Nyagasera, someone who crossed their path and who wasn't wearing the clothes, the hat, or had a flag would be beaten.

Bonding social capital within the members of the MDR reached new levels as their party continued to consolidate its power in Akatwa and Nyagasera. Vertical involvement came when the leaders began ordering *kubohozas*, an act of forcing people to join the party (Des Forges 1999). A *kubohoza* was performed by sending a group of party members to one person's house who the leaders wanted to join the MDR. In the mildest of cases, this chosen person was given a hat and a card, indicating that he should join the meetings. Some interviewees reported that once they were given the hat and card, then the *kubohoza* group left their houses. However, many interviewees also told of more violent *kubohozas* that involved beatings and continual harassment until they agreed to join the party and wear the hat. The most extreme *kubohoza* was done to Gohinga, the Counselor of Ngali, who remained a member of the MRND until late 1992. One day a group of MDR members was driving a car to the commune meeting, but first stopped at his house to try and force him to come to the meeting. They parked the car in front of the counselor's house, began cursing at him and asking him to come out of the house. When he showed himself to them, they beat him and forced a hat on his head. He refused to get in the car with the group and they eventually left, but not before threatening his death the next time he refused. This same incident was repeated one month later, and at that time Gohinga accepted the offer to join the MDR and reluctantly went to the meeting in Bikele.

10.1.3 The Agents of the Development State at Work

"Leaders were the intelligent people in the cells, sector, or commune. They could read, write, or were rich so the people followed them," said one interviewee.[6] These leaders were key to the rapid spread of the MDR's popularity in Akatwa and

---

[5] Interview August 23, 2004, Akatwa.

[6] Interview August 17, 2004, Akatwa.

Nyagasera. These strong personalities organized the meetings and gave announcements for when the next congregation would be. With jobs that afforded them a higher status in society, such as *businessmen*, teachers, or the *agronomist* and agricultural monitors, they were the people who had the potential to foster bridging social capital between communities. Instead, they manipulated their positions in the communities to easily disseminate the party ideology to Hutu inhabitants in all the cells as well as party paraphernalia of hats, t-shirts, and flags. Knowing how the people were already accustomed to high levels of social organization, these leaders were able to pervert this towards the organization of party meetings, demonstrations, and *kubohozas*. It is important to note their positions of power in the pre-genocide period because, in most cases, they used their dominant positions to become leaders during the genocide as well.[7] Figure 10.1 describes the positions of the key leaders in the relational network of the sector.

One of the most influential leaders for all of Ngali was Farrad Nwayo, a vice prefet in Gitarama who eventually became the National Vice President of the MDR, before the genocide started. He was born in Nyagasera and returned often because his family still lived there. When the political parties started, Farrad often came to meetings in Ngali, making speeches to the people, presiding over the elections of who would be local leaders of the MDR and hanging flags outside of their houses. Sometimes he came in his car to drive people to meetings at the commune or prefecture. Since he had been to secondary school and became quite an important figure in the government, many people admired him and joined the MDR under his persuasion. A few months before the genocide, Farrad left the country to study in Europe and remained outside until after the war. His role in the genocide is still debated and his trial was supposed to start at the time of our research.

The *agronomist* and agricultural monitors were the first to join the political parties. Twagamungu was the communal *agronomist* in the years leading up to the genocide. Originally born in Nyagasera, he moved to a nearby sector with his wife and children. However, his father Kayega and brother Ngirumpatse, who were very active members of the MDR as well, still lived in Nyagasera. The three of them worked together as leaders of the Nyagasera MDR and the Ngali sector. They also brought their friend, Innocent, a teacher in a nearby sector, with them to the Nyagasera/Ngali meetings and, consequently, he became a very active member. This family seems to be one of the leading MDR organizers for all of Ngali. Since Twagamungu had connections to the communal administration through his job, he was able to spread messages from the burgomaster Babgabo to many people in a very short time, thereby showing again the ability for the vertical integration at the local level.

Two other leading figures of the MDR were the agricultural monitors, Celestin Zimana and Egide Mawiza. Twagamungu was their boss who went with each of

---

[7] The MRND and other parties also had leaders; however, in terms of the development of the genocide in Akatwa and Nyagasera, not many of them plaid a vital part in the organization of the attack groups. Therefore, the research focuses mainly on the MDR leaders.

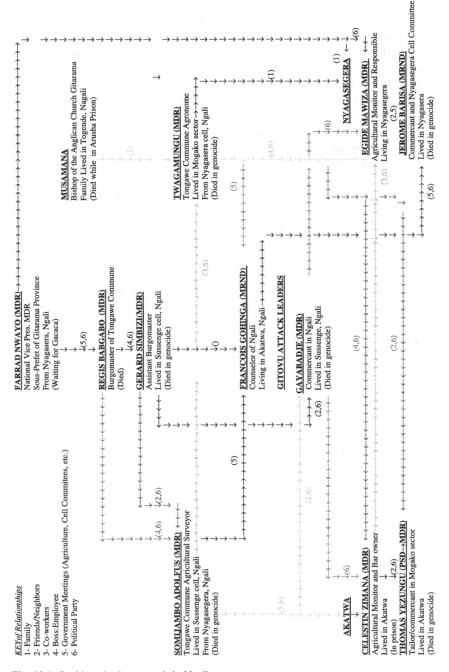

Fig. 10.1 Positions in the network in Ngali sector

them when they visited the fields and *paysannat* of Ngali to help with the coffee trees. Zimana was born and lived Akatwa. In addition to being an agricultural monitor for Ngali sector, he also owned a bar in the center of Akatwa where he flew the MDR flag. Mawiza was not only an agricultural monitor but also served as the Responsible of Nyagasera. He reportedly read out the minutes of each meeting and presided as the secretary for the MDR in Nyagasera. As responsible, many people respected Mawiza and saw his membership in the MDR as a reason to join for themselves.

Twagamungu and his agricultural monitors worked closely with Somijambo Jean, the agricultural surveyor of the commune. As the surveyor, he had a list of families to visit each season in Akatwa, Nyagasera, and Sussenge (another cell) to collect data about their fields and to find out how much each produced. This information was recorded to keep track of the *paysannat* statistics and agricultural records for Ngali.[8] Jean joined one of the major agricultural associations in Ngali, and became a youth leader for the sector. This meant that he was in charge of encouraging and assisting the youth, such as helping them to organize the *umuganda* and to join associations. Well-known and respected due to his high ranking position in the sector and a job that enabled him to know many people, it is not surprising that Jean became one of the most prominent leaders in the MDR for all of Ngali. He lived in a nearby cell but was born in Nyagasera; therefore, he returned to Nyagasera for many of the MDR meetings and was always present at the sector and commune gatherings as well.

Businessmen were also powerful MDR leaders. The most dominant of them in Akatwa was Thomas Yezunga. His house was in Akatwa, but he worked as a tailor and *businessman*, first in Nyagasera and then in Mogako (another cell). Originally he started as a member of the PSD, serving as the sector leader; however, the PSD gained very few members. Since he worked in Mogako, he was good friends with Twagamungu and lived as a neighbor to Zimana. They both gave him a friendly *kubohoza* early in 1992 and he switched to the MDR, immediately rising to be a leading member in Akatwa and Ngali. When people joined the MDR, they went to Thomas's shop in Mogako so he could sew clothes for them out of black and red colored material. Becoming a member of the MDR was lucrative as well as increased Thomas' status.

Another successful businessman, Gayabaje, became a principal figure for the MDR in Ngali. He was born and lived in Sussenge, Ngali sector. Having a car enabled him to deliver hats, flags, t-shirts and cards to all the cell leaders. Gayabaje was also neighbors and good friends with Gerard Simbizi, the Assistant burgomaster of Tongawe Commune and a staunch MDR member as well. Through

---

[8] Remark that, in Chap. 6, I showed the link between the Paysannat settlement scheme and the massacres in the 1990–1992 period. Here, I show the link between the agricultural monitors, agronomist and agricultural surveyor working in the Paysannat and their subsequent engagement in the genocide. The link between Rwanda's Developmental State and the implementation of genocide is thus found at the macro-level (the social engineering of Rwanda's agrarian space) as well as the local/micro-level (the work of agents of the State in the organisation of the genocide).

Gerard, Gayabaje became another virtual mouthpiece for Babgabo the burgo-master and he wielded much clout with the populace of Ngali.

Two leading MRND were also paramount in the turmoil of the political parties. Most prominent was the Counselor of Ngali, Francois Gohinga. While his sector was virtually taken over by the MDR, he continued to hold weekly MRND meetings and went to all the cells to promote his party. Eventually he was given a violent *kubohoza* and joined the MDR. The other MRND leader was Jerome Barisa, a rich *businessman* living in Nyagasera. He had a car and was constantly taking people to and from MRND meetings at the Commune and various sectors. When the MRND and MDR eventually merged to Hutu Power, Barisa became one of the most outspoken members, and subsequently continued that role during the genocide.

10.1.4 The Rise of Hutu Power

As the fire of the political parties continued to swell, divisions between Hutu's and Tutsi's became more severe and pronounced. Bonding social capital was rein-forced within the Hutu participating in the MDR and consequently breaking down any bridging social capital that was once in existence. By late 1992, six of the eight agricultural associations had disbanded in Akatwa and Nyagasera and over half of the *icybinas* had dissolved. Family relations even became strained as the political party took precedence over people's lives. The cell committee in Akatwa was mixed, with the responsible and one member being Tutsi. Committee meetings used to be friendly and open; however, with the advent of political parties, the relaxed atmosphere changed to one of suspicion, secrecy, and fear. It grew so uncomfortable and strained that the committee disbanded and ended meetings in 1992. In Nyagasera there were very few Tutsi and the cell committee was com-prised of Hutu only. When the MDR came, they all ditched the MRND except for one member, Jerome Barisa, who remained a leader of the MRND.[9]

Not only did the cell committees break down, but the *umuganda* ceased as well. The previous social organization of the cell eroded and the precedence of the MDR took its place. People followed the leaders of the political party, who were mostly MDR. The old government rules and duties were disregarded, further demon-strating the politicization of the community bonds. Six Tutsi interviewees that had been involved in agricultural associations or *icybinas* talked about these groups becoming separated and excluding them from participating any longer. Following the same trend, citizens of Ngali didn't keep up the maintenance of their coffee trees. The agricultural monitors and *agronomist* perfunctorily came to fine farmers

---

[9] Previously he and Mawiza, the responsible of Nyagasera, were best friends, lending money to each other, and giving one another cows. But when Jerome didn't join the MDR with Mawiza, their friendship dissolved and they actually fought each other during an MDR street demonstration.

up until 1994, but it is reported that most infractions by MDR members were
ignored or could be forgotten with a small bribe. However, Tutsi still had to pay
for each tree that was overgrown. One survivor from Akatwa explained,

> Mawiza, the agricultural monitor, sometimes made us pay money for no reason. We had to
> give him beer and then he gave us a fine that was higher than the normal amount due to the
> commune. If a person wanted land, Mawiza and Twagamungu had the power to divide it
> up among the people. Tutsi continuously got small areas and Hutu were given the biggest.
> One time that I wanted land for my son I had to give Mawiza a large sum of money. That
> was how it was. Mawiza used his job to spread the word of power and genocide.[10]

It wasn't only Tutsi who suffered under the MDR's accession to power. Those
Hutu who chose not to join a political party, or who were married to Tutsi spouses,
often experienced harassment and fear tactics from members of the party. The
party bonds replaced familial bonds in some instances. One man from Nyagasera
who married a Tutsi woman talked about his family's treatment towards him when
he didn't join the MDR:

> My father had been a member of Parmehutu in 1959 and then joined the MDR again in
> 1991. He had never liked that I married a Tutsi woman, but it didn't become a problem for
> our relationship until 1991 when the MDR brought back his old feelings. When I didn't
> join the MDR myself, my father and brothers called a meeting for us to drink together and
> talk. They asked me why I didn't join and I told them that I wanted to be neutral and to
> support the party that won. They cursed me and my wife. I didn't feel safe around them. I
> went to one meeting and I disliked how the MDR leaders were cursing Habyarimana and
> Tutsi people. They were promising to get jobs for young people and to bring so much to
> Nyagasera. I didn't join the MDR and never went to a meeting again.[11]

Sometime in 1992, even greater organization within the MDR occurred as
leaders reportedly formed small groups from the cells and other followers who
showed commitment to the MDR philosophy. It was noted in a few interviews that
in 1992 and 1993, leaders like Zimana, Jean, Twagamungu, Thomas, and Nwayo
went to two meetings either at the commune or Ruhango, a bigger town near to
Tongawe. These meetings were not announced for all members of the MDR. In
Nyagasera, a small group of members was formed to listen to all radio stations and
to spy on Tutsi families thought to be helping the RPF. One man who admitted to
being a part of this group said that they listened to Radio Murabura, the RPF radio
station, to find out when the Tutsi were going to kill the Hutu.[12] The group spied
on Rusebago's house, an elderly Tutsi man in the cell, to find out if he and his
friends were sending money to the RPF. Whatever they heard on the radio or had
heard in private conversations, their job was to go to the cabaret and to tell all the
members of the MDR about their findings. They spread the message heard on the
Hutu radio station RTLM that the Hutu in the country should kill the Tutsi before

---

[10] Interview September 23, 2004, Akatwa.

[11] Interview September 14, 2004, Nyagasera.

[12] Interview September 16, 2004, Nyagasera.

they came and killed all of them. The leaders encouraged them to continue with the small group and to find out as much as they could.

With the loss of many members and growing popularity of the extremist ideology, the MRND joined forces with the MDR in 1993 to create MDR Power, or more commonly known as Hutu Power. Before it became power, there was fighting between the MRND and MDR, but when they united, their energies were all harnessed towards the anti-Tutsi message. Bonding social capital was now within the Hutu who were not just MDR, but those who wanted to exterminate the Tutsi. A woman interviewee who saved two Tutsi children recounted this change:

> The MRND people changed to the MDR and it became MDR Power. When it became Power it added the thought of killing Tutsi people. People who organized the genocide were the leaders, chanting 'Power, power, power.' MDR and MDR Power were different. Sometimes they came and forced people to join. If you refused then they beat you or asked for money. The leaders did this themselves.[13]

Sometime in November 1993, active participation from all citizens in Ngali was required at the night watch, or *irondo*, which was ordered by the provincial and communal governments. Each of the seven cells in the sector was assigned to guard the frontier of Gitarama and Ngema one night in the week and the Counselor and Responsibles would organize the people each night. Everyone was told that RPF soldiers were coming and they had to carry stones on their heads to the border and defend Ngali. Both Hutu and Tutsi went to the night watch together with the idea that they were defending their communities against the RPF. Later, in the days just before the genocide, the *irondo* was used as a way to organize attack groups and to trap Tutsi; however, at that time the people were united in the defense of Ngali.

In December 1993, adding to the mounting secrecy, some of the political leaders began taking boys and men from all of Ngali to go for training at Ngema-Gihinga and the Commune office in Bikele. Thomas, Zimana, Twagamungu, and Innocent, leaders listed above, identified and selected those whom they felt most suitable and obedient for the training. These sessions continued until close to the time that the genocide started. These men went inconspicuously to different houses with orders for those who were to go to the training, but it was never talked about at political meetings and only Hutu boys and men were chosen. On the days of training, they went on foot early in the morning so no one would see them leaving. Burundian refugees were used to assist in the training, instilling violent fighting tactics. During these sessions, the recruits were also repeatedly told that the RPF was coming to kill them, and brothers and sisters of the RPF were in their communities. If MDR Power won the elections and defeated the RPF, the recruits were promised payment and a good job. An ex-prisoner from Nyagasera talked about his experience in the trainings at Ngema:

---

[13] Interview September 21, 2004, Akatwa.

They already had an Interahamwe in Ngema in 1990 and started having the killings early so that is where they had the training. The Ngema people weren't afraid to kill. I was in the second group sent to get training, which didn't finish because leaders were called away and didn't come back. The first group that went got guns. The second training was near to the time of the genocide. Radio RTLM talked about distributing machetes but we never got them. We listened to Kambanda on the radio saying that they would give a gun to every cultivator to take to the fields. RPF soldiers were so lazy that we would be able to just hit them on the head with a gun and continue working. But we didn't receive them. On the way to training, before Habyarimana died, we met at the river with Ngema people who were bringing sorghum from the valley. They said that we must kill Tutsi and if we refused they would come and kill the Tutsi themselves.[14]

When the Responsible of Akatwa, a Tutsi, received word that these trainings were taking place he made an inquiry to the government for an investigation. As a result, the Vice Prefect came to arrange a meeting for the people of Ngali to discuss the rumors about these trainings. He said he didn't know if these trainings were true and, if they were, then he would punish those who were arranging it. In reality, the government officials were all a part of the training and the Vice Prefect did nothing to curtail the operations. As these essential ingredients for the genocide to become a devastating success began unfolding months before the genocide was actually carried out, the leaders and small extremist groups kept their operations rather covert. Many people in Ngali truly remained naïve to what was about to happen in April 1994, but the organized networks that were planning the killings were already strongly bonded together and determined in their mission.

10.1.5   The Agents of the State Turn Genocidal

On the radio we heard about Habyarimana's death. We were all dancing because we thought this was our freedom. We were all very happy. We did not know that what was going to happen next was even worse.[15]

This statement, made by an elderly Tutsi man who was thrown in prison in 1990 for suspicions of aiding the RPF, reflects the thoughts of the general public in Ngali on April 6, 1994. The plane crash killed both Habyarimana and the President of Burundi who was accompanying the Rwandan president on the trip. Both Hutu and Tutsi alike rejoiced at the end of Habyarimana's reign thinking that all of their lives would improve with a new government. Although the situation remained seemingly calm in Ngali, preparations for the genocide were rapidly coming to fruition.

On April 10th the agricultural monitor Zimana and the agricultural surveyor Jean asked specific people from Akatwa and Nyagasera to come to a meeting in Togende. It was said that this meeting was for people who wanted to start an

---

[14] Interview September 16, 2004, Nyagasera.
[15] Interview August 26, 2004, Nyagasera.

agricultural association and that Anglican Bishop Musamana[16] from Shyongwe Diocese in Gitarama was supposedly offering five million RWF to initiate its formation. This was a lie told to those who didn't go to the meeting. In reality, Twagamungu was there organizing the distribution of machetes to cell leaders and talking about the attack groups. Bishop Musamana, Twagamungu's cousin, used to live in Togende and his family was still living there at that time. He had a lot of money with connections to the government as a priest and supporter of MDR Power. Zimana and Jean took these machetes back to Akatwa and Nyagasera, distributing them secretly to people who were privy to information about the planned attacks.

At 5:00 p.m. that same day in Imodoka, a central meeting point in Ngali sector, a group of young boys chopped down a large tree and formed a blockade on the main road to stop any car from entering Ngali. Foremost in this group was Gerard Simbizi, the assistant burgomaster. Upon his orders, the group went to Umereka's house, a successful Tutsi businessman who lived near to the road block, and began hurling stones. Naturally, the family was frightened and fled to the Counselor Gohinga's house to hide. When they told him about the road block, he went down to Imodoka to find out what was happening Gohinga went to speak with Gerard, who was still there with the group of people; everyone had machetes. Gerard explained to the Counselor that he had seen "tall people" go into Umereka's house and it had to be the RPF. But when Gohinga tried to insist that he was wrong, Gerard took a machete to his neck and his group broke the Counselor's bike. They said that he had to be careful who he helped and then released him. Gohinga ran back home and arrived around 2 a.m. The story told by Umereka's family and Gohinga becomes convoluted at this point because it is unclear as to whether he warned the family. In his version, Gohinga came home and told the family that it was dangerous for them and that the group wanted to kill Umereka. According to Umereka's surviving family members, Gohinga told them that they should not worry and could return home. No matter who is correct, the family returned home and no police or government officials ever came. The roadblock remained intact and a group stood watch every day and night.

On April 14th, the killing began when Gayabaje (the businessman), Gerard (assistant burgomaster), Phocas (communal police officer), and Nahayo (assistant burgomaster's friend), entered Umereka's house. These men forced their way inside at 7 p.m., shot him and then cut his body to pieces, leaving his dead corpse in the house while they chased after his older son. The entire family ran away to hide and fortunately escaped the attack. Three days later, on the morning of the 17th, the family came back together and tried to bury Umereka's body in the yard. While they were digging a hole, the attack group returned coming to loot, burn their house and eat their cows. Again the family ran away, but they all escaped to different places. The mother and older sister became refugees in Burundi. The two older sons were murdered while hiding and the youngest boy, age 11, ran to the

---

[16] Bishop Musumana was sent to the Arusha Tribunal and died in prison while awaiting trial.

larger town of Ruhango, hiding in a church until the war ended. In the years before 1990, Gerard, Nahayo and Umereka had been good friends and neighbors. Umereka had lent them money and they gave each other cows. However, in 1990 those men began harassing him about harboring RPF soldiers, frequently searching his house and store. Tensions only worsened when they joined the MDR, culminating in Umereka's death. Nahayo was sent to prison for merely one day and received a gun when he was released. No investigation was ever made, and Gerard remained the assistant burgomaster.

On the day that Umereka's family dispersed, April 17th, people saw burning houses over the hills in Mogako, the sector bordering Ngema and Ngali. The Counselor ordered everyone from Ngali to go and defend the sector from the incoming attack. All Hutu and Tutsi went en masse to the border expecting to stop the group from Ngema and Mogako. "I thought that it was the Ngema people coming to steal our cows, like they had done many times in the past to both Hutu and Tutsi families," said one man who had been at the attack. At 2:00 pm the Ngali defense arrived and gun shots rang out, which signaled the beginning of the looting and killing of cows. Most people did not know that the attacks were directed at Tutsi, and so some of them, Hutu included, fled the scene to hide in the fields. That day the attacks advanced as far as Rugindo cell before everyone returned to their homes. Among the defense group were the assistant bourgomaster Gerard, the agronomist Twagamungu with his brother and father, agricultural surveyor Jean, the agricultural monitors Zimana and Mawiza, businessmen Thomas, Gayabaje and Barisa, all leaders from the political parties. They had prior knowledge as to what was going to happen at the defense of Ngali and informed all the Hutu who stayed that they should begin killing Tutsi as it was their work.

The next day, April 18th, the defense group trotted off to the border again, but this time a large group of the Hutu participants were wearing banana and coffee leaves as their "uniform." When they arrived at Rugindo, many Hutu began turning on the Tutsi who had returned to the defense without knowing their fate. The attacks then continued on to Nyagasera and Akatwa that day, and the attack groups from each cell began burning houses and killing there as well. In many interviews, the people initially denied the existence of attack groups from Akatwa and Nyagasera, placing sole blame on the attackers from Mogako and Ngema. But when questioned further about how the attackers knew which houses to burn and who to kill, the responses changed. "The attack groups mixed together and the people from Akatwa showed the Mogako people where to go" said one Akatwa woman.[17] A man who was at the defense candidly stated, "Many people say that the attacks were from Mogako and Ngema people, but that isn't true. Ngali people did it themselves. People in Akatwa and Nyagasera had their own attack groups."[18]

---

[17] Interview September 10, 2004, Akatwa.

[18] Interview September 16, 2004, Nyagasera.

10.1.6 Formal Organisation of Genocide Solidifies

> Road blocks started everywhere and they asked for your ID's. That is when the genocide
> started. People were acting like animals, like the devil. They wore banana leaves, were in
> attack groups, and stole and ate everything they could. People were killed in their houses,
> or on the paths to where they were hiding. They mostly threw people in the toilets alive.—
> A Hutu woman from Akatwa.[19]

After the chaos broke loose at the defense, all the attack groups set up numerous
road blocks in each cell, stopping to check the ID card of anyone who walked by.
If it said "Tutsi" or if they didn't have the card with them, they were considered to
be the enemy and killed on the spot, leaving their bodies on the road or dumping
them in a nearby toilet, which was a deep hole in the ground. Every morning, the
various attack groups met at the center of each cell and listened to their leaders
regarding whose house to go to or where a Tutsi may be hiding. They burned all
the houses and stole everything they could, even roof tiles and the bricks of the
house. All cows were eaten and the attackers rooted up the Tutsi' fields, leaving
nothing behind. Each night, they returned from what participants called having
gone to *gukora akazi*, "do the work", as stated by a Hutu participant.[20] In effect,
they were replacing the *umuganda* with this new type of cooperation. The groups
celebrated with singing, dancing, eating, and heavy drinking. Attack groups were
about twenty to thirty people. Not everyone who was in the attack groups participated in the killings. Many people joined just to steal and eat cows. Also, the
leaders themselves rarely involved themselves directly in the killings, instead
choosing to direct the group where to go and who to kill without implicating
themselves in the murders. Twagamungu was the main leader for Mogako who
brought his men to fight with the Nyagasera and Akatwa attack groups. Twagamungu not only distributed the machetes given to him by his cousin Bishop
Musamana but also gave kerosene to the groups, which was used to burn the
houses. Jean had his own group in Sussenge cell, but was active in helping all
groups in Ngali. Thomas and Zimana led the Akatwa *igitero* or attack group.
Mawiza and Barisa directed the Nyagasera group. Gayabaje was a floating leader
for all Ngali attack groups.

The first killing to happen in Akatwa cell was that of Daniel Nimezi, a Tutsi
Adventist priest and farmer. When the attack groups began, Nimezi had escaped to
another sector, but networks of extremist Hutu were so strong that he was
immediately discovered in his hiding place, brought back to Akatwa, and killed in
front of his burning house. Zimana and Thomas were there and gave the orders to
kill him on the road. The current responsible of Akatwa took me to the field where
Nimezi had lived. He explained how he watched them kill his friend while hiding
in the banana field, fearing for his own life. After he witnessed the killing he fled

---

[19] Interview September 21, 2004, Akatwa.

[20] Interview September 16, 2004, Nyagasera.

with his family to Burundi. In the next month and a half, 170 out of 200 Tutsi in Akatwa died. Twenty-one were actually killed in Akatwa and all the others died while escaping to other sectors, communes, and to Burundi.

In Nyagasera, Rusebago and his wife Gihozo were the first Tutsi to die in the cell. Both were elderly, over sixty years old, and could not make it across the valley to Burundi like most of their family had done when the attacks began. Instead, they tried hiding in their coffee fields, but when Mawiza, the responsible, saw them, he blew a whistle indicating to the attack group that he had found someone. The group took Rusebago and Gihozo to the road block, laid their bodies down on the tree trunk, cut their bodies into pieces, and then dumped them in a nearby toilet, which was a deep pit. Nyagasera only had two Tutsi families living there at the time of the genocide and ten of the twenty-five people from those families died. Since Nyagasera is surrounded by the valley, many Tutsi fled through Nyagasera on their way to Ntarama and Burundi. Some escaped, but a majority were murdered before they crossed the border.

The stories about participation vary. Some people said that all men were forced to go to the road blocks and if they didn't, then they were punished by having to give a cow or money. If one did not want to join an attack group, then it was often reported that he was beaten. However, one prisoner from Nyagasera told a different story. For him it was a choice to join, believing that he was saving his country from the RPF and seizing the opportunity to eat meat:

> Yes, I killed someone and I went to prison for six years. I killed Marion Veraze and participated in all the attack groups that went to steal and take cows. I saw the attack group meeting in the center of Nyagasera and I joined them to go to Marion's house. She was married to a Hutu man and they had a small child. We went to her house and demanded that her husband give us a cow. He had many, but he refused to give us one, so we took his wife to the toilet. At the toilet, we told her husband that he had to kill her. He put the child behind his back and cut her with his machete. We all took turns cutting her and then put her into the toilet. The attack group was about twenty to thirty people. The attacks were so violent because the group was many people and the person would run away and fall, so then each person in the attack would take turns beating him. I thought that all Tutsi would kill us so I didn't want to leave any in the country. Maybe if I didn't kill them then the RPF would come and kill me. I knew that it was a bad thing, but I wanted to eat meat and it was like an order so I did it. We went in groups to steal and sometimes you met a Tutsi who wouldn't leave his cows, so then we fought with him and sometimes people in the attack group died. Each attack group had a leader, someone who was strong and showed leadership, dividing the cows between all the people in the attack.[21]

But for some others who went to jail for killing, they did not seem to have a decision about whether to join the attack or not. An ex-prisoner from Akatwa broke into tears explaining how he had been forced to kill and could not live with himself after having committed murder:

> At 10:00 am I was in my house drinking beer with many people. I was hiding two Tutsi in my house, a woman and a son, both my mother's cousins. An *igitero* (attack group) came

---

[21] Interview September 16, 2004, Nyagasera.

and so all the people in my house ran away. I tried to lock the door, but I didn't do it in time. The two Tutsi were hiding in the back in the kitchen. The young boy was afraid when he saw the attack and tried to run, but they saw him fleeing. They caught him and found his mother still hiding in the kitchen. Then the attack group beat me and took us all up the hill where they showed us the father who had just been killed. They said to me, 'If you don't kill them then you will be like this in a few seconds.' Then they beat me more and the woman told me to kill them to save myself because if not then they would kill all of us anyway. I did it, but I didn't want to. The group left me to go and kill more people. I went to the road block everyday after that because I was afraid that if I didn't go then they would come back and make me do it again. They never came back to force me again, but everyday I was praying and crying so much because I regretted the killing.[22]

From mid-April until June, the attack groups swept through Akatwa and Nyagasera, killing, pillaging, stealing, and eating everything that they could find. The bonds between the participating Hutu, both members of attack groups and those opportunists who went along to steal and eat meat, were fortified even further. In Akatwa, 85 percent of the Tutsi population had been murdered, their houses burned, cows eaten, and fields uprooted. Nyagasera lost nearly 40 percent of the two Tutsi families. The genocide did not break down the social organization among those who committed these atrocious acts.

It wasn't until early June that these bonds unravel. As *indanini* (literally, big stomach or the greed for eating other people's meat) took hold, the attack groups started stealing from everyone, even Hutu who had been complicit in the genocide. In one specific instance, Gerard, the assistant burgomaster brought an attack group from another sector to steal from a Hutu man's store in Akatwa. Phocas, the communal police officer who had killed Tutsi together with Gerard, organized another attack group to kill him. Phocas was angered because they were supposed to divide what they stole, but Gerard was now trying to take everything for himself. When Gerard arrived in Akatwa, Phocas and his attack group were waiting for him and they killed him on the spot. One Hutu observer recounted, "Gerard cried as he was dying saying that he had killed so many Tutsi and now Hutu were killing him. The dogs came and ate him."[23]

At this time, the RPF had made its way to Akatwa and Nyagasera, only to find that nearly all Tutsi were dead or had fled to Burundi. Many of the identified leaders were killed by the RPF as it attempted to purge those who were participants in the killings. Tutsi families and other moderate Hutu returned from refugee camps in Burundi only to find that their houses burned and all their possessions gone. In Akatwa, they lived in tents for another four months, receiving food from the Red Cross. Some families received aid from international organizations and churches in order to rebuild their houses. In Nyagasera, the people returned what had been stolen to the two Tutsi families and reconstructed their houses. Some of the accused murderers were taken to jail, but most remained in liberty, going on with their daily lives.

---

[22] Interview September 23, 2004, Akatwa.

[23] Interview September 2, 2004, Akatwa.

10.2 Other Communes and Sectors

As part of the qualitative field work we undertook the same type of analysis in six other locations in the prefecture of Gitarama. In each location we attempted to answer the same questions as raised in the beginning of this chapter. The results are presented in a comparative way, explaining which mechanism for participation we found in each of the locations, rather than with a narrative for each location separately.

We can distinguish events that have common characteristics from events with characteristics that only occurred in one location. The latter have a local, context-specific explanation. In one cell in Ntabona sector for example, one interviewee told us to have killed someone because he ran away with his wife.[24] Jealousy in love was in this case the motor behind the killing. These kind of killings, with a clear micro-motivation, are not unrelated to or independent of the general situation and the course of events during the genocide. In this section, we analyse the importance of individual motivations, social capital and collective action to explain the course of the genocide.

As we discussed earlier, presence of social capital facilitates cooperation in a rural community. Social capital helps to solve the mobilisation/coordination problem, it facilitates social control and it can be perverted to benefit the few. We now address the question how social capital influenced collective action in the locations of our field work, in particular participation in collective violence. *We organise this discussion around several salient features of peasant communities in rural Rwanda: the degree of autonomy of peasant organisations, the authority of leaders, the use of selective incentives, the adherence to norms of behaviour, the dynamic of political power and the use of rumours.* I refer to Sect. 8.3 for theoretical discussion.

10.2.1 Peasant Organisations: Autonomous or Instrumented?

In sector Birate, associational life was flourishing. All associations were individual private initiatives of the local population. That is why almost always friends, neighbours and/or family members joined the association. The members knew

---

[24] Ntabona is a pseudonym to ensure confidentiality and guarantee safety for Ntabona's inhabitants that were willing to participate in the research activities. All of the names of Ntabona's inhabitants appearing in the text are pseudonyms as well. The local dynamics in Ntabona, both during and after the genocide are also described in: Ingelaere, B. (2005), "Changing Lenses and Contextualizing the Rwandan (Post-) Genocide", In: F. Reyntjens and S. Marysse, *L'Afrique des Grands Lacs. Dix ans de transitions conflictuelles,* Paris, L'Harmattan, pp. 389–414. And: Ingelaere, B. (2007), *Living the Transition. A Bottom-Up Perspective on Rwanda's Political Transition* Discussion Paper 2007.06, Antwerp, University of Antwerp, Institute of Development Policy and Management.

each other well and trusted each other. In other words, social capital was strong. As Taylor wrote, this forms the ideal basis for participation of the members in collective action. The groups were small since most of the organisations for agriculture and tontines counted ten or maximum twenty members. Detection of shirking was easy. The contribution to collective action in the genocide can be interpreted in two ways. You can consider active killing and plundering as a contribution. Conversely you can regard hiding Tutsis or staying at home and not killing or stealing, as a contribution to collective action that consists in opposing the genocide. In cell Birate the collective action can rather be seen as obstruction to the genocide. During the interviews, we received a lot of names of inhabitants who hid Tutsis for one or two days or even for several weeks. Bystanders as well as survivors cited those names. The associations were small, members knew if somebody was hiding Tutsi, did nothing or actively plundered and committed murder. In the sector members of several associations had decided to oppose the genocide thereby increasing the probability that other members would do that too. They did not only hide members of the association to which they belonged, but also others they knew, like family or friends[25].

The association named *Ingabo* is a good example of the strength of social capital. We did not receive a complete list of all its members before the genocide, but after the genocide, in August 1994, *Ingabo* inquired into the degree of participation of its members in the massacres: 95 % of the members had not taken part in the genocide. Ingabo was well-known among the local population. When Ingabo decided to pursue a policy of not taking part, the local population could follow this example. A well developed community ties can be strong enough to resist genocide. A key element preventing the involvement of Ingabo in the genocide or the abuse of Ingabo as a vehicle for the genocide is the fact that Ingabo seemed to have been a genuine peasant organisation, not an organisation that was set up by politicians to gain influence among the peasantry. 1991 then was a crucial year for Ingabo. If it had allowed political competition to destroy, split or instrumentalize Ingabo, it would most probably been used for political and genocidal purposes in 1994. The fact that Ingabo succeeded in remaining an independent peasant organisation during the political troubles of 1991 laid the basis for its independence in the subsequent years. Peasants then, when they see that alternative or autonomous forms of organisation are possible, meaning outside of MRND or MDR, will feel empowered vis-à-vis communal authorities.

From our field work, we have examples of the opposite, of organisations that are so-called by and for the peasantry, but which in reality are vehicles of local politicians. In the commune of Munenge for example, in a sector close to the road Kigali-Gitarama, we found that a charismatic leader, named Alfred Takir, was the president of *Impuyabo*, an umbrella-organisation of local peasant organisations.

---

[25] Interview, sector Birate, September 2004. Every interviewed Tutsi who survived the genocide gave names of neighbours, friends and family members—who were often member of the same association to which the interviewee belonged—who protected them.

The success of *Impuyabo* was noticed by President Habyarimana who invited Alfred Takir to become a member of his presidential office. In 1993 the local population sensed that Takir did not cultivate the land anymore and decided that he did not merit the title of president of the association any more. Our interviewees however confirm that Takir remained president till 1994. Given the MDR tendency in the whole prefecture of Gitarama, president Habyarimana chose a successful rural organiser to become his direct collaborator in the commune of Munenge.[26] As a result Impuyabo and Alfred Takir became the focal point of the genocide in Munenge. They financed and organised the killings. Takir was considered the highest authority in the commune. *Impuyabo* became the vehicle to organise the local killings. What we see here is the opposite of the Birate case, in Munenge, a well-known peasant organisation does not retain its independent or autonomous identity, but becomes a vehicle of political control and local influence of Kigali politicians, in this case President Habyarimana himself.

In the two cells of the commune of Tongawe, close to the prefectural border with Rural Kigali, where we performed our field work, we find a third example of the importance of the (in)dependence of rural, agricultural, peasant organisations vis-à-vis political leaders for the unfolding of genocide. The two cells count eight agricultural organisations and over twenty tontines. These horizontal organisations offered many chances for contact and cooperation among the cell residents. By all accounts, membership in both of these groups was ethnically mixed and there were no reports of exclusionary tactics before 1990. All these horizontal associations could be seen as fostering trust and a culture of cooperation for communities mutual benefit. However, it is important to realize that such associations between the residents of the two cells were co-opted by the heavy vertical integrations coming from the state down to the local level. The agricultural associations could be seen as a burgeoning of civil society in the cells, but they were completely dependent on the government to allot them a piece of communal land and could have their land taken away at any time.

The committee in one cell in Tongawe had a Tutsi Responsible and one Tutsi member. In late 1991, they both noticed that tensions grew between themselves and the other members. Committee meetings used to be friendly and open; however with the advent of political parties, the relaxed atmosphere changed to one of suspicion, secrecy and fear. It grew so uncomfortable and strained that the committee virtually disbanded and ended meetings in 1992. As the fire of the political parties continued to swell, divisions between Hutu and Tutsi became more severe and pronounced. The bonding social capital was reinforced within the Hutu participating in the MDR, but weakening bridging social capital. By late 1992, six of the eight agricultural associations had disbanded in the two cells and half of the tontines had dissolved. Thus, Tongawe seems to be a case were prior tot the war and the advent of multipartism, associational life was well-developed and ethnicity

---

[26] I refer to (Sect. 6.1.1) where I described the fostering of personal ties of loyalty by Habyarimana.

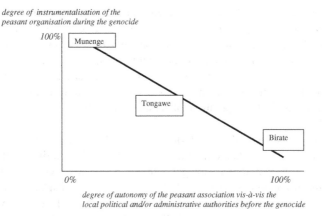

degree of instrumentalisation of the
peasant organisation during the genocide

Fig. 10.2 The relationship between the degree of autonomy of a peasant organisation before the genocide and its instrumentalisation during the genocide

was not an issue in membership of associations or tontines. These associations functioned well in a peaceful environment. As soon as the political environment turns hostile, horizontal social capital is not strong enough to withstand political interference. This indicates that the associations in Tongawe were not autonomous peasant organisations, but disbanded as soon as political cleavage hit their area. Figure 10.2 plots the three cases we just discussed in one graph, relating the degree of autonomy of the peasant organisation to its instrumentalisation during the genocide.

10.2.2 Leaders and Authority

Here the organisation of economic and political life in the sector of Ngali, commune of Tongawe [see Sect. 9.1, part (9.1.3)] gives an excellent example of the role played by respected persons in the community such as the agronomist, the agricultural monitors and the agricultural surveyor, the assistant burgomaster and the businessmen In was only logical that exactly these people became the leaders of political parties after 1991.

   In sector Ntabona, the first attack on the cell of Rama was countered by burgomaster Akayesu and members of his police force. Insurgents coming from the other side of the river raided the cell, helped by some local inhabitants. The counter-attack by Akayesu restored order by driving the attackers towards the river and killing their accomplices. This event can be considered as an intervention of vertical social capital. State-driven vertical social capital countered and tempered the success of the formation of communal-level Hutu groups. The influence of this kind of social capital lingered on until the 20th of April when the news was spread that this kind of help could not be expected anymore from the level of the commune. Burgomaster Akayesu received orders from the government in exile in Gitarama and was overpowered by the presence of Interahamwe-leader Désiré in the region. This changed his course of actions. Not only did the presence of Désiré prevent a new reaction of the commune authorities, his presence also influenced the actions of Rucago who had contacts with other Interahamwe operating in the region. The change in nature of the vertical social capital, from protective towards hostile against the Tutsi population, also changed the horizontal social capital that dominated.

In the period between the attack on the cell of Rama and the 20th of April the situation remained calm due to the influence of the local authorities and elite: "The conseiller told us that it was not good to kill the Tutsi. We were at war with the RPF, the Inkotanyi. And a lot of them are not even Tutsis. That is what he explained during informal reunions."[27] But the influence of the group of Rucago grew and attacks on the Tutsis started. The local authorities did not have the power and intention to actively resist these attacks. They could only sooth tempers and protect some of the Tutsis looking for refuge.

When it became clear that Rucago and his group had the intention to continue the killing and looting, the protective attitude of the elite of the sector changed into a reactive position. As mentioned before, it were the names of persons who can be considered as the elite of the sector that occurred on this list. This because of three reasons:

1. They were wealthy, so a lot of goods could be pillaged;
2. They had good relations with the Tutsi population. Not only through family relations, but also in daily contacts;
3. They had shown a protective attitude and refused to participate with the attackers.

The news that these people were going to be the next targets, shifted again the dominance of horizontal social capital. Rucago was killed, the members of his team were afraid that the same would happen with them and stopped the lootings and killings. The nature of the horizontal social capital changed again because of the intervention of the higher authorities who called together a reunion in the woods of Masaka between the sectors of Ntabona and Kagenge. They called for action and this state-driven vertical social capital destroyed the protective horizontal social capital. The Tutsis who were still hiding were killed.

10.2.3 Selective Incentives, Threats and Sanctions

Our interviewees in Munenge commune pointed out four mechanisms to increase participation:

---

[27] Interview Ntabona, 29th September 2004.

1. A fine of 5,000 RWF was issued to someone who refused to participate in the night patrols as well as in the killing operations;[28]
2. Threats were delivered in case of refusal to participate, " if you do not co-operate, we will bring you to Alfred Takir";
3. Physical punishment was administered in case of refusal;
4. Non-participants were believed to hide Tutsi and thus considered traitors, with all potential consequences that come with it.

The police sergeant Tegibanze in Birate gave free beer and mobilized young persons during several weeks. Several interviewees mentioned that the leaders threatened people when they failed to participate. Detection of free riding was very easy because the group of perpetrators was small. The police sergeant was always seen with the young people when the killings took place and when they were burning down houses. In other words, he was monitoring their behaviour. In addition, perpetrators always got the first pick when the goods of the murdered Tutsi were distributed. They were also allowed to rape the women. This can be seen as direct rewards or returns on their participation, what is exactly the definition of a selective incentive. In interviews conducted in the central prison of Gitarama, half of the interviewees mentioned economic considerations as reason for participation, the typical answer on such questions was "it is a question of food and money". Incentives as in Birate and sanctions as in Munenge are powerful mechanisms to make collective action happening.[29]

During out interviews in Zerta, we often encountered the importance of wealth, the status that came with it and the effect of unemployment on recruitment. "It was easy for Faustin to become an Interahamwe, he was in his mid-twenties and had no job. From the MRND he got money and was able to buy better clothes".[30] Faustin was often seen with Calver Kamana, Zerta's wealthy businessman and MRND stalwart. A former prisoner told us that the MRND was not liked in this area, but that people supported it out of their own interest. They wanted to get a job from Kamana, they liked the money they got from him. In the case of young unemployed men, personal interest more then ideology seem to drive their adherence to a leader. They go were the money goes.

In Birate, Zerta and Ntabona, assailants gathered in the *cabarets* to meet, to recruit potential participants and to discuss their plans of attack. In Zerta, Claver Kamana owned a cabaret in Mihedo where such meetings took place. The garden of the cabaret was used as a training ground for newly recruited Interahamwe. Kamana never did the recruiting himself, he always used intermediaries like friends and employees. "The MRND was run from the bar of Kamuhanda. If you wanted to talk

---

[28] One interviewee told us that he paid someone to kill in his place every time he was asked to kill.

[29] The result of these prison interviews are reported in the January 2008 issue of *Panopticon*, a leading criminology journal in Belgium and the Netherlands.

[30] Interview, Zerta, August 2004.

to anybody from the MRND, you had to go there".[31] Another well-known leader of the Interahamwe in Zerta, René Tebira, explained that the distribution of money and the promise of jobs was a policy of the leadership of the Interahamwe. He recalls his attendance of a large meeting of Interahamwe in Kigali:

The meeting was headed by Kajuga, assisted by the two vice-presidents of the Inter-ahamwe, George Rutaganda, from Murana commune, and Phéreas Ruhumuriza, from Masango commune, near Murana and Jerone, in the district of Kabagali. There were no national leaders from the MRND. They talked about the organization of the MRND party, and how to behave during official meetings. They also gave us instructions to work hard to get young people as new members, because the competition between the parties was tough. They also told us how to do that. First, to talk about the ideology of the MRND. Second, to tell them that the other parties worked together with the RPF. Third, to offer these youngsters assistance with whatever their problems were: if they were sick, or needed a job. For instance, they said that if there was a free post inside one of the government departments, they could give it to them." At last, they told us that if one of our members was attacked, they should organize and help each other. That, I knew, happened very often those days, not in my sector, as we were all MRND, but in other places. I knew a tradesman going by the name of Shyirakira, that by giving beans tried to get peoples membership, while his younger brother, Mbyariyahe, was MDR. Maybe there were not many open fights, but giving people money and goods to join parties was common practice. After the meeting I talked with Kajuga about my financial problems, as I needed money to buy more beer for my shop, and Kajuga gave me some money. [32]

In Ntabona, Rucago gave orders to others where and when to attack. In the first phase they threatened the Tutsi population and ordered them to leave their houses. They pillaged the houses and stole the cows. Mazimpake played the drums and another person used a whistle. These were the signs that an attack was going on and the signal for the local population to join the attack. So it was possible to avoid being forced to participate. "You could stay at home."[33] They tried to increase the level of participation by obliging passers-by to participate in the attacks. They did not go into the houses of the other Hutus to demand their participation, but they forced people to join their group when they passed somebody on their way. When somebody did not want to participate a fine was issued or a cow or other animal could be confiscated. The amounts varied between 1,000 and 5,000 Rwandan francs. "Someone paid 5,000 Rwandan francs because he let a child pass by that was chased by the group."[34] A lot of inhabitants joined the group because of this mechanism and the evident social pressure at the time or because of other, more personal reasons:

My wife, a Tutsi, was hidden together with her sister in my house. I had brought her away in broad daylight so everybody would expect that she was not in Ntabona anymore. But at

---

[31] Interview, Zerta, August 2004.
[32] Interview, Tebira René, August 2004.
[33] Interview, Ntabona, August 2004.
[34] Interview, Ntabona, August 2004.

night I went through the fields and woods to pick her up again and hide her in my house. When I heard there was an attack, I followed the group to avoid creating any suspicion.[35]

In the beginning these attacks had only the intention to chase the Tutsi away and to steal their property. It were the leaders who took the most valuable objects, the rest was abandoned and handed over to the followers. The leaders also used the meat of the battered cows to incite and persuade others. Around the 20th of April, the situation changed and the attackers started to kill the Tutsi. Of course, this can be linked to the general events in the province of Gitarama, as described earlier.

When selective incentives, threats and sanctions were used to bolster participation in the genocide, we also observe a dynamic of non-participation. During different occasions several people went to the commune office in Taba to ask for reinforcements to handle the situation. They received the answer that nothing could be done and that they had to take care of their own security. The responsable of the cell of Rambura of the Ntabona sector went to the commune together with one of the members of his committee but returned when they met the engineer-agronomist Fabrice, Tutsi and personal friend of Jean-Paul Akayesu, who was living in Kigali but found refuge in Ntabona: "Fabrice told us that it was of no use to go to the office of the commune, he had just been there himself with the same intentions."[36] The conseiller and responsable felt powerless and could not take action against the ongoing events. But together with a large group of inhabitants they tried to sooth tempers during conversations along the pathways. The responsable mentions the fact that he organised a small meeting with his committee and some farmers to discuss the situation. Some interviewees indicated that there were two groups formed after a while: the group of attackers taking action and the people who did not want to participate. The latter group was not overtly active in their resistance but showed their disapproval through non-participation and by the conversations they had with the population.

In Tongawe, it wasn't only Tutsis who suffered under the MDR's accession to power. Moderate Hutus, those who chose not to join a political party, or who were married to Tutsi spouses, often experienced harassment and fear tactics from members of the party. The party bonds replaced familial bonds in some instances. One man from Nyagasera who married a Tutsi woman talked about his family's treatment towards him when he didn't join the MDR:

My father had been a member of Parmehutu in 1959 and then joined the MDR again in 1991. He had never liked that I married a Tutsi woman, but it didn't become a problem for our relationship until 1991 when the MDR brought back his old feelings. When I didn't join the MDR myself, my father and brothers called a meeting for us to drink together and talk. They asked me why I didn't join and I told them that I wanted to be neutral and to support the party that won. They cursed me and my wife. I didn't feel safe around them. I went to one meeting and I disliked how the MDR leaders were cursing Habyarimana and

---

[35] Interview, Ntabona, August 2004.

[36] Interview Ntabona, August 2004.

Tutsi people. They were promising to get jobs for young people and to bring so much to
Nyagasera. I didn't join the MDR and never went to a meeting again.[37]

10.2.4 Norms, Tipping Equilibrium and Perpetrator
         Behaviour

The death of Habyarimana increased the contest for political power at every level
of Rwanda's administration. Burgomasters and conseillers whose power was
contested in the previous months by younger challengers or a contestant from
another party could barely withstand that pressure after April 6. We have already
described how the préfet of Gitarama was able to avoid a radicalisation until the
arrival of the Interim Government on April 18. As long as the préfet's authority
was not undermined from above, he was able to fight off radical people with a
lower administrative rank. That did not last for long. When the radicals saw that
the Interim Government was not supporting the préfet anymore, they were able to
take over the province. At the same time, the burgomasters of Gitarama, several of
whom had until then opposed the genocide, understood that their position was
untenable. Without support of the government, they realised they would no longer
be able to control the radical elements in their communes. Consequently, these
burgomasters changed their behaviour and became perpetrators of genocide
themselves. This behavioural change, from opposing the genocide to advancing it,
is a powerful observation. It is powerful because it demonstrates in detail how
personal choices are interwoven with the political situation. Not only burgomasters
and conseilleurs had to make these choices, but many ordinary citizens found
themselves in this difficult situation. We also observe such positional change
before the genocide. In Zerta commune, when Claver Kamana was ousted in 1993,
many people changed from MRND to MDR.[38]

   The logic of participation can be illustrated from the unfolding of genocide in
Ntabona commune: initially the group of Rucago was rather small, it were the
leaders who killed the Tutsi, but "the number grew because the people wanted to
steal".[39] The people who where forced to participate or who joined the group out
of opportunistic reasons did not kill. The group of attackers consisted of three
elements: the leaders, the poor who participated to gain some goods and the people
who were forced to participate. The number of attackers grew to 50 people during
certain attacks. The logic thus runs as follows:

1. A violent leader tries to introduce a new norm. This is the political contest at
   the local level. He is surrounded by several loyalists, a group of radicals, often

---

[37] Interview, September 2004.

[38] Interview, Zerta, August 2004.

[39] Interview, Ntabona, September 2004.

ideologically motivated to kill the Tutsi. Most people however do not participate at this stage. They wait and see;

2. As Rucago becomes more powerful, and by the nature of his violence is able to
sideline or subjugate moderate people, as he also hands out money and makes
promises, more and more people follow him;

3. Through this bandwagon effect, violence gains momentum, Tutsi are killed,
goods are stolen and women are raped;

4. When Rucago plans to kill members of the local Hutu elite, he is killed himself
and the level of violence decreases.

In Ntabona, a large part of the Hutu population was neither motivated by
ideology nor by personal profit, they just wanted to get through this dreadful
period. Doing as others were doing (adherence to the norm of the day) was one
way to overcome that period. In Ntabona, the norm to kill Tutsi was not followed
by everybody and only lasted as long as Rucago was powerful and alive. As soon
as he is dead, violence decreases only to resurge with the arrival of another
powerful Interahamwe leader (Mulat Désiré). The introduction of a killing norm
did not succeed in Birate either. We have already seen that social capital in Birate
commune was well-developed and able to withstand the drive for genocide. For
such a norm to develop, one does not only need persons who follow the norm, but
also persons who punish those who do not follow the norm. In Birate, such a norm
never developed. Only a small number of Tutsi was killed in the sector[40]—with
exception of cell Makiri[41]—and the even more survivors in mixed marriages. The
data collected in the sector deny the existence of killing norms and punishing
behaviour. The interviewees cited 18 names of people who actively killed Tutsis
and destroyed their houses, among them the three leaders of the local population[42].
Three of them were liberated in the meantime because they confessed. In the
interview we had with him, he said he was accused of killing three members of a
Tutsi family and he confessed he was a bystander at the moment other persons

---

[40] We could not see the official list mentioning the victims of the genocide, drawn up in 1998.
We met a Tutsi teacher who helped with an investigation on the victims of the genocide and she
mentioned 187 people killed in sector N. The former coordinator of 1998 however tried to find
that list, but had to rewrite it because the original list was not available. He only wrote 60 names
and mentioned that there were for sure more than 100 victims, but could not give us an exact
number. In comparison with other regions in the province of Gitarama, 100 persons out of more
than 4,000 families living in the sector is really a small number.

[41] The inhabitants of cell Makiri in Birate were not members of an association or a tontine and
practiced Ubudehe less frequently than in the other cells of the sector. In Makiri more people
were killed: of every Tutsi family several members were killed while in the other cells most of the
time only the head of the family was killed. Not many Hutus of Makiri hid Tutsi or helped them
to flee. The community basis that existed in the other cells was missing, giving way to other
mechanisms.

[42] Sometimes the interviewees did not remember the names of the perpetrators they knew. For
that reason we can believe there were more than 18 perpetrators. However it will not be much
more, because all the interviewees, with the exception of two Tutsi, stated that just a small group
of men killed Tutsi and burned their houses.

(among them some of the eighteen who are cited and other people whose names he did not remember anymore) killed the Tutsis. Eleven interviewees claimed they did nothing and stayed at home during the genocide because they were afraid. Two interviewees stated literally they refused to participate when the Interahamwe and the local leaders asked all persons they met to take part in the massacres. Some interviewees stated that the three leaders also threatened individuals, but nobody could or would give us names of those who were individually threatened or punished for non-participation. The two interviewees who refused, did so because they disagreed with the ideas of the Hutu Power and because they thought Tutsi to be normal people who had done nothing wrong, even though they were too afraid to really help Tutsi. Eight of the 41 interviewees did help Tutsi: three of them were friends, three of them neighbours, one protected his Tutsi wife and one was the head of the sector. The interviewed Tutsi were helped by family in the half of the cases, by Hutu friends, by neighbours and by the coordinator. Other persons knew that Tutsi were helped and by whom, but did not punish them. Other interviewees cited names of people who helped other people, but did not punish them by giving their names to the group of killers.

In Ganira, the opposition was being silenced. This happened very clearly by the killing of the burgomaster who had been able to protect the Tutsi refugees for already several weeks. By killing him, the local power structure collapsed and a vacuum was created that was very favourable for the attackers. Another strategy that the organizers of the killings in Ganira used weakened the resistance of the Tutsi in the parish and scared Hutu to provide them assistance. At first the local population provided the refugees at the parish with some support by giving them water and food. But after the killing of the burgomaster the genocidaires were able to set up a complete structure of barriers in the area so that it was not possible to provide them any help. According to some respondents there are a number of Hutu killed who still tried to help the refugees.

10.2.5 The Dynamic of Political Power

The protection given to Tutsi varied with the balance of political power at the local level. When the burgomaster or conseiller were opposed to the genocide, few Tutsi were killed. When these authorities bowed to pressure or when their authority was overrun by other, more powerful people, more Tutsi were killed. Such more powerful forces could come from outside the commune.

Examples of these effects can be found in Ntabona (see Fig. 10.3) and in Ganira commune. Because of the resistance of the burgomaster of Ganira (which included the sector Itabi) against the killings that started in large parts of the country, the parish of Itabi had become an important place of shelter for the Tutsi of Ganira as well as other communes. The first major attack at the parish took place around the April 20. Interahamwe from Zerta and Kiri together with military men lanced an attack, but the resistance of the refugees and the burgomaster with his policemen

Level of protection
granted to Tutsi

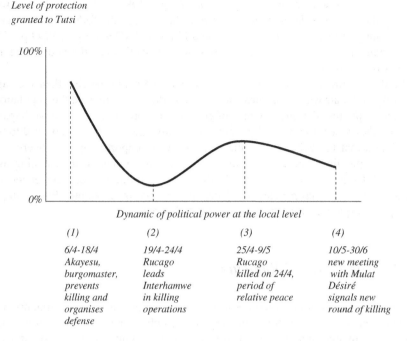

Dynamic of political power at the local level

(1)	(2)	(3)	(4)
6/4-18/4	*19/4-24/4*	*25/4-9/5*	*10/5-30/6*
Akayesu,	*Rucago*	*Rucago*	*new meeting*
burgomaster,	*leads*	*killed on 24/4,*	*with Mulat*
prevents	*Interhamwe*	*period of*	*Désiré*
killing and	*in killing*	*relative peace*	*signals new*
organises	*operations*		*round of killing*
defense			

Fig. 10.3 Dynamic of political power and the level of protection granted to Tutsi in Ntabona sector, Kiri commune

was too strong and they forced the attackers to flee. Confronted with resistance in Ganira, but also in other parts of the province of Gitarama, the genocidal interim-government together with Interahamwe and the military augmented their pressure and looked for a way to overcome the resistance. After the failed attack, they decided to kill the burgomaster, who as the highest local authority was their greatest obstacle. The next day the burgomaster was killed in an ambush. On April 22, a day after the murder of the burgomaster, Interahamwe killed the first Tutsi, a family who had fled from Kiboga, on the market in Kigirora. On April 25 the final attack of the parish was executed. By that time it had become clear that the majority of the policemen had taken the side of the killers, which meant that there were no local authorities left to protect the refugees or to assist the population to resist. Renforcements had come from all over the region to guarantee the success of the attack.

In Ganira, the role of the army was outspoken. Before April 1994 several political meetings inciting the population had taken place, but after April 6 this was taken to a higher level with strong support of the army and Interahamwe. Des Forges (1999) recognizes the role of the military in spreading the killings throughout the country when she writes: "the military encouraged and, when faced with reluctance to act, compelled both ordinary citizens and local administrators to participate in attacks, even travelling the back roads and stopping at small

244   10   The Developmental State at Work

marketplaces to deliver the message" (Des Forges 1999, p. 8). In Itabi this was exactly the case. On the market of Kigirora they spread the following messages: "We want you to destroy Tutsi houses and kill Tutsi" (Des Forges, 1999 p. 277) and "some of you are already eating cows (from Tutsi that had fled) but where are the corpses of dead Tutsi?"

Soldiers at the above-mentioned market place were empowering their message by firing in the air with their guns. Besides spreading fear amongst the population, several people told that the presence of guns also encouraged people to participate, because they saw it as a sign of government involvement. "The guns proved to the population that the execution of the genocide was supported by the government and the population thought she had to help the government with searching and killing Tutsi all around the place". But besides military men, the genocidal message was also propagated by local and well-known people. For example Onesphore organized two meetings at the marketplace.

10.2.6 The Power of Rumours

In Ntabona, our location in the north of Seon commune, a series of rumours was spread. The messages were indicating and emphasizing the ethnic difference between Hutu and Tutsi. It were Tutsi who accentuated their difference or, at least, the Hutu population had the perception that Tutsi were accentuating their ethnic difference: "The Tutsi had provocative expressions like: 'we will see who is going to win soon, the partridge or the gazelle'. Or: Tutsi asked the Hutu: 'Did you ever see a goat living together with a sheep'".[43] The difference between the two ethnic groups was expressed in the subtlety of language. Elegant and noble animals like partridge or goat indicating Tutsi were compared with lesser animals representing Hutu. In second place, these rumours were bringing the distant war with the RPF to the local level, to the life of the local inhabitants. "Tutsi had been digging holes where they were going to throw the bodies of the Hutu or they had been collecting bananas to make beer they were going to consume the day they were going to throw the Hutu in the holes."[44]

Rumours were spreading that all Tutsi were accomplices of the *Inkotanyi*, the soldiers of the RPF who were coming from Uganda and were engaged in a civil war with the Rwandan army. These rumours were fostered by broadcasts over the radio and via the popular newspaper *Kangura*. It was especially Rucago who spread these ideas and opinions on the local level. After his return from the battlefield, he spread the word that "we are at war with the Tutsi"[45]. Rucago often went to Kigali where he had contact with groups and leaders of the *Interahamwe*.

---

[43] Interview Gitarama, September 2004.

[44] Interview Gitarama Prison, September 2004.

[45] Interview Ntabona, August 2004.

Upon his return to the sector, he had money to buy drinks in the cabarets where he looked for support for his ideas. "Rucago proclaimed his ideas in the cabarets. He told us he had been on the battlefields with the *Inyenzi;* that we had to be careful."[46] He did not distribute weapons, but he did hand out uniforms. He founded a small group of enthusiastic allies who were also spreading his message, but most of the people kept some distance.

The rumours did not stay vague or general, but were focussed on certain individuals living in the commune. The threats and propaganda broadcasted over the radio were translated into a lived and embodied reality. For example, Remy Takande, a Tutsi, was suspected of leaving the region from time to time to get in contact with the *Inkotanyi.* In the local cabarets people were discussing these topics. "But we knew that this was not true, because he was always around."[47] "An atmosphere of distrust was growing when the *Inkotanyi* started their attack in 1990. The Tutsis started to live in small groups, but this was because they felt unwanted. We heard on the radio and there were rumours going around that they were accomplices. But we never saw that they were really implicated. They were always together with us."[48] These rumours were heightened by the fact that the population could actually hear the ongoing war between the RPF and the FAR from time to time. Ntabona is situated in the North of Gitarama and the sound of shelling was audible from a distance.

Another major influence were the stories of the refugees who fled the war in *Byumba* and were living in the commune on the other side of the river *Nyabarongo* in a centre called *Mukebeke.* They mingled with the population and had sporadic contacts with inhabitants of Ntabona. Stories about *Inkotanyi* burning Hutu alive in their houses stirred the imagination and strengthened the fear: "They told us that the Inkotanyi were only here to kill the Hutu. They often came to us to ask some help and then they told us stories about the way the *Inkotanyi* burned people in their houses."[49] "There were refugees coming from Byumba who were giving information that the RPF killed in a brutal way. These messages and rumours were the catalysts of the massacres."[50]

Although many inhabitants had doubts regarding these declarations and rumours. They had a significant influence on the social relations. Conversations stopped or words were cried out when Tutsi passed by, some families wouldn't open the door when Tutsi came by and sometimes crops on the fields of Tutsi were pulled out or demolished. Séverine, a survivor, gives the example of a local teacher in the primary school, Francois Mirase, important leader of the MDR, who would not pass the invitation to pay the tuition fee sent by the school in Gikongoro, where her child was attending classes. Simply because of the fact that the family was

---

[46] Interview Ntabona, September 2004.

[47] Interview Ntabona, August 2004.

[48] Interview Ntabona, August.2004.

[49] Interview Ntabona, September 2004.

[50] Interview Gitarama Prison, September 2004.

Tutsi. The deterioration of the social relations reached a peak in the period of February–March 1994.

10.3 Conlcusions

In Giterama, the push towards genocide did not come from the prefectural or local authorities. The préfet and several burgomasters did not want to execute nor cooperate with the genocidal forces spearheaded by the interim government. They mounted resistance but where overwhelmed by political and military power. After April 18th most local authorities nevertheless accepted the genocidal program or stopped their resistance. The case-studies in seven sectors in Gitarama demonstrate the role of the agents of the state in the organisation of the genocide at the local level. Those agents, such as the assistant bourgomaster and the agricultural monitors had a lot of sway over the population before the genocide by virtue of the high standing that came with their job. They were leading figures before the advent of political parties and subsequently became the leaders of these parties. Instead of using their status for bridging Hutu and Tutsi together, they became the catalysts in the amplification of the networks, bonds and trust among those who would soon kill Tutsi. Such organization and leadership by the agents of the Second Republic's Developmental State, was what enabled radicalisation to move forward at such a rapid pace and have successful, albeit devastating.

Farmer associations such as tontines and agricultural organisations had mixed ethnic composition before 1990. Such horizontal organisations are ideal to foster bridging social capital between ethnic groups. In six of the seven localities they however proof too weak to stand up to the ascent of Hutu Power. The degree of autonomy of the agricultural associations vis-à-vis the Developmental State influenced the behaviour of the leaders and the members of such associations. When that autonomy was large, as for example in Birate, the association was not a vehicle for mobilisation in the genocide. In the absence of vertical interference, autonomous organisations could work against the genocidal norm. When the agricultural association was dominated by the agents of the Developmental State, as for example in Munenge, the association became a vehicle of power and mobilisation at the local level and did not counter the rise of the genocidal norm.

Wether by choice or by friendly or forcecul kubohoza, they joined the MDR in stead of the MRND. In late 1993 they united in Hutu Power. While the competition between MDR and MRND was real at the national level and in other communes, the MDR was far more powerful in our localities and overwhelmed the MRND easily. Did this matter for the implementation of the genocide? Not really, these leaders joined together regardless of previous political adherence to execute the genocidal project. This offers additional evidence that the genocide was executed as a national, state-sponsored project rather than the project of a political party.

In the second and third week of April 1994, even after months of intense propaganda, ordinary Hutu farmers who participated in the defense of their locality after the death of Habyarimana had to be told by their leaders that they should not attack Hutu from other sectors or communes who were attacking their community. They had to be told that the Tutsi were the enemy. The leaders of course knew very well what the objective was of all these attacks.

10.4 Appendix: Who are the Agricultural Monitors?

Bart (1993 pp. 508–509) writes that an agronomist was appointed in each commune, assisted by several agricultural monitors. Their task was to teach modern agricultural techniques to farmers and to convince them to adopt these techniques. The adopters were then officially called 'progressive farmers'. Most often, these farmers were among the well-off who had the means (land, inputs) to experiment with or implement new techniques. Newbury (1992) points out the ambivent role accorded to these agricultural monitors.[51] *One the one hand* they were agents of the state and in this capacity they were required to implement the directives of the Ministry of Agriculture. This included, among other things, to police the farmers who were not observing the orders of the ministry. When farmers, eg would not plant and maintain their coffee trees, they could be fined by the monitors (as explained in Chap. 4). *On the other hand*, the monitors witnessed the hard life of many farmers, the lack of inputs available to them such as fertilizer, seeds and land. In this capacity they could have served as the voice of the farmers informing the communal council and the ministry of these difficulties and asking that action be taken in favour of the farmers. Most of the available evidence shows that the agronomists and the agricultural monitors subscribed to their first task, not to the second. Bagiramshi, Bazihizina and Barnaud (1986) list five reasons why this was the case (p. 422): [52]

1. the message of the agricultural monitors is not based on an analysis of local conditions and as a result not adapted to these conditions;
2. extension services were conceived in isolation of other policies such as access to credit, commercialisation, taxation, price policies or manufacturing and would only bear fruit when considered together;
3. seldomly, the experience of the farmer was taken into account. As a result monitors were surprised to encounter resistance from the side of the farmers when introducing innovations;
4. operational procedures changed according to the source that financed an innovation, handicapping effective planning;

---

[51] Newbury, C., 1992, Recent debates over Governance and Rural Development, pp. 207–208.
[52] Bagirameshi, J., Bazihizina, C and Barnaud, M., Pour une Nouvelle Pratique de la Vulgerisation Agricole au Rwanda, *Revue Tiers Monde*, XXVII, n.106, Avril–Juin 1986, pp.419–437.

5. monitors nor farmers were supposed to question the directives given by their superiors and as a results did not take responsibility for their actions.

As a result, extension work in Rwanda was considered as a top–down mechanism where the agricultural monitor told the farmer what to do (p. 426). Frequently, agricultural monitors combine their job with a position as responsible de cell or conseiller de secteur, the two administrative levels below the level of the commune.

Chapter 11
The Endogenous Genocide

In terms of objectives reached, in the rate of popular participation in collective action in general (e.g. umuganda, anti-erosion campaigns,…) and in the participation of the killing of the Tutsi minority in particular, Rwanda we a 'successful' country. Can political economy help us to find deeper level explanations for the success of the establishment of a killing norm and the success of collective action in Rwanda? In this conclusion we look at the role of population density and the institutions of a Party-State in explaining collective action in Rwanda.

11.1 Dictatorship and Institutional Failure

During the second half of the eighties, David and Catherine Newbury (2000, p. 872) write, Rwandan academics and intellectuals began to write openly about the difficult conditions faced by rural cultivators, the exploitative practices of merchants who purchased coffee and food from peasants, and the inadequacy of government programs to provide alternative markets for peasant production. In 1985, Jean Rumiya argued that government policies in post-colonial Rwanda had intensified rather than reduced social inequalities.[1] This called into question the government's claim of an egalitarian society, one of the pillars of the Second and First Republics. A citation from the review essay by David and Catherine Newbury (2000, 873–874) is particularly revealing in this regard:

> André Guichaoua's research showed the extent to which strategic areas of economic and social life in the countryside (commercial outlets, agricultural supplies, consumer goods, credit, transport) were dominated by people outside the rural milieu (traders, absentee landlords, civil servants, and military personnel). The concentration of power and the polarization of wealth benefited only the elites in the capital.
>
> In a well-grounded economic analysis, Fernand Bézy issued a particularly scathing indictment. Citing the results of a government survey published in the mid-1980s, which estimated annual per capita expenditures for consumption among Rwanda's peasants as less than $150 (U.S.), he condemned the 'pauperization of the peasants'. Writing in a

---

[1] Rumiya, J., Rwanda d'hier, Rwanda d'aujourd'hui, Vivant Univers 357, May–June 1985.

P. Verwimp, *Peasants in Power*, DOI: 10.1007/978-94-007-6434-7_11,
© Springer Science+Business Media Dordrecht 2013

prophetic vein in 1990, he argued that the problems were not just economic but political, with a risk of serious social conflict if current conditions continued. New approaches were needed, he concluded, to ensure food security for rural dwellers, protection from merchant exploitation, and the establishment of many small, labor-intensive industries in different regions of the country to provide employment and produce basic essentials. But achieving such a program would require nothing less than a re-ordening of current political structures, a 'transformation of the society'. His advice went unheeded.

Critiques by Rwandan intellectuals and studies such as those of Guichaoua and Bézy delineated important facets of Rwanda's political economy in the 1980s. Combining economic analysis with sensitivity to power and politics, they showed how government policies, highly placed politicians, and others tied to the powerful were implicated in the reproduction of inequalities that permeated Rwandan society.

An integral part of dictatorial rule under Habyarimana was the automatic membership of each Rwandan in the MRND and the weekly participation in animation sessions glorifying the president. Towards the end of the eighties it became clear that the institutions built during the Habyarimana regime, meaning the monopoly power of the MRND party and its president over all party and state institutions, together with the policies undertaken by these institutions (such as umuganda, coffee policy and food self-sufficiency policy) were unable to prevent crisis, famine, rising poverty, corruption and self-enrichment.

Rwandans know that disobedience to officially sanctioned norms can be very costly. MRND membership and animation sessions were dictatorial institutions to convince peasants of the great powers of the dictator, to discourage resistance and to imprint official demands in peasants' minds. Local authorities, foremost the burgomaster, often did not need to give orders to the peasants, a word or gesture was enough for the peasants to guess what the burgomaster wanted. The weekly communal labour (*umuganda*) was not a voluntarily contribution of labour as the regime would have liked everybody to believe, but a compulsory activity for each adult. The failure of these institutions became clear in 1991: at the moment when the rural population saw that dictatorial power diminished (when Habyarimana had to accept a multi-party system) peasants refused to attend umuganda and the animation sessions and dared to become members of a political party other than the MRND.

The leadership of the Second Republic was unable to organise a transition to a democratic government and to agree on the terms of a return of Tutsi refugees living in the diaspora for 17 years (1973–1990). For all these reasons, as we have written earlier on, the institutions themselves, the MRND, its president and the Akazu in particular, became part of the problem. *The institutions of dictatorship were no longer able to guarantee the economic well-being of the population because these institutions were instead highly redistributive to the powers that be.*

This reminds at what authors like Tsebelis and Olson have written, to wit that economists usually assume that a society develops efficient institutions, institutions that promote the well-being of everybody. Institutional development under the Habyarimana regime is one of the examples that show that this orthodox approach is not correct. Institutions appear to be not the result of an apolitical design to reach a situation beneficial to everybody, but rather the result of a truly political process in which not so much efficiency but re-distribution towards the powerful is on top of the agenda. Under the multi-party system, the renewed MRND, now called MRNDD, continued to be the leading force in all but two prefectures (Butare and Gitarama). The president continued to seek direct popular support and the MRNDD forged ties with CDR and MDR Power, extremist parties whom it had helped to create.

11.2 Population Density and Access to Resources

There exists a branch of economic theory that links resource endowments with institutional change. According to Platteau (2001) it is especially population growth and population density that are the driving forces behind institutional change. Platteau argues that economic development is difficult in sparsely populated areas. It is more difficult to raise the standard of living in a country with a low population density and highly dispersed settlement compared to a dense and concentrated population. The underdevelopment of transport infrastructure is responsible for high transaction costs and hinders the development of product and factor markets. This reasoning also applies to public goods and to collective action. Government services will be undersupplied in remote and sparsely inhabited regions. In contrast to many Asian countries, these conditions are highly prevalent in many African countries. Lack of transport infrastructure, dispersed populations, remote areas, absence of health and educational facilities, poor communication lines constitute a vicious circle of underdevelopment of markets and underprovision of collective goods.

The condition of low population density *was not* prevalent in Rwanda. As we have stated before, Rwanda was the most densely populated country in Africa and among the most densely populated countries in the world. In this respect, it resembles much more the conditions of an Asian country like China, India or Vietnam than of the average African country. For the study of economic and institutional development in Rwanda, it is therefore worth looking at some densely populated Asian countries.[2] As Platteau argues,

> The densely-populated, stably-settled farm population of Asia had traditionally been the convenient basis for rulers to expropriate tax. Since peasants had been the major bearer of the tax burden, a kind of agricultural fundamentalism had developed to regard peasants as the foundation of society. According to this ideology, it is legitimate for a ruler to tax away surplus above a peasants' subsistence but he must fulfill the responsibility to maintain their sustenance by providing infrastructure such as flood control, major irrigation and drainage systems (Wittfogel 1957). This tradition seems to underlie the Asian development strategy of providing key public goods for agricultural development while taxing farmers for the sake of industrial development (Platteau and Hayami 1997; Hayami 1997, Chap. 3).

---

[2] For a detailed analysis of the significance of agricultural land, peasant ideology and the freeze of social order for genocide in the history of East Asia, I refer to Ben Kiernan (2007), Blood and Soil.

As we have argued in the second chapter, the speeches of Juvenal Habyarimana reveal that he indeed regarded the peasantry exactly as in this citation. This vision did not come out of the blue: much of the history of the centralisation of power and the penetration of the state in the rural areas has to do with taxation by forced crop cultivation and by the compulsory supply of labour. In a very well researched review essay, Catherine and David Newbury (2000) rely on research by Leurquin (1960) and Dorsey (1983) to argue that the policies of forced crop cultivation (especially coffee) placed the colonial state directly in the production process.[3] When one wants to understand the history of Rwanda in general and the history of the genocide in particular, one has to study and analyse the connection between state activity and peasant agency in the rural areas. In the review essay, the authors argue that the omission of politics or of rural actors from an analysis will lead to misinterpretations of Rwanda's history. I believe they are correct, reason why I have focussed on the relationship between the state and the peasantry in this book. And I add that, while many Tutsi were in effect also cultivating the land, the regime's ideology considered the Tutsi as bourgeois and feudalists, and thus not as the foundation of Rwandan society.

What sets Rwanda apart from some densely populated Asian countries is the absence of access to the sea. Rwanda is surrounded by other countries and the distance to the nearest port is about 1,500 miles. The high transport costs to this port make Rwanda a case in between: *Internally*, population density is very high, transport is relatively well-developed and transaction costs are reduced. *Externally*, Rwanda is isolated from and marginal to world markets. Both these conditions have shaped Rwanda's economic and institutional development. In our approach, we focussed on the internal condition of a dense, but nevertheless remote, population. The external condition has contributed to the idea that Rwanda is isolated and has to rely on its own forces. The result is that the leadership underdeveloped and undervalued the benefits of trade with neighbouring countries.[4]

A compact, densely populated country such as Rwanda, should experience the inverse effects of a sparsely populated country. In terms of the supply of public goods and collective action, this would entail:

1. lower (per capita) costs of public service provision
2. lower reluctance to live in rural areas for professionals
3. easier access to schools, health centres, electricity and drinking water
4. lower administrative costs of tax collection and fewer options to escape taxes
5. better flow of information and easier organisation of collective action.

---

[3] Newbury, D and Newbury, C., Bringing the peasants back in, *The American Historical Review*, vol 105, number 3, June 2000, p. 868.

[4] A good example of Rwanda's inward-looking attitude is the desire of the Habyarimana regime to be self-sufficient in food. This policy minimized the import of food from neighboring countries, a policy causing starvation in southern Rwanda at the time of a local crop failure. See Chap. 5.

In general, these 5 conditions were met in Rwanda during the Habyarimana regime. Most were indeed better than in other African countries. Health centers, schools, roads, access to drinking water, local administration, the collection of taxes and several forms of collective action were part of rural life. In fact, when Rwanda was considered a "developmental state" by western donors, it was precisely because of the presence of state institutions and public goods in the rural areas. Before discussing the pro's and contra's of strong collective regulation and state presence in the rural areas, one first has to understand to logic behind collective action. A first and important element of this logic is in effect Rwanda's population density: high population density not only makes the provision of public goods feasible, it also makes this provision attractive from a ruler's point of view. Per capita costs of delivery are low and tax revenue will benefit from increased economic growth. High population density makes it also feasible to actually (in practice) collect this tax revenue.

Thus, the strong presence of state institutions in Rwanda's rural areas can be explained by the political economy opportunities shaped by Rwanda's population density.

High population density also requires complex regulation of access to resources. Under rising population density, resources become scarce and collective action to regulate the access to these resources becomes more and more important. Several forms of collective action were highly developed in Rwanda, exactly, we argue, because of high population density and the resulting social and political control. This is true for *umuganda*, the weekly activity of communal labour in which all adult males had to participate. Collective labour activities under control of state and local institutions have a long history in Rwanda. According to Guichaoua's work on umuganda (1989), levying taxes and organising communal labour where the two most important activities of the burgomaster (the local authority). In fact, the word 'umuganda' will be used to describe euphemistically the action of killing in the massacre of the Bagogwe in 1991 in northern Rwanda (FIDH 1993, p. 33). It is also worth mentioning that the militia *Interahamwe* literally means *"those who stand, act or work together"*.

Without collective action, the resource base will be depleted. From Platteau (2001) we learn the typical ways in which groups deal with resource scarcity. Either the community takes steps towards regulating the collective use of the resource, or it accepts its division and the consequent emergence of individualised rights. At this point in our reasoning, we have to discuss the Property Rights School. This school argues that private property is generally desirable on efficiency grounds. It is also their contention that private property constitutes an institutional innovation that is expected to emerge spontaneously under the combined impact of population growth and market development. As it happens, property rights theorists have a rather static view of the capacity of communities to deal with resource scarcity, especially under conditions where privatisation is very costly. A number of scholars have tried to qualify property rights theory arguing that collective regulation of a resource may evolve under population growth when privatisation remains prohibitively costly (Kikuchi and Hayami 1980; Ruttan and

Hayami 1984, 1985; Binswanger and McIntire 1987; Hayami 1997). Kikuchi and Hayami point out that under these circumstances, the social structure becomes tighter and more cohesive in response to a greater need to co-ordinate and control the use of resources as they become increasingly more scarce (Platteau 2001, Chap. 3). They argue that in pre-modern Japan under Tokugawa, population growth was gradual, which gave village communities sufficient time to develop the organisational capacity for mobilizing communal labour to build and maintain local irrigation facilities (Hayami 1997, 92). On the basis of detailed studies in South India (1988), Wade (1988, 185–188, and 211) found that villagers concerted their actions when net material benefits provided to all or most cultivators are high. Wade is confident, Platteau writes, that villagers will somehow succeed in overcoming the incentive problems associated with collective action.

According to Platteau (2001), the qualified property rights approach to institutional change offers a coherent explanation of a number of observed phenomena, but it remains problematic in so far as it assumes a priori that the main force behind institutional evolution is the search for a more efficient utilisation of resources. This however only occurs under restrictive conditions. The Coase Theorem—that efficient solutions will be realised when transaction costs do not matter or when parties bargain—is only valid when the value maximisation principle applies.[5] Dictators or presidential clans however are not in the first place interested in the efficient allocation of resources from a general welfare point of view, but in an allocation that re-enforces their position. This is usually not an efficient solution of the problem, but a re-distributive one. It takes the form of a redistribution of wealth to the advantage of the dictator's favourite group. In Rwanda's case the Akazu or presidential clan in particular and the Hutu population of northern Rwanda in general. Laws and practices that regulate access to schools, to fertile land, to jobs in the administration, to the military and to work-permits can all serve as examples of regulation that benefits the dictator and his ruling group, but that are not consistent with the value maximisation principle.

11.3 The Three-Fold Significance of Population Density in the Final Solution of Rwanda's Problem

11.3.1 Mobilising and Controlling Peasant Labour

We have discussed why, in general, it is very difficult (for a group or a regime) to organise collective action, as it is not rational from an individual's point of view to

---

[5] Milgrom and Roberts (1992, 36 and 38) define this principle as follows: an allocation among a group of people whose preferences display no wealth effects is efficient only if it maximises the total value of the affected parties. Moreover, for any inefficient allocation, there exists another (total value maximizing) allocation that all of the parties strictly prefer.

contribute to collective efforts. In Rwanda however, state institutions and especially communal authority has penetrated the peasant's daily life to such an extent that it allowed collective action to take place. Both authorities as well as peasants had a lot of experience with collective action.

In their review essay, David and Catherine Newbury (2000, 876) repeat that at numerous occasions (in several publications) they have argued that one cannot understand the genocide without understanding the political economy of Rwanda over the 1980s and 1990s. I entirely agree with them, and I am taking the political economy explanation of the genocide one step further.

In his well-known speeches Habyarimana talks many times about the virtues of hard work and manual labor in particular. Both the coffee policy (coffee being a labor intensive crop) and the umuganda policy are prime examples of the importance of labor control and labor policy to Habyarimana. The strong effort to mobilize and control labor by the regime can be explained from a political economy viewpoint: given the near absence of mineral wealth or other resources in the country, Habyarimana could not act as if he were Mobutu Sese Seko. For Mobutu, the control of the mineral wealth allowed him to buy off everybody to stay in power. Mobutu did not need to make use of peasant labor. Moreover, he did not need to gain the loyalty of the peasant masses. Things were a little different for Habyarimana. Since he claimed to be the president of the *majority people* and since the country had no mineral wealth, Habyarimana had to rely on the use of peasant labor. *I purposely say 'use'* because I believe that Habyarimana did not 'exploit' the peasant population, as we saw with my treatment of taxation in Chap. 3. Of course, umuganda policy could be regarded as the exploitation or abuse of peasant labor (certainly when it was used for private purposes), but on the other hand Habyarimana had to make sure that the peasantry did not turn against him. Part of the realizations of umuganda benefited the population who had built them. As we have described earlier, umuganda can best be viewed as a system of labor taxation, in part for the common good, but also intended to control and mobilize peasant labor. The same reasoning can be applied to the coffee policy (see Chap. 4): it was forbidden to rip out coffee trees once a peasant had planted them and peasants were fined when they did not maintain the trees well. But, again, the peasants were offered a relatively high price for their coffee. Here again, Habyarimana uses coffee policy both as a means to raise income AND at the same time to build political loyalty with the peasantry, albeit with a repressive stick for non-compliance. Just as with umuganda, the coffee policy can be seen as a form a taxation of peasant labor power, the only resource that was abundant in the country. The importance of and reliance on labour, especially manual labour as the principal source of value is also written down in the MRND party manifest: in a section titled '*the guiding principles of the economic policy of the MRND*', one reads that labour is not only the prime source of value and wealth and a right, but it is also a moral quality.[6]

---

[6] Manifest et Statuts du MRND 1975, le 5 Juillet, Les principes directeurs de la Politique Economique du MRND, p. 100.

On the relation between communal labour, peasant mobilization and genocide, it is worth citing Des Forges (1999, 234):

> Prefects transmitted orders and supervised results, but it was burgomasters and their subordinates who really mobilized the people. Using their authority to summon citizens for communal projects, as they were used to doing for Umuganda, burgomasters delivered assailants to the massacre sites, where military personnel or former soldiers then usually took charge of the operation. Just as burgomasters had organized barriers and patrols before the genocide so now they enforced regular and routine participation in such activities against the Tutsi. They sent councilors and their subordinates from house to house to sign up all adult males, informing them when they were to work. Or they drew up lists and posted the schedules at the places where public notices were usually affixed.

The mobilisation of the people by the administrative hierarchy, assisted by the military, mirrors the task assigned to each of them in the 1975 Manifest of the MRND. The local and national leadership had to guide the peasantry in their efforts for the development of the country. The military it was stated (see Chap. 1 of the Manifest) would not stay out of social and economic activities but would be integrated in the mobilisation of the People.

One could synthesize Habyarimana's policy towards the peasant as follows: "*if you do what I say, you will be rewarded*". This approach tried to make the (Hutu-) peasants believe that they were taking part in the governance of the country. Habyarimana after all was a Hutu president, and because he was from the 'majority people', the poor peasants were made to believe that they themselves were part of the government, hence the title "*Peasants in Power*" of this book. This management and control of the peasant labor force ("for the well-being of the peasant masses") will find its ultimate application in the execution of the genocide: it is indeed a most innovative idea to have the genocide executed by the population itself. This idea did not come out of the blue, but was rooted in the understanding that the peasants were the base of Rwandan society. In the same way as they worked for the development of the country, they will be using their labor power for the killing of their Tutsi neighbours. In fact, the more one thinks about it, the more the evil genius behind this idea becomes clear: using the country's only abundant production factor in the execution of the genocide assured a speedy, cheap and as complete as possible execution.

Here again, the peasants were made to believe to be acting for their own benefit when they participated in this evil form of collective action. It is in that respect that we can understand the use of economic incentives during the genocide. Just as they were given a good price for coffee to keep up political loyalty, they were given free beer, money, permission to loot, to take Tutsi women as concubines or sex slaves, the promise of land parcels, and so on. The same mechanisms as before applied: "if you put your labor power at my disposal, you will be rewarded." Having the peasant population participate as much as possible in the massacres can be regarded as yet another form of labor taxation for a collective purpose: in exchange for this taxation, the genocidal regime delivered the disappearance of the Tutsi from Rwandan soil. *In its implementation, the destruction of the Tutsi of Rwanda was a successful form of collective action, rooted in the mechanism of*

*control over the (labour of the) peasant population and pushed forward by an
extremist elite that promoted a killing norm. The organisation of the genocide and
the path of economic development chosen by the elite had in common that they
relied on the collective labour of the peasant population. With Rwanda's population density, this strategy was very attractive and very efficient.*

11.3.2   Population and the Re-design of the Polity

To the picture painted in the previous sections, one has to add that *the Habyarimana Regime considered both the size of the population AND the ethnic composition of the population of Rwanda as an integral part of the Rwandan institutional
set-up.* I discussed the absence of family planning, the pronatalist attitude and the
Malthusian beliefs of Habyarimana in the second chapter of this book. He rega-
reded the population as a force and considered the country overpopulated. The
leaders of the Second Republic believed that, were very aware of and made sure
that Rwanda's population size and the ethnic composition of that population were
part of the political game. *The size and the composition of the population were
crucial in the way these leaders thought about and discussed the political economy
of Rwanda.* This was the case in defining *the problem*: 'the country is overpopulated', Habyarimana said, 'the majority people are not afraid of the Tutsi', radio
RTLM proclaimed. And it was also crucial in designing the *solution*, to wit using
Rwanda's abundant labour force to build a civil defence force and to engage its
youth in militias that would kill Tutsi (see the section on 'the majority people' and
'the great mass' in Chap. 8). One could use the following catchphrase to describe
the Second Republic: population size, population density and population composition matter. Colonel Pierre Célestin Rwagafilita declared in October 1990: "their
number is small, we will liquidate them".[7]

This means that population size and population composition are not excluded
when discussing solutions to problems in the political economy of Rwanda. Since
they are essential factors upon which the leadership of the Second Republic had
built its ideology, its power and its legitimacy, these endowments were also
considered essential in the solution of problems. Onwards from the point where
population size and population composition had become political variables, they
enter the space of change, the space of design, the space of manipulation and
innovation. The bottom line is that political leaders start believing that these
factors can be changed.

The small, extremist group that spearheaded the genocide after the death of
Habyarimana claimed that the extermination of the Tutsi would once and for all

---

[7] Assemblée Nationale Francaise, mission d'information commune, Enquête sur la Tragédie
Rwandaise (1990–1994), Paris, Décembre 1998, Tome I, p. 276 (translation from French by the
author).

solve the ethnic problem of Rwanda and destroy the domestic Hutu political opposition. Donat Murego, holder of a PhD in political science and leader of the MDR-power wing of the MDR, saw the massacres as a way to complete the 1959 revolution and also a means to position his party for future elections. The extermination serves several purposes at the same time: their will be no Tutsi constituency for future elections and thus no popular support for a Tutsi-lead party while at the same time the social and political bonds between extremist politicians and ordinary perpetrators are strengthened (see Chaps. 9 and 10). In this sense the genocide was a 'final solution' to their 'ethnic problem'.

The genocide can be considered as a final attempt to solve the institutional deadlock that the regime faced. The genocide was the (ultimate) response of the elite to solve its own problems. That elite had defined Rwanda's problems in ethnic terms: by declaring the Tutsi to be the enemies of Rwanda, the regime gave its own idiosyncratic definition of the problem. The genocide can thus be considered as an ultimate political act to change the ethnic composition of Rwanda by making use of the country's only abundant factor of production: peasant labour.

11.3.3 Land Scarcity and Peasant Perpetrators

The third level of significance of population density in Rwanda's genocide is the importance of access to land (and other economic opportunities) for ordinary citizens. Agriculture is the most important source of income for the vast majority of Rwandans, both in terms of subsistence (crops for own consumption) as in terms of the sale of crops. Because of population density all cultivable land is taken into cultivation and peasants farm their plots very intensively. Since land is such a valuable asset, peasants prefer crops with a high value per unit of land (described in Chaps. 2 and 4), thereby applying a lot of labour to the land to maintain its fertility, avoid erosion and increase the output.

In earlier work on perpetrator profiles (Verwimp 2003, 2005), I have shown that land renting peasants were over-represented among the perpetrators of the genocide. This comes as no surprise when we consider the absence of economic opportunities for land-scarce peasants. This is not just an individual response of a poor, desperate person who al of a sudden sees an opportunity to steal a cow, a radio, extract cash from Tutsi and hopes to get a plot of land when he 'engages himself in defense of the Nation'. This whole set of behavior from the side of poor peasants is rooted in Rwanda's institutions. The vulnerability of these poor people, in purely economic terms the tiny size of their field, the lack of education, the danger of crop failure and hunger, cannot be separated from the institutional—and thus political—organization of Rwanda. The vulnerability of the relationship of a peasant family vis-à-vis a landlord, an employer, or a powerful local office holder is a political one. Local elites have used the vulnerability of poor people, of which some were eager to participate.

The local businessmen, administrators, police officers and so on were strongly represented among the perpetrators. This shows that our political economy approach does not only capture the poor, but looks at the relationship that each ordinary Rwandan had with the institutions of the state. The more involved one was with an institution, as client or as a patron (who himself a client vis-s-vis a more hierarchical patron) the higher one's probability to become a perpetrator. The results of my earlier empirical work show that this was the case for access to land and access to paid labour. The land and labour markets in Rwanda under the Habyarimana regime cannot be regarded as institutions outside of politics or power.

One element in this conundrum that has been under researched until today and upon which I hope that future research will shed light is the enrolment of displaced people, in particular young people, in the interahamwe. As a result of the war in the north of the country it is estimated that about 1 million people were camping in bad conditions just north of the capital in 1993. There is some evidence (far from conclusive) that the regime was particularly successful in recrutement among these displaced youth.

11.4   Endogenous or Exogenous?

The contribution of this book and issues for further research

The underlying question in a lot of scholarly and public debates on the Rwandan genocide is on the role and importance of endogenous versus exogenous factors. Advocates of the latter argue that fear caused by the RPF attack was the prime mover in the genocide. The build-up of the RPF is not independent of the development of Rwanda's institutions during the Second Republic. Had the Second Republic allowed the Tutsi refugees to return to Rwanda in the 1970s or 1980s, an invasion would not have taken place. We will never know what Rwanda's history would then have looked like. On the one hand, the attack was the decision of a group of Tutsi officers united in the Rwandan Patriotic Front and living in Uganda. A decision made because the Habyarimana regime stood under great pressure to solve the refugee question and was about to make concessions. On the other hand, the regime did not make concessions in the past 17 years (1973–1990) to solve this question and Habyarimana, as I showed, did not have the intention to allow the refugees to come back. He wanted them to settle in their host country and argued that Rwanda was overpopulated.

The exogenous shock of the attack—argument invoked by the advocates of the thesis of fear—upset the regime as well as the population which responded with an extermination campaign to eliminate the threat. In Chap. 7 on civil war and the 1990–1992 massacres as well as Chap. 8 on the mechanisms, I show that I do not share this reading of the genocide. This does not mean that I disregard external or international influences in the run-up to the genocide.

The organisation of the coffee economy, as explained in Chap. 4, shows how the revenue of the state and the monetary income of the peasants depend strongly on the price of coffee. This chapter clearly shows the importance of the international price of coffee, an element that is exogenous to the institutions of the Second Republic. The internal organisation of the coffee economy however was a Rwandan affair. I have shown that the price paid to the producers was both a means to increase the volume of coffee produced as well as an instrument of political loyalty. The coffee crisis which started at the end of the 1980s was an international phenomenon, with sharp declines in the international price. The impact it had on the Rwandan state in the first place but also on the Rwandan peasantry was the result of the way the Rwandan coffee economy was organized. In particular, it was unsustainable to continue to use the price paid to the producers as a mechanism to buy political loyalty from the peasants.

As can be inferred from this book, my argument is that the Rwandan genocide is first of all an endogenous genocide. Endogenous in the sense that is was the result of the development of Rwanda's own institutions during the Second Republic. As explained in the second chapter, Ferdinand Nahimana, professor of history and later ideologue of genocide, quotes Habyarimana in his 1988 book when he writes *"Rwanda has to rely on its own forces"*. This expression was already explicitly mentioned in the preamble of the 1975 MRND party manifest, which reads *"We have to convince ourselves every day that we first of all have to rely on our own forces. This is a constant of our Movement"* (MRND 1975, 90). This is not an expression of genocidal intent, but it captures the core of the Second Republic. It tells us what the Second Republic was all about. It was an inward looking, highly administered society where the elite glorified and relied on the labour of hard working peasants united in a unique political movement. The elite envisioned a homogenous society where there is no room for politics and were everybody is engaged in the realm of development.

Having said that, external and international factors have plaid an important role. I believe future research should especially look at the impact these factors had on the domestic polity, especially on the balance of political power and on the relationship between the state and the peasantry. In the writing and the conclusion of this book I am not able to do full justice to several interesting contributions on the role of external events, decisions of the international community or the influence of the civil war on the genocide. In fact, I hope other researchers take up this challenge and weigh the contribution of this book with that of scholars who put more emphasis on the civil war in their explanation of the genocide.

A model of strategic interaction may shed light on the period before the genocide.[8] Most genocides have indeed occurred during civil wars. Civil war

---

[8] In a 2003 paper, (Verwimp 2003) not included in this book, I have made my own contribution to this debate from a game-theoretic perspective. The model highlights the strategic interaction between the government, the domestic opposition, the RPF and the international community. Under certain conditions, the actions of a player influence the options of other players as well as the pay-offs of these options. In brief, with the external threat of a rebel movement and the

allows the development and use of strategies that were not available in the absence of civil war. The problem of a strategic approach is that it does not yield an analysis that is grounded in Rwanda's history. It helps us to understand how the choices made by different players influenced each other on the eve of the genocide, but does not really bring us closer to answer the question on the causes of the genocide.

Perpetrators of the Rwandan genocide, leaders as well as rank and file, argue that they killed the Tutsi because they were at war. How do we have to understand this? Do these perpetrators really believe that the wanton killing of 650,000 men, women and children is a act of war? Did they want to win the war? Why then did the regime not devote all its energy, resources and manpower to fight the RPF on the battlefield? Clearly, a lot of resources, especially weapons and manpower were devoted to the extermination of the Tutsi population, not to the war with the RPF. If we want to answer the question why the regime as well as parts of the population engaged in genocide, we cannot be satisfied with the observation that the killing of Tutsi is a act of war, or that this is the way the Hutu population reacts when it is attacked. This needs to be explained. We need to explain why *Rwanda works like this*. That is what I have tried to do in this book.

An approach which puts the civil war at the centre of analysis to explain the genocide also fails to adequately explain the *'how?'* question. This question, on how the genocide was implemented, to wit by mobilising the rural population as much as possible, is at least as interesting as the question *'what are the origins of the genocidal intention?'* Regimes that have build an ideological and organisational apparatus, such as Rwanda's Second Republic, will use this apparatus to find answers to threats to the apparatus. Genocide is the result of a gradual policy involving identification, hate propaganda, militarization of society, resource allocation, and so on. *Regime leaders, by the time they take the ultimate step to execute the genocide, have a pretty good idea how to do it.* In the 1993 FIDH report mentioned in Chap. 6, the content of a meeting that planned the massacre on

---

(Footnote 8 continued)

increased activities of the domestic opposition, a government may have or use options that it did not have or was not able to use prior to the threat. In the paper, I use a nested games approach (Tsebelis 1990; Lohmann 1997) to model strategic interaction. As the option of cooperation (the Arusha peace agreement) becomes more likely in a game where a player is engaged in multiple arena games, such a player may seek to redesign the rules of the game (institutions) because he realizes that the linkages between different games changes the structure of the game and thus of his pay-offs. Cooperation in the nested game will lead to a higher pay-off for all players taken together, but not for the player whose non-cooperative strategy has yielded him a higher individual pay-off in the non-nested version of the game. This player may then want to reduce the nested game with multiple players into a game between two players only, Hutu and Tutsi. The elimination of the domestic Hutu opposition can be regarded as an institutional innovation in the nested game. It simplifies the game and allows the regime to reach its highest pay-off with its non-cooperative strategy. The genocide then can be seen as another institutional innovation, as a final solution of the game. Because the perpetrator would never have to play the game again. In the model the role of the international community is to condition aid on the observance of human rights and in this sense make the cooperative strategy more rewarding for players.

the Bagogwe was revealed. The group that decided to kill the Bagogwe had met several times before, giving the participants the chance to link issues over time as well as over different topics. The meeting that decided to do the killing discussed at the same time the means to be used for the operation (FIDH p. 38). These means were trustworthy burgomasters, 15 million RWF and the help of policemen. In fact, the gradualism of the path to genocide is as much a search for the best way how to do it as it is a reflection on whether or not one should do it. *If, gradually, advances are made on the logistical side and genocide becomes a feasible option because leaders realise they can actually do it, the ultimate decision to implement it may be only a formality.*

That is in my opinion also the way we should look at the Interahamwe. The question whether or not to use and train Interahamwe for killing operations and the question whether or not to massacre Tutsi influence each other. In the beginning (1991–1992) Interahamwe were used to intimidate people opposed to the MRND and the Habyarimana regime. Soon however, the regime used them in killing operations, as in March 1992 in Bugesera. This means that by that time regime leaders had enough confidence in the Interahamwe to have them assist in a local killing campaign. From previous local massacres in 1990 and 1991, the regime had already learned that the reaction of the international community to such a massacre was soft and that it was fairly easy to enlist parts of the local population to participate in the killing, especially when rumors and propaganda are used. In 1992, regime and militia leaders observed the advantages and possible disadvantages of using the Interahamwe in a killing operation. The organisors of these massacres learn from these events. They learn how certain means can best be combined to reach certain ends. They learn about the feasibility of their aims and the effectiveness of their means.

The endogenous approach to the Rwandan genocide used in this book accounts for the intimate link between two questions: 'Why was genocide commited?' and 'How was genocide commited?' I contend that the development of the institutions of the Second Republic answers both questions. *The Hutu Power elite not only wanted to retain power, they also wanted to maintain the agrarian order that cemented their power. And they implemented this by using the rural masses to defend that order. From the 1990–1992 massacres the elite learned that this strategy would work.* The agrarian order and the powerful position of the Hutu elite in it are two sides of the same coin. Their position of power and privilege in Rwandan society could only be maintained when Rwanda remained an agrarian society of hardworking peasants. Their power was an integral part of the existing order and at the same time a guarantor of that order.

When, as Habyarimana frequently said, the peasants of Rwanda are the foundation of Rwandan society. *When* all Rwandans are members of the MRND by birth. *When* the president of the MRND and all positions at different levels in the party or occupied by the same people who occupy a state position at the corresponding state level. *When* the MRND is a pyramid where all militants know their place in the hierarchy. *When* the president and the MRND consider themselves to be the sole guarantors of the State and of the whole Nation. *When* it is the ideology of the MRND that all militants should contribute to the objectives of the movement, especially by supplying their labour. *When* all great projects emanating from the leadership of the Second Republic such as umuganda, the paysannats settlement scheme, the nationwide anti-erosion campaign, weekly animation sessions and coffee cultivation rely heavily on peasant labour for their execution. *Then it is no surprise that the next campaign, the defense of the established order guaranteed by the President and the institutions of Party and State, is proclaimed to be everybody's responsibility. Hence the idea that 'the people' themselves will execute the genocide.* This idea and its implementation, which is an answer to the question 'how are we going to do it?', do not come out of the blue. The mobilisation of the peasants to execute the genocide follows directly from the way the Second Republic was organized and ruled, from the institutions of Party and State.

About the Author

Philip Verwimp is Associate Professor of Development Economics at the Solvay Brussels School of Economics and Management, Université Libre de Bruxelles, where he holds the Marie and Alain Philippson Chair in Sustainable Human Development. He is Fellow of ECARES, member of the Centre Emile Bernheim and co-founder and co-director of the Households in Conflict Network. He is author and co-author of articles published in the American Economic Review, the Journal of Development Economics, Economic Development and Cultural Change, the Journal of Agrarian Studies, the Journal of Conflict Resolution and the Journal of Peace Research, among others.

P. Verwimp, *Peasants in Power*, DOI: 10.1007/978-94-007-6434-7,
© Springer Science+Business Media Dordrecht 2013

Bibliography

Acemoglu, D., & Robinson, J. A. (2006). Economic Origins of Dictatorship and Democracy, Cambridge University Press

Adelman, H., & Suhrke, A. (1999). *The Path of a Genocide: the Rwanda Crisis from Uganda to Zaire.* : Transaction Publishers.

Adelman, H., & Shurki, A.(1996), *Joint Evaluation of Emergency Assistance to Rwanda.*

Association Rwandaise pour la Défense des Droits de la Personne et des Libertés Publiques, (1992), *Rapport sur les droits de l'homme au Rwanda*, Kigali; décembre

The African Commission on Human and People's Rights, Examination of State Reports, 9th Session March 1991: Libya - Rwanda – Tunisia.

African Rights (1994), Resisting Genocide, Bisesero April-June 1994.

African Rights (1995), Rwanda : Death, Despair and Defiance.

André, C and Platteau, J-Ph. (1998), Land Relations under unbearable stress : Rwanda caught in the Malthusian Trap, *Journal of Economic behaviour and Organisation*, vol 34, 1998. First published as a Cahiers de la Faculté des Sciences Economiques et Sociales, no 164, January 1996.

Akerlof, G.A. (1984), A theory of social custom, of which unemployment may be one consequence, in Akerlof, G.A., An economic theorist's book of tales.

Arrow, H. J. (1972). Gifts and Exchanges. *Philosophy and Public Affairs, 1*, 343–362.

Axelrod, R. (1984), The Evolution of Cooperation.

Axelrod, R. (1997). *The Complexity of Cooperation.* Agent-based models of Competition and Collaboration: Princeton University Press.

Bardhan, P, (1997), Method in the Madness? A Political-Economy Analysis of the Ethnic Conflicts in Less Developed Countries, *World Development*, vol.25, no 9.

Bart, F. (1993). *Montagne d'Afrique.* Bordeaux: Terres Paysannes.

Bates, R. (1981). *Markets and States in Tropical Africa.* : University of California Press.

Becker, G. S. (1974). A theory of social interactions. *Journal of Political Economy, 82*, 1063–1093.

Belgian Senate (1997), *Report of Rwanda Commission of Inquiry*, December 6, 1997.

Berlage, L., Eyssen, H., Goedhuys, M., Sleuwagen, L., & Van den Bulcke, D. (1993). *Rwanda :Disequilibrium.* World Bank, Country Background Paper, April: Reform and the Manufacturing Sector.

Berlage, L., Verpoorten, M., & Verwimp, P. (2003). Income mobility in post-genocide Rwanda, report for the Flemish Interuniversity Council on Development Cooperation June (VLIR-UOS), Leuven, June.

Bevan, D., Collier, P., & Gunning, J. W. (1989). *Peasants and Governments, an Economic Analysis.* Oxford: Clarendon Press.

Bézy, F. (1990). *Rwanda : Bilan d' un régime 1962–1990.* : Louvain-La-Neuve.

Bhargava, A. (1997). Nutritional Status and the allocation of time in Rwandese Households. *Journal of Econometrics, 77*, 1997.

Binswanger, H., & McIntire, J. (1987). Behavioural and Material Determinants of Production Relations in Land-Abundant Tropical Agriculture. *Economic Development and Cultural Change, 36*(1), 73–99.

Blam, W. (1997), Genocide as 'modern' political instrument, original text published in German in H. Schürings (ed.) Ein Volk verlässt sein Land. Krieg und Völkermord in Ruanda, Köln, 1994. Authors translation from the French version published in Jean-Pierre Chrétien, Le défi de l'ethnisme, Karthala.

Blarel, B.,Hazell, P., Place, F., Quiggin, J., The Economics of Farm Fragmentation : Evidence from Ghana and Rwanda, *The World Bank Economic Review*, Vol. 6, no. 2

Bonneux, L., (1994), Rwanda : a case of Demographic Entrapement, *Lancet*, 344, no 17.

Brandstetter, Anna-Maria. (1997). *Ethnic or Socio-Economic Conflict?* (pp. 439–440). International Journal on Minority and Group Rights: Political Interpretations of the Rwandan Crisis.

Brandstetter, A. M. (1999). *Die Rhetorik von Reinheit*. Gewalt und gemeinschaft: Bürgerkrieg und Genozid in Rwanda, Zeitschrift für Ethnologie.

Brush, S. G. (1996). *Dynamics of Theory Change in the Social Sciences, Relative Deprivation and Collective Violence, Journal of Conflict Resolution, 40(4)*. : December.

Byiringiro, F., & Reardon, T. (1996). Farm Productivity in Rwanda : the effects of farm size, erosion, and soil conservation investments. *Agricultural Economics, 15*, 1996.

Capéau, B., & P.Verwimp (2012), 'Dictatorship in a Single Export Crop Economy', *Journal of Theoretical Politics*, April, 24, pp.210-234

Caunce, S. (1994). *Oral History and the Local Historian*. New York: Longman group.

Chandler, P., Kiernan, B., & Chanthou, B. (1988). *Pol Pot Plans the Future, Confidential Leadership Documents from Democratic Kampuchea, 1976-1977*, Monograph Series 33/Yale University Southeast Asia Studies, New Haven.

Chrétien, J. P., Dupaquier, J.-F., Kabanda, M., & Ngarambe, J. (1995). *Les Médias du génocide*. Paris: Karthala.

Clay, D., Kampayana, T., & Kayitsinga, J. (1989). *Inequality and the Emergence of Non-Farm Employment in Rwanda, paper presented at the Annual Meetings of the Rural Sociological Society*. : Seattle.

Clay, D. (1995), Promoting Food Security in Rwanda through sustainable agricultural productivity : meeting the challenges of Population pressure, Land Degradation and Poverty, International Development Paper no. 17, Michigan State University, Departements of Agricultural Economics and Economics, chapter 3.

Clay, D., Reardon, T., Kangasniemi, J, (1998), Sustainable Intensification in the Highland Tropics : Rwandan Farmers' Investments in Land Conservation and Soil Fertility, *Economic Development and Cultural Change*, 1998.

Clay, D., Rwandan Agricultural Household Survey 1989-1992, Michigan State University and Food Security Project, Rwanda.

Cohen, Y. (1994). *Radicals*. Reformers and Reactionaries: Chicago University Press.

Cohen, Stanley. (2001). *States of denial, knowing about atrocities and suffering*. Cambridge: Polity Press.

De Lame, D. (1996). *Une Colline entre mille ou me calme avant la tempete, Transformations et Blocages du Rwanda Rural*. Tervuren: Musée Royale de l' Afrique Centrale.

Des Forges, A., (1999), *Leave None to tell the Story*, Human Rights Watch.

de Walque, D., & Verwimp, P. (2010). Demographic and Socio-Economic Distribution of Excess Mortality in the 1994 Genocide in Rwanda. *Journal of African Economies, 19*(2), 141–162.

Discours et Entretiens de Son Excellence le Général-Major Habyarimana Juvénal Président de la Republique Rwandaise, et Président-Fondateur du Mouvement Révolutionnaire National pour le Développement, Office Rwandais d'Information, Kigali, 1973, 1974, 1979, 1980, 1981, 1982, 1985, 1986, 1987,1988.

Dorsey, L. (1983). *The Rwandan Colonial Economy, 1916–1941*. Dissertation: Michigan State University.

Duncan, T., Frankenberg, E., & Smith, J. (1998). Lost but not Forgotten, Attrition in the Indonesian Family Life Survey, Paper presented at the Conference on Data Quality in Longitudinal Surveys, Institute for Social Research, University of Michigan, October 1998

Enquête Démograpique et de Santé, Office National de la population. (1992). Federation International des Organisations de Droits de l' homme, Rapport sur les violations de droit de l' homme au Rwanda depuis le 1e Octobre 1990, Paris, Mars 1993.

Galtung, A. (1964). A Structural Theory of Agression. *Journal of Peace Research, 1*(2), 94–119.

Gasana, E., Butera, J. B., Byanafashe, D., & Karekezi, A. (1999). *Rwanda, chapter 8 in Comprehending and Mastering African Conflicts, ed.* Adedaji: A.

Gascon, J.-F., (1992), Pauvreté a Gikongoro, Résultats de l'enquête réalisée aupres des ménages indigents, Projet de Development Agricole de Gikongoro, Document de travail, n.156, Juin 1992.

Gatete, C. (1996). *Food Security and Food Aid in Rwanda.* June: Wihogora.

Ganguly, K. (1992). Migrant identities: personal memories and the construction of selfhood. *Cultural Studies, 6*, 27–50.

Griffin, R. (1995). *Fascism : a reader.* : Oxford University Press.

Guichaoua, A. (1989). Destins paysans et politiques agraires en Afrique Centrale : L' ordre paysan des hautes terre du Burundi et du Rwanda.

Guichaoua, A. (1991), Les Travaux Communautaires en Afrique Centrale, *Revue Tiers Monde*, t.XXXII, n. 127, July-September, p.551-573

Guichaoua, A. (1992). *Le problème des refugies rwandais et des populations Banyarwanda dans la région des Grands Lacs Africains.* Geneva: UNHCR.

Guichaoua, A. (1995). *Les Crises politiques au Burundi et Rwanda (1993–1994).* : Université de Lille.

Guichaoua, A. (2010). *Rwanda de la Guerre au Génocide: les politiques criminelles au Rwanda (1990–1994).* Paris: La Découverte. 622p.

Gupta, D. K. (1990). *The Economics of Political Violence.* New York: The Effect of Political Instability on Economic Growth.

Gurr, T. (1970). *Why Men Rebel.* : Princeton University Press.

Habyarimana, J, Discourse at the first encounter with public servants

Habyarimana, J, Speech at the opening of the 1980 new year, 1979

Harff, B. (2003). No lessons learned from the Holocaust? Assessing Risks of Genocide and Political Mass Murder since 1955, *American Political Science Review*, vol.97, no.1

Hayami, Y et Platteau, Ph. (1997). Resource Endowments and agricultural development, Africa vs Asia

Hayami, Y. (1997). *Development Economics – From the Poverty to the Wealth of Nations.* Oxford: Clarendon Press.

Hirshleifer, J., (1977), Economics from a biological viewpoint, *Journal of Law and Economics*, 20

Horowitz, I.L. (1976). *Genocide: State Power and Mass Murder.* Transaction Books, New Brunswick.

Human Development Reports, UNDP, 1990 and 1994.

Human Rights Watch, (1994), Arming Rwanda, New York.

International Commission on Human Rights Violations in Rwanda since October 1990, FIDH, March 1993.

IWACU, documentary film, February 1990.

Janssen, S. (2002). The Violence of Memories Local narratives of the past after ethnic cleansing in Croatia. In. *Rethinking History, 6*(1), .

Jefremovas, V. (1991). Loose Women. *Virtuous Wives and Timid Virgins: gender and control of resources in Rwanda, Canadian Journal of African Studies, 25*(3), 378–395.

Jon, R. (1999). *Conte memory, research, and the law: future directions in Trauma & Memory Linda M.* Williams and Victoria L. Banyard eds: Sage publications London.

Kalt, J.P., & Zupan, M. (1984). Capture and Ideology in the economic theory of politics, *American Economic Review*, 74 (3), June, pp.279-300.

Kangasniemi, J. (1998). *(1998), People and Bananas on steep slopes : Agricultural Intensification and Food Security under Demographic Pressure and Environmental Degradation in Rwanda*. Ph.D Disseration: Department of Agricultural Economics, Michigan State University.

Kangura, June 1990, No. 3 and No 5, November and December 1990 and nr 18, July 1991.

Keiner, H., (1992), Allmahlich schwand die Bewunderung for 'Habis' regime, *Frankfurter Rundschau*, November 5th, 1992.

Kiernan, B. (1996). *The Pol Pot Regime, Race, Power and Genocide in Cambodja under the Khmer Rouge 1975–1979*. New Haven: Yale University Press.

Kiernan, B. (1998). *'Genocide and "ethnic cleansing"'*, in *The Encyclopedia of Politics and Religion, ed.* Washington, D.C., Congressional Quarterly: Robert Wuthnow.

Kiernan, B. (2007). *Blood and Soil*. New Haven and London: Yale University Press. 724p.

Kikuchi, M., & Hayami, Y. (1980). Inducements to Institutional Innovations in an Agrarian Community. *Economic Development and Cultural Change, 29*(1), 21–36.

Kimonyo, J. P. (2000). *Revue critique des interprétations du conflit Rwandais, Cahier n°1*. Centre des Gestion des Conflits: Université Nationale du Rwanda.

King, M., Rwanda, (1994), Malthus and Medicus Mundi, *Medicus Mundi Bulletin* 54.

Kuran, T. (1995). *Private Truths*. The Social Consequences of Preference Falsification, Harvard University Press: Public Lies.

L'Umuganda dans le dévélopment national. (1990). *Présidence de MRND*. Janvier: Affaires Economiques.

Länderbericht (Country Report) Rwanda, Statistisches Bundesamt, BRD, 1992.

Large, D. (1997). *Where Ghosts Walked : Munich's Road to the Third Reich*. New York: Norton.

Laub, D. (1995). *'truth and testimony: the process and the struggle'*, in *Trauma: Explorations in Memrory, ed.* Cathy Caruth (Baltimore: Johns Hopkins University Press.

Lemarchand, R., (1970), *Rwanda and Burundi*.

Les Retombées de la Famine dans les Préfectures de Butare et de Gikongoro, Bureau Social Urbain-Caritas, Kigali, Février 1990, 26 p.

Letter by the Minister of Interior and Communal Development to the military commander in Gisenyi asking to send troops to Kibuye Prefecture to support an operation in the sector of Bisesero, Commune of Gishyita, dated June 18, 1994.

Leydesdorff, S. (2004). *De mensen en de woorden*. Amsterdam: Meulenhoff.

Letter of the Préfet of Kibuye Prefecture to the Minister of the Interior and Communal Development, on May 5, 1994.

Letter of the Préfet to all the Burgomasters concerning the self-defense program of the population, on April 30th, 1994

Leurquin, (1960). *Le niveau de vie des populations rurales du Rwanda-Urundi*. Editions Nauwelaerts: UCL.

Liao, T. F. (1994). *Interpreting probability models*. Quantitative applications in the social sciences series: Sage publications.

Little P.D., & Horowitz, M., 1987 and 1988, Agricultural Policy and Practice in Rwanda, *Human Organisation*, vol.46, pp.254-259 and vol. 47, pp. 271-273

Longman, T., (1995), Genocide and socio-political change : massacres in two rwandan villages, Issue, A Journal of Opinion, vol.XXIII/2, pp.18-22

Mamdani, M, (2001), When Victims Become Killers, Princeton University Press.

Marysse, S., De Herdt, T., & Ndayambaje, E. (1994). *Rwanda*. Cahiers Africains, Institut Africain, Paris et Bruxelles, Karthala et CEDAF: Apprauvissement et Ajustement structurel.

Myerhoff, B. (1986). Life not death in Venice: its second life. In V. Turner & E. M. Bruner (Eds.), *The anthropology of experience*. Urbana, IL: University of Illinois Press.

Milgrom, P., & Roberts, J. (1992). *Economics*. Prentice-Hall International: Organisation and Management.

Moore, B. (1993). *Social Origins of Dictatorship and Democracy.* : Beacon Press.

Nahimana, F. (1988). *Conscience chez-nous, confiance en nous.* Ruhengeri: Notre culture est la base de notre developpement harmonieux.

National Agricultural Survey. (1984). *Department of Agricultural Statistics.* Rwanda: Kigali.

Ndahayo, E., (2000), Rwanda : le dessous des Cartes, l' Harmattan.

Newbury, C. (1987). *The Cohesion of Oppression: Clientship and Ethnicity in Rwanda 1860–1960.* New York: Columbia University Press.

Newbury, C. (1992). Recent Debates on Governance and Rural Development. In M. Bratton & G. Hyden (Eds.), *Governance and Politics in Africa.* Boulder and London: Lynne Rienner Publishers.

Newbury, D., & Newbury, C., (2000), Bringing the peasants back in, *The American Historical Review*, vol 105, number 3, June, pp.832-877.

Ngirumwami, J.L., Ministry of Agriculture, Résultats de l'enquête Commerce Frontalier au Rwanda, June 1989

Nsengiyaremye, D., La Transition Démocratique au Rwanda (1989-1993) in Guichaoua, A., (ed.) *Les Crises politiques au Burundi et Rwanda (1993-1994)*, Université de Lille, pp.239-263.

Ntezilyayo, A., L'agriculture, une priorité dans la reconstruction nationale in A. Guichaoua, A. (ed.), Les Crises politiques au Burundi et Rwanda (1993-1994), Université de Lille.

Ocir-Café, Proces-Verbal de la Reunion du conseil d'Administration de l'Office des Cafés, mars 25, 1992, Kigali, Rwanda

Office of Population, Rwanda, *The Demographic Problem in Rwanda and the Framework of its Solution*, 4 volumes, 1990.

Olson, M., (1965), The Logic of Collective Action,

Olson, M. (2000). *Power and Prosperity.* Outgrowing Communist and Capitalist Dictatorships: Basic Books, New York.

Olson, M., & Mcguire, M., (1996), The Economics of Autocracy and Majority Rule : The Invisible Hand and the Use of Force, *Journal of Economic Literature*, pp.72-96.

Place, F., & Hazell, P, (1993), Productivity effects of Indigenous Land Tenure Systems in Sub-Saharan Africa, *American Journal of Agricultural Economics*, February 1993, p.14-15.

Platteau, J Ph. (2001). *Institutions.* Social Norms and Economic Development: Harwood.

Pottier, J., (1993), Taking stock, Food Marketing reform in Rwanda 1982-1989, *African Affairs,* pp.240-251

Prunier, G. (1995). *The Rwanda Crisis.* : History of a Genocide.

Ravallion, M. (1997). *Famines and Economics.* : Journal of Economic Literature.

Reardon, Th. (1997). Using Evidence of Household Income Diversification to inform Study of the Rural Nonfarm Labor Market in Africa. *World Development, 25*(5), 1997.

Renton, D., (2001), The Agrarian Roots of Fascism : German Exceptionalism Revisited, *The Journal of Peasant Studies*, Vol 28, No 4, July 2001

Report by the Préfet of Kibuye of the day to day events in all the communes between April 6 and April 10 dated on April 11.

Report of the meeting of the security committee of Kibuye Prefecture on April 11, 1994.

Republic of Rwanda, Compte-rendu de la Réunion tenue au Minagri en date du 02/05/1989 sur la situation alimentaire du Rwanda en Avril 1989, Ministry of Agriculture, p. 4.

Republic of Rwanda, Rapport sur la Situation Alimentaire de notre Pays, Ministry of Agriculture, Octobre 1989, translation by J.Pottier, ibidem, 1993, p. 20

Reyntjens, F. (1985). *Pouvoir et Droit au Rwanda.* : Musée Royal de Tervuren.

Reyntjens, F., Démocratisations et conflits ethniques au Rwanda, in : P.Wymeersch, (ed.) Liber amicorum M.d'Hertefelt, Bruxelles, Centre d' Etude et de Documentation Africaines, p.209-227

Reyntjens, F. (1994). *l'Afrique des Grands Lacs en crise 1988–1994.* Paris: Karthala.

Reyntjens, F. (1996). Rwanda : Genocide and Beyond. *Journal of Refugee Studies, 9,* 3.

Rumiya, Jean, (1985), Rwanda d'hier, Rwanda d'aujourd'hui, Vivant Univers 357 (May-June 1985).

Ruttan, V., & Hayami, Y. (1984). Toward a Theory of induced Institutional Innovation. *Journal of Development Studies, 20*(4), 203–223.

Schumpeter, J. A. (1963). *History of Economic Analysis.* : Oxford University Press.

Seltzer, W. (1998). Population Statistics, the Holocaust and the Nuremberg Trials. *Population and Development Review, 24*(3), .

Sen, A. (1977). Rational Fools : A Critique of the Behavioral Foundation of Economic Theory. *Philosophy and Public Affairs, 6,* 317–344.

Sen, A., (1981), Poverty and Famines.

Sibomana, A. (1999). *Hope for Rwanda.* Conversations with Laure Guilbert and Hervé Deguine: Pluto Press, English-language edition.

Simbalikure, A., Under-prefect of Busoro Under-Prefecture, Letter to the Burgomasters of the Communes of Gishamvu, Kigembe, Nyakizu and Runyinya, June 1st, 1994.

Skocpol, T. (1979). *States and Social Revolutions : a Comparative Analysis of France.* Russia and China: Cambridge University Press.

Staub, E, (1989), The roots of evil : the origins of genocide and other group violence, Cambiridge University Press

Stigler, J. (1981). Economics of Ethics? In S. McMurrin (Ed.), *Tanner Lectures on Human Values, vol II.* : Cambridge University Press.

Straus, S. (2006). *The Order of Genocide: Race.* Power and War in Rwanda: Cornell University Press.

Sykes, G., & Matza, D. (1957) summery from: 'techniques of neutralization; a theory of delinquency', p. 206-213. In: Munche, J., Mclaughlin, E., & Langan, M. (eds.), (1996), Criminological Perspectives. A Reader. London: Sage publications

Tardiff-Douglin, D., Ngirumwami, J. L., Shaffer, J., Murekezi, A., & Kampayana, T. (1993). *Apercu sur la politique cafeicole au Rwanda.* : Kigali.

Taylor, H. O. (1960). *A History of Economic Thought.* : Harvard University.

Thiry, I., & Verwimp, P. (2008) Daders van Genocide bevraagd: een bijdrage vanuit de criminologie met veldwerk in Rwanda, *Panopticon,* januari.

Thomas, D., Public Policy and anthropometric outcomes in the Côte-d'Ivoire, *Journal of Public Economics,* 1996

Thompson, P. (1988). *The voice of the Past. Oral history.* Oxford: University Press.

Tilly, C. (1975). *From mobilisation to revolution.* : Addison-Wesley Reading.

Tilly, C., Tilly, L., & Tilly, R. (1978). *The rebellious century, 1830–1930.* Cambridge: Harvard University Press.

Tonkin, E. (1992). *Narrating our Pasts.* : The social construction of oral history. Cambridge; Cambridge University Press.

Tsebelis, G. (1990). *Nested Games : rational choice in comparative politics.* : University of California Press Berkeley.

Tullock, G. (1987). *Autocracy.* Dordrecht: Kluwer.

Twizeyimana, P., & Uwimana, V., *Portrait de la Pénurie alimentaire actuelle au Rwanda. Dévoilement d'une famine cachée sous la verdure,* CCOAIB, Kigali, Novembre 1989, 43 p. Several attempts to get a copy of this report in Rwanda failed.

Udry, C., (2003), Fieldwork, Economic Theory and Research on Institutions in Developing Countries, Yale University, mimeo

Udry, C., & Bardhan, Development microeconomics

UN special rapporteur's report on Rwanda, August 1993

Undated letter addressed to the Minster of Interior and Communal Development concerning the management of Gisovu Commune.

US Department of State, *Country Reports on Human Rights Practices for 1993,* Report submitted to the Committee on Foreign Affairs of the House and the Senate, 1994

Uvin, P. (1998). *Aiding Violence: the Development Enterprise in Rwanda.* : Kumarian Press.

Uwezeyimana, L. (1996). *Crise du café, faillite de l'Etat et implosion sociale au Rwanda, Serie MOCA, Montages et Café, no 4.* : Université de Toulouse.

Valentino, (2000), Final Solutions : the causes of genocide and mass killing, Security Studies, Vol.9, no 3, spring

Verbeek, M. (2000). *A Guide to Modern Econometrics.* : John Wiley and Sons.

Verdoodt, A., & Van Ranst, E. (2003). *A Large Scale Land Suitability Classification for Rwanda, Laboratory of Soil Science*, Ghent University, p. 80.

Verwimp, Philip (1999), Development Ideology, the Peasantry and Genocide: Rwanda representedin Habyarimana's speeches, Working Paper 13, Genocide Studies Program, Yale University. The revised version of this paper is online as "The One who Refuses to Work is Harmful to Society, 2006, at www.hicn.org.

Verwimp, Philip (2001), The Political Economy of Coffee, Dictatorship and Genocide, *European Journal of Political Economy* vol.19 p.161-181

Verwimp, Philip. (2003). *Development and Genocide in Rwanda, doctoral dissertation.* Economics Department: Catholic Univeristy of Leuven. 335p.

Verwimp, Philip. (2003). Testing the Double Genocide Thesis for Central and Southern Rwanda. *Journal of Conflict Resolution, 47*, 423–442.

Verwimp, Philip (2004), Games in Multiple Arenas and Institutional Design on the eve of the Rwandan genocide, *Peace Economics, Peace Science and Public Policy*, web based journal published with the Berkeley Electronic Press, www.bepress.com/peps, Winter

Verwimp, Philip. (2005). An Economic Profile of Peasant Perpetrators of Genocide. *Journal of Development Economics, 77*, 297–323.

Verwimp, Philip (2011) The 1990-92 Massacres in Rwanda: a case of spatial and social engineering?, *Journal of Agrarian Change*, Vol.11, n.3, July, pp.396-419

Vidal, C. (1991). *Sociologie des Passions.* Paris: Editions Karthala.

Vidal, C., Question sur le rôle des paysans durant le génocide des Rwandais tutsi, *Cahiers d'Eudes africaines*, 1998

Von Braun, Joachim, Hartwig de Haen and Juergen Blanken (1991), Commercialisation of Agriculture under Population Pressure, Effects on Production, Consumption and Nutrition in Rwanda, International Food Policy Research Institute, Research Report 85, 1991

Wade, R. (1988). *Village Republics – Economic Conditions for Collective Action in South India.* : Cambridge University Press.

Wagenaar, W. A., & Groeneweg, J. (1990). The memory of concentration camp survivors. *Applied Cognitive Psychology, 4*, 77–87.

Weber, B., & Vedder, A. (2001). *In the Kingdom of Gorilla's*, Simon and Schuster, New York

Wiggins, S., (1995), Changes in African Farming Systems between the mid-1970s and the mid-1980s, *Journal of International Development*, vol.7, n°6,1995, pp.807-848

Willame, J.-C., 1995, Aux sources de l'hécatombe rwandaise, Cahiers Africains vol.14, Paris et Brussels, Karthala et CEDAF.

Wintrobe, R. (1998). *The Political Economy of Dictatorship.* : Cambridge University Press.

World Bank (1987) Community Development in Rwanda. Washington DC.

World Bank, (1991), Rwanda agricultural strategy review.

World Development Reports, World Bank, 1993.

Index

P. Verwimp, *Peasants in Power*, DOI: 10.1007/978-94-007-6434-7,
© Springer Science+Business Media Dordrecht 2013